Praise for

NORTH STAR
OVER MY SHOULDER

"Buck relates his wide-eyed first flying experience at sixteen
with an enthusiasm normally relegated to the pages of romance
novels. . . . His descriptions of these early flights in bare-bones
vehicles have a white-knuckle intensity. . . ."
—*Publishers Weekly*

"[W]hen he talks about his early flying days, or about his
war years, we feel a sense of adventure we haven't felt since
Tom Wolfe's *The Right Stuff*. . . . We can only hope there
will be a second volume of this marvelous memoir."
—*Booklist*

"Bob's life above the clouds and below is remarkable. His
well-written memoir reflects this full life in a
lighthearted, high-spirited style."
—*Vermont Journal*

"One comes away from this book feeling that today's pilots
may have missed something wonderful."
—*St. Louis Post-Dispatch*

"Bob Buck is an excellent raconteur. . . . It is awe inspiring
to share, albeit vicariously, in the memories of an octogenarian
who looks back at his life and understands that his journey has
been an interesting and meaningful one."
—*The Roanake Times*

"You don't have to be a pilot to appreciate this book. An interest in
flying or the joy of a tale well told will suffice."
—*Aviation Week & Space Technology*

ALSO BY BOB BUCK

Weather Flying

Flying Know How

The Art of Flying

The Pilot's Burden

NORTH STAR OVER MY SHOULDER

A FLYING LIFE

BOB BUCK

SIMON & SCHUSTER PAPERBACKS

New York   London   Toronto   Sydney

SIMON & SCHUSTER PAPERBACKS
Rockefeller Center
1230 Avenue of the Americas
New York, NY 10020

First Simon & Schuster Paperbacks edition 2005

SIMON & SCHUSTER PAPERBACKS and colophon are registered trademarks
of Simon & Schuster, Inc.

For information regarding special discounts for bulk purchases,
please contact Simon & Schuster Special Sales at 1-800-456-6798
or business@simonandschuster.com

Book design by Ellen R. Sasahara

Manufactured in the United States of America

1   3   5   7   9   10   8   6   4   2

The Library of Congress has cataloged the hardcover edition as follows:
Buck, Robert N.
North star over my shoulder : a flying life / Bob Buck.
    p.   cm.
Includes index.
1. Buck, Robert N. 2. Air pilots—United States—Biography.
3. Airplanes—Piloting. I. Title.
TL540.B7449 A3   2002
629.13'092 B—dc21   2002283338

ISBN 0-7432-1964-3
0-7432-6230-1 (Pbk)

For Jean, Ferris, and Rob.
This is how it was.

＊

For Alexia Dorszynski,
a lovely lady who inspired me to keep writing this book
when I'd about given up, gave me sage advice,
and most of all showed what courage really is,
delivering a lesson on how to live without cowardice. . . .
No day passes that I do not remember her.

Acknowledgments

There are always people to thank for their help, and only Heaven knows all those who deserve it, but a few stand out strongly and I thank them here:

Deep is my gratitude to Jeff Neuman, who edited the book—a wonderful, understanding man. We never argued, and he was quick to see the point of things in fields he'd never been near before. I am a very lucky person to have worked with Jeff. He plays a good round of golf, too.

I thank Captain Robert C. Sherman, TWA retired, a man and computer who has kept all the pertinent information about TWA's past and its people; if he doesn't know, he knows where to find it.

My oldest and dearest friend, Captain Robert A. Wittke, TWA retired, remembers all the people, places, and stories I forgot.

Bernard J. Dowd, the B-17's crew chief—a tower of knowledge and strength.

William Paris, C.M. Spitfire pilot in North Africa during the big war, then home to Ottawa, Canada—my informant north of our border.

Kitty Werner, my computer guru—I would never have made it without her because I am a computer ignoramus.

Finally, thanks go to Captain Robert O. Buck, Delta Airlines, who remembers many things, and keeps me up to date on how it is out there now.

Contents

CHAPTER I

Night Flight

IT WAS LATE FALL, with the brilliant colors already turning dull. The leaves of the large chestnut close by our old stone house lay on the ground, curled and brown and brittle. The sky was overcast, but without definition—no way to identify the clouds, it was simply gray and dreary.

I looked back as I turned the car from the dirt road onto the two-lane blacktop, and waved to my wife, Jean, who was watching me go; she waved back, and after that I only looked ahead.

I felt that emptiness and sadness I always faced when leaving home and family, the nagging feeling of not having had the time for all the important things to do or say.

The country road soon reached the Delaware River; after that the roads grew bigger, and the occasional auto became many as others slid into the flow. Finally the route became the steady nose-to-tail stream of highway leading to New York City and its disheartening surroundings. As home dropped back behind me and the airport loomed, the sad feeling retreated to a quiet place in the mind's back storage, while my primary thoughts turned to the evening's task.

This night I'd fly a Boeing 747 from New York across the Atlantic to Paris, as I did four or five times a month, hauling people, mail, and cargo—a pleasant task despite the problems that weather, crew, and air-plane might toss my way. Whenever I drove to an airport the same thoughts occupied my mind, mostly about emergencies and what I would do if one occurred.

The act of flying an airplane is a daily chore and I'd long since become proficient at it, the repeated reactions and movements automatic, but emergencies almost never happen so there's no rehearsal for them except for a few hours twice a year in a simulator. And that doesn't cover all of them—ditching the plane in mid-Atlantic, for example. So you review these things, playing mental games of how to cope if the improbable should come true, and the time spent driving to the airport gives you a good opportunity to do it.

What if an engine catches fire? Pull back the throttle, cut the start lever, call for the emergency checklist. How necessary is this review? I'd been thirty years a captain and only had one fire, on a Constellation—a "Connie"—taking off from Frankfurt, Germany. Just as we broke ground there came the shattering confusion of a loud bell and a bright red light. "Engine fire!" Quick action on the remembered items: throttle closed, fuel mixture off, fire extinguisher lever pulled, "Read the engine fire checklist!" All the pre-trained, well-thought-out operational actions took place, right by the book. But in the back of my mind was the thought of a wing burning off, which told me, "Get the son of a bitch back on the ground as fast as possible."

I wrapped the plane into a tight turn I had learned long ago while flying fast around pylons in small-time air races and stunt shows. "Tell the tower we're coming right back," I said. The tower operator, accustomed to orderly traffic flow procedures, tried to direct us to follow another aircraft, a normal aircraft on a normal flight. A few firm words advised the tower to get others out of the way, that we were in a hurry for terra firma.

We landed okay—total flight time was probably five or six minutes, and the fire was out before we touched down—but it had been a fire, caused by a complicated turbine failing and tearing things up. Those few minutes presented the contrast of carefully taught and programmed reactions versus the kind of seat-of-the-pants flying you store up during long hours of flight time—some call it "fright time," and a pilot needs some of that in his or her dossier. The modern way is right and necessary, but periodically there are difficult and perhaps emergency situations that demand the basic stick and rudder skills of quick, intuitive action.

But now it was time to quit thinking about that day in a Connie, and to come back to the 747 I was going to fly tonight. How about a hydraulic system loss? An electrical? Instruments? I go over each one—and the tough ones, too, like a crash landing with fire, and how to get 400 people off the plane; review your actions, think of the twelve doors, know the other crew members' responsibilities, because they're yours, too. It sounds matter-of-fact in the manual, the drawings all neat and precise, but planes generally don't crack up so neatly; it'd probably be a shambles.

My mind slides back to a noon takeoff from Paris, headed for New York with a light load of only 177 passengers. We climbed toward the Channel because our route was to go over England and north, out to sea over Northern Ireland. There was a scattering of fluffy cumulus clouds around 5,000 feet, the sky above blue, the Normandy countryside green and lush below.

"Flight eight-oh-three, Paris." It was our company radio calling. The copilot answered.

"Go ahead, Paris—eight-oh-three."

"Eight-oh-three, we have a telephone [they never say "call"] saying there is a bomb on your flight set to explode at 1340!"

All eyes to the cockpit clocks—that was about forty-seven minutes from now. Shit!

Scared? No—because I didn't think it was real. The natural reaction of "This wouldn't happen to me" numbs you unless there's a real accident in progress.

Logic also said that a bomb was unlikely, as most such threats are hoaxes. But we're just off the ground with seven hours ahead of us to New York, and hoax or no hoax you have to play it for real.

A quick return—Paris air traffic control (ATC) was cooperative when the problem was explained. "You are cleared direct Orly, number one to land." The French grasp situations quickly and act that way, too.

The purser, Buddy Ledger, an efficient old-timer, was called up front: "It's like this," I explained. "We may have to evacuate, so get 'em all ready." Cool as a cucumber, no more excitement or emotion than if I'd simply wanted a cup of fresh coffee.

We started a descent, dumping fuel as we descended, but there wasn't time to get down to landing weight before arriving; as we neared Orly there were just twelve minutes left before the big bang was scheduled, so no time for hanging around the sky. Orly's runway is long, so an overweight landing was less risky than a possible bomb.

I had briefed the passengers during our return, telling them exactly what was going on: "Ladies and gentlemen, this is your captain. We've been notified there is a bomb on board set to go off in forty minutes, so we're returning to Orly. I don't think it's for real, but we cannot take the chance. We should be well on the ground before the time. Please follow the instructions of your purser and cabin team."

That was giving it to them straight. I've always believed in being truthful to passengers about problems. Let 'em have it as it is—some might faint, but they'll know the score when we revive 'em.

Safely down, and then on the ground we were directed to a deserted area of the airport; they didn't want us to be at the terminal if we blew up.

How do you feel during all this? Annoyed, mostly, still not believing in the bomb, but playing the game. Judgments, actions, compromises all needed because of a phone call.

Out at our lonesome area on the far end of the field—we were almost out in farm country, the terminal a couple of miles away—I couldn't see any steps being towed out to us. To play the game right we should get out of the airplane fast: evacuate, slide all the passengers down those long chutes that inflate when the door is opened. That's a regrettable procedure, because someone always gets hurt. I look at the copilot and flight engineer; they're staring at me, expecting a decision. "Let's go!" Action: engine shut down, checklist items all done fast. I flip the switch to ring the bell that will tell the cabin team to start the evacuation, but I didn't want any misunderstandings so I also picked up the intercom. "This is it, evacuate the aircraft!"

"Go!" I said to the two crew members, and they disappeared from the cockpit. I took a minute to double-check that we'd turned all the proper things off, set the brakes, and so on. We'd been thorough, so I was mostly satisfied—but not completely because in a big complex airplane there's always a feeling that you may have missed something; it's like leaving your house with that question of "What did I forget?" gnawing at your mind.

Last check done to the best of my ability, I rushed out of the cockpit and down the stairs expecting to see a mob of people headed for the doors, but they were already gone, the cabin empty. What a job Buddy and his gals had done. Just to be sure, I ran, circling the length of the cabin to be certain we hadn't missed anyone, and then got to the front door and its chute. Before jumping into it I hesitated a second—gad, it looked a long way down there; well, it's almost three stories. I jumped, fanny first, feet up, into the chute and slid to the bottom.

The passengers had all been moved away from the airplane and cars and buses were racing out to get them. One man came up to me—sensitive-looking, with eyeglasses, suit and tie, and a worried look.

"My violin, it is very valuable—will it be safe? Please take care of it."

"If the airplane doesn't blow up, your violin is safe."

I turned to Buddy and asked, "Anybody hurt?"

"No. One gal, a dead-heading hostess [a flight attendant not working but traveling along to her next destination], turned her ankle. Everybody else okay, including an eighty-two-year-old lady with a cane."

A big sense of relief, because all the people in that airplane are your worry.

We waited a couple of hours and nothing happened. After long discussions among mechanics, airport police, and Lord knows who else, it was decided the airplane was safe. Somehow I was elected to go back on board first.

At the airplane there was a lift with a platform, and I climbed on accompanied by the commandant of the airport police, a proper Frenchman in full uniform topped by his blue kepi—always neat and impressive. We were raised up to the front door, and in an automatic gesture of politeness I held back for him to go first. Ah, no. He bowed graciously. *"Après vous, Capitaine,"* he said, a hint of amusement in his smile.

We looked around the cabin, toilets, and closets. I searched the overhead racks and found the violin in its case. There were about ten handbags with money and whatever else such bags may hold that the hostesses had left on board; the rule in evacuating is not to worry about belongings, just get yourself off!

I deplaned with ten handbags hanging from my arms and the violin case in hand. The passengers were at the terminal being fed, and when they saw me, the women grabbed the bags for a quick check of their belongings, and the violinist repeatedly bowed and thanked me for his instrument.

Later that night we flew the airplane to New York. You reflect, in the long quiet hours over the sea, how much can be affected by so little: one person—the authorities concluded later it was an angry employee who'd been fired—can disrupt so many.

✳

I'M STILL DRIVING toward JFK, trying to focus on a review of important issues for the flight. The task gets weary and stale; emergency procedures drift out of focus as my mind wanders from airplanes to lighter things: Paris tomorrow, and thoughts of what to do there.

Paris, like any other layover, is a release from responsibility; until the next day I've got nothing to do, nothing to account for except getting to bed for a good rest. I'll have twenty-eight hours to spend in the city I find to be an alluring obsession, one that once you've seen and understood becomes a haven from mundane reality. Experience her with an open mind, and her culture, intellect, beauty, freedom, smells, feeling, and movement will create an almost mystic love. I daydream of an early morning arrival, in the thick mist and cold air that will warm during the day; then the hotel, my room with its brass bed, simple chair, and small marble-topped table of some Louis period, the armoire to store my clothes, a clean bath with the normal fixtures plus a bidet, that civilized apparatus of plumbing and porcelain. The bed has a warm, inviting quilt. From being up all night you will be foggy-tired, relaxed, not concerned about anything in particular and know how good the embrace of that bed will feel.

When people learn that you're an international airline pilot, they often ask how you overcome jet lag. The answer is simple: you don't. No matter how many times you've crossed the sea, jet lag drags on you physically and mentally. You can only get some smarts about it and try to dodge it as much as possible by strategies like napping and thinking ahead to the next period of work and necessary wakefulness.

Sleep will come instantly and the alarm's ring will seem to as well. You've set your clock for 2:00 in the afternoon—it's essential to carry your own alarm; when you ask for an oddball wake-up in mid-afternoon, 90 percent of the time they simply forget. That's more of the smarts that develop with the job.

It's awful to get up after a three- or four-hour sleep; you feel draggy, with an empty, almost sick feeling inside. Gad, it would be good to roll over and go on sleeping, and it would be so easy to do. But no, get up—sleep any longer and you won't be able to go to sleep that night.

Because I've lived this Paris routine so often, the daydreaming on the drive to JFK seems real. Get up, shower, shave, dress, and go out. The immediate goal is something to eat, but not too much because dinner is not far away. Down the slope of Rue Balzac for a block to the Champs-Elysées. The afternoon air will be temperate as the sun shines with frail warmth through the fall haze. The street is busy, with cars going by at great speed in a thunder of engines not unlike the start of an auto race; some are trying to find a parking place on the wide sidewalk. People are walking, all kinds of people. Tourists stroll, looking in windows, but the French are in a hurry. Chic ladies dressed as only the French can hurrying to some destination; young people in jeans and sloppy T-shirts—the world infestation of the jean that homogenizes the young, along with middle-aged folks trying to hold that youth but looking a bit silly; you think of this blue-bottomed army as acting and thinking alike, all with the same values, but that's probably unfair. On Avenue George V, past the Hotels Prince de Galles and George V, fancy cars with chauffeurs wait for fancy people with money. You see them come out: a man in an expensive tailored suit, lovely tie, hair pomaded to slick it down flat and shiny, along with a very fancy blonde with great legs ending in high-heeled shoes, a sexy dress, and makeup to decimal-point perfection. Is she a movie actress or a business girl (to use the French connotation)? Either way, it's amusing.

Then on to a café near the Place de l'Alma; there are chairs and tables outside, a zinc bar inside, the bartender imposing on his elevated floor surrounded by polished machines that make espresso and hot milk. The complexity of the handles, knobs, and dials rivals my 747 instrument panel.

I sit outside. A waiter approaches, small circular tray under his arm, wearing a long white apron and a bored, detached look. I know exactly what I want; I've thought about it since floundering around my hotel room earlier. *"Un croque monsieur et un demi-pression, s'il vous plaît"*—a sandwich of thin bread buttered on one side, Gruyère cheese and ham between, well grilled so it comes warm with the butter shining on the outside—enough fat to jump the cholesterol reading 100 points in a minute, but very good. The *pression* is draft beer from Alsace, a province along the Rhine that for a period, until the end of World War I, was German, so the beer is good. I suppose some people would be shocked to think of a pilot drinking before a flight, but a beer isn't much drinking and the next flight is about seventeen hours off.

The company rule says no drinking while on a trip at all. Well, I'm not a drinker—never real booze—but a beer, or wine, in France? It's ridiculous to think I wouldn't have a glass with a meal.

I think about the one time the wine did get away from me, at a simple dinner with my beloved French friends, Riton and André. Riton was a real old-school Frenchman who knew all the ways of living well—work was something one did in order to live and not the other way around. He knew every stone and every street in Paris, was an amusing conversationalist, and got serious only rarely, and then generally to express his total dislike for the grand Charles de Gaulle. Riton was one of the best golfers in France and that's how I'd met him many years back, during the more relaxed days of piston airplanes and less frantic schedules when we had two or even three days' layover in Paris.

On the evening in question they took me to dinner knowing I had to get to bed early for a flight to Tel Aviv the next morning. We dined at the Grand Comptoir, an old bistro on the edge of Les Halles market; the food was very good and the wines excellent, chosen from small vineyards the proprietor knew. Riton ordered a Fleurie, a red wine from the Beaujolais region—my first encounter and, my, it was wonderful and is still one of my favorites. I drank sparingly, knowing I had to fly in the morning. But the conversation was warm and good, and I took little notice that I was drinking more Fleurie than was prudent—Fleurie is a quaffing wine, not one to sip.

At a good hour we departed and they dropped me off at the hotel. I readied myself for bed and crawled in, stretched out, and closed my eyes. A dizziness instantly overcame me, and my eyes popped open. What's this? I wondered. I closed my eyes again and my head spun with a nausea that said if my eyes stayed closed I'd throw up. My eyes opened again and I stared into the darkness. "My God!" I admonished myself. "You're drunk!"

Or at the least I had had too much to drink—and in just seven hours the phone would ring for crew call. I couldn't possibly fly that soon. This was terrible. I thought it over, made my plan, and picked up the phone to call the airport.

"This is Captain Buck. I'm ill, I'm sure I ate a spoiled mussel [nothing will flatten you more]. I won't be able to take my flight—have you got someone to cover it for me?"

A pause. "Captain Utgard is set up for eight-oh-one to New York; we can turn him around and send him back to Tel Aviv."

Poor Ed, what a dirty trick I was pulling, but the lie was better than flying "a bit less than efficient," as one old captain put it.

After sleeping until noon the next day I got up well recuperated and flew Ed's 801 to New York in the late afternoon.

Not long after, I saw Ed and apologized for the turnaround I'd caused him and confessed to the real reason. He laughed—but then he thanked me! He was glad of the extra turnaround, it made it possible to pick up some pay time he'd lost because of a previous cancellation. But it was a strong lesson, and something I never repeated.

✳

M Y DAYDREAMING STOPPED and I awakened to the present, to my automobile on the Belt Parkway. I turned off the parkway into JFK airport. The reverie had served its purpose, to put thoughts of home back in storage, where they couldn't distract me from the job or the days ahead. This was not an instinctive process, but one I developed through the years of going and coming as an airline pilot.

You cannot allow the distraction of thoughts of home and family when you're trying to land through low ceiling and fog, or when battling thunderstorms or snow and ice. Nor can you lose sleep or wrap yourself in melancholy over the separation from family thousands of miles away. A more selfish urge is at work here, too: there are the sights and sounds of foreign places to enjoy, and why spoil the experience by mooning about home? But flying off to distant places wasn't a selfish choice. The overseas flights paid best, and since the flights were long, the flying time built up quickly, and that meant more time off between trips—more time at home. And any hesitation over my enjoyment of the travel was mollified by the thought, "Someday I'll show these places to Jean and the children."

It's a dual life, really, because the airline and its people are a family, too. We were closely knit, knew one another's thoughts, character, and problems. It was an intimate relationship that the family back home wasn't part of.

So pulling open the door to the vestibule that led to the stairs and to the offices on the side of the hangar was also a homecoming. The guard greeted you, other crew members were coming and going, and most you knew and could exchange a quip with by way of hello. You had departed home two hours ago, and here you were, home again—a different home, but home nevertheless.

As a pilot you don't just get to the airport, climb into an airplane, and go; you sneak up on it in stages. Stage one is a stop at the schedule desk, where a clerk sits behind a counter with a telephone receiver seemingly always glued to one ear, calling to notify crews of future duty, or scrounging up someone to fill in for someone else who called in sick, all the while checking in people like me. When I motion I'm aboard, she checks my name off the crew list, gives me a nod—and never misses a word to whomever she's talking to on the phone. I lean over the counter for a closer look at my crew list and note that O.B. Smith is tonight's first officer, or copilot, which makes for a warm feeling because O.B. is quiet, efficient, and a pleasure to be with.

A copilot can make a trip or ruin it; get someone who talks too much, gripes about the company, tries to impress you, tells long and boring anecdotes, or is overly aggressive in suggesting ways to run the flight, and the taste is unpleasant. A1 was one of those. He was a captain on domestic, but bid copilot international and the 747 because it paid more and had the romance of flying to Europe and other distant places. But he couldn't stop being captain and started tuning radios and adjusting navigation items without telling me. I finally had to lecture him strongly: "You bid copilot, now damn it, be a copilot and not a co-captain. We'll do things my way, and if you don't like it bid back to domestic." It worked and he settled down, but his resentment always showed.

Now and then there'd be a milquetoast who wouldn't get things done unless you told him each item you wanted. A good copilot is a balance of these things, following, doing as told, but strong enough to point out any error you may have made.

All in all my copilots were fine, like O.B.: a big man from Iowa farm country who came to flying via the navy. (For some reason, naval aviators always seem to come from farms, way out in the middle of the country, far from the sea.) Farm people impress me because they generally have common sense, and if there's one trait a pilot should have in abundance it's good old-fashioned common sense. Farm people also have a way of recognizing that certain things, even unpleasant things, have to be done; they don't bitch about the chore, or cuss out the company because of some obnoxious procedure, and they don't get vocal or outwardly scared when things get tough like the weather going down at your destination when the fuel reserves are low. If that were to happen, O.B. wouldn't change appearance a mite; he'd just settle in to computing fuel, getting weather information, and being generally useful in a matter-of-fact manner. Yes, it's a good feeling to have O.B. in that right seat beside you.

A glance at the rest of the crew: S. C. Bushy, whom everyone just called Bushy, as flight engineer, or second officer; another good man who knows the airplane's innards and workings. The cabin team is twelve hostesses and a flight manager. A few names I recognize at a glance; a couple of attractive gals with a certain verve who'll burst into the cockpit bringing coffee or food and a wise remark, a spark to wake us up for a few moments during the dull grind of a long night.

Then to the mail room and my mailbox crammed with the latest stuff you have to know before a flight.

Paper, lots of it. We're so damn wasteful—probably one of the worst inventions of all time has been the copier, since it encourages the making and distributing of more copies than are actually needed; computers breed waste, too, as their printers spew long ribbons of paper. For all this paper, the land gets scalped as trees are torn down, and chemicals are dumped into rivers. I've seen the damage from the air, mountainsides made barren, ugly gook flowing out the mouths of rivers and streams into lakes and oceans; acrid smoke that drifts for miles and blots out the sun from a town, city, or countryside. These things can't hide from a pilot's eyes.

I take the papers from my mail folder and lug my black salesmanlike case to a long counter with low stools where pilots sit and bring their operation manuals up to date before flight. The chatter of gossip and tall tales flows from the half-dozen pilots working at the long bench.

The key item in my not-so-briefcase is a beat-up leather-covered six-ring notebook with charts for each airport on route and many off route in case some emergency or bad weather diverts you away from normal routes or places. One packet in the mailbox contains the latest revisions, perhaps a couple of dozen thin paper sheets. There have been changes since you last flew the route and you'd better know about them: a different radio frequency, runway repairs in progress, airport changes; here's one for Geneva, Switzerland—the airport elevation has been changed from 2,000 feet to 2,014 feet. That's the mark of Swiss precision: someone remeasured it, probably with new instruments. The fourteen-foot change doesn't mean much to me, and I'm certain Geneva's airport hasn't suddenly risen fourteen feet, but it has to be corrected. The old page for Geneva is thrown aside and replaced by the new one.

San Francisco: "I left my heart . . ." Yes, there's still a part of my heart in San Francisco from my young copilot days. On the San Francisco page, a tower frequency change: the old page is tossed out and the new one put in place. The binders and luggage we carry are big because we carry the information for all the places and routes, from San Francisco to Bombay. It seems silly, and a big burden, but internationally one never knows where the route may be.

Our office was part of the hangar, as many are. They're afterthoughts, stuck onto the side and never well ventilated, and not much light gets into them. The hangar is long, and the offices are located along a corridor that stretches from one end of the building to the other. At the end of the corridor is the entrance to Dispatch and Weather. When you pass through that door you're suddenly in the middle of the action: clerks moving about, writing stuff at their desks, gathering messages, handing them to the dispatcher, who sits in the center of it all worrying about airplanes and flights. The right side area is international; Flight 907 is hung up in Bombay with mechanical problems; Milan is fogged in, what happens to the passengers, mail, and cargo? Concerns like that for every destination from New York to Hong Kong. A partition divides the room and on the left is another dispatcher with a cadre of clerks who handle the North Atlantic; the immediate problems of weather, fuel, loads, and air traffic delays. It's where I do business.

Bill Hussey is on duty, a crisp, pleasant, and sharp individual. We shake hands and pass the pleasantries. "You've got plane 310, it came in on eight-oh-one, no mechanical problems—you're all set: 395 passengers; Paris looks a little shaky."

Paris is shaky because it may fog in, but that's nothing unexpected; it's fall and not only is Paris shaky, so is all of Northern Europe—it always is. At this time of year, around October, a high pressure area sits over Europe and gives it those warm hazy days when the light filters through the chestnut trees, creating patterns of soft sunshine and shadow on the ground. But the evening air cools, and as dawn approaches this can form fog—and our flights arrive in the early morning, around 7:00 A.M. As the day warms the fog burns off: in early October it clears by 8:30 or so; in late October, it may hang on until 9:30 or 10:00, by late November, with the longer and cooler nights, the fog is thicker and it's near noon before it burns off. By December it may not burn off at all. I once spent five days in Paris because no airplanes could get in. They weren't days of complete freedom because you had to be handy in case the fog burned off, but the five days weren't a hardship by any means and, as pilots say in such circumstances, I was there so long I thought of running for mayor. Now it's early November, and the fog situation is chancy. The cure is to take on enough fuel so you can go to the warmer south of France—Marseilles, for example. But sometimes the payload, or poor winds, make it difficult to put that much fuel on board.

Now over to the meteorologist and his weather map, the man who will tell me what I'll find en route, up in the high sky with its invisible winds that flow from various directions at different speeds and sometimes tumble and churn, creating turbulence. The meteorologist—we generally call them weathermen—was Terebelski, a man who'd come to the United States from Poland in some shuffle during World War II that I never dug into deeply enough to learn the details. Terebelski was old-world, his Polish accent still much alive. "Good evenink, Keptain." Medium size, thin gray hair, pleasant smile, and all business—which he knew very well.

Terebelski's world was up in the troposphere and stratosphere. The troposphere, where we live, is the space where things happen; jet streams move, low and high pressure areas slide over us with their bad weather or good. It's the world of action, that dome of air above us that's about 30,000 feet thick over the poles, 50,000 feet over the equatorial regions. As we take off and climb in the troposphere the temperature decreases, roughly 2°C for every thousand feet we climb. This varies day to day with weather patterns.

Above the troposphere is the stratosphere, which extends up to about 125,000 feet. It's different from the troposphere in that as we climb in the stratosphere the temperature increases with altitude, gets warmer. The air is dry, too, so the weather is clear.

Where the troposphere and stratosphere meet is called the tropopause; in flying talk it's known as "the trop." It really isn't anything except a point of change from troposphere to stratosphere. Often, at the trop, one can see a fine line of dust particles, stuff from where we live down below that can't go any higher because the warmer stratosphere prevents its climb, just like the pollution in Los Angeles stays there because of an inversion—warmer aloft, like the stratosphere.

What does all this mean to me in a jet airplane? Well, I want to get as high as possible because up high, simply put, we get more miles per gallon. The catch is temperature; if the airplane is heavy, the altitude it can climb to is limited by temperature. If it's too warm for the airplane's weight, performance deteriorates, because warm air is thinner, so it has fewer molecules for the wing to grip and the engine to use. There's no danger, but if you're heavy and beginning a long flight you cannot climb into the warmer stratosphere until enough fuel has been burned to reduce the weight. The game, then, becomes how high can I climb before reaching the stratosphere? Where's the trop?

The trop isn't always at the same altitude or location and varies with the weather conditions under it and the seasons of the year. The stratosphere isn't the badlands; there's less wind and turbulence in it, and if you're westbound against a head wind, getting up into the stratosphere will lessen that head wind. The stratosphere is a lid that keeps the jet streams and turbulence in the troposphere, so lots of times you'd like to get up into the calmer, benign stratosphere, as long as the temperature isn't too high for the airplane's weight. So a pilot wants to know where the trop is and how high, and that's where experts like Terebelski come in.

We look at the weather map he's drawn. It includes the United States, the North Atlantic, and deep into continental Europe. "There is southwest flow New York to Gander [Newfoundland], no turbulence, good tailwind, maybe 70 knots, at 45 west," Terebelski tells me, and his hand moves and his finger points to the area off the coast of Newfoundland, about 380 miles east of Gander. As I listen to Terebelski my eye sweeps over the entire map and from experience I can tell in a glance what the trip is going to be like, but I listen anyway for his thoughts about whether or not the situation is likely to change, and what the chances of that happening are. The bond between pilot and meteorologist is like that between patient and doctor, and can't be understood or appreciated by someone outside the action; one looks to the meteorologist to explain the often unexplainable, and to tell you honestly about what he doesn't and can't know, and why, and what to expect if the unknown appears as you fly toward or through it. This bond started with my earliest flights, and has been the same with all the meteorologists I've dealt with since.

Terebelski continues, "At 45 west the jet stream turns north," and his hand follows it on the map. I know what he'll say next because I know that where the jet stream bends the air will be rough and we'll bounce in turbulence. I wonder how he visualizes this, if his mind makes a picture of the turbulence or if he just thinks in principles and formulae. He isn't thinking of it the way I do, picturing the airplane jouncing, seeing myself reaching to get the seat belt sign on, reducing power so as to slow to turbulence penetration speed, being a little apprehensive in the dark night, hoping it doesn't get real nasty. Much in flying carries such concern: "I've got this under control, I can handle it, but I don't want it to get much worse." I look at the tropopause level and see that it will be up to 35,000 feet, right near my cruise altitude, which will aggravate the turbulence. "There will be turbulence," Terebelski says, "perhaps moderate, but not for long. Beyond that, in stratosphere, no turbulence, but the wind will only be about 30 knots tailwind—no problem from there to Paris, perhaps a short area of turbulence just before descent where jet stream swings back north, but not so strong." We both stare at the map for a moment longer and he adds, "Possible the jet stream will turn north a little earlier, maybe 50 west." This means the big tailwind might fade away earlier and my speed will slacken so we'll be ten, even twenty minutes longer in the air. I think about that a moment, how it means more fuel burned, less reserve at Paris, less hanging around time before I go off to an alternate if the fog doesn't lift. A little worrisome, but finally just part of the flying facts of life.

I thank Terebelski and walk to the counter where our flight plan will be checked over, but my mind hasn't moved on yet; I'm thinking about the meeting of those forces that will influence my airplane above the North Atlantic, a meeting between winds that cruise for thousands of miles in great sweeps and my 747, a mere speck up in that vastness. The meeting will be, in a way, a contest between those invisible forces and my knowledge and experience, a contest to which I look forward not with fear, but with comfortable anticipation.

Dispatcher Hussey joins me at the counter where the computer flight plan is spread out. O.B. and Bushy are already there, looking down at the printout with its lines showing fuel, 206,500 pounds of it; payload; takeoff weight, 710,000 pounds; time to Paris; the wind component and whether it's a head wind or tailwind. Tonight it's a modest tailwind. The flight legs are listed: JFK to Nantucket, then Yarmouth, Nova Scotia, and other towns in the Canadian Maritimes; over Gander, Newfoundland—and from then on just numbers because we'll be over the ocean, where there are no markers, just the moving sea. The locations there are lines visible only on maps as latitude and longitude, or "Lat-Lon" as the trade calls them. Our flight plan says 50 west/50 north; then 40 west; 30, 20, Cork, Ireland; Land's End, England; Dinard, France, in Brittany; and then Paris.

The first thing you glance at is the flight time: this plan says six hours and fifty-eight minutes from wheels lifting off until touching down on the runway at Orly Field. Hussey says, "We plan Geneva as an alternate." This can be a problem because Geneva, like most of Northern Europe, has its moments of fog in autumn, too; if Paris is too bad for landing, and you chase off to Geneva as an alternate, you risk the chance that it may go bad as you get there—a situation commonly referred to by pilots as "folding in your face." The anxiety in this situation is that you might run from one deteriorating place to another, never finding weather good enough to land, until the fuel ran out, and that would be disaster. No, the only place that's by-God, for-sure safe would be down on the Mediterranean, a place like Marseilles—but using that as an alternate takes more fuel and cuts back on any extra fuel available for holding. Holding comes when you arrive over Paris and it's fogged in, but you know it'll clear out, so you hold, circling, waiting for the sun to warm things up and thin the fog enough to sneak in. The strict no-no is holding so long that your reserve fuel is used up and going to Marseilles becomes impossible.

Hussey's view is simpler; he looks over the fuel numbers and says, "That'll give you about an hour hold at Orly, with Geneva alternate." I say to myself, Maybe half that if I use Marseilles. I nod, and realize that asking for more fuel will mean reducing payload, and you hate to do that.

"Okay, we'll go with it," I tell him—and I think that no matter how carefully the plan had been created, the final decision will come tomorrow morning as we arrive over Europe, gritty-eyed and tired, when Hussey and all the people here in the office are home in bed. Then I, the captain, will make the final decision of whether to hold or go to an alternate, one that I will choose—but that's what you're paid for.

And now the flight has stirred into reality. All the hack things—driving to the field, checking in, bringing manuals up to date, reading bulletins, walking down the long corridor—the motions that lacked substance are done. Now an actual airplane, and the fuel it will carry, the passengers, route, and weather, and time of flight are all pulled together as Flight 800. You're no longer really in New York, nor yet in Paris, but for certain you're going there and part of your psyche is already on the way.

✳

THE FIRST PART of the crew's voyage covers the few miles from the hangar to the terminal, and that's done in an inglorious school bus the company utilizes for such transport. A hostess, sitting across from me, asks, "What kind of flight tonight, Captain?"

I look over at her, a pretty brunette whose eyes are bright with youth, and the sight of her makes everything feel better.

"Peachy," I say, "just peachy." But then I become a little more serious and tell her it will be a fairly quick flight, mostly smooth, and the weather in Paris will be good enough so we'd get in—even though inside I was a little wary about that. "A little turbulence, but not enough to upset any meal service longer than a few minutes."

By now the bus has stopped at the terminal and we get off. I walk into it and head for the airplane. I pass the counters, with people lined up waiting for ticketing and checking baggage. The line is long and the baggage piled high; I see a young lady in the line, and next to her is a mound of bags. I wonder why anyone a slight five foot two or so would need all that clothing and stuff. The people standing in line reveal their personalities; some are patient and look off into space with the same vacuous gaze you see on cows in a field, and others are fidgeting, looking around and over the ones ahead to see how it's going, moving their luggage a little further along, rudely crowding the person in front; some are talking with friends or traveling companions, animated by the excitement of the coming trip, moving along in the line conscious neither of position nor the passage of time.

I stop by the newsstand and look over newspaper headlines, browse the magazine titles, but decide I'll be better off with the books I have in my suitcase. A man stands next to me, restless, and then says, "Where you going, Captain?"

"Paris—Flight 800."

"Oh, I'm on your flight." A slight pause and then, "Good weather tonight?"

I can tell immediately he's nervous, worried about flying. "It's fine, we should have a nice flight." I don't mention the chance of Paris being fogged in; he'd stew and fret all night if I did.

"Been doing this a long time?" Now he wants to know how experienced I am, and I know he's looking me over, appraising me. I'm awfully tempted to say it's my first trip, simply from an ingrained dislike of people who submit to fear—an unfair judgment I suppose—but despite this distaste I'm not sadistic, so I tell him the truth.

"Long time—since the war. Well, I've got to get things going, I'll see you later."

Now down a corridor that is like a tube stretching out toward the passenger loading area. The tube is crowded with people coming and going, a mass of motion. People on the move—how did we develop into such a wandering tribe? Where are these people all going, and why? Isn't anyone satisfied with their own hearth, the quiet and comfort of home? I believe that World War II created a lot of this. The war developed the airplane, released its capabilities, demonstrated that it could fly across oceans and go to far places. In those airplanes were many GIs, learning that the world had no travel restrictions: oceans could be spanned, the tallest mountains crossed. When the war ended the camouflage came off the airplanes and bright commercial colors replaced it; the flight crews took off khaki and put on a blue or some other color uniform resplendent with gold stripes, but we headed out over the same oceans to distant lands and cities of history and renown. The GIs wanted to show their families where they had waged war, and the heretofore provincial American public learned it was easy to go to Paris, Rome, London, and other places. Humanity began its trek toward creating one world, and the airplane did it—which isn't necessarily something to be proud of, because the mass of tourists we've flown overseas have changed Europe; the individuality, the gentle ways of another land, its customs and culture have been stained by the commercialism designed to attract the tourists and, to some extent, screw them. If one knows a country from before, happily, it's still possible to ferret out the old, to find in quiet corners what the tourist doesn't see: what once was, and still is. But the airplane is creating one world, and often doing it badly.

Near the entrance to the jetway and airplane the crowd has thickened, waiting for boarding. I work my way through the people, a bit self-conscious because so many eyes turn to look me over, to see what they've drawn for a captain. It's a relief to get away from that scrutiny and into the empty jetway, and walk down it toward the airplane.

You'd never know it was an airplane—all you see is the door and lights inside—but as I cross the threshold my foot comes down on something solid and familiar. I'm on board and it feels good. Immediately in front is a galley and two hostesses are there checking equipment, fussing with this and that, opening and slamming shut doors after they're certain the food, trays, and all the necessary service stuff is on board. One of them is that pretty young brunette from the bus to the terminal.

The airplane is clean, tidy, and neat before the passengers come aboard. Everything looks ready, seats all proper with the seat belts crossed on each one, a little white napkin on the headrest, pillows and blankets arranged. It's hard to believe that in a few short hours the passengers will have it in shambles.

I address the pretty young lady: "Would you mind nuking a hot dog for me and bringing it up to the cockpit?"

"No, I'll be glad to; only take a few minutes."

I ask for that to hold off hunger; it's after six o'clock and I haven't had time for any dinner. We'll be busy in the cockpit until after departure and in climb; then the cabin team will be serving drinks and getting the passenger dinners served; it'll be ten or eleven o'clock before they have time for mine, so the hot dog to fill the gap.

I walk through the long cabin to chat with the attendants, interrupting them as they go through their checking routine, reviewing everything from the fire extinguisher and first-aid kits to whether or not the caviar is on board. One night it wasn't, and a hostess came into the cockpit that night: "Captain, is there any chance you could come back and talk to a passenger? He's really upset because we don't have any caviar. I'm afraid it's my fault. I thought I checked it, but I guess I didn't."

I smiled, a gesture meant to let her know I wasn't upset about the damn caviar problem. I struggled out of the seat, put on my uniform jacket and cap, and stepped into the first-class section. The man in question was standing by the galley.

"Understand there's a little problem. May I help?"

He proceeded to launch into a tirade about the lack of caviar. He was flying first class and expected it, he'd never ride this airline again, and on and on.

I tried to mollify him and be as pleasant as possible while inwardly feeling repugnance at his asinine attitude. When you consider all the serious factors that go into flying this big airplane across the sea safely and efficiently, and then you're confronted by a jerk who thinks caviar is the most important detail, it's galling. I apologized still, made limp excuses, and asked for his business card. He was VP of some company and almost certainly in first class by way of an expense account. When I got back to New York I worked out a plan with our meal people and had a can of caviar wrapped up fancy and sent by messenger, along with a letter from me, to his office. It took a long time to compose the letter because I wanted to be polite and tell him how sorry we were, but at the same time, between the lines, to let him know what an ass I thought he was. He never acknowledged the gesture.

Tonight there are twelve cabin attendants and I banter and chitchat with each of them, telling them how the trip will be, letting them know if there'll be any turbulence and where because cabin attendants hate turbulence, which often seems to come during meal service when they're juggling meal trays and serving drinks. I also want them to know we aren't sacrosanct in our great perch up front, and to come up if they have problems, we'd be glad to help, and anyway, drop by once in a while. I don't say it, but it's nice to have a pleasant young lady drop by in the long hours of night—and it works both ways, giving them relief from the squirming mob, in the lower section.

Once I step through the cockpit door, the world changes. The soft lights of the cabin, the decorated interior, the cabin attendants all slick and prettied up—all that is set aside and now I'm back in the flying world, recognizing once again that this is an airplane with instruments, levers, throttles, circuit breakers, switches, and a multitude of other things that mean serious business. The seat I'll sit in, the cushions beaten down by hours of various rear ends punishing them, pressing them flat so they're uncomfortable, is ready for me. I slide in and adjust it for my height and where I like to sit.

You make thousands of landings over the years, and if you're perceptive you've learned that sitting low tends to make you level off a little too high, while sitting up high tends to make you fly into the ground and not level off enough. No pilot makes good landings all the time. Some days the landings are slickers, and you hardly know when the wheels are on and start turning; other days the landings are firm, meaning one crunches down hard. They come in streaks. For a week or so your landings are perfect—grease jobs, as the trade calls good ones—and then for a week or so you cannot seem to get a grease job and every landing is firm. You're like an athlete in a slump. So your notions about where you like to sit are like the way some batters stand, or how high a golfer tees the ball. I like to sit high, and I jack the seat full up so I can see the runway as close to the nose as possible for low-visibility landings—and this way I don't have to fiddle around trying to find some precise spot; I just sit down and run the seat full up and it's set. It did take me a bit of doing to learn to level off properly and not thump the airplane on the ground. All of which is a lot of conversation just about getting the seat where you want it.

Getting settled in is like creating a nest, putting things where and how you like them for comfort, to be within easy reach and to satisfy habit. I adjust the seat, then place my black brain bag on the floor to the left with its top open so I can easily reach in for the navigation gear when needed, or for a piece of candy I may have stashed there. In the bag is my personal radio headset that I dig out and plug in, adjust to my head, and place the little hearing aid–like piece in my left ear, the right ear free so I can communicate with the copilot and flight engineer or anyone who might come in the cockpit and stand next to me. Wearing the headphone over my left ear for all these years of radio communications and static, before very high frequency radio came in, has made me about half-deaf in that ear, but volume control lets me get it up where I can hear it; at home my wife impatiently repeats things louder. The maps—the approach plates—for our New York departure and the confusing taxiways on Kennedy Airport go on a little shelf to my left; earlier I put a pencil in my shirt pocket along with a penlight to use when the cockpit is dark. I adjust and put on the safety belt; I still call them that because that's the terminology I grew up with. For psychological reasons related to not scaring passengers, they're now referred to as seat belts, as in "Please fasten your seat belts." In the cockpit we also have shoulder harnesses, but I don't attach mine until we've started and are ready to taxi. Now I'm settled in, ready for work.

Meanwhile, O.B. is settling his own nest, getting things organized for the night's work. Bushy comes through the door and enters the cockpit. "We're fueled and all else looks good," Bushy tells us. He's studied the logbook, which has a history of recent flights, the notations by previous crews about things that needed fixing—snags, the Canadians call them—and the mechanic's guarantee that the gripe had been fixed. He's double-checked the fuel on board. Now he's on board and going with us. Bushy is the kind of man who would do it all thoroughly and conscientiously even if he weren't going along, but knowing he is makes you feel even better.

O.B. is set and holds the checklist in his hand ready to read it, giving me a look that says without comment, "I'm ready when you are."

This is the beginning. "Parking brake?" O.B. calls out, and I reply, after checking it, "On." There are checklists that we read at various times in the flight: the first is a long list of systems and instrument settings, sort of like pre-launch on a space flight; the next is a short "Before Starting Engines" list; then as we taxi to the runway there's a taxi checklist ("Flaps take off, stabilizer set, spoilers down"); and then at the end of the runway we'll read the "Before Takeoff" checklist.

These checklists either demonstrate man's inability to remember all the items, or show that the airplane is now too complicated for the human, who needs crutches like the checklist to keep safety under control. Either way, the checklist is necessary but not infallible. Pilots are sometimes interrupted during the reading of the list by an outside occurrence such as a radio call, and don't pick up at the next checklist item, missing one or two when they resume reading it. A few pilots do silly things like memorizing the checklist so they can spill it out like a litany with all the dangers of forgetting; a few old-timers thought checklists were a poor reflection on their aeronautic prowess and disdained their use, although most of those pilots are gone. But the fallibility of the lists has shown up in a few serious accidents, where simple things like putting the flaps down for takeoff were forgotten. This makes you wonder about modern airplanes and the system they fly in: has it all become more than a human can handle 100 percent of the time? It's a complicated subject and it demands study and argument. I realize that my safety is as much at risk from the weaknesses of the system as anybody's, but I chose the trade and I like it, and I recognize the possibilities—which makes me thorough and careful, precise and watchful.

We're all settled in now, ready to go as soon as passenger and cargo loading is finished and we're cleared to start. The busy confusion of getting it all together settles down, and in the cockpit for a moment there's nothing to do, a moment of relaxation that doesn't last long as the mechanic on the ground calls me by the telephone that connects the airplane and outside. "Captain, clear to start three." We're alive again, starting each engine as the ground gives us clearance. As the engines come to life, the airplane changes from an inanimate object to a living entity, sensation coursing through its structure, instruments alive, lights glowing. It was a large, dead mass of metal I sat in before starting, but now there is movement, the engines rotating, giving slight motion to the structure, setting the fluids, electrical systems, and air pressures all to flowing. Now I relate to the airplane, am in touch with its soul. There's strength and a pledge that links us, that says together we'll complete the task and complete it well. "All clear, Captain. Have a good flight." The mechanic signs off and tucks the telephone into the nose wheel well, where it stays until the French mechanic takes it out in Paris tomorrow morning and calls up to me, "Bonjour, Captain."

I look out the left side at the ground, where an airline agent stands ready to salute when all is ready to go. It's a formal thing, this salute, something that says, "I release the airplane to you." I return the salute, signifying, "I accept the airplane and the responsibility." I've done this a thousand times, but no matter how common the action, it's a serious moment, a moment that reminds me of the charge and the dignity of the task.

Now we wander through the maze of taxiways at JFK accompanied by a discordant symphony of radio chatter from the tower directed at the various aircraft: a mishmash of voices, instructions, queries, and cautious steering in the dark. All sorts of vehicles dart about as we leave the terminal; this is the most ignoble and worrisome part of the trip, the careful creeping along the taxiway three stories below, being transported on wheels also three stories below and hidden way back under the wing. Approaching the runway end I pull up behind another airplane, an Air France flight also headed for Paris. A long line of aircraft is ahead waiting to take off. I count them: ten planes. There's about a three-minute interval between takeoffs, so three times ten means thirty minutes before our turn comes—and we're burning precious fuel while we wait. We inch along, one after another, until finally it is our turn.

I pull out on the runway and carefully line up on the pavement that stretches over two miles before us, a pathway through the dark outlined by lights going down the left and right sides. The last "Before Takeoff" checklist is complete, shoulder harness attached, and I make a quick, habitual, personal check of what we call the killer items: takeoff flaps down, stabilizer set, spoilers down, fuel valves on, the directional gyro heading reading the same as the runway direction. The tower clears us for takeoff.

I wiggle and settle in the seat, then carefully push the throttles forward. The noise isn't one of power and thunder in the cockpit; it's more like a big buzz saw. Slowly we gain speed, and then the pace quickens, the runway lights go by faster, the landing gear bangs as we hit rough spots on the runway—not potholes, but they feel like them. Bushy slides his hand below mine on the throttles and trims them to the takeoff power setting, while I still keep them in hand in case I suddenly have to snap them back and abort the takeoff should something go wrong. Takeoff is a time of intense concentration for all of us, working seriously and tightly together, keeping straight, alert, watching airspeed, checking across the board as needed. And then O.B. calls "Vee one," an announcement that means we've passed the speed at which we could abort; now we must keep going. Then he calls "Vee R," which is the speed to pull back the wheel, rotate the airplane, and let it fly. I double-check the speed as I pull back and raise the plane's nose to 15 degrees as shown on the artificial horizon—or ADI, as they call it now, for attitude direction indicator, but it will always be an artificial horizon to me. And I think about the instrument I'm using and its symbol for the horizon, a barlike indication only a few inches long. My eyes are clamped on it, making certain I've got the nose at exactly 15 degrees. A three-inch reference to move this big airplane: 700,000 pounds, 200 feet long, 350 passengers, all directed by a little bar not much larger than a toothpick. Little symbols, do your job well.

Then the rumbling noise stops, a smoothness comes over the airplane, and we're in the air. I call for the landing gear to be retracted and O.B. moves the small lever. The collection of big wheels and struts twists and folds into the airplane, the doors clump closed, and the landing gear, still and silent, is in repose until tomorrow when, on command of the same small lever, it will unfold, twist, and finally lock down in position to support us on the runway at Paris.

The departure is a routing of twists and turns, changes in speed, hesitation at various altitudes, all designed to weave us through other traffic, inbound and outbound. The careful, precise task demands high concentration, but finally the air traffic controller tells us we are cleared on course and can climb unrestricted to cruise altitude of 35,000 feet. The power is advanced, the nose pointed up and eastward. We've shaken off the finicky routes and rules for getting away from JFK, and now our wings reach out and take up the broad task of flying across the sea in the cold mysterious thin air high above it. I sit back and relax. New York and the U.S.A. are behind me, off the tail, out of view, out of thought.

*

THE TENSE ACTIVITY of departure over, we sit back doing small chores as we climb.

This big mass of airplane is pushing its way up at a rate of 2,000 feet per minute to 35,000 feet—amazing, especially when I think back to Lindbergh staggering into the air at Roosevelt Field on Long Island and heading for Paris. He crawled up to an altitude of 200 feet and stayed there for many hours simply because the *Spirit of St. Louis,* with its burden of fuel for forty hours, couldn't do much better. And now, forty-three years later, we zoom to 35,000 feet—impressive progress in such a short time of man's history.

Climbing is one of the three parts of every flight: the climb to altitude, the level-off for cruising, and finally the descent to land. Sometimes climbing isn't easy. I remember being copilot on a DC-2 taking off from Winslow, Arizona, on a dark night before Christmas in the late 1930s. We needed to reach 14,000 feet to be safely above the inhospitable terrain around Flagstaff, and the 12,670-foot Humphreys Peak. At 11,000 feet we're barely climbing, which brought oaths from the captain: "What's wrong with this son of a bitch?" Twelve thousand feet and the climb had almost ceased despite all the power our two engines would allow. In shocking realization it became evident we couldn't get to 14,000 feet— and we had to, because outside there was no visibility, only clouds and snow. The decision was obvious: we turned back to Winslow. There were two reasons for our inability to climb high. One, which was a theory only, was that air rushing down the mountain slope in the stormy night pulled down the contiguous air the plane was trying to climb in, so we were fighting to climb up a waterfall of air. The second reason, discovered when we were back on the ground, was that the airplane had been overloaded by some 3,000 pounds! Mail and freight were crammed on; in the holiday season's frenzy, there was no thought of checking weight—just get it on.

But now we've reached 35,000 feet and we level off. The automatic pilot has taken over and keeps the airplane on an even keel and fixed to the altitude. The inertial navigation system (INS) is sending its signals to the autopilot, telling it the course to fly, so all we have to do is sit back and relax. To a casual observer, an airline pilot has a very easy job: get the airplane off the ground, climb to altitude, set up the autopilot, and do nothing until it is time to descend and land. What the casual observer doesn't see is the inside of the pilot's head, where questions constantly present themselves, demanding answers. A pilot constantly scans, with eyes and mind: a look at the instrument readings, note the position of switches and levers, check the autopilot to be certain it hasn't wandered off in direction or altitude, scan the distant sky outside searching for other aircraft while at the same time surveying the sky for changes in the clouds that suggest a storm or turbulence ahead. And the questions: Is the airplane in good form, or is there a slight irregularity of some system that's not dramatic at the moment, but still bears watching so you'll know what to do should it get worse? And that Paris weather, how is it doing? How is our fuel use—normal, so we'll have the proper reserves at Paris, or are we using more than planned due to higher air temperatures or head winds? And in the back of the mind is the "what if" stuff: What if an engine fails? Where's the nearest safe airport, or do I keep going? What if the pressurization goes sour and we need to descend to an altitude at which we'll burn much more fuel—what then? These questions don't make you worried or even anxious, but the good pilot knows the possibilities, however remote, and your job is to keep them all in mind and know what to do if they happen.

Then there's your sensitivity to that mystical phenomenon called a hunch—an inexplicable feeling that something isn't right or isn't going as you'd like. Some days you feel it strongly; some days the hunch factor is low, and the flight is more comfortable. Is there something to these hunches, or is it just that your psyche is functioning differently that day? I cannot honestly recall any events I could tie to a hunch, but feeling such uneasiness made me extra diligent, and perhaps that's why nothing ever seemed to happen, at least that I can recall.

At altitude, set for the long cruise ahead, there's a feeling of peace and calm. It's a time to look out at the sky, a change from the cockpit and its intricacy of instruments, switches, lights, knobs, and levers to the vastness outside. A great dome of darkness has covered the sky above us. Night, as one flies east, comes as a curtain rising from the eastern horizon, gradually climbing toward the zenith to darken a quarter of the sky, then half; looking back, westward at this stage, there is still daylight—the red-orange color of the fading day. The advance of night is quickened by our rushing toward it, increasing the speed by 500 miles an hour; the curtain pulls farther west to cover three quarters of the sky, then finally all of it, and daylight is shut out. The stars and planets appear, becoming visible like fireflies, the nearest and brightest first and, as our eyes adjust to the dark, the less bright become discernible until the sky seems alive with points of light, thousands of them.

At this perch, 35,000 feet above the earth, the air is unstained by haze or pollution and the stars shine with brilliance you rarely see from earth. From the days of celestial navigation I know certain stars as intimate friends: Sirius, Rigel, Arcturus, Altair, Vega, Deneb, Acrux, Antares—fifty-seven I knew and used, the specific ones depending on our location above the earth, whether we're over the Northern or Southern Hemisphere—and if north, as we are tonight, Polaris, the North Star. It's not the brightest, but I feel it's the most steadfast because it consistently sits close over the North Pole; a glance at it tells which way you're headed. Tonight it's over my left shoulder, so we're going east.

I like to regard stars the way the ancients did, as parts of constellations, each with its legends, all there to see and recognize. I understand the science, I know about the immense distances of space, the fact that the light of a star I see may have begun its journey a million years ago. But such theories spoil the romance; I prefer to see Cygnus the swan flying across the sky, and Taurus the bull protecting the seven sisters of the Pleiades from the mighty hunter Orion, who is climbing up the eastern sky. There is pleasure in this feeling of detachment from earth and surroundings.

I press my head against the window on the left so I can see out without distraction from the inside. The glass is cool on my forehead and I feel almost as though I'm out in space. The cool glass reminds me that only inches away the temperature is 50 degrees below zero, but this does not detract from the fantasy of being out there in the enormous space that has no limits.

How did fate allow me the good fortune to be here, pilot of a Boeing 747 across the Atlantic, the king of assignments? It all began a long time ago, while I was still a young boy making his first tentative step toward the sky.

CHAPTER 2

Hooked

I WAS ABOUT FOURTEEN and was walking from my aunt's house toward an open field on a sunny afternoon, hoping to find a baseball game. But at the field I stopped, transfixed by the sight of a young man holding a model airplane. His right hand held the fuselage high and his left held the propeller, which was hooked to a tightly wound rubber band. As I watched, he shoved the model forward and released the propeller, which spun and the model flew. It climbed slightly, curved, and when the rubber band had exhausted its winds—a matter of seconds—the propeller stopped and the model glided back to earth and nosed up in some tall grass. It was a model of the airplane in which Louis Bleriot had made the first flight across the English Channel in July 1909.

It was a moment of wonder, excitement, and total captivation. From that instant on I was wedded to aviation. The young man, Bill Mumford, became my friend; he was two years older and already a craftsman with tools. We used, and relished, his father's workshop, a treasure trove of drills, lathes, workbenches, and drawer after drawer filled with screws, nuts, bolts, and parts to fit anything. Bill showed me how to build models, and that's what we did.

A year later my enthusiasm zoomed even higher when Lindbergh made his epic flight to Paris. It wasn't just hero worship; as little as I understood weather and navigation, I knew that the problems posed by trying to fly an ocean required incredible courage and foresight to even think of tackling them. I have looked up to Lindbergh all my life, and the more I learned, the more he became a hero—one I would meet one day. He wasn't just a pilot, but a scientist. I hated the tag "Lucky Lindy": any luck in that adventure he created, because he was the best equipped pilot to try the flight, an airmail pilot familiar with battling through the night in foul weather—storms, ice, snow, fog. His scientific mind determined the best type of airplane to use, outfitted with the latest instruments. He carefully plotted his course and studied the weather he'd face. He knew, when he took off, all that was possible to know, and he was as well prepared for it, relatively, as Neil Armstrong was when he blasted off for the moon.

One day Bill suggested we build a glider—not a model, but the real thing, one we could fly. We talked of it almost in hushed tones, because we weren't sure what our parents or others might say. But we built it, Bill doing most of it because he was the better craftsman. It was a simple primary glider with an open fuselage, a plywood seat, and a stick and rudder bar that stuck out from the edge of the fuselage over the empty air below. The wings were wood spars and ribs, linen covered. We dubbed her "Diving Dottie." When we unveiled our plans our parents were cool to the idea and a little baffled, but eventually overtaken by our determination.

And then it was time to take the craft into the air. It was my first solo flight, my first everything, and there was no instruction—just go. I sat in the glider, safety belt fastened, hand on the stick, feet on the rudder bar, while a long rope attached the glider to an automobile that began to move forward. The glider ran smoothly over the ground. As we gained speed I pulled back on the stick and the glider lifted, climbing to an altitude of about fifty feet—that was high enough for the first flight—and I pulled the release and dropped the rope and was now in free flight. But I didn't fly; I simply sat there dumb, awed by it all. A swift mush downward, a hard crunch on contact with the earth, the rudder bar snapped in half, and my rear end broke through the plywood seat. I had mushed to the ground.

Bill ran up from his observation spot near the automobile. "You didn't put the goddamn nose down—you never got the nose down," he said. "I yelled at you—why didn't you put the goddamn nose down?"

I didn't know why I hadn't, but that was it: first solo, first crackup.

There was no serious damage to me or to it, and the glider was back flying a day later.

I was hooked, but I was fifteen and that was too young to fly an airplane even then, so that meant messing with the glider until my sixteenth birthday in January and my first lesson—a Fleet airplane, open cockpit, cold, with my instructor, Pa Bowyer, in the front cockpit; he was a quiet man, with an airman's blue eyes and a gentle touch. The Kinner engine popped loudly with its five cylinders and uneven-length exhaust stacks that made it sound as though it were missing fire. The inside of the cockpit was made up of steel tubing with an outer shell of thin blue linen that let the daylight show through. The air blasted your head and the raw sky was right there; I could look down at the earth and feel a sense of our height above it.

On my first lesson, my first loop: a shallow dive and then the nose rising and the earth disappearing, only the sky in view, and then the nose coming straight down and the earth coming up—a gentle pull brought the nose level and the topsy-turvy world was back in place again.

As the lessons progressed I learned more stunting, as we called it. Carefully raising the nose with back pressure on the stick, the Kinner slowly popping as it idled, controls getting soft in your hand, a quietness as the airplane lost speed, then a quiver through the structure as the yellow wing came up and heaved over—and the nose dropped straight down and turned to start a spin as the tail rotated around the nose and the New Jersey ground whirled fast as it came up toward us—my first tailspin. Rudder opposite and stick forward to stop the spinning, then a delicate pull back while you gently opened the throttle and you were back level and organized. It was a frightening feeling, but stimulating, too.

The instruction covered the basic stuff from flying straight and level to turns, takeoffs, and landings, but Pa Bowyer took me through all the stunts and unusual maneuvers as well. No one ever soloed a student without showing him how to get in and out of a tailspin, or to do loops and maybe snap rolls. A student who couldn't do those things wasn't considered completely schooled and safe.

Then one day, after we'd been practicing landings, he stopped at the end of the runway and I saw him wiggle out of his cockpit and step down off the wing root to the ground to stand next to me.

"It'll trim a little more tail-heavy—and get off quicker. Go ahead, take her around."

With a rush of feeling, in a detached, almost dreamlike state, I opened the throttle and the Fleet rolled down the field, bounced a little, and climbed into the sky. The flight was short, just circle the field and land, but I was conscious of being alone—not afraid, but feeling a border had been crossed, that I was a step further along in being a pilot. That first solo, that first successful flight, lives in the memory of a pilot, and even now I can see the nose of the Fleet ahead with the propeller whirling in front, the familiar countryside I knew, and the runway. It was the start of a very long journey.

✳

WE FLEW FROM a country airport with grass runways except where tail skids had worn dirt streaks into them. They were called runways, but they weren't the long strips of concrete festooned with lights and markings one knows today, but just clear strips through the old farm pastures where we could run down and take off or land. The long one, oriented northeast to southwest, was 2,700 feet; the medium was northwest to southeast, and the short one, 1,600 feet, ran north to south with trees and an electric wire across one end that made it tight to use. Between them the grass was rich enough to cut for hay.

The main building was an old farmhouse. Two of the rooms were used as offices, meaning they had a couple of desks and a file cabinet, while the other room was for diversified and miscellaneous storage ranging from parachutes to paint cans. The upstairs had a couple of bedrooms that were used for overnight stays and perhaps a dalliance now and then. In back of the house was a two-hole outhouse painted green.

The big building, fifty yards from the house, was a hangar of recent construction and quite modern, except for the floor of messy cinders, which is where the money ran out during construction. The airport was operated by a recently formed company run by two gentlemen who didn't know much about airplanes, but they'd noticed the surge of interest in aviation ignited by the Lindbergh excitement and had the big idea that aviation was the place to make money. Little did they know.

To the rest of us such high-powered ideas were vague and unimportant, what mattered was the place to fly and the presence of the airplanes. The airport never grew into anything lucrative, but simply went on its country way with the sweet-smelling grass and the blue sky.

The activities of the airport were student instruction, passenger rides, selling airplanes, and taking people places if they wanted to go somewhere—but few did, and not many bought airplanes either. There were a lot of students, and the passenger rides sold briskly on the weekends. We paid for a half hour of instruction when funds allowed; the rest of the time we just hoped someone would take us along on a flight.

During the week it was quiet, and there was time to talk with the two instructors and your fellow students who were hanging around the airport trying to become a part of this new endeavor. We'd sit out on the ground chewing any stems of long grass within reach, and talk flying. On rainy days we gathered in the office and sat on beat-up wooden office chairs or the old, low, uncomfortable couch with the broken springs that slumped you sideways. These sessions were called hangar flying, even though they were seldom in the hangar. Bits of wisdom would come out of someone's tales of adventure, and would sink into our neophyte minds. I remember a remark by Warren Noble, the number two instructor, about having trouble getting out of a spin; the airplane was rotating, but it whipped on one side of the spin each time it came around, and at that point he goosed the engine, shoving open the throttle briefly—and on the second try the controls took, the spin stopped, and everything turned out fine. The memory of that tale served me well not long after.

Hangar flying has dropped off in modern times because there's so much formal instruction, and experienced pilots just don't sit around talking with young people as much anymore. You still see it to some extent in rural places in the Midwest where there are country airports. Those who get to take part in such sessions are fortunate because the stories help you learn a lot of the feel for flying, something you can't get from a book.

The airplanes we learned on were mostly biplanes: two Fleet trainers—blue and yellow—with 90 horsepower engines and dual cockpits, the front for the instructor with the student in the rear; and two Spartan biplanes with a rear seat for the pilot and front seat with room for two. One Spartan had a Walters engine of 120 horsepower or so, and the other had a Wright J-6 five-cylinder sporting 165 horsepower. This latter airplane was painted red, white, and blue, which made it very flashy and the pride of the fleet, and the one we students dreamed of flying. It was tricky to start and would load up easily, which got raw gas into the induction system—when it caught it would backfire with a loud "plop" kind of noise and would catch fire. Anyone hearing this noise knew what was happening and, without even looking, grabbed the nearest fire extinguisher and ran like hell to the flight line and put the fire out. Miraculously, no fire was ever serious enough to damage the airplane.

The other airplanes were two red Cessnas, enclosed monoplanes: sleek and modern with no struts and not much sticking out to slow them down. They were ahead of their time, and today's most modern airplane of the same power performs no better than they did. One had a 110 horsepower Warner engine and carried four people at over 100 miles an hour; the other had a Comet engine of 160 horsepower and was fast enough that Pa Bowyer flew it in the National Air Races at Cleveland, Ohio, and although he didn't win, his finish was creditable. We neophytes were in awe of the Cessnas; being so slick, they required some fine stick and rudder work to land because they didn't have flaps, which made it difficult to reduce speed and get down in the confines of the airport. Those open biplanes with their tail skids taught you the skill of slipping, fishtailing, and S turning, maneuvers seldom seen today, but good to have tucked away in a pilot's bag of tricks.

Weekends, and especially Sundays, were when the airport could make money by giving passenger rides. A crowd always gathered, lured by a stunt show and a parachute jump arranged as the come-on, and we had to put up a rope to keep people off the field. We weekday loyalists were given tasks to perform: sell tickets, escort riders to the airplanes and strap them in, push the airplanes around, help refuel, and all such.

The stunts and rides would today make an FAA inspector go pale. Warren Noble often hopped passengers in the red, white, and blue Spartan biplane; his standard pattern was a takeoff, a short tour of the surrounding country, and then a dive for the airport, roaring across only a few feet off the ground and then pulling up in a loop, rolling out on top to level, followed by a side slip and landing. One day the engine quit right on top of the loop—a cam ring broke, and that makes for instantaneous cessation of all power, from full out to zero in a second. But it was old hat to Warren, and he just rolled out of the inverted position, slipped a little, and landed perfectly—real stick and rudder airmanship.

The parachute jump was the big event of the day and it was held off until five o'clock or later to keep the crowd around. John C. Krajick—Sarge—was the mechanic and an expert parachute man. He was tall, with china blue eyes that crinkled when he smiled, and he was always dressed in tan coveralls. His long hitch in the Air Corps—the 22nd Observation Squadron—had been in parachutes; before the Sunday jump he'd repack the parachute to be used, stretching it out on a long table, straightening the shroud lines, carefully lapping over each panel of the canopy and then lacing the shroud lines into loops of material in the canister that held the chute. The chute was folded over in an accordion fashion so it was an orderly pile of silk about eighteen inches square and a foot high; this was encased in the canister and pounded down to fit. Flat wooden sticks were used to tuck in the ends.

Sarge was a showman, and he did all this where the crowd could watch and listen to his remarks such as, "If it doesn't open he can bring it back and I'll give him a new one." Sarge never jumped himself, and one day when I suggested I'd like to make a jump he lit into me unmercifully: "What the hell for?"

"Well, if I ever had to jump I'd know how."

"Listen, sonny, going up and jumping out of a nicely flown level airplane isn't going to be anything like the real thing, when it may be spinning or a wing folded back over the cockpit. It's foolish to jump for nothing—the chute will open if I pack the sumbitch, but you might land on a rock, break your leg, spend the summer in the hospital. No, forget it."

I did, and I never have jumped. Of course, chutes were different then, almost like oversized streamers out behind you; they slowed the fall to survivable limits, but the descent was fast, and the jumpers hit hard and bowled over. Today a sport parachute can be steered, and if used properly it'll deposit you softly back to earth with about as much inconvenience as stepping off a footstool.

The first accident I ever witnessed was the chute jump. It was late afternoon and there were a lot of people, the atmosphere thick with airplanes, noise, and excitement. Curly Crasto was the jumper, and the crowd gawked skyward as the small Fleet biplane climbed, watching for it to reach altitude and for Curly to crawl out and dive off the wing root.

"There he goes!" and the small black form of a man fell through the sky, a long way because he was delaying opening the chute to thrill the crowd, conning them into thinking it wasn't going to open—a standard crowd shocker of the time. Finally Curly pulled the rip cord and the chute streamed out, but something was wrong—he was flat on his back when the chute opened and it came up between his legs and around his body. The shroud lines didn't stream out clean, but went over the top of the canopy, folding it in half so that Curly didn't have an open chute, but in effect two streamers fluttering in the air behind him as he plunged toward the ground twisting and writhing in a futile attempt to get it untangled.

I was standing next to our car as my doctor father rushed up, pushed me aside, and jumped into the car and headed for the impact point. A frightened feeling enveloped me and I didn't want to go along; I stayed fixed, immobile, not knowing what to do. I was afraid to, afraid of what I might see, and this fear bothered me later on, bothered me for many years and still can if I think about it—one of those flaws you question about your character, always wondering if it is really a flaw.

My father returned and simply said, "He died a moment after I got there."

A woman who'd been a bystander during the packing operation started yelling and pointing her finger at Sarge: "He did it, he did it—I saw him beating on the parachute!" One of the airport regulars got close to her and told her to shut up, that she didn't know what the hell she was talking about.

The incident spooked me and I thought of Curly dead, cold, never to move or talk again, or to be there, or anywhere. But I also remember rationalizing that I wasn't a chute jumper and wouldn't be; the protective subconscious that all pilots carry around was already beginning to work for me.

It was at about this time that the Department of Commerce, which then regulated aviation, decided to issue parachute rigger licenses. Sarge was eager to get the first one and he rushed to take the exam; he passed all the tests perfectly and was issued license number twelve, as I recall. He became livid: "Those sonsabitches, I should be number one!" He tracked down information on who got the other eleven, and he claimed they were all Department of Commerce people. He cussed about this for months.

My goal was to get a private pilot license, and to do that I needed ten hours of solo flying. They came in tiny dribbles, each one important and cherished, carefully testified by Bowyer's initials—CDB. Looking back to my logbook from those days I see entries of "15 minutes—landings," meaning I was practicing landing; "18 minutes—aerobatics." And so it went for a month, and by then the bits and pieces added up to ten hours and enough for a license.

Periodically the Department of Commerce inspector visited the airport to give license tests and look over the airplanes, checking that they were being maintained properly. His name was George Ream, and he was a square-jawed, dark-complexioned, cigar-smoking man who looked mean, and whose reputation fitted his looks; the idea of being under his scrutiny was scary. Many years later I got to know Ream better and found him a thoughtful, tolerant, pleasant man, but on that day he was Satan to me.

The written test was simple, mostly on rules of the air. It wasn't multiple choice like today, but the kind where you wrote out that balloons had right of way over airplanes, that the airplane coming on the right had right of way, and other such stuff you'd studied carefully in Department of Commerce regulations. Then came the flight test.

Ream looked me in the eye. "Here's what I want you to do: make three takeoffs and landings, touching down just opposite where I'll stand on the airport, then go up to 3,000 feet and do two turns of a spin to the right, and stop the spin facing me—then do the same to the left—come in and land." Inspectors didn't ride with private pilots, they observed the tests from the ground—I never knew why, but I suspect everyone felt it was safer that way.

I did what he asked and lucked out on the spins, stopping both in the direction he dictated.

"Well," he said after I landed, "I guess you're safe enough. Don't do anything foolish." He made out the license and eventually I received an official one, number 13,478, the number that stayed with me from then on, moving along with each advance in grade of license.

With this license I was approved to carry people and to go where I wanted as long as I didn't do it for hire—to do that took a commercial license, which meant 200 hours solo and a tougher written exam, plus a minimum age of eighteen. A private license today requires cross-country flying, night flying, forty total hours with twenty of them instruction designed so you can't jam it all into forty hours; most people applying for a private license have closer to sixty hours.

But back then the ten hours said you had enough experience, and the next day, my father bravely went with me, my first passenger. After that came a string of relatives: my mother, my seventy-six-year-old grand-mother, who admonished me not to fly too slow or low just because of her age. They all enjoyed the flights, never realizing how tenuous the safety margins were with their lives in the hands of a sixteen-year-old boy with ten hours of purely local flying experience. But with my white piece of paper, I could legally fly any airplane, anywhere, day or night, fair weather or foul.

CHAPTER 3

Records

I EARNED MY LICENSE just three years after Lindbergh's flight to Paris, when the publicity generated by record flight attempts of all types fueled a nationwide enthusiasm for flying. A record or a daring flight looked like the road to fame and fortune, but few people recognized that Lindbergh had been first and best, had wrapped it all up, and any effort to duplicate or better him would be an anticlimax, even shabby—and the idea of making money that way was laughable.

But at sixteen you don't reason like that. I caught the bug, too. There was a small experimental biplane, a close copy of a World War I Nieuport fighter, that showed up at the field; called the Air Cub, it was being promoted as a sport plane and trainer. There were many projects like that across the land, most of them created on a shoestring and all expecting to cash in on aviation's great future. They craved publicity, and this group decided that an altitude record attempt by a sixteen-year-old—me—would do the trick.

They let me fly the airplane, and it was sprightly. The large wing area and the small fuselage—I stuck out of it a goodly way—gave it quick climb and slow landing. I thought it was fabulous. Pa Bowyer wasn't as enthralled, and he suggested I be careful with it: don't spin it, don't strain it, and always wear a parachute.

The record try was perfect for the airport promoters; I'd do it on a Sunday afternoon to draw a crowd. When the day arrived, it brought with it a sky heavy with cumulus clouds that suggested showers. It wasn't a great setup for a record attempt, but the crowd was there, so I took off and climbed. Clouds built up and surrounded me, seeming to climb as fast as I did. They cut out my view of the earth until I could only see it in glimpses. The towering clouds were unfriendly, menacing, pressing in—I knew not to get into one because I had no instruments for what we called blind flying and even if I had, I wouldn't have known how to use them. A gnawing fear said to get out of there, forget the record, just get back to earth. I picked a twisting trail down through the narrow corridors between the clouds, weaving and turning to avoid slipping into one—trying to hold back the feeling of panic—and descending until at last I was underneath the clouds, low and skimming the earth as the rain cut at my exposed face. I searched for something familiar—and there it was, through the rain and blurred visibility: the reservoir, only a mile from home, and in a moment I was back on the good, safe solid earth. I'd spent an hour's fright time with about three years experience packed in it—but no record.

The harsh lesson taught me that weather and flying went together and I'd better learn about it. I was also fortunate in that I'd had some humility infused into my flying character without paying a heavy price. But the experience didn't turn me away from records; the air was too full of excitement, almost daily someone was off trying something, and everyone wanted to be a part of it.

My next effort was a coast-to-coast flight for the junior transcontinental speed record. Pa Bowyer sat me down for a stern, fatherly talk about waiting for weather, playing it so that if there was any doubt I would sit on the ground and wait it out. (Only time spent in the air would count toward the record.) I respected his lecture—and I respected the memory of those big wet clouds that had scared me in the Air Cub. Weather was the first antagonist.

I realize now that a sixteen-year-old has more mature judgment than grown-ups believe—or want to admit. The nature of my judgment was much the same then as it has been through my flying years; of course some guidance is needed, but teaching a young person to fly—in an airplane or a glider—is safer than turning him loose in a car or on a motorcycle. You can tell a teenager to be careful in a car, but the sermon has a tendency to make rapid transit between ear openings. Teach them to fly, however, and as lessons progress they'll understand that they'll soon be flying alone— well above the earth, not attached to it—and that disciplined flying and concentration provide the only safe way back. Under those circumstances you don't have to preach self-preservation, the need to understand how things work and to do things properly becomes crystal clear. I've seen a lot of young people learn flying at early ages, and they have all been safe and responsible; my son made his first solo flight at age fifteen, and has carried on in an aviation career. I have never had to question his judgment, and I don't think he's unusual.

As for the record, I could have done it about as fast in an automobile. The respect I'd acquired for weather had me calling the Weather Bureau, talking it over carefully with meteorologists, taking heed, becoming interested in the science, and waiting when it seemed prudent to wait. It took me five days to get to California.

I had no radio for navigation or ground communication. There was only a sketchy series of radio beams, called radio ranges, across the country; they were used by the airmail pilots and very few others, and beginning pilots weren't taught how to use them. Control towers were a rarity, and if there was a tower and you didn't have a radio they'd signal landing clearance with a green light—it was red if no—and the lights were used more than radio. All towers still have signal lights today in case of radio failure, though they hang unused most of the time. Further communication wasn't necessary because there wasn't any air traffic control; it was a free sky to go as you wanted, where you wanted, and in whatever weather. Very few pilots knew how to fly blind—even the airmail pilots and the few airliners hadn't adopted the technique yet. Navigation was by compass and map. The maps were sketchy; I used Rand McNally state maps that showed towns and railroads, but no roads, elevations, or terrain. Each state map was on a different scale, so as I flew from one state into another I had to readjust my idea of distance. Rand McNally made a set of maps for me, a coast-to-coast scroll of their state maps rolled up on sticks that I could unroll as I progressed—Frank Hawks, who held the transcontinental speed record and was considered the king of speed flying, had encouraged them to do this as a favor for me.

My airplane was a Pitcairn Mailwing (PA-6) open biplane, pilot in back, two passengers in a front cockpit. The engine was a Wright J-5 of 220 horsepower—the type Lindbergh flew to Paris. The Mailwing cruised about 110 miles an hour. This same type of airplane was used in the air-mail service, with a mail bin replacing the front cockpit. I put an extra gasoline tank in the front cockpit, removing the windshield and covering over the hole. We named the airplane the *Yankee Clipper* because of my New England background—this was long before Pan Am started calling their airplanes Clippers, and I often wondered if Juan Trippe, PAA's president and founder, saw something about my airplane in a newspaper and said to himself, "Say, that gives me an idea." We'll never know.

I took off from Newark on a windy day, and computing my course from the winds forecast, I took up a compass heading and flew west. The ground matched the map in my lap for a while, but as I flew over the Allegheny Mountains and looked down, the railroads twisted along valleys, went through passes, and disappeared into tunnels, and it was difficult to relate to the map. The long mountain range that first flows east-northeast to west-southwest subtly changed to more north-and-south, and that confused my tracking because it's natural to continue crossing the mountains at the same angle you've been flying, but that's not right and it sent me off in a wrong direction. Just a few hours out I was confused, filled with anxiety, a little frantic. Then I saw a grass airport in a valley. I landed, and asked, "Where am I?"

"Indiana. Indiana, Pennsylvania."

I looked on my map—not bad, not far off course. In a moment I was back in the air, hanging on to the compass. Past Pittsburgh and into Ohio where the mountains subside, the railroads straighten out and make sense with the map. The compass in the airplane became secondary to the iron compass on the ground, and I tenaciously hung on to the railroad, following its right side.

Indianapolis the first night: weary, my face windblown and -burned, my lips cracked and sore, my arms tired from fighting the heavy aileron control forces in the turbulence.

The next day, Wichita. The railroad had been good to me, and I'd learned that just plotting a compass heading from forecast winds wasn't how it worked—the textbooks made it look that way, but the real world puts ifs, buts, and maybes all over the theory.

Wichita required my first weather judgment: low clouds, and poor visibility between there and Amarillo. I sat a day and waited. The next day it wasn't much better, but the visibility was good despite the low clouds—I took off and flew squeezed between the cloud bases and the ground, but the ground was flat, all wheat fields and ranches that I could race over only a few hundred feet up. The good visibility made it safe and exciting; I dolphined up and down following the undulations of the land, seeing it in detail and feeling that I was going like hell over the close-by ground. The highest obstructions were oil rigs that were easily avoided—TV hadn't been invented, so its towers weren't sticking up a thousand feet or more as they do today to menace the hedge-hopping, scud-running pilot.

Beyond Amarillo the Far West began, and there was the solid Santa Fe Railroad to hold on to. Buttes and mesas, red rock, arroyos, and always the far, far visibility of a kind an Easterner had never seen; then you came around the corner of the majestic Sangre de Cristo Mountains and there was Albuquerque—what an eye-opening thrill for a young man in the air.

At the Albuquerque hotel I met my first real airline pilot, Joe Kuhn, a nice man. I asked him about the way west, how you get into the Los Angeles area. "I'll show you," he said, pulling out some hotel stationery and patiently drawing maps for me emphasizing the points I'd see. The maps Joe made were dimensional, with mountain peaks sticking up and passes in perspective. He drew the important checkpoints, the things that really stood out, in exploded detail; he wasn't an artist, but he knew how to put it down. Then he carefully went over the route point by point, telling me what to look for, which side of a mountain to be on, where to expect a railroad to cross a road—he explained it all. It made the flight easy: hotel stationery in one hand, stick in the other, and it all rolled out before me just as he said it would—over Winslow, Arizona, and the big meteor crater; past Flagstaff and the high mountains around San Francisco Peak; Kingman, then the Colorado River into California—the sandy desert and mountains. Cajon Pass came up as he said it would and I slipped through it to fly out over a land of orange trees, open country, unlimited visibility—smog hadn't been invented and it was the land of milk and honey. The airport, Alhambra by name, was easy to spot, with its big octagonal hangar, the maintenance base for Western Air Lines, standing out prominently. I landed, shut down, and took a deep breath of air perfumed by orange blossoms and perhaps a trace of eucalyptus—it was heady in those days.

A week later I headed back, but only as far as Kingman; beyond there was bad weather in the mountains around Flagstaff. Five airline pilots clustered in the small building at the airport; they were flying together back to Newark, in a Fleetster that had a high wing, a single Pratt & Whitney engine, and an open rear cockpit plus a small cabin forward that seated six passengers.

The pilots were being transferred to Newark. The flight was a contentious setup, with one pilot flying from that single cockpit in the back and the other four suffering in the cramped cabin, wondering about weather and unable to see ahead or know what the rear cockpit pilot was up to. The man doing the flying was Alton Parker, a pilot from the Byrd Antarctic expedition and a captain for Transcontinental Air Transport, TAT; the passengers were all captains, too.

In Kingman they had a lively argument about the weather ahead and if they should go—it was decision by committee. There was some discussion about flying on instruments, and the cabin-bound pilots were not in favor of that—instrument flying wasn't universally used except in short segments. One pilot, Bob LeRoy, was expressing himself firmly to Parker. "Just because you flew in the Antarctic doesn't make you a hotshot around here—I know where that throttle arm goes and I can get at it—you pull up in the clouds and I'll pull that son of a bitch closed!" It was said in a kidding tone.

They took note of me, and LeRoy struck up a conversation. I asked him about the weather ahead. "Oh, hell, it's okay, just stick to the railroad and once you're past Flagstaff it's a cinch into Winslow."

This group was being sent east because TAT and Western Air Express had merged on the transcontinental route. Up until then TAT had carried passengers coast to coast by railroad and airplane; passengers rode overnight on the train from New York to Columbus, Ohio, where they transferred to the airline—a Ford Tri-Motor airplane—and flew through the day landing at Indianapolis, St. Louis, Kansas City, Wichita, and finally Waynoka, Oklahoma, where they crawled back on a train for an overnight journey to Clovis, New Mexico, then back on the airplane again headed west in daylight with stops at Albuquerque, Winslow, Kingman, and finally Los Angeles—actually Glendale. It was a tiring, bouncy, noisy voyage.

Now, after the merger, the railroad part would cease and the new airline, Transcontinental and Western Air, Inc., would fly the mountain portions, making it all air, coast to coast. The pilots were getting in position.

They didn't go much faster than I did, and we overnighted together in Albuquerque and Wichita. They went up to Kansas City, the main office, but I went straight on to St. Louis. Spending time with them had been wonderful for me, a chance to live among the gods, to listen to their stories, jokes, constant banter, and laughter. They were human, too, but they were still on pedestals; they took me in, and I felt T&WA was my airline.

It took five days again going back, but it went faster and I could feel that I was developing a certain experience, a craftiness. Getting lost was no longer a big problem; I cut corners, and when the railroad went up north, such as to Gallup, New Mexico, I went straight across and used the compass for direction until the railroad came back to me at Albuquerque. The bends in rivers meant more to me, the way a railroad twisted, other features: they began to translate from paper to the real world, to what I saw and what that hill or river and valley actually looked like. Maps began to get in my blood and mind.

The last day, past Pittsburgh, into the Alleghenies: snow showers, reduced visibility. I hung on to the compass, and got a few position checks by picking up a name from a water tower in a town. One was a shock: West Virginia Pulp and Paper! West Virginia? My God, I was way off course! But I took a closer look, and under the big sign were the letters spelling out Tyrone, Pennsylvania. I was fine, but more important, without realizing it, I had started using the compass and then checking my position to learn if the winds were as expected, what the variation or deviation was, and how to adjust the compass heading accordingly. I'd use the same principle someday with fixes on stars, or radio beacons, or anything else that came up.

Coast to coast, in twenty-three hours and forty-seven minutes of flying time. The record—for what it was worth.

✶

THE T&WA PILOTS I had met drifted into Newark. Bob LeRoy was looking for a house with his family still in California, and my folks invited him to stay with us until he got settled. He'd only been there a day when he asked for a lift to the airport the next morning, because there was going to be a pre-schedule survey flight over the mountains for which he'd be copilot. The captain would be Charles Lindbergh!

We arrived early. The operations people and a few newspapermen gathered near the Ford Tri-Motor; the Ford engines were ticking over, and LeRoy took me aboard as he took over the job of sitting in the pilot's seat, watching over the airplane as the engines warmed up. But soon a mechanic came up front and said they were all wanted in the office for a preflight conference, so LeRoy turned over the watching job to me. "You sit here, keep an eye on the airplane—there's the throttles, the switches, and that's the brake [a big lever in the center]." I worked my way into the captain's seat, checked the things he'd pointed out and waited—in a glorious, superior, heavenly aura; here I was, a part of the airline. I sat there about ten minutes and then felt some action back at the rear door. I turned to see what was happening, and there, coming up the aisle, was Lindbergh. Our eyes caught and his face lit up in that big boyish grin you occasionally saw in pictures. He stuck out his hand. "How's she goin'?"

I could hardly speak, but I mumbled something and slid out of the seat to make room for him. "Thanks," he said—friendly, likable, one of the gang. I cannot describe the feelings, but they were there, overwhelming: I'd met my hero and he was true.

The next night they returned and I was there to pick up LeRoy. A fairly large group from the press had gathered. One newspaperman I knew pulled me over toward Lindbergh, "Here's our famous young flier, Bob Buck." Lindbergh shook hands in a formal, polite fashion.

"How about a picture?"

"No," Lindbergh quickly and coolly answered.

This was a huge contrast from the day before, in the airplane. Today I understand: it was the press; he never liked the press and froze up in its presence. I had lunch with him years later and had a long, private conversation—he was again the boyish, smiling man I remembered walking up the aisle of that Ford Tri-Motor.

✳

FLYING SEEMED MOSTLY a man's world in the 1930s, but there were many fine women pilots. I remember an air derby to Florida in 1933, when a covey of private pilots gathered and flew to the Miami Air Races, lured by the offer of free lodging at the Biltmore and a tank of gas. One of the airplanes, a two-seat Monocoupe, was flown by Tiny Goddard, a New Yorker from a well-off family. She flew for fun and she had what I call the "fire," that burning desire to know everything there is to know about flying. People with the fire practice, listen, and learn. The outside world of publicity isn't important to them, what they crave is more knowledge so they can fly better. Tiny flew alone in her little airplane to Miami and back; she navigated and made weather judgments with no radio to help, just a map with her finger tracing the route.

She was the first woman aviator I knew, and she showed me that women can fly as well and love it as much as any man in the sky. In later years, having flown with a number of ladies, I concluded that women have a delicate touch with the controls that is actually better than most men.

There was a pretty gal that flew at our Vermont airport. She had the fire and did anything she could to gain experience and flying time. Bonnie Tiburzi was her name, and she flew charter work in the Bahamas, ferried airplanes, taught students, and did, as she says, "basically all the flying no one else liked." She applied in 1973 for a job as pilot for American Airlines. After scrutinizing her record and watching her fly a simulator they hired her, the first woman pilot to go with a major airline. She started as flight engineer—the first woman ever in that job; advanced to copilot and finally to captain, flying Boeing 767s to Europe. In between she married and added the name Caputo, had two children, and took early retirement after twenty-six years with American in order, she said, "to be a proper mother for my teenagers." There's no one in aviation I admire more.

There was another woman in Vermont who fell in love with flying, Vanda Crook. She took lessons in Montpelier and obtained her private license, but that wasn't enough for Vanda; she packed all her worldly goods in an automobile and drove to Florida, where she studied with Flight Safety and when she was finished she had a commercial license and rating to fly by instruments. Back in Vermont, she took on any flying job that would teach her more and help build her hours. Finally she applied to a local commuter airline, Air North, an outfit that flew all the toughest weather in Vermont, New York, the Adirondacks—that's what she wanted, the fire was burning. She started as copilot and became a captain. I had the distinction of riding as a passenger on what may have been the first commercial flight with an all-woman crew: Vanda was captain, Sarah Wastvedt first officer, and the flight attendant Carol Anne Varney (now Farmer). We flew Burlington, Vermont, to Boston—it was sometime in 1982, and I felt happy and comfortable.

Air North became Brockway, and finally the regional airline Commut-Air. Vanda is now VP of operations for the airline, and I can't tell you how proud I am of her.

Then there is Debbie, Debbie Gary, who said she fell passionately in love with flying on her first ride in an airplane, at age twelve. She was living in St. Thomas, Virgin Islands, with her family, and as soon as she was old enough she learned to fly gliders, flew passengers, instructed in them. Then on to airplanes; Jim Holland, an aerobatic show pilot, taught Debbie aerobatics. They became an aerobatic pair, flying in shows all over the country. Debbie worked fiercely for more knowledge. She became an air show pilot—the first woman in a jet aerobatic team, spending a year with Canada's prestigious Carling team. She gave aerobatic instruction as well as doing shows. She married, had two children, and flew little for a few years, but then was back at it flying for the movies when they made the Pancho Barnes story. She has flown ninety different airplanes, most of them made for aerobatics, and done over 200 air shows. She's flown all over the country and knows weather and navigation. Her fire, she tells me, has never gone out, and her quest for knowledge is constant. In 2001, Debbie was doing a wing-walking act, flying the airplane while another woman rode on top of the wing—perhaps the first all-woman act of its kind.

I mention these great women pilots because they're different from the merely famous, like Amelia Earhart. A.E. may have had the fire, but she really never pursued it. I don't know if that's because she didn't want to, or because she was thrust into the world of spectacular flights so early in her flying life, was pushed too hard, and tried to fly airplanes she wasn't up to. She had about eight accidents, mostly during landing or takeoff. Generally pilots didn't think she was a good pilot. She never learned such vital elements of navigation as the best radio procedures and techniques, which had much to do with her missing Howland Island on her fateful flight. Many of us were not surprised at the final misfortune.

She was a nice lady. I met her once, a brief and strange meeting in New York at the office of her husband, George Palmer Putnam. I was there about a book Putnam had published. Someone had invented an airplane training device; it was very simple, a model airplane about eighteen inches across, mounted on a stick with a swivel so it could move in any direction. String ran from each control, down to a board with a control stick. One could sit on the floor, move the stick, and see how the controls worked. It wasn't much more than a toy, but someone was promoting it.

The device somehow got to Putnam's office. Amelia was around, so her opinion was sought. She came into the room and we were introduced, hardly more than a "How do you do." She studied the gadget as it was explained, and then she sat on the floor in front of it, wiggled the stick and said something about it being useful, got up off the floor, shook my hand, said goodbye and was gone. So when I say my meeting with A.E. was brief, I mean brief. My main memory of it is that as she sat on the floor moving the stick, her dress hiked up, and I noticed she was wearing pink bloomers.

There are about 37,000 woman pilots as I write this, about 6 percent of all licensed pilots; some achieved fame through records and such, but the ones I think of as great role models are the ones like Tiny, Bonnie, Vanda, and Debbie—they had the desire, they learned how to do things right, they pursued knowledge and experience, and they're a credit to aviation and its safety.

✶

M Y OWN PURSUIT of records next took me to Havana, Cuba, and back. I was getting more sophisticated—only one stop to Miami, then down the Keys, and from Key West out across the ocean to Havana. On the maps the 100-mile hop looked like nothing; heck, I thought, I'll probably see the Cuban coast right after leaving Key West.

But what a shock! The Keys disappeared quickly, and ahead was only the sea, with a haze over the water that reduced visibility. I didn't like the feeling: land was gone, the land I'd used for forced landings; now it was all water, unfriendly, lonesome, no place to land if I needed help. A very tight, anxious feeling growled in my lower innards. I didn't like this water flying. Then I saw a dark form ahead, the coastline, and I crossed over a beach— but no Havana. I studied the map and decided I was east, so I flew west, and in a few minutes the city showed up.

Going back, the fact that I hadn't hit Havana right on the nose worried me because Key West was a small target: get a little west and you'd go up into the Gulf of Mexico with land a long way off; too much east and you'd be out over the Atlantic with a lot of ocean—remember, no radio, no beam, just a compass. A pilot had done just that on a record flight only a month or so before—gotten east and started out across the Atlantic, but luck slid one of the Bahamas under the airplane and her rear end was saved.

I knew that a passenger and freight ship ran between Havana and Key West every day, and so I timed my departure to pass the boat right about midway as a checkpoint. I plotted the winds and then flew the compass very carefully, precisely, my eye glued to the heading I wanted. The lonesomeness of being alone over the sea didn't go away, but the task of navigation became paramount and pushed that scared feeling to one side. But the midpoint came, and there was no boat. I looked right and left as far as the haze allowed, but saw nothing, just the empty sea. I got a very tight feeling, really worried. But then I had a thought: I racked the airplane up in a steep bank and looked underneath, and there it was, the ship, majestically cutting through the sea right smack below. I'd come up so dead-on that the long nose of my open biplane had hidden it from view. What a relief. The time then went quickly, and soon the water turned from deep blue to greenish blue, and I saw the fine white line of a sandy shore and Key West came into focus through the sea haze—I flew over it right on course. What a testing yo-yo of emotions, from fear to the heights of giddy gladness.

Then one stop back to Newark, landing in the dark on Newark's black cinder surface. On the flight up I had a sure feeling, a falling away of uncertainties; I felt more that I was leading the flight and it wasn't leading me.

My next project was to fly into Mexico City. People told me the mountains around it were often barricaded by clouds I'd have to climb through to get on top; it would be necessary to fly blind, on instruments, and I didn't know how.

These were the early days of instrument flying, and I'd met Howard Stark, one of the Eastern Air Transport pilots who had done a lot of the pioneering work. He'd poked his nose in the clouds and learned how to use instruments, and he wrote a book about it, *The 1-2-3 Method of Blind*

Flying. It wasn't a big book, only a quarter-inch-thick paperback, but it was big in importance. The book cost one dollar, and I still have my copy.

I built a hood for the back cockpit of the Mailwing so I couldn't see out, only in at the instruments. My glider friend, Bill Mumford, was enlisted as safety pilot to fly the front seat and keep me out of trouble.

The main instrument was called a turn and bank—a needle connected to a gyro that went left and right with the nose. Under the needle was a ball bank indicator—a curved carpenter's level that had a steel ball instead of a bubble. The other instrument was the airspeed indicator. So the 1-2-3 method was: one, center the needle on the turn and bank with the rudder; two, level the ball with the ailerons—the bank controls; and, three, pull or push—gently—the elevators to get the airspeed where it should be.

It was guaranteed to get you out of any fix, any wild maneuver. I practiced. It demanded attention and a quick scan of needle, ball, and airspeed indicator. It was clumsy at first, but it worked and I gradually developed a certain facility. I could fly straight and level, make turns, climbs, and glides, get in and out of a tailspin and even loop and roll.

A chance call from a friend in New Hampshire set me up for a final exam in flying blind. I was invited to visit a summer camp and maybe sell some rides. My problem was bad weather, rain and low ceilings in the New Jersey area. In New England it was better: Manchester, New Hampshire, had only high clouds. But the ceiling was too low and the visibility too poor to work my way up there. In those days everything was flying contact—flying based on what you could see down below.

The weather hatched an idea: why not fly on instruments? I knew how, and the setup was perfect—low ceiling at departure, but good weather at my destination. I could take off, climb to a safe altitude (say, 3,000 feet), and hold a compass course northeast until I broke out of the clouds. I went to the Westfield, New Jersey, airport and got the airplane out. The airport manager came up and wanted to know just where I thought I was going.

"Manchester, New Hampshire."

"In this weather—hell, the ceiling is only about 500 feet!"

"I'm going to fly instruments, climb up to 3,000, and just cruise on up there." He shook his head, but he didn't stop me.

I sat there warming her up. The rain fell gently, puddling on the fabric of the wing, swirling behind the interwing struts. The world looked dreary, and the trees near the airport had a blurred, impressionistic look. It seemed foolish to be going flying, and I was nervous—more than a little.

I ran up the engine, taxied to the runway, and lined up. A quick look at the security of familiar things and, as we often did in flying, a muttered, "Well, here goes nothing."

I poured on the coal, raced down the grass strip, and skimmed into the air. I climbed a little, thought a second about trying it down low, but I could see only a quarter of a mile ahead, so I quickly realized that was impossible. But it was a hard thing to do, to climb into that stuff, something I'd never done before—few had—climbing into the clouds you had always tried to stay out of, that represented mystery and danger. In a moment a few of the gossamer shreds that hang from a cloud's bottom passed between the wings—I looked down for the ground and assurance, but it was gone—and a gray mass enfolded me. I could have panicked easily, but reason took over and nudged me: "The instruments, you jackass, the instruments!"

My eyes went to the turn and bank and airspeed indicator. I steadied the airspeed, gently made a turn using the turn indicator to the heading I wanted, and climbed. With the first few bumps the turn indicator slipped off center, and a feeling of searing fright came over me as I worked to steady it in the middle. It settled down and did what I asked it—I was flying blind.

At 3,000 feet I leveled off, pulled the power back to cruise, and dared to look around—there was whiteness everywhere, not a break in it, no ground, no blue sky, just white above, below, all around. But the instruments said we were steady-on, and despite the worry a feeling of comfort edged its way in. I was well above the ground, not down near trees and hills trying to hedge-hop in bad visibility wondering where the next dangerous obstruction was—no, up here I was safe. I slid back further in the seat and gradually relaxed, felt as though the whiteness was protecting me, that the world now was the snug cockpit and the instruments on the panel that translated how the airplane was doing in space. The airplane and I were released from the earth, not bound to it—we were of the sky only, truly flying. I held the course, believing those dials and needles. It was a remarkable, exciting awakening, a feeling of accomplishment and progress.

The time ticked by and an hour passed, fifteen more minutes, then a

pilotage—by reading the map. But around St. Louis some oil started to leak back into the cabin, a slow but steady leak. Some of the welds on that ridiculous oil tank had given way—that damned government man. I hated him and I carried a grudge against government aviation people and rules for years after.

The engine was running, with no indication of an oil temperature increase or pressure loss. We'd press on until it quit; maybe we could still break the record, which was a point near Indianapolis marked with a big diamond on our map.

More and more oil flowed inside, soaking into our shoes, ruining our sandwiches, but the engine kept going. We passed the record point but felt little elation—the worry about the oil was too consuming. We kept on. Then, between Dayton and Columbus, the oil temperature started rising— a sure sign we were running out of oil. I didn't want to ruin the engine—I couldn't afford to—so over the Columbus airport I cut the switch, stopped the engine, and we slid into the fresh green grass of early May between the concrete runways, 1,986.94 miles from takeoff—a new record by nearly 178 miles. We received a Diplôme de Record from the FAI, all in French, official, *Distance en ligne droit (3,197 kms 679)*.

The victory was dulled by the furious frustration of having enough fuel left in the tanks to make Newark easily with the daylight and good weather ahead. But we had run out of oil, scuttled by a sticky government man. Damn, damn, damn!

Not many weeks later I was at Newark Airport talking with Dick Kirschbaum, a *Newark Evening News* reporter who covered aviation.

"TW&A is going to hire some pilots. Why don't you try for it?"

"Me, an airline pilot!" I'd never thought of it.

"Listen, as a friend: you can't go on forever breaking records, doing these crazy things—there's no way to make money, and you may break your neck. You want to get married—what do you have to offer that gal?"

It was a shock at first, those sincere words. I had met a lovely gal, and there was never any money for records—if a little was made on one flight, it was quickly spent on ambitious plans for another. The dreams of records for fortune were past. Slowly, relentlessly, it sank in, and the idea of being an airline pilot became important and finally consuming. I had to get that job.

CHAPTER 4

Co-Education

✳

I FILED AN APPLICATION with Transcontinental and Western Air, but it was a nervous application because I had only logged 1,300 hours and I'd heard they wouldn't take anyone with less than 1,500. The one thing I had going for me was that most of my time was flying cross-country: not just around an airport, but off to strange places requiring navigation, weather flying, and judgment. I hoped that would count for something, maybe make up for my lack of hours.

Dick Kirschbaum got me an interview with Pat Gallup, the Eastern Region general manager—an airmail pilot, quiet man, little mustache. Gallup looked over the application and didn't throw it back at me. "Hull's coming into town next week," he said. "I'll set up an interview."

Harlan Hull was chief pilot, a veteran of early airmail flying who'd served with the U.S. Marines before joining T&WA. *Veteran* might be a misleading word for those pilots: they were veterans for certain, but they were still young, in their late thirties. The dark and stormy nights, the ice and thunderstorms and fog, and the crudeness of those early airplanes along with their sketchy navigation systems and primitive instruments had given them a lifetime of experience in very fast doses.

Hull was pleasant, with an easy smile and an open, relaxed manner, his uniform hat shoved back off his forehead. We sat, legs dangling, on top of a spare desk in the old terminal at Newark. He was getting ready to take a trip to Kansas City.

It wasn't an interview, but more like a bull session between pilots. He didn't make me feel like a fledgling; he just asked me about where I'd been and what I'd flown. I think I know the exact moment he decided to hire me. We were talking about flying cross-country, navigating, and I said to him, "Well, I've learned one thing about getting off course: it doesn't pay to make a big correction and get back on course right away, it's better to make a shallow correction—refigured—toward the airport you're headed for. It saves time and fuel—keeps you from zigzagging." And I demonstrated, as pilots do, with my hands cocked at different angles. It wasn't a big point, but looking back I realize it was something that showed experience. I could see it was something he valued.

"Okay," he said as he swung off the desktop, adjusted the bill of his hat down to proper military position, and got ready to go. "The next class will be in August. You'll get a telegram." And so I did.

He never looked at my logbook or mentioned my flying time. I guess he realized the fallacy of logbooks, that they were, and I suppose still are, suspicious because it's easy to write in hours that have never been flown and to phony up the endorsement—"Parker time" we called it, after the Parker pen. When pilots brag about having thousands and thousands of hours, more worldly pilots often smile knowingly at such "facts."

Hull was the ideal chief pilot. I realize that might sound like hero worship of the man who hired me when I was so young, but I feel the same way today. He had the one basic quality that all chief pilots should have: he could fly as well as or better than any of the pilots who worked for him. He had their respect, he was fair, and he was always technically ahead of the pack.

T&WA gave me a pass to go from Newark to Kansas City for their training school. The flight was on a brand-new DC-3. Jack Zimmerman was captain and his cousin Don Smith was copilot. Those aren't just names—they're legends.

Jack, slender, quick-acting, sharp, and youthful, had an infectious laugh that made his face sparkle. You had the impression he might be a new captain until you looked into his eyes and saw the age and experience deep inside them—a certain place where the laughter faded and toughness and realism lived.

He'd flown the mail in open cockpit airplanes in the hard days when you fought through bad weather thanks to a combination of the ignorance of the age and its unsophisticated equipment. He was a benign swashbuckler; girls liked him and he liked girls. The hostesses on Jack's flights were most always happy gals.

He was a good pilot—an excellent pilot—but a bold one. He'd stick his nose in weather others might quail from, and he had a certain impatience with prissy caution.

Don Smith, the copilot, Jack's cousin, worshipped Jack, and flew with him whenever the schedule allowed. Don was quick with a wheezy laugh at Jack's jokes and quips. Their cockpit was a jovial place, but it turned serious when weather or the situation demanded and they displayed their skills.

I climbed aboard, showed the hostess my pass, and took the seat she indicated. It seemed only a few moments before she approached me and said the captain wanted to see me up front. With feelings of timidity, awe, and a smitch of importance I worked my way forward and through the cockpit door.

"I'm Jack Zimmerman—this is Don Smith. So you're going out to school. Great." I was at ease immediately—Jack was that kind of guy. "Stay up here and we'll show you how it's done." He laughed at his own boastful remark.

As we talked I looked over the cockpit. It was a lot different from my Monocoupe. It had two throttles, propeller pitch controls, carburetor heat, and instruments I'd only read about: the directional gyro and the artificial horizon. These two gyroscopic instruments were much simpler to use than the turn and bank indicator I was used to; the directional gyro gave you a compass heading without the unstable movement of a magnetic compass, and the other put a horizon, with wings representing the airplane, into a single instrument right in front of the pilot—dip a wing and it showed immediately on the instruments; raise or lower the nose and that showed, too. These two made instrument flying easier and less fatiguing.

It was a great flight. Don, in his kind way, assured me I wouldn't have any trouble in school. He warned me about the most important things to learn, such as the heater operation, and told me the captains were all different enough that I'd have to be a psychologist to get along: "Just do it their way and you won't have any trouble."

Once we reached cruising altitude and the cockpit settled down to the quiet tedium of clear weather cruise, the hostess came forward to offer coffee. The companionway behind the pilots was narrow and she squeezed in close to me, looking at me with large brown eyes, smelling good of perfume, one arm around me because it was necessary in the cramped quarters. This was impressive—good-smelling and smooth-feeling girls right there in flight.

Jack caught my flustered but acute appraisal of the situation. After she'd gone back to get the coffee, he kidded me. "How do you like this hostess idea?" He laughed, and added, "Take it easy, leave a couple for us." (TWA called the young ladies hostesses, visualizing them as the hostess to the passengers. I'll continue to call them hostesses in this book and skip today's dual-gender, cold appellation of cabin attendant.)

Hostesses—all of them registered nurses—were new to the line, and some pilots thought they were there solely for their sexual gymnastics. This of course turned out to be far from the truth, but the feeling was not surprising when you think about this hearty band of rough-and-tumble pilots suddenly having attractive gals made part of their crew to share trips and overnight stops in the same towns and hotels!

In all fairness, most pilots were straight arrows with never a thought of the hostesses as anything except a little sister to be protected. Most pilots truly were like that, but not all—this was an era when flying still bore an aura of apprehension, and even though the DC-3, improved radio aids, and more blind (instrument) flying would make it safer, there were still enough accidents to consider it a dangerous game. The live-for-today feeling of pilots going off to war hadn't been totally bred out of the airline pioneers. But as far as Jack's kidding me about the hostesses went, I was far too anxious about making the grade in copilot school to think about much else.

I had no baseline to judge myself against. I was a prep school dropout who had learned to fly, soloed, and then had never been checked, supervised, or disciplined again except for the rote government tests for my licenses that demonstrated how I could jump through the bureaucratic hoops but didn't tell a crumb about my judgment or ability. I was certain that most of the others were being hired from the military where they'd been checked all their flying lives; they'd have had experience that made them fairly relaxed with others looking over their shoulders, and they'd have had a college education. Would I look like a bumpkin and stand out stupidly in class, to be quickly dismissed and sent off?

I'd flown much of the United States; gone to Cuba, Mexico, and Canada; had taught myself to fly blind by needle, ball, and airspeed; had read all the books I could get my hands on, had even taken some courses—but none of that eased my near panic. After all, I'd never flown a big airplane, one with two or more engines; for that matter, I'd never flown an airplane with a radio in it either for communications or navigation, since my navigation had all been by compass and map. The anxiety gnawed at my insides.

Like most fears, they were groundless. School was informal; there were seven students in the class, one of them military, the rest of us civilians. One, Roger Don Rae, was famous from the world of racing and exhibitions. Rae and I were the only ones to eventually become captains and fly to retirement.

The instructor was Bob Overman, a line copilot ready to be made captain. The school was in a hangar, where Bob stood at a blackboard and pounded out words of wisdom that were mostly admonitions about captains, advice like not tuning the radio without first getting the captain's approval. We had to be careful not to do anything that even suggested we were overriding the captain's authority; it took extreme caution to prevent the outbursts of anger that, for some captains, were always near the surface.

The school covered company policy and procedures, the DC-3 airplane, and the rules set by the Department of Commerce that were soon to be called the Civil Air Regulations. (The Bureau of Air Commerce had just launched a two-year comprehensive airways modernization program at about this time—1937—that was to cost the American taxpayers the staggering sum of $7 million.) They didn't worry about testing your ability to fly; you were an apprentice, and the captains would be your mentors while you as a copilot were learning the broader aspects of flying, weather especially. The airlines flew in weather that others did not; getting through and trying to keep on schedule was the main objective. There were few outside pilots who had flown in enough storm and darkness to be able to step in and fly as an airline pilot. Going with an airline meant you had achieved a unique and privileged rank where the eagles' heads were encrusted with snow, their feathers ruffled by winds and turbulence. The airline was its own school, and most of the skill and knowledge was passed along by a variety of captains who had many different pet ideas that the copilot had to sort out as either good stuff or bad. Some authorities were trying to establish procedures and standardization, but it was just a glimmer in the distance.

The airways weren't complicated, nor were the airplanes, so the captain usually could do it all if he had to. Of course there were certain wild times when the captain got very busy, especially when he had a new copilot at his side. Probably this contributed to some accidents, but flight training for copilots wasn't in the cards—it cost too much money. The airlines couldn't afford to fly an airplane just for training; when airplanes flew they had better be bringing in revenue.

Overman handed out some of what we'd need for school: an airplane manual, an operations manual, flight plan forms. The manuals were thin compared to the fat ones of today. The operations part contained instrument approach plates—maps—with the procedures for finding your way down through bad weather to each airport.

We had to buy a calculator from the company store—a Dalton Mark VII, which was a circular slide rule on one side and a bunch of lines and degree marks on the other. This exalted device was for keeping time and fuel, making estimates, computing the drift and winds—all of which was necessary for making out the flight plan. Pilots had to be adept and fast with it; the object was to be able to use it so proficiently that you could "make it smoke."

The school taught operational matters like the instrument approach at Newark; mechanical items about the airplane—nuts-and-bolts stuff we still call it, even though today the subject may be sophisticated electronics systems; and TWA's way of keeping a log sheet and making out the complicated flight plan before each flight. This involved figuring wind effects for each flight leg—and there might be many between departure and arrival; working out climb time and distance, and fuel consumption to your destination and an alternate.

There was a lot in school about the airplanes, the DC-2 and DC-3. Copilots had to know how to extend and retract the landing gear without screwing up and dumping the airplane on the ground, and we had to manage the heating system, as Don Smith had warned. The heater was tricky to use; it was a steam heat rig with water that dripped, ideally in a controlled fashion, on the hot exhaust stack to make steam that went through a radiator, over which outside air blew to send the heat into the outlets for the cabin and cockpit. The outside air came in through a hole in the nose of the airplane that was simply called the nose duct valve. There was a knob under the bottom of the instrument panel on the copilot's side to adjust this rush of air—not enough outside air and the radiator would boil over; too much and the heater would freeze and the only thing warm on the plane would be the captain's wrath.

The copilot also had to put water into the system. This meant getting out of your seat, stepping back a few paces to the water tank in the forward baggage compartment, opening a valve, and letting water into the system—referred to as "letting water down." In the DC-2 it was bit by bit; the DC-3 claimed it was automatic, but it took a trained eye to keep tabs on the automatic part because it often went sour. So you were juggling air and water from inside and out, calculating how much air to allow for the amount of water you had in the system, but the captain kept a suspicious eye on the action and offered suggestions—which amounted to commands—thereby lousing up your plan and getting the boiler frozen. Then it was the copilot's fault, although he didn't feel he was to blame and muttered to himself that if that old bastard would keep out of the act everything would run okay.

On one brilliant night of cold Arctic air about a year and a half after I came out of copilot school, with temperatures so low everything worked at reduced efficiency from personnel on the ground to airplanes in flight, Captain Jim Eischied and I were between Columbus and Indianapolis in a DC-2 with a frozen heating system. The cold was more than it could handle, and despite my spending most of the flight trying to juggle water and air at 30 below zero, the system froze. This one probably was my fault, but I like to think it was simply colder than the system's design could handle—and Jim was a kind man and didn't show disgust or anger. When we landed at Indianapolis it was frigid in the airplane. The mechanics went through the procedure for unfreezing, but it didn't work—the boiler had burst and they didn't have a spare in stock.

The termination of the flight was the next stop, St. Louis. We went into the warm terminal and put it to the five passengers, all businessmen: if they wanted to go with no heat, but with all the blankets we could find, we'd get 'em to St. Louis—but mind you, it would be damned cold, and would take a bit under two hours. In the terminal, warm and refreshed, their spirit of adventure was high—sure, let's go.

God, it was cold. We sat with coats, hats, and gloves on, plus blankets over our shoulders. The passengers were buried beneath blankets, and the hostess—coat, hat, boots, and blanket wrapped around her—tried to serve coffee. It began okay, but the 30-below air inexorably, cruelly, crawled and crept in—to your feet, through the weave of the blankets and coats, into the leather of gloves, through the walls; Arctic cold is like that. It was numbing, and the passengers, though none said a word, looked grim, and their eyes revealed second thoughts about their enthusiastic willingness to go.

St. Louis, finally, and the ordeal was over, but when we climbed out of the deep freeze Jim and I were shivering, the kind that will not stop. We shook all through the cab ride to the hotel, stomped into the lobby, and instead of stopping at the desk Jim swung his arm in a follow-me gesture.

"Come on!" And he headed for the bar.

"We can't go in here, we're in uniform!" I cried; we were about to break the holiest of company rules.

"The hell with that—this is medicinal."

At the bar he snapped, "Two brandies."

We drank them down, we weren't spotted, and nothing came of it, but I'm certain it didn't worry Jim anyway—he was almost a teetotaler and the company knew it. (What we didn't know then was that a hot cup of soup would have been better—alcohol makes a condition like ours worse. But we slept it off and we were flying again the next afternoon, headed for Newark and home.)

In school we worked through the manuals, made practice flight plans, and tried to get sharp with the calculator. Overman stuck to his "Beware of the Captain" theme, with periodic swings of his arm representing the chop of an axe.

When school was over I wasn't sure what came next, but then I ran into Dick Hanson, a captain I'd met in Newark, in the hall in Kansas City.

"You finished school yet?" he asked me.

"Yes, sir."

"Had a flight yet?"

"No, sir."

"Are you set up on one?"

"No, sir."

"Come on with me, we'll go down to Dispatch and get you a flight right away."

"Thank you, but I'm not that much in a hurry—I can wait until they call me." I was scared to get my feet wet.

"Hell, your seniority doesn't start until your first flight," he told me. "You want to get out as soon as possible and get that number. That seniority number is how you'll live from now on: advancement, where you live, everything."

"Oh, I didn't know how all that worked."

"Jesus, you don't know anything! And join ALPA as soon as you can—you'll be an apprentice member."

"ALPA?"

"That's the Air Line Pilots Association—our union."

I was from a good bourgeois Republican family, where the word *union* wasn't exactly a hallowed one. I kept my tongue, but I wondered how I'd eventually face that.

"Hey, Lee," he said to the dispatcher, "get this kid on a flight—he's finished school."

Lee was Lee Flanagin, chief dispatcher. "Oh, another new one—well let's see—yes, there are some courtesy hops this afternoon, he can copilot on those."

Courtesy hops were made to promote business—thirty-minute flights over the city for travel agents, businesspeople, and folks who might buy a ticket. Not a lot of people used air transportation back then, and headlines about crashes kept them away; courtesy hops were part of the constant effort to sell flying as safe, efficient travel.

"Who's the captain?" Dick asked.

"Larry Fritz."

I felt my knees go limp. Fritz was the vice president of operations and had a tough reputation that terrified people at my level.

"I'd just as soon wait for another flight," I said.

"Hell no—put him on that, Lee."

And that was that.

I was ready two hours before flight time, all neat and shined up, waiting in the dispatch office. Finally Larry Fritz charged through the door, a scowl on his face.

"Where's the copilot?"

"Right here, sir, my name is Buck."

"Okay, let's get out of here."

I tagged behind as we walked to the airplane. He sat on the left in the captain's seat, and I strapped myself in the copilot's.

"Now," he said, "I understand you're just out of school so I'll handle everything. Don't touch a damned thing unless I tell you—and then explain what you're gonna do before you do it!"

"Yes, sir."

We were supposed to make three hops, but we made four. After the first one he allowed me to raise the landing gear and lower it—but not before I carefully explained what lever I was going to move and which way. Then he allowed me to make the necessary radio reports, which were simply what time we'd taken off and then what time we landed. I loosened up a bit, but I was nervous and afraid to make any moves.

After the second hop we waited for the unloading of the passengers and the loading of the next bunch. It seemed to take a long time, and Fritz began to mutter.

"What the hell are they doing back there?"

He was about to send me back to find out what the hell the delay was when the hostess came into the cockpit, stood between us, and said, "You won't believe this."

"What?"

"After the last flight there was a mix-up, and they signaled you away from the gate before the old group got off and the new one got on."

"You mean," he said, "that we took the same group up twice?"

She nodded yes. I waited for the roof to fall in—but it didn't. Instead of raging he broke into laughter.

"Those dumb bastards" was all he said—and he kept laughing about it.

The other hops were made in good spirits, with Fritz occasionally shaking his head and laughing. As we parted, he patted me on the back and said I'd do.

So now I had my seniority number, 148, meaning I was the 148th pilot hired. (Before I retired that list got to be more than 4,000.) Many times through the years I've given silent thanks to Dick Hanson's pushing me onto that first flight. One number can make a huge difference in life—the difference in living where you want, in flying bigger airplanes, in flying to Paris or exotic places rather than the humdrum back-and-forth between New York and Chicago—and for lots more money, too.

My first actual line trip was from Kansas City to Albuquerque—part of the hotshot transcontinental sleeper flight. Yes, a sleeper in 1937. It was a heavy Hollywood flight filled with movie people; we gave orchids to the ladies and even served pheasant, though it might not have been perfect because we didn't have frozen food and microwaves; the food was stored in thermos-type containers in a somewhat pathetic attempt to keep it warm. The effort toward food and service, however, was sincere, and it started early in the game.

While passengers were important, each flight had a deeper import: the U.S. mail in the cargo bins made you realize a vital component of what you were doing. The romance of carrying the mail goes back to the Pony Express and then to the airmail pilots in their open cockpits, helmets, and goggles. They're gone now, but much of the U.S. mail today is still flown in airliners, and deep within each pilot is an appreciation of the importance of carrying those canvas U.S. mailbags with their authoritative locks.

When the load was too much, or more fuel was needed, the priority order for what got removed was: freight first, then passengers, but the mail remained even if it and the pilots flew an airplane of empty seats. Passengers who learned about this when they got the heave-ho could become pretty irate.

The flight I was going to fly originated in New York, went to St. Louis, and then to Kansas City, arriving in the middle of the night. We'd pick it up at Kansas City and fly it to Albuquerque, where a crew based in Los Angeles would take it to L.A. for an early morning arrival. This was the big time, the best of its day, and the importance was not lost on a new copilot.

We all envied the Los Angeles crew, because the ultimate in flying life was to have enough seniority to live in L.A. That was seniority first-class, and all the captains living in what was then the promised land were old-timers. We never realized we'd be flying oceans one day, covering the world; our dream was simply to be a senior captain and to live in L.A. and fly to Albuquerque!

It was the rule that you had to be in the dispatch office one hour before flight in order to look over notices, revise manuals, and make out the flight plan. This night—my first—I was there two hours before, apprehensively waiting for the captain and wondering what sort of ogre he'd be.

When he showed, it was Jack Wade: boyish-looking, big smile, big teeth, calling out greetings to all and coming over to me with his hand out. "You Buck—the new boy?"

"Yes, sir."

My immediate problem was the flight plan. This was a big sheet of paper covered with lines and boxes to be filled in, noting winds, courses, speeds, the amount of fuel we'd use (this was called fuel burn), and other things that gave an idea of the flight to come. Planning is the link between preflight and actual flight; it tells what you can expect en route, and when you put pencil to paper the flight begins, for the first time, to come alive.

The key to the accuracy of all flight plans is the forecast of the winds that the meteorologist provides. If the weather information is good, so is the flight plan; if it isn't, then the actual flight may be a lot different from the planned one.

So first we had to go to the weather office and look things over. The weatherman made his own map then; it wasn't done by an impersonal computer as it is now.

We stood over the weather map as the meteorologist explained what was going on.

"Nuthin' much there tonight; big high, light winds—no fog, no thunderstorms."

"I must be livin' right," Jack said. Then, to me, "Let's make her out for 10,000."

Translated, that meant I'd take the winds the meteorologist gave us and make out the flight plan based on our flying at 10,000 feet.

With my calculator and charts and graphs that detailed the airplane's performance, I started to fill in all those blanks on the form. It was a torturous job for a new copilot that consumed forty-five minutes to an hour; after six months on the line I could do it in ten to fifteen minutes while shooting the bull with another copilot working on his flight plan next to me at the long counter all dispatch offices had.

The world hadn't gotten around to the electronic calculator, so we used the plastic one we'd gotten at school. The back of the calculator was covered with lines and a movable dial that was a compass rose. The lines represented heading, airspeed, and track, and with all this it was possible to figure winds, drift, ground speed, and a bunch of related things.

Though I'd practiced making out flight plans and use of the calculator in the hotel room, I was still pretty clumsy and far from being able to make that thing smoke. This first for-real flight plan was a lip-biting chore. Jack helped me, laughing at my clumsiness and kidding me about being too serious: "Hell, you don't need three decimal places!"

He signed the finished product and turned it in.

We gathered our stuff together—me clumsily—and went out into the night, walking along the ramp toward the terminal to wait for the airplane from the east. I was all new: new uniform, new stiff suitcase, and my new black salesman-type case for manuals, navigation gear, flashlight, and small tool kit—I'd lug that black bag for the rest of my airline life. In later years, I'd tell my wife, "Bury that damned thing with me—I'll never know how to get to heaven, or wherever, without it."

My hat sat square on my head, tall and stiff, without the crushed, careful sloppiness of the hats experienced pilots wore. My shoes were shined, and anyone who glanced at this long skinny kid would have known it was his first trip.

Looking into the night, north, I picked up the two landing lights of our inbound flight, as the pilot finished a left turn and lined up to land south. The airplane was almost soundless, sneaking into the field. The twin lights descended steadily, and then two squeaks as the tires contacted the pavement and spun up. Flight 5 was on the ground K.C.

Forms began to show behind the landing lights taxiing toward us out of the night. The propellers picked up light from the terminal and became whirling disks of brilliance. The fuselage reflected patches of silver light, but the side away from us was in the dark and not visible. The airplane became bigger and bigger, and for the first time I heard the engines idling softly, a staccato murmur. When it stopped it seemed huge, the biggest airplane I'd ever seen—and even now, with 747s behind me, in my mind's eye that DC-3 on that sultry August Missouri night is still the biggest of them all.

The area burst into activity. All had held back, waiting for the last turn of the propellers for which all ground people have great respect, since being hit by one would mean certain death.

The long set of steps that reached to a small door just behind the cockpit was busy with mail and baggage coming down, while a mechanic, flashlight in hand, looked into the landing gear wells behind the engines, checking for anything that might not be just right, and another rubbed his hand over the tires and inspected them for any cuts or excess wear. The activity, the quickness—like a pit stop at Indianapolis—spoke of men who knew what they were doing, who understood the seriousness of their job, and who wanted to get on with it. Their striving for perfection—their development of competence, procedure, and responsibility—was building a foundation of reliability for the industry that lives to this day and is an important foundation of its record of safety.

I've been lucky in life to have a sense of knowing when something is special—when I should allow it to envelop me, and to remember. This was one of those times, and the emotion was almost overpowering.

The incoming crew got off—strangers to me—looking important, too, with their uniforms and gold braid bright in the light, carrying their black bags. The captain was medium height, a little fat with a mustache and a high voice.

"Hi, Jack—how goes it?"

"Good—good. How's the airplane?"

"Runnin' like a sewing machine."

"Good flight?"

"Once we got past St. Louis—east there's a mess of thunderstorms, but we lucked out."

Translated, that meant they had wended their way through a line of thunderstorms and managed not to hit a cell.

The copilot was a lot older than I—a big blond handsome man, but gentle, as his smile revealed. "Your first trip?" he asked me.

"Yes."

"Well, don't let it scare you—we all feel green and clumsy at first, and you've got a real nice guy to fly with. Relax."

"Thanks."

We climbed the short set of steps at the passenger door and entered the cabin. It was dark and quiet. A hostess appeared in the dim light. She spoke in soft tones. The idea was not to awaken the passengers who were supposed to be sleeping, but they'd have to be solid sleepers not to wake up from all the banging of fueling, loading, and all the rest.

"Good weather?" she wanted to know. They always wanted to know if it was going to be good—good meaning smooth, so passengers wouldn't get sick and so serving wouldn't be difficult.

The DC-2s and 3s, light in wing loading, fluffy compared to a modern jet, rode rough air in a wallowing, tail-swinging way that seemed designed to make people ill. Great heaves up and then sinking down—and all the while the tail swung back and forth so you were swishing through the sky. Today's jet, with heavy wing loading, hits bumps sharply like a racing boat clipping across the top of a wave; the jet jolts rather than wallows, and people don't get sick as they did in propeller days. The jet, too, is up out of the weather on top of most turbulence—although there's still some that shakes them up at times.

"Beautiful weather—smooth as silk," I told her.

"Thank God—I didn't get much sleep today and I'm not in the mood for any rough stuff."

I noticed she was good-looking, but it was only a passing moment of appraisal—I was too busy.

We went forward through the narrow aisle. There were a few rows of seats in the back and then berths forward—all curtain-covered like a Pullman train. We quietly worked our way through the dark area, brushing the curtains, wondering what glamorous figures were sleeping behind them. This walk was uphill, because the airplane had a tail wheel and sat on the ground with the nose high and the tail down. I wondered if the sleeping passengers were sliding downhill in their dreams.

Jack went through the cockpit door first and motioned me to come on and get the door closed to keep the front-end noise of loading out of the cabin.

I closed the door and was in the cockpit—the office—with a heavy screened-over baggage area to my right, the two pilots' seats and the instrument panel ahead. It was a sudden change from the quiet, dark, curtained cabin; the plush is gone, replaced with the spartan requirements of instruments, levers, switches, fuel valves, and seats that pilots are never satisfied with. The smell of the cockpit hits you first—an aroma collected through hours of flight and ground time when mechanics work on the airplane. There was an odor of metal, of spilled fluids, the dusty stale smell of mail bags, a little whiff of food that had slopped on the floor during a turbulent moment and—hidden down in the confusion of floor, cables, and plumbing—had had time to spoil. A scent, too, of sweat permeated the pilots' seat cushions and the black control wheel. All these "perfumes" had been accumulated since the airplane was built, had become part of it. It isn't particularly unpleasant, just part of the trade; blindfold any pilot and lead him into a cockpit, even a new one, and the first whiff will tell him where he is.

Clumsily I got into the right seat. The entry to any airplane seat has an awkwardness, gives you an opportunity to kick some important things or to take a bruising bang on a shin. Experience includes developing a deftness and a pattern for getting in and out of pilots' seats.

I put my small zippered navigation folder under the seat and fastened my safety belt. I looked around and began checking items. There weren't checklists yet, and every pilot had his own system for covering the cockpit to see that fuel valves were set to the proper tank, radios checked, instruments, electrical switches—all of it ready and proper.

Once all the equipment was cleared away, the engine started, and the ground electrical cart was disconnected and pulled to one side, a passenger agent saluted Jack, who returned it.

We carefully taxied down a strip outlined by yellowish individual lights, a string of them down the sides, and finally to the runway. The engines were run up and checked and we lined up to go. The runway stretched out ahead, two long parallel rows of lights delineating a path toward the black void of night. Jack opened the throttles, positively and smoothly. The engines came up to power, pounding it out almost in a scream; the power is strong, and I felt it through my body as the airplane gained speed.

The noise of the power, the feel of acceleration, the sight of the runway rushing toward me faster and faster was a wild kind of feeling, almost of abandon. It was and is thrilling, and never, in thousands of takeoffs, has this feeling changed—it is always exciting, whether I'm in a small Cessna 172 or a mighty 747.

With a gentle pressure back on the control wheel Jack raised the nose and the airplane left the bumpy, wild world of the ground—weight successfully transferred from wheels to wings. "Up gear!" Jack ordered and I reached down, unlocked the gear, pulled out and raised the hydraulic lever, and the landing gear folded and crawled up into its well.

"Make it off at fifty-three."

I reached under the seat and pulled out my navigation case—it was leather with TWA's logo on the front, along with the words "The Lindbergh Line," a piece of my destiny linked with that day in the Ford Tri-Motor at Newark. On top was a log sheet that showed the route to Albuquerque divided into segments separated by radio range stations or checkpoints. Under Kansas City I wrote 01:53—our time off the ground. There was an entry place for the time we pulled away from the station called "Time Out," and another for the time a fuel tank was turned on and off so that careful tabs were kept on fuel use and on what remained. As the flight progressed the blanks were gradually filled in, telling in numbers the flight's progress, condition, and history, all of it there so you knew how things were going.

After putting down 01:53 I estimated the next checkpoint, Baldwin City, Kansas. The flight plan said it would take twenty-four minutes before Baldwin City slid under our wings. On the form I added the twenty-four minutes to the 01:53 and radioed it to Kansas City.

I was clumsy with the radio. I pushed the mike button: "Flight 5—ah— to Kansas City—ah—go ahead."

This procedure was much different in terminology than it is today, but regardless, I didn't say it crisply, with several "ahs" and hesitations.

"You let go the mike button before you were finished," Jack said. "Call 'em again." I did and this time I held down the mike button until I was sure I'd finished talking.

We reached cruising altitude, and Jack pulled the propeller controls back to lower the RPM, the manifold pressure was set, and then the mixtures leaned out. The noise diminished from harsh climb power to an unstrained, soothing, steady beat. He adjusted the autopilot and sat back propping one foot up on the pedestal near the fuel valves—there was a shiny place on the corner of the pedestal where all the pilots propped their feet and had worn off the green paint and polished the metal.

The night was beautiful and clear, the sky infinite and dressed with stars, the ground below a black abyss without depth or form. But the scattered lights of an occasional small town announced that the earth was still there.

A flick of light showed an airways beacon. The beam of light you see from a beacon on the ground doesn't reach out like a long finger to the pilot; it's more like a small flash as it goes past his eyes. Under the beacon's white light were two red lights, aimed in the course direction, that flashed in Morse code to denote which beacon it was. They went in sequence and repeated every 100 miles—beacons were about ten miles apart. W (.– –) represented the first beacon; the next flashed the code for U (..–), the one after V, and the others down the line: H, R, K, D, B, G, and M. If the beacon was located at an airport there weren't course lights, but one side of the beacon would flash green. Copilots had to know the sequence by heart, and we used various gimmicks to help us remember—one was the saying, "When Unknown Visibility Has Reached Known Deterioration By God Make It." Pretty absurd, but useful.

Open-cockpit airmail pilots depended on these beacons more than we did in the DC-3 days. They were learning to fly bad weather—to fly, as it was called then, blind. Their navigational help was sketchy, and part of the system was the beacons. They knew where each one was, and the compass heading to the next one.

Jack Zimmerman once told me how they'd fly what he called "contact instruments." On a desperate night of fog or snow, or whatever nature threw at them that reduced visibility and ceiling to almost zero, they'd fly low—very low—and they'd catch the light from a beacon. Over it, they'd take up the heading to the next beacon and—just barely above the terrain, essentially flying blind—search in the nothingness to try to see the flash of the next beacon. By clock they knew how many minutes of flying until it ought to be in sight. If they missed it, they went back to the one they'd left and start out again until they did pick one up. If they made any miscalcu-

lation—flying suddenly into absolute zero fog, if there was a hill they'd
forgotten—they crashed. The appalling, tragic loss of pilots in those hazardous times is understandable when you realize that this type of flying—
the most dangerous kind—was part of their routine.

We droned on through the clear night. My head was down much of the
time keeping up the log, noting checkpoints, and sending the information
to the ground stations.

One bothersome problem was light. The captain wanted the cockpit
dark so he could see out, and the airplane didn't have any kind of small
light to direct onto your lap. So you held a hooded flashlight in one hand
and wrote with the other. Copilots were always on the lookout for pen-
lights that would do this job well. It was years before the manufacturers
put proper lights in cockpits for the copilot's or captain's lap work area.

Between bouts with the logbook I could look out into the night. The
mountains showed plainly, with shadows hiding the deep valleys and the
spookiness of the peaks silhouetted against the night sky. The complexity
of the airline—the logs to keep, the things to remember that didn't seem to
have much to do with flying; the captain on my left, aloft on a pedestal of
experience and skill—humbled me until I nearly forgot I had flown, too,
that I was also a pilot. But looking down into the dark shadows at the eerie
mountain peaks, I had time to think back to the Monocoupe working its
way across this same sky, its landing gear off, the cool air of 10,000 feet
rushing across its wings, the small engine purring softly—and it reminded
me I was a pilot, too, not as lofty as the man on my left, but good enough
to revive a fragment of confidence.

Jack landed the DC-3 in the quiet dark on the unpaved runway in
Albuquerque. After the landing run, as we taxied back, he opened the side
window and stuck his head out for a minute, then pulled back and yelled
over to me, "Slide your window open, smell that sage—it's wonderful."

The engines shut down and we gathered our stuff together, ready to
hand the flight over to that Los Angeles crew. I still felt ignorant and
green, but now I was a part of it—and it was a part of me.

I felt the change, once we'd left the airplane, from the glamour of gold-
braided uniforms and official importance to the mundane events of ordinary
life. We checked in at the office, where we saw the tired clerk on duty, scrib-
bled-over notepaper left in disarray on the counter, a bulletin board clut-

tered with notices ranging from official company stuff to dogs for sale. A few howdy words and sign the sheet for next day's flight, then out of the building, Jack with his uniform jacket off, collar unbuttoned, tie pulled down, lugging his navigation kit and small bag over to a disreputable auto.

"Crew car," he explained. "Pilots own it, add up the bills and charge at the end of the month—it doesn't amount to much. Outbound crew brings it out to the field, and inbound, us, takes it back. Get in."

The hotel was one of Conrad Hilton's first, called the Franciscan. My room cost $1.24—a special pilot's rate. I shared it with the captain. Two rooms were separated by a bath between them; the other was a pilot's room too.

There were noises from the bath, intestinal.

"Hi, Dutch," Jack called out loudly.

"Hi, Jack," the voice responded.

"That's Dutch," Jack explained. "I can always tell it's him. L.A. captain; health nut, eats fruits, nuts, and vegetables, knows all about that stuff—will only eat the bottom half of a grapefruit, says all the nourishment collects there. You can tell it's Dutch in the bathroom by the noises."

The next day I drifted around Albuquerque; pilots walk a lot, sometimes for miles, to stretch from the confinement of a cockpit, and to see what's around—to be tourists.

We ate that evening at Phil's. The pilots automatically went there, it was their place. They looked slightly askance at anyone else who came in. A steak dinner cost $1, and we sat at a long counter to eat it. Phil appreciated the pilots and took pride in his food. One night as he paid up, Ted Hereford, an L.A. captain, was asked by Phil not to come back. Ted, shocked and amazed, asked why.

"You didn't eat the fat," Phil told him. "My steaks are good steaks—you're supposed to eat the fat. Don't bother comin' back."

It was a month before Ted made peace with Phil—and from then on he ate the fat.

The flight back to Kansas City was different; there was a schedule mix-up and the airport called me to say I'd be on a different flight with a different captain. I didn't like that—Jack had become familiar, a security blanket. My layover quietude was broken, and the thought of an unknown captain preyed on my mind.

The airplane was a DC-2, not the fancy DC-3 we'd had coming over. The flight made stops—Amarillo and Wichita before Kansas City. That meant a three-leg flight plan, more difficult and time-consuming, but I couldn't get to the airport early because I was expected to ride out in that shameful auto with the captain, and captains liked getting to the field as close to schedule as regulations allowed so they wouldn't have to hang around.

It started fine. The captain—whose name I'd rather not mention—was a pleasant, polite man. When we got to the field I tore into the flight plan and stumbled through it, but I needed his help on the last few items or we'd never have finished in time. He was decent about it and my spirits rose.

We walked out to the airplane in the cool early morning dark; a slice of dawn was just cutting the sky in the east. As we approached the airplane he said, "When I call for 'up gear,' I want it up fast. This thing doesn't fly worth a damn on one engine with the gear down—in case one quits the gear has to be up, so get it up fast!" A steel-like quality had come into his voice that shattered my peaceful feeling.

Getting the DC-2 gear up wasn't a matter of flipping two levers and letting the hydraulic system do the work as in the DC-3—no, in the DC-2 you had to flip one lever to unlock it and then grasp a pump handle and frantically pump sixty to seventy strokes until the gear was up. I'd never pumped a 2's gear, so I didn't know how tough it was, didn't know the tricks—but I'd heard some wild tales.

We rolled down the field, slid into the air, and the captain shouted, "Up gear!"

I flipped the first lever, grasped the pump handle, and started pumping. My God it was tough! I worked my arm up and down with total, but inadequate, effort. Albuquerque's mile-high altitude tore my breath to gasps. Would the damned thing never get up? Then, when exhaustion had me on the verge of collapse, the captain shouted, "Faster, goddamn it, faster!"

I tugged and heaved and finally the pump would go no more—the gear was up.

The words "You just have to do that faster" were my reward.

"Yes—gasp—sir."

Later I learned some tricks: at the command "Up gear," flip your safety belt off, quickly slide a cover off the locking lever on your left and briskly move it up, then grasp the pump handle with your left hand and the bottom of the seat with your right and throw your body up and down (all 155 pounds in my case) and stiff-arm the gear handle while your right hand, holding the seat, supports you. It was still a gut-wrenching job but it did go faster.

There was a difference, too, depending on how the captain flew. A bad guy would climb out steeply, and the slightly increased G force would cause extra load on the gear that made the pumping more difficult; a good guy would hold the airplane down, climbing flat and slowly, until you got the gear up.

You also had to pump the flaps down—and up. This wasn't as difficult as the gear, except for the last quarter of "Flaps down," which required hard effort. So good guys only used three-quarters flap for landing, but bad guys wanted full flaps. You leaned on the handle exerting the extra force for that last 25 percent—which didn't make much difference in landing anyway—muttering to yourself about the prick in the left seat. Copilots soon knew who the good guys and bad guys were.

This captain proved to be slightly schizophrenic—or at least a paradox. A delightful gentleman much of the time, he was also quick to anger, cussing red-faced and mean at something I'd done that didn't suit him— like being slow at getting a checkpoint noted and reported, or my landing gear retraction time, which never satisfied him. I was disturbed, confused, and damned unhappy—with a developing feeling that if this was the way the job was going to be they could just shove it!

I didn't realize that this captain had certain fears of flying and was nervous at times—which may be a euphemistic way of saying he got scared. It came out in anger. (He eventually died of a heart attack—on the ground.) Some pilots display fear with anger; others keep it in, and you'd never know it until you learned to recognize a certain set to their jaw, a change of skin color toward gray, or sometimes a slight shaking of the hands and perspiration under armpits. Many pilots—probably most—get "nervous" at times, but it doesn't change them; they work along with the problem, and though the fear is there, it's controlled and subdued into a secondary place. An experienced copilot learns all these subtle characteristics, and after you were on the line awhile you could judge what kind of pilot the captain was on the very first leg of your first trip with him.

There weren't that many who flew nervous; most took it all in stride, but you didn't feel comfortable with the ones who were.

After more sharp words directed my way than I care to remember, we landed in Kansas City and my torture was over. On the ground he was gracious, told me I'd do fine, that all I needed was some practice and experience. I was glad to have the experience of my first round-trip on the line behind me, and I couldn't help thinking I'd seen some of the best and worst the flying life had to offer.

CHAPTER 5

Apprentice Time

M Y FIRST ASSIGNMENT was Newark, New Jersey—back in home territory.

Newark was the eastern terminus of the airline; there were no La Guardia or Idlewild/John F. Kennedy (KIDL) airports yet. There was an old airport on Flushing Bay called North Beach, and Mayor Fiorello La Guardia was trying to develop it as New York's airport. He didn't like the idea that to fly to New York City it was necessary to de-plane in New Jersey.

One evening during the squabble about airports, he flew to New York from Washington, D.C. The flight landed at Newark with the usual announcement of all off for New York City, but La Guardia refused to get off. "My ticket," he announced in his squeaky, liquid voice, "says New York, and this isn't New York—I demand to be taken there!"

It threw the airline into quite a quandary, it was reported, although there was some suggestion that it might have been a cooked-up caper. Either way, they cranked up the airplane and flew him to Floyd Bennett Field in Brooklyn, way out on the far end of Flatbush Avenue. He'd made his point, and eventually New York's airport was created on the old North Beach site and named for him. But when I started my copilot career none of that had happened and we were flying out of Newark.

Each airline had its own terminal—not a terminal by today's standards, more like an appendage on a hangar. TWA had a small round building, perhaps fifty feet in diameter, with an iron anchor fence between it and the airplanes. There were no jetways; passengers walked out to the airplane and climbed a low flight of stairs into the DC-3. There weren't many steps because the DC-3's rear door wasn't far above the ground. On rainy days the passenger agent had a circular container full of umbrellas, and gave one to each passenger to get to the airplane's steps where another agent retrieved the umbrella. When everyone was loaded, door closed and ready to go, the agent pulled the stairs, mounted on wheels, back out of the way.

The airport itself I always think of as black. The runways weren't paved, but were just black cinders on top of fill. The area had been a swamp and a garbage dump, and occasionally bottles and junk from below would work its way to the surface.

There was a control tower, one of the first, manned most of the time by Whitey Conrad. The conversation was a lot more informal than today, and there were relatively few radio contacts. Whitey knew many of the pilots, who all knew him, so it was often, "Cleared to taxi, Jack," and, "Thanks, Whitey."

I hadn't been back a day when I was set up for a flight with Captain Lloyd Olson—naturally, called Ole. The airplane was a DC-2 with stops at Camden, New Jersey (the airport for Philadelphia—New Jersey seemed to have a monopoly on airports), then after Camden it was Harrisburg, Pittsburgh, and finally Chicago. There would be lots of pumping the gear and flaps up and down.

I was quite a sight going to the airplane: a large suitcase with enough clothes for a week when it was just an overnight, my black navigation case, and a portable typewriter because I had a crazy idea I might find something to write about on layover. I must have looked ridiculous.

Ole was no problem, although his quietness had me spooked and wondering what he was thinking. I didn't recognize that he was what today we call a laid-back person. I doubt he would have shown emotion if both engines quit.

The trip went smoothly and he was patient with my fumbling, and helpful with a short, no-words-wasted remark when needed. Between Pittsburgh and Chicago he decided it was time for a lesson on my status as copilot.

We were flying through the smooth, clear early evening sky, passing Akron. Ole had it on autopilot and sat with his right foot braced on the pedestal, the other on the floor—left arm vertical from the armrest, cupped hand holding his chin, a model of relaxation as he gazed out the window at sky and ground.

I wasn't so calm. We were running low on fuel from the right tank, and it was about time to shift to the full left tank. The gauge hit zero, and I glanced at Ole—not a flicker of concern. The needle sat on zero and my eyes went to the fuel pressure gauge, which would go down as soon as the last of the fuel came out of the tank, quickly followed by a red warning light. We flew on. I was afraid to say anything; some captains would consider such a reminder as treading on their territory, challenging their awareness and skill. I watched the pressure gauge needle—it flickered and started down—and I glanced at Ole. Nothing. I squirmed as the needle hit zero and the red light popped on. To hell with Ole, what was the matter with him? I reached down, changed the fuel valve to the full tank, pumped the hand-wobble pump for pressure, and the engines ran on—we were in business.

Ole took his hand away from his chin and looked over at me. Was I about to catch hell?

"I wondered," he said calmly, "when you'd get around to changing that tank."

He put his chin back in his hand and resumed studying the sky and ground through the window. But he'd taught me a lot in that moment, changed my level from a nervous new boy to feeling that I was a part of the crew, useful, with things to do. Brief though the incident was, it put my feet on the first step up from neophyte.

Chicago was the Municipal Airport (later Midway Airport)—a busy place. Air traffic control did not cover the country, only certain airways and terminals. The control towers took over in the vicinity of the airport. There was national concern for air traffic safety—the pleas then were for more controllers, more funds, and requests by the airlines to keep private pilots out of the terminal areas. The date was 1937, but it could just as well be 2002—the problems haven't changed or been solved.

That day with Ole, however, was clear, there were no delays, and we landed close to schedule, checked in our paperwork, and took the "limousine" into town. *Limousine* was a word loosely used; crews went into town in these vehicles leased from a private operator, and during some economy drives and union battles the crews had to pay for the ride. The limousines were old, used to the point of obsolescence, dirty, loose, and rattly, smelling of stale cigarette smoke, their seats uncomfortable and squashed down with broken springs. The drivers were hired wherever the company could find them, and ranged from surly silence to too much annoying talk. Their skills ran the gamut, too, and some rides were scary—the pilots worried more about their safety in the limos than in airplanes. Crews were generally silent on the way to the hotel—tired after long flights, the ride frequently coming in the early morning after flying all night. No one wanted to talk and everyone slumped as best as possible in the old seats and nodded or slept, mouth wide open, disheveled, gray-looking, and unshaven.

In Chicago we stayed in an old hotel on the South Side—the Hyde Park, not deluxe by any means, and past its prime, an example of decayed elegance. It was big, and painted over often enough so there was a thick crust on radiators and woodwork; the lobby sprawled, with old armchairs and sofas of faded upholstery scattered about. Young, uniformed pilots checked in and out, watched by old ladies and widowers who sat in their favorite chairs living out their loneliness.

We stayed together, sharing a big room with two double beds. This wasn't a particularly happy arrangement. There's a certain primitiveness when one person has to put up with the other's habits and idiosyncrasies. One smokes, the other doesn't. One wants to read late with a bright light, the other wants to sleep—it goes on and on, but to aggravate the situation there was also the captain-copilot relationship in which the copilot was subordinate and generally had to do what the captain wanted. Of course, many of the pilots were considerate and asked the copilot's desires and paid attention to normal decencies. But not all.

As copilot you had to listen to long discourses on many boring subjects, such as how the captain had fixed up the attic of his house. Some delighted in debate and wanted to argue about almost anything when you wanted to read or simply not talk; others were tight-lipped and never said anything.

The double room also presented problems if the captain was bent toward the ladies; one told me that if I came up to the room and the "Do Not Disturb" sign was out I was to bug off. I spent one night sleeping in the lobby while my young, single captain entertained a damsel in "our" room.

Of course there were good guys, interesting to be with, but you still would have preferred to rest when you wanted, read when you wanted, and go and come without concern and without having to wait for the bathroom.

Many years later, in the early 1950s, our union contract mandated single rooms—a great step forward. The Air Line Pilots Association, ALPA, was founded in 1931 after many years of trial in the 1920s when people were fired if they became involved in union activities. ALPA has long been a leader in fighting for greater safety, working with the airlines and making them shape up when necessary. It was ALPA that made the airlines purchase radar when it became available in order to improve thunderstorm detection. The airlines will deny this, but that's the way it was.

Layovers with Ole were painless; he was quiet and thoughtful and a little sly, too. When it came time to pack and leave for our trip back I was a mite late, and was hurrying about trying to get all my junk together and downstairs to the limo.

I dashed about while Ole sat patiently waiting, his little overnight bag packed and ready. Finally I closed my bag, got it in one hand, flight kit in the other, and the typewriter I'd never used tucked under one arm. I started for the door.

Ole: "That your shirt on the bed?"

"Damn." I grabbed the shirt, opened the suitcase, stuffed in the shirt, and made a dash for the door.

Ole again: "Those your slippers by the bed?"

"Damn." I got them, repeated the confusion and jammed them in. Ole got up and we finally left. He didn't chide me or crack a smile, but he had quietly needled me and loved it. My next trip the typewriter stayed home and the suitcase had much less in it.

For three months I flew out of Newark. It was a good three months because it covered the end of summer, then late fall and finally early winter—a cross section of weather that began with thunderstorms and ended with snow and ice.

Flying is weather and weather is flying; the two intertwine until it's impossible to separate them. Airline reliability and safety are dictated by Mother Nature: the accidents because of wind shear, thunderstorms, ice, and fog make for a list of weather-caused problems that still haven't been conquered, and there are others. Reliability suffers when major snow-storms close airports and back up traffic, or hurricanes and thunderstorms bring flying to a halt. Weather is the great dominating influence, and as I got more involved with the airline I learned that this great X factor was always there, calling for skill and prudence, at times demanding a halt to all operations.

Weather affects flying not just in an overall sense, but in very specific detail: Is there going to be enough room between the base of the clouds and the earth—the ceiling—and enough visibility to see the airport for landing? Will there be ice that creates drag and slows the airplane until it can't fly? Are thunderstorms and their turbulence going to obstruct the way so we have to turn back, or if the decision is to penetrate them, what risk is there that the airplane may be torn apart? Will severe winds at the airport cause shear? Will head winds cause a fuel shortage? Each of these alone causes problems, and they often work in concert to make things worse.

Playing the weather game, you learn basics that never change and never will. Basic number one is the fact that weather does not always turn out as predicted. "State of the art" it's called, and the meteorological state of the art is, and will be for a long, long time, such that weather will always present surprises. Mother Nature makes it capricious, and like anything of whimsy it's hard to know in advance what's coming. Forecasting weather is an inexact science; it is critically important to realize and understand that ceilings may be lower, that you may encounter ice, thunderstorms, turbu-lence, and strong winds that were not expected to be there. You have to take this as a fact of flying life and not be upset or angry about it; this is the norm, meaning that weather forecasts must be viewed with skepticism at all times.

Because of this, the clever pilot always has an out. Having an out is a big part of flying, and it's there to save the day when the weather doesn't behave as it should.

The out doesn't only apply to weather, but includes things like mechanical failure, air traffic problems, the airport suddenly being closed because the airplane ahead of you had a flat tire and couldn't get off the runway for you to land. The list is long enough that the idea of an out becomes part of the character of good pilots and you don't think about it, except to have it.

One of my early trips out of Newark I drew the hotshot Flight 7, the Los Angeles–bound sleeper—Dick Hanson captain, the man who had set me up on my first flight at Kansas City. Hanson had a special fixation—they all did to some degree—on knowing the route, every little town along the way. He gave me one month to learn them all between Newark and Kansas City.

"What's that town?" he'd ask as he indicated some small place in the hills of Pennsylvania—a small cluster of lights.

"Nanty Glo," you'd say if you were lucky and on the ball—a place north of Johnstown.

Dick was a positive pilot; he didn't vacillate, and he knew what he was going to do and did it. He was almost brusque at times. He flew well, his movements fast and sure.

We flew uneventfully to Chicago, refueled, and took off for Kansas City. A front was forecast to move through Kansas City and give clear sky for our arrival. Dick checked the weather—a broadcast at fifteen minutes after the hour from the Burlington, Iowa, radio range station as we flew over—and it didn't show Kansas City as improving.

Dick fidgeted. "That son of a bitch isn't clearin' out as fast as they thought."

Approaching Kirksville, Missouri, we were on instruments, and white streaks of snow zipped into the landing lights when Dick turned one on to see what was out there in the dark. A bluish flash lighted the clouds.

"God damn—a thunderstorm." But it was a high one, the base of it above us in the warmer air running up over the lower cold air we were flying in. We didn't get a bump.

But now we were at Kansas City. The ceiling was less than 200 feet, and the old Kansas City airport, nestled close to town in a bend of the Missouri River, wasn't an airport where you could land with a ceiling of 200 feet.

The front was north of us now, but rather than clearing out, a low fog had settled over the river valley. As we flew across town, the colorful top of the Power and Light Building was sticking up through.

We milled around. "I'm gonna take a look," he said—meaning an attempt at letting down over the airport to the minimum altitude, hoping a higher spot in the cloud deck would let us see to land.

On the beam, listening to its signal, he flew carefully. The cockpit was dark except for the lighted instruments, and there was a certain tightness in the atmosphere. Dick, head down, eyes locked on the instruments, me looking through the windshield into the dark nothingness, trying to get a glimpse of something useful on the ground—and glancing back inside quickly and frequently to the altimeter, checking to see how low we were.

At minimum altitude, nothing. "No good!" Dick exclaimed, and opened the throttles to climb.

Now on the radio with Kansas City's dispatcher: "What do you think? Is it going to get any better? I can hold for half an hour." This meant we had enough fuel on board to wait half an hour for improvement and then go to our alternate—our out that Dick and the dispatcher had agreed on before we left Chicago.

"Dick," he said, "we don't see any improvement for a few hours."

"Okay, I'm going to Wichita." We climbed and took up a southwest heading. Then to me, "Get the gal up."

It was the hostess's job to tell the passengers we were Wichita-bound and there would be arrangements made for the Kansas City passengers to return and the Los Angeles ones to continue as soon as a crew could be flown down from Kansas City. We had exceeded the legal eight hours and couldn't continue. The eight-hour limit was established around 1934, as part of the Railway Labor Act, which governed how the airlines could treat its pilots and crews.

While Wichita was an inconvenience, it was a safe place, and the old rule of having an out made the flight an annoyance rather than an adventure.

Back then, weather information was gathered and presented by a knowledgeable human being, the meteorologist. Working with him on a regular basis, you came to know how to read his character so you could tell when he lacked confidence in the forecast and was conning you a little; some were very open and would tell you frankly that they weren't sure just what in hell was going to happen. Today you talk to a computer or its servant, and you can't read character from a sheet of paper covered with the symbols that a printer clicks out.

Back in the '30s, you first went over the general picture with the meteorologist—where the highs and lows were, anticipated movements of fronts (a fairly new concept in weather forecasting then), ceilings and visibilities along the way. He'd point out the areas of turbulence en route, of thunderstorms, ice, winds and their velocity, and then the important additional consideration: Was it a good situation, easy to forecast, with strong signals saying that these conditions were likely to stay where he said they would? Or were there quirks in the setup that made the forecast iffy, a chance that things would go sour—and what should a pilot watch for that will tell him when to forget about the forecast and to alter the original plan?

Pilots became very good at reading weather, and at times vied with the meteorologist on forecast accuracy—Hanson, for example, was an excellent weatherman. But regardless, the approach to weather was an honest one—no one pretended their predictions were statements of fact, true beyond question. The modern weapons of computerized weather reporting haven't improved forecasting, and they've eliminated the pilot's intimate discussions with a meteorologist that would highlight what might go wrong, and what signs to watch for that it was going wrong. A good pilot must still be wary, computer forecast or no; weather is still capricious.

I was quickly learning these things and developing a deep interest in the weather; more often in daily life, my eyes traveled skyward at cloud and wind. The first thing I did in the morning was go to the window and look at the weather and the sky—and sixty years later it still is.

The copilot's life was a endless procession of flight plans, radio checks, figuring out what you should or should not do for which captain, filling in logbooks, filling out pay cards—everything except flying. As a new copilot you never got a chance to take off or land the airplane; a good captain would let you fly in the air, but that was almost like you were a new student being tested to see if you could hold it straight and level. The sacred final act of flying—landing—was reserved for the captain. I can appreciate some of their feelings because they didn't know how well this new boy could fly, what my background was, so they weren't about to let me land, but it didn't stop my yearning to fly—to do the real flying, to take off and land.

The ultimate crunch to my ego came on my first flight with Captain Charles Kratovil, a first-generation Czech from St. Louis who in his early pre-airline days had unknowingly flown some of the first-string bootleggers of St. Louis to Chicago.

Charlie was a warm person with a positive nature. He spoke each word distinctly, with a sort of stop at the word's end—seemingly for emphasis. He cocked his head slightly as he talked, and he laughed during much of the conversation.

On our first trip together, a DC-2 en route to Pittsburgh, he called the hostess up front. "Please—bring—me—an—air—sick—container," he said. They were quart cartons back then, like the kind ice cream is packed in.

"You feel sick?" she asked with some concern.

"No—I—am—not—sick. Just—bring—the—container—and—then—go—back—and—stay—there."

After she'd departed, Charlie got out of his seat and explained this to me.

"Robert—I—don't—want—to—hurt—your—feelings—but—I—don't—know—you—and—how—you—fly—and—I—have—got—to—pee. I—do—not—want—to—leave—you—alone—up—here—and—go—back—to—that—john—and—be—that—far—away—in—case—something—should—go—wrong."

He proceeded to relieve himself into the carton, covered it and stashed it away in a corner of the front baggage bin. At Pittsburgh he carted it off somewhere to dispose of.

While this was an intriguing operation, the blow to my ego was severe. I was starting to wonder, Did I know how to fly? On my next day off I went to Hadley Field near New Brunswick, borrowed a friend's airplane, went up alone and did a few loops and spins followed by a series of landings just to convince myself I really was a pilot.

Getting a landing, as we called it, wouldn't come for some time—not until I was flying out of Los Angeles, where I was sent to fly vacation relief. This was in the winter, the only time vacations were given; the airline business was severely seasonal, and our east-west routes were busy in the summer—we put on more flights to fill the demand, and every pilot was needed. But winter was dismal, and the passenger loads dropped to depressing numbers—a few businessmen or people on family emergencies were about it. Flights sometimes flew empty except for the U.S. mail and a little cargo, so there were excess pilots. North-south airlines like Eastern thrived in the winter with their Florida trade, but in turn they flew light loads in the summer. This was all before deregulation, and an airline was only allowed to fly its specific routes.

Flying out of L.A. was interesting, because I was flying with the most senior pilots on the line—the pilots who started the business. There would never be anyone more senior.

They were distinctive, the last of the rugged individualists from airmail days, and each did things his own way. One trait they had in common, however, was that they did the flying—copilots got very few landings. A copilot landing was an event, and the news was passed around: "Hey, Cy let me land at Winslow last Friday!"

I flew a lot with Dutch Holloway, a good-humored, kind man—the original health food man I'd met in Albuquerque. He spoke with a slight lisp, the result of a forced landing in a single engine Lockheed Orion mail plane in the desert near Albuquerque; the plane slid along on its belly and threw Dutch forward into the instrument panel, tearing his lip badly and giving him a lisp for life. He was a for-real old-timer and had flown in World War I.

Dutch loved mining and was constantly involved in searching for gold, going into the desert, packing in like an old prospector and digging and exploring. He knew a lot about geology, and each trip was a lesson in rocks, strata, and formations as we flew over the fascinating and geologically rich country between Albuquerque and Los Angeles. His chatter was constant and enthusiastic as he noted points of interest and talked of the earth's history. This was before public address systems in airplanes, and so the passengers sat uninformed, and they no doubt wondered what in hell kind of flying was going on as Dutch pointed out things to me, wandering, making turns and changing altitude for better sighting. It was something I hadn't expected in the austere atmosphere of an airline, but to some pilots it was like we were still barnstorming. We weren't under air traffic control and there was no radar watching our progress, so altitude and course changes didn't matter, and besides, there weren't enough other airplanes in the sky to worry about.

Dutch gave me my first landing; it came after about four months on the line and a lot of promises. Dutch kept promising me a landing off and on for about two months, but each time we'd be in a logical situation for which he'd have a reason why it wasn't advisable.

"It's just dusk—that's a hard time—it wouldn't be fair to give you a landing now." I didn't care a damn about being fair, I just wanted to do it.

Or, "There's a nasty crosswind—I'd better handle it."

Then one foggy night at Burbank set me up for the big event. Burbank was fogged in along with the rest of the L.A. basin; we couldn't land, but the beauty of L.A. fog is that the desert almost always remains clear, and it's only a short hop to get there. That night our alternate was Saugus, a dirt strip twenty miles from Burbank, but made of the desert—clear and dry.

The company sent a limousine to pick up the four passengers and the hostess—Dutch and I were left to spend a night of isolation in the airplane. The dusty strip was deserted—no people, no town, just a beacon rotating and flashing its green code proclaiming it was an airport. We settled into passenger seats with blankets and pillows for a quiet night's sleep—after first scrounging through the galley and finding a couple of leftover dry sandwiches for dinner.

Sunup in the stillness of the desert, lighted by the clean early light—pink and gold in the pastel blue sky, still, soft, and quiet, the desert fragrance of sage and clean sandy earth, all beautiful and pure. We stirred and brought the radio to life, and Dutch called Burbank.

"Go ahead, Dutch," came the radio operator's reply—it was Tiny, a big man with a small, hoarse-sounding voice as though he had perpetual laryngitis.

"How's it look, Tiny?" Tiny knew well that Dutch meant the fog.

"It's still solid, but looking a little lighter."

"Okay—I'll call you in half an hour."

Dutch shut off the radio and told me, "It'll be okay in about an hour—we might as well get things fired up." Pilots knew their local weather, and if Dutch said it'd be okay in an hour you could bet on it.

We inspected the airplane, mostly checking the tires for damage from the dirt and stone strip, drained the fuel sumps to check for water in the gasoline, and then the big chore: "We'd better pull 'em through." This was the arduous task of pulling the propeller blades through to turn the engine and be certain no oil had collected in the bottom cylinders that might cause a lock and damage when we started the engines. The props were big and well off the ground and tough to turn, but I figured it wouldn't be too bad with Dutch's help.

"I'll watch the switches while you pull 'em through," he said.

I was flabbergasted. Why the hell did the switches need watching? Normally you checked them to be sure they were off so the engine wouldn't kick or start while you pushed and tugged on the big props—but the only reason to sit and watch them was to make certain no one else accidentally turned one on, and we were out in the desert with no one around for miles! I looked to see if Dutch was kidding, but he wasn't, and he crawled up in the airplane, opened the side window, and shouted down.

"Switches off!"

I pushed and pulled, leaning all my 155 pounds to the task, and finally, somewhat out of breath, got it done on both engines.

With that taken care of, I climbed up into the cockpit, where Dutch greeted me with news: "I called Burbank—it's lifting, and Tiny said he can see half the runway. By the time we get down there it'll be good enough."

We started the engines and taxied to the end of the strip. Dutch lined up and said, "Okay, you fly it."

An unexpected treat after all the promises. I placed my hands and feet on the controls, happily thinking of flying and the additional pleasant thought that for once I wouldn't have to pump up the landing gear.

I walked the throttles forward and we rolled, but not straight; the DC-2 wanted to wander off and I pushed the rudder to correct, but I overcorrected and the nose turned the other way, so we were snaking a path down the runway. Dutch shouted which rudder to push and how much, but he was laughing so hard the instructions were impossible to understand. I was discovering how squirrelly a bird the DC-2 was on the ground—very prone to go off on tangents.

Finally we had enough airspeed to fly, and I eased back on the wheel and we flew, up into the element where control response was normal.

I opened my mouth to speak the magic words, "Up gear!" But to my astonishment Dutch beat me to it.

"Okay, I've got her—up gear!"—and he took over the controls while again I had to throw myself into the task of pumping up that damn gear.

Gear up, he gave me the controls again and I flew to Burbank where the visibility was still marginal, but the fuzzy outline of roads and trees was enough reference to find the runway. I landed, not too bad a landing, but once on the ground it wanted to go off on its own. I worked hard to keep it on the pavement.

So I'd had my first landing and moved up a bit mentally. I flew another month with the old-timers, but got no more landings.

My days flying with Dutch were joyful ones. I never felt angry or ill of him for making me turn the props, or for his extended promises to let me fly; it was all part of the fun. Dutch was a grand person, and one I loved; as his copilot, I may have been largely along for the ride, but I learned a lot about flying, too, particularly weather flying. And eventually that knowledge and experience became the foundation on which the captain-copilot relationship and the organized cockpit and crew of today is based.

CHAPTER 6

Early Airplanes and How We Flew Them

THE DC-2S AND 3S we flew were crude compared to the jets of today, but they were pretty reliable airplanes, by which I mean their engines ran for hours without trouble. There's never been enough credit given to the engines of those airplanes; we tend to get starry-eyed about the good old DC-3, but we shouldn't forget some loud hurrahs for those good old engines, too.

As a whole, though, the DC-3 had its faults. It didn't fly well on one engine with a heavy load. Part of making sure you have an out is being prepared for when things go wrong, and the DC-3's limitations made this difficult. On many mountainous routes, if you lost an engine, the airplane couldn't maintain altitude above the peaks. (The expression "lost an engine" often confuses laypeople when pilots talk about engine problems. Since I'll be using it frequently as we go along, let me clarify that saying, "I lost an engine," doesn't mean it fell off the airplane, but simply that it stopped running. Of course, a few have fallen off airplanes, and when that rare event occurs aviation people are more apt to say, with wide eyes, "I really lost an engine—I mean the son of a bitch fell off!")

In flight, at reasonable altitudes, a DC-3 would stay aloft on one—but in the critical part of flight, taking off, especially at a high altitude airport, it just wouldn't fly. In the late 1930s, Hal Hess and Bronson White lost one right after takeoff at Albuquerque, which is about a mile high. Try as it might, and giving its all, the good engine wouldn't keep 'em flying and they descended, under control, to the desert and slid to a stop with little damage and no injuries.

There was an official hearing after the incident, and all the participants including government inspectors and company officials were there, including Captain Hess and Copilot White, who were somewhat under a cloud. The group gathered in a hangar to look at the engine, which had been removed from the airplane and was on a stand showing a few scuff marks and dirt from its slide across the desert. The company was trying to prove there wasn't anything wrong with the engine and that the real problem had been some vague screwup by the flight crew—a normal strategy considering liabilities.

The VP of flight for the region pointed to the engine and said, "There's nothing wrong with that power plant."

White cocked his head and crisply suggested, "Well, why don't you fire 'er up and let's hear it run?" Great scowls from the mighty.

Bronsie, as we called him, went on to captain and became one of the finest line instructor and check pilots. His sparkling career included flying a Constellation all by himself—solo and alone in the airplane—to get it away from Kansas City when the Missouri River flooded the airport. This was complicated by the flight engineer's panel being located behind the copilot's seat, so White had to go back there to be sure the fuel was on the right tanks, check the generators and other things, then go to the pilot's seat, start it up and double-check everything on the instrument and gadget panel behind him—he was a busy man that day. Another time he was aloft near Kansas City in a Connie, working with a copilot who was trying to advance to captain. Way below he spotted a Braniff passenger trip headed for Kansas City. Bronsie couldn't resist the chance—like a World War I pursuit pilot, he dove the Connie for speed to catch and pass the Braniff, but to add an extra fillip he shut down the two Connie engines on the side visible to the Braniff pilots and passengers, and he feathered the propellers—turned their blades perpendicular to the airstream to halt any windmilling—so the props were stopped cold and motionless as he zoomed closely past, waving. Of course he then pulled up and turned back out of view so he could quickly restart the two engines, but he'd made his point to Braniff's passengers and crew: that TWA could pass them even with half the engines shut down.

There was substance in Bronsie, and despite his dashing, unconventional ways, he was part of the industry's growth, and many good pilots fly today because his instruction taught them the airplane and his sense of command gave them confidence. It's a little sad that all that has gone—it just wouldn't fit in today's rigid, simulator-driven, FAA-scrutinized world.

Even aside from the DC-3's marginal performance with an engine out, it wasn't all that good a flying airplane. Its stall characteristics—what happens when the speed is too low to keep flying—were tricky, and if you got frisky with it you could wind up in a tailspin, as I did one night while giving instruction to a new copilot in late 1941. We were practicing steep turns and got into one too slow and too steep. It flipped one wing up over the other and spun! Not for long because I got to work quickly and recovered before it had developed seriously. The main damage was to the airplane's interior, more specifically to the toilet area; on transition flights (as training and checking flights are called) the maintenance crew is supposed to remove the "honey bucket" from the DC-3's lavatory, but they'd forgotten to do this, so as our G forces went slightly negative when we flipped into the spin, the honey bucket's contents dumped all over the lavatory interior and into the cabin as the lav door flew open in the chaos of the maneuver. The maintenance crew no doubt had great regrets about forgetting to take the bucket out as they cleaned up the mess.

The DC-2s and 3s also had performance limitations. Their maximum practical operating altitude was about 12,000 feet, which did not get you on top of much of the weather but rather left you down in it, wallowing in rough air, battling ice and periodically plowing into the fury of thunderstorms. The airplane could climb well above 12,000 feet, but it began to gasp for air and struggled to stay up there. Also, any operation above that altitude required oxygen for the passengers by law, but we only carried it for the crew.

The crew oxygen system was crude; rather than fancy masks that meter out oxygen in the physiologically proper amounts, we had a rubber hose with a wooden nipple on the end that one stuck in one's mouth. The oxygen flowed constantly and we breathed through our mouth to get it. Many shunned its use because rumor had it that oxygen would make the fillings fall out of your teeth.

We were pretty cavalier and naive with the oxygen and played tricks with it now and then as we flew, like pointing the end of the hose toward the captain's pipe or cigarette to surprise him as it flared up in a foot-high flame! A captain you knew well, of course.

The airplanes leaked while flying in rain—the 2 far more than the 3—and a frequent comment when radioing the ground about the weather was, "Light rain outside, heavy rain inside!" We carried rubber ponchos in our DC-2 flight kit and when we encountered rain we'd spread the poncho over our laps to keep from getting soaked. It was messy at best and the paperwork got wet, and water dripped onto the floor and soaked into your clothing where the poncho didn't cover you adequately or had slipped off your lap. As if that wasn't enough fun, snow could seep through the windshield joints—enough so that an inch or more would build up on the inside, which gives you an idea of the temperature in the cockpit.

The airplanes were unstable on the ground, and the tail had a tendency to want to beat the nose to the end of the runway. You tried to land carefully on the front wheels with the tail in the air, because this was a way to land successfully more consistently. Of course some pilots, as a matter of pride, tried to land the classic three-point way, tailwheel and front wheels touching the ground at the same instant in a smooth contact. But the result often wasn't smooth, and the airplane could drop in with a crunch or bounce in a sort of porpoising, galloping way.

When the design of future aircraft moved the tailwheel up front and made it a nose wheel, landing and keeping a true path on the ground became easy because the geometry of the landing gear changed in relation to the airplane's center of gravity; now it was natural, by the laws of motion, for it to go straight. With a tailwheel location, however, all those laws told the airplane it should be going ass-end first, so it tried to swap ends and make itself a nose wheel airplane. The pilot's job was to fight this instinct and keep it under control. This was just part of the game and we didn't think about it, but when the nose wheel came along we all had that "Where has this been?" feeling. We didn't get nose wheels until the C-54 during wartime—later this became the DC-4 when the war was over.

The brakes on the DC-3 were operated by pressing on the top half of the rudder pedals with one's toe; more pressure on one than the other gave you braking on that side and aided steering. These brakes were effective and easy to use. The DC-2 brakes were another matter: a handle came out of the upper left portion of the instrument panel, and you grasped it and pulled out for braking—both brakes. If you wanted right brake only, for steering, then you'd push the right rudder pedal while tugging at the brake handle, which took considerable strength—this gave you brakes on the right, but not the left wheel. While doing all this your right hand was free to use the throttles, together or individually—right or left engine—to get some steering ability, because often the brakes were weak and pulling as hard you could didn't produce enough stopping. Of course if airplane controls were needed—like keeping the elevator shoved forward while taxiing with a strong tailwind, or up into a head wind—then you put that hand on the control wheel and you couldn't use the differential throttle. Captains yelled at copilots to push the wheel forward or back when trying to taxi in strong, gusty winds so they could keep their hands on the throttles. Often the plane took on the role of adversary, as it always wanted to cock into the wind and fought you madly when you wanted it to go another direction. The tailwheel was free to swivel to aid in steering, but it was also possible to lock it in the straight-ahead position to help keep the airplane track straight; you did this by pulling a lever located under the throttles that would pull a long cable that set a pin into the tailwheel mount. Locking and unlocking the tailwheel was a masterful part of taxiing, but it demanded use of the right hand, which was already busy with throttles and flight controls—both the DC-2 and DC-3 had this feature. If the wind was too strong, shoving against the fuselage's side, the tailwheel locking pin would shear, causing muttered oaths from mechanics when they had to replace it.

I'd always thought that being captain on a DC-2 would relieve me of the manual labor of pumping the gear and flaps, but once on the left side I discovered that the damned brake took almost as much strength and effort.

Visibility forward in times of rain, snow, or freezing rain ranged from marginal to zero. For ice, we carried in our navigation kit a putty knife so we could open the side window, reach out in the cold blast, and scrape enough ice off the front windshield to see for landing. The opening you scraped off was generally about the size of a dollar bill. We didn't have windshield wipers either; eventually wipers were installed, but they were only effective at slow speeds when the wind blast wouldn't smear the water across the windshield faster than the wipers could clear it. Another added system delivered alcohol through a copper tube with little holes in it that went along the bottom of the windshield outside. We could pump alcohol through the tube so it would spray out the little holes onto the windshield and, in theory, melt the ice for the wiper to knock away. Its effectiveness nestled in about the 40 to 60 percent range; cold, thick ice wasn't fazed by it at all, and so the old putty knife went back into action.

There was some heat in the airplane that you could direct onto the windshield through a flexible tube, but the heat level was so low it was only effective against frost or the lightest ice. More often the metal tube, breathing out its warm air, found itself nestled inside the front of the captain's coat, keeping his body cozy.

The DC-3 was sluggish in aileron control (bank and unbank); the elevator control was light and responsive, the rudder heavy. So what pilots call harmony in an airplane's control, meaning all the controls feel proper in relation to the others, was poor in the DC-3.

The DC airplanes had slightly swept wings—that is, the wingtips were further back than the root where they fastened to the fuselage. In theory this reduced drag, but it also gave them a tendency to wallow in rough air, the tail swinging back and forth in what's called Dutch roll. It made the ride in the cabin uncomfortable and caused much of the airsickness that was routine stuff in those days. A good pilot could combat this tail swinging by using the rudder, but the heaviness of the control and the effort of pushing one's feet forward and back on the rudder pedals for long periods was tiring, so much of the time the pilot rested his feet on the floor while the tail swayed through the sky and passengers heaved and retched.

A unique aspect of the control wheel hookup made for strained relations between pilots. The wheel was mounted on a metal tube called a column, which contained the chains and cables the wheel was hitched to. The tube didn't go straight down to the floor, but was constructed so it went from the wheel over to the side and down the cockpit wall into the mysterious innards of the airplane where cables and pulleys live. Since the cockpit room was not abundant, this column tube could get in the way, and long-legged pilots often flew in sort of a sideways position with their knees bent toward the aisle to keep them away from the wall.

It's normal practice when first getting in an airplane and checking it over on the ground to grasp the control wheel and push it full forward and full back and to turn it full side to side to check that the controls are free and that nothing is restricting them. Experienced pilots learned to check first to see where the other pilot's legs were before doing this, because these were dual controls and if one pilot moved the wheel, the other pilot's control wheel moved, too. Copilots unaware of the implications of their actions grasped the wheel and briskly pulled full back only to hear an outburst of foul oaths as the column along the wall bashed into the captain's kneecap.

The DC-3 control wheel was not a full circle but was open on the top third, so turning it to check ailerons could create an additional wounding when one of the ends, much like a bull's horn, dug into the captain's groin, compounding the anger and ill feeling. These were not necessarily separate actions, but could be done simultaneously by turning the wheel while pulling on it, which didn't give the victim much chance to squirm away from either thrust. Captains were also guilty on occasion of being thoughtless in this manner; good guys called out, "Control check," before starting the action to give the other a chance to get vital parts out of the way.

The cockpit's interior was noisy with the big engines clanking and roaring not too far away; the right front cargo door always seemed to rattle, how severely depending on the engine power being used, and a sort of harmony developed. On DC-3 takeoffs the rattle became a loud buzzing noise, but we didn't worry about it because we knew what it was.

We wore radio headsets; as a captain you wore the left earphone to receive radio communication, while keeping the right headphone piece behind or in front of your right ear so you could hear the copilot. So your left ear was hearing the radio noise of crackle, snap, and a hissing sound like fat frying in a hot pan, while the right was bombarded with the cockpit noise. Actually the radio noise was more powerful and damaging than the cockpit noise; most old captains can hear better in their right ear than their left. I find this useful when I'm trying to sleep in a noisy environment—I sleep on my right side, my good ear buried in the pillow, while my airline-deafened left ear sticks up in the noise it doesn't hear.

There was an evolutionary difference between the DC-2 and the DC-3. The 2 was advanced from the old biplanes, to be sure, but the elements, the outside, still seemed awfully close. There was a lot of noise, it was cold, it leaked, snow gathered inside the windshield. The propellers were not constant speed, but two-position. You made a climb in low pitch—the propeller blades at a flatter angle so the engines could turn faster and give more power—as the airplane's engines ran louder but smoother at the faster revolutions per minute. When altitude was reached you set up the airplane for cruise: level off; pull the power back; reach down to two levers, ganged together, and pull them up. A shudder went through the airframe as the propeller pitch changed and increased; the noise level lowered, the power was pushed up to the correct manifold pressure; and you lightened the fuel mixtures carefully by watching an indicator.

At this point you were in business, unless you were in some kind of weather: rain, snow, clouds. Then you needed carburetor heat, because the DC-2 Wright engines were wonderful refrigerators and created ice in the carburetor throat that would eventually stop the engine if you didn't do something about it. Using the carburetor heat, pulling back a lever for each engine, disturbed the fuel-air mixture, so that had to be readjusted and delicately balanced by moving a lever connected to the carburetor on each engine and watching the engine instruments for results. With all this done, one could sit back and relax.

There was an autopilot, a crude hydraulic system with a big control panel containing a directional air-driven gyro that had to be set with the compass—then a duplicate under it that was the autopilot's. You synchronized the two by twisting two knobs to line them up, and then the autopilot could be turned on. The directional gyro precessed (wandered off), as gyros do, and it was necessary to realign the two frequently; this could be done by turning off the autopilot, resetting the gyros, and then turning it back on—this method caused little motion or jerking that passengers could feel. If a pilot was lazy he would grasp both knobs, one in each set of thumb and forefinger, and carefully turn them together, resetting the gyro without much airplane action—but if he was hasty the airplane slewed around to the corrected heading and passengers must have been startled.

If a climb was needed to get atop some clouds, then the mixtures were enriched, the propeller levers pushed down for low pitch, throttles advanced, and the level-off procedure reversed—once the new cruising altitude was reached, the props were put in high pitch and all the adjustments made again. We'd often try to sneak up a couple of thousand feet in high pitch with all items set, too lazy to go through the routine, but it was a struggle and slow.

We flew a lot of weather. When the 2 came on the scene it was a big technical advance over previous airplanes and the pilots thought it could fly any weather, so we flew a lot of ice, thunderstorms, and most anything nature could toss your way.

The 2, with its thick, high-lift wing, could carry a lot of ice. It built up on wings, engine cowls, propellers, tail, anything that stuck out. The propellers were equipped with alcohol that centrifugal force threw out onto the blades, loosening the ice so it flew off in chunks. Some chunks hit the side of the fuselage with a great banging noise. Since it came off unevenly, the prop would be unbalanced after tossing a big piece of ice, and vibration shook the airframe. Ice on the fin disturbed the airflow over the rudder, making the tail swing back and forth.

A typical experience in ice meant sitting in a cold cockpit, windows covered over in a fan-shaped plume from the lower aft corner toward the middle front, frost or snow covering the inside of the windshield frames, pieces as large as eight inches growing forward from the windshield's edges outside, hunks of ice banging against the fuselage and the airplane shaking as the tail swung left and right, right and left, and the action was transferred to the rudder pedals your feet were on so you felt them saw back and forth beneath you. The side windows were frosted, but you could wipe them clear enough for a look out at the engines. The nose cowlings collected ice on their leading edge, and I've seen it so bad that the ice built forward until the back of the propeller was shaving it! But still the airplane flew. The indicated airspeed would slow, and you'd push up the throttles for more power to overcome the loss, but it didn't always take, and the airspeed sometimes went down to alarming numbers approaching stall. There were deicer boots, rubber strips along the leading edge that expanded when air was blown into them—the idea being that the blown-up boots, swelling by inches, would break off the ice that had formed on the leading edge. They didn't do a good job. Often the broken ice would spin crosswise and hang on to the wing, causing even more drag; or the ice came off the leading edge, but eight inches back of the boot there was still ice; and some ice it cracked but didn't break, leaving drag-producing stuff on the wing. Sometimes when I used the boots I lost airspeed as compared to a smoother wing with ice on it. So you didn't count on the deicer boots to get you through ice of long duration; you turned them on for amusement mostly, to see what they'd do, not as serious protection from disaster.

In the meantime, you worked to get out of the ice, descending if it was likely to be warmer under the clouds. If the airplane was still flying crisply you might try to climb above the clouds. Over the Allegheny Mountains, east of Pittsburgh, the cloud tops would be at 10,000 or 12,000 feet, and it was a race to see if you could get on top before you accumulated so much ice you couldn't get there. Sometimes there was a front pushing through and you knew that going up or down wasn't going to do any good, so you flew on, knowing that you'd eventually fly out of the front into clear air, or at least get between layers—if the ice didn't do you in before that. There were some accidents because of ice, but not as many as you might think considering the anxiety it caused. But the rule we all followed, to keep the fearful potential under control, was to do something about ice the moment it started to form—try to escape it before it got serious. These were bleak experiences fraught with much apprehension.

One kind of ice put gulping fear into all pilots: freezing rain. The ice formed so quickly, and in such immense amounts, that something had to be done instantly when it started to form. The rule was, turn around or climb. It was logical to climb because the rain had to be coming from an above-freezing region—it starts as liquid as it falls and only forms ice when it strikes the cold airplane down in the below-freezing air. So when ZR—freezing rain's teletype symbol—started to form, the drill was immediately to low-pitch, pour on power, and climb, staring at the outside air temperature as you did, anxiously waiting for it to go above freezing. It was a damned tense time.

As in all these things, certain conditions or situations can occur that call for something different, as they did for Captain Red Miller approaching Chicago. He told me he was in descent and only twelve miles from Chicago Municipal Airport when freezing rain started to form. Climb, turn around, or go for the airport? Red decided to run for the airport—hell, climbing practically within sight of the field didn't add up. The ice formed at a terrifying rate, and the boots didn't faze it. The airplane slowed, Red put on more power, then more, and finally within sight of the runway he was wide open—with the airplane sinking, unable to hold altitude. It was a contest of not running out of altitude before reaching the airport. He made it, touching the runway solidly, engines wide open. At the terminal, the ground personnel had to hammer ice from the passenger door to get it open.

The 2 carried fourteen passengers in pretty pleasant conditions—as long as the heater didn't freeze. The cabin was fairly well soundproofed and the seats were excellent; they weren't jammed in as on today's airplanes, and had a back that could be cranked full flat to sleep on. They rotated, too, so one could turn around and face the person behind to converse, play cards, whatever. One of the Vanderbilts who frequently flew coast to coast with us always purchased two tickets, one for his body and the other for his feet to rest on the seat ahead, reversed. I look back at those seats as the best we've ever had.

The engines, 710-horsepower Wrights, were allowed to run 525 hours before being completely torn down and overhauled. Flying between Kansas City and Chicago one time I heard the company radio-call Captain George Duvall on another flight with an urgent message to turn immediately and fly back to Kansas City. It was a strange request, but on the ground I learned that somehow the records of that airplane had been mixed up, and it actually had 920 hours on the engines since overhaul. Today's jet engines are never overhauled; they remain on the airplane for tens of thousands of hours being checked carefully, certain parts replaced, but the idea of taking them off the airplane, tearing them all down, and overhauling them is gone, unneeded—their reliability is almost perfect compared to the old piston engines.

The DC-3 didn't really perform any better than the DC-2, maybe a bit less snappy, but it was still a move up in sophistication. The landing gear and flaps went up and down by simply moving two levers—no more hand pumping! The brakes were toe brakes on top of the rudder pedals, leaving the pilot enough hands to work controls, throttles, and tailwheel lock; the propellers were constant speed, the carburetors less apt to ice, the cockpit better soundproofed, the heat improved as long as you didn't freeze the boiler. It didn't leak much and it had windshield wipers. The cockpit came closer to what's known today as a shirtsleeve environment. The airplane was bigger and went from fourteen to twenty-one passengers, and some models had sleeper berths. The gross weight was 24,400 pounds versus 18,000 for the 2; the engines were 1,100 horsepower each against 710—and the 3s would gain gross weight and power through the years. When the war came, the DC-3 became, in the Air Corps, the C-47: same dimensions, but beefed up to carry heavy cargo on the fuselage floor, so the empty weight went up. To me, it wasn't the same airplane as our first DC-3s. The originals felt lighter, flew more sprightly, and gave me more seat-of-the-pants feel. The C-47s came from the DC-3, make no mistake—it was a close kin, but to me it wasn't the old 3 I'd cut my teeth on.

As I look back, I see the DC-3 was the first step to modernity, a change from being part of the outside with the wind whistling and the inside wet from rain, to sitting in blasé comfort—of course, the DC-2 wasn't any open biplane with singing wires either, but there was a difference, a development not quite fully achieved, that made it closer to the old era. Then the DC-3 came to give a quick peek at the environment that jets now have, a complete distancing from the elements and from thinking how to combat them. The jet requires judgment and management by numbers and computers; the general idea is that in the protected, computer-managed environment, seat-of-the-pants judgment isn't needed or even wanted. I hope this works just fine, but I also hope that when an unexpected or unpredicted emergency suddenly arises, the pilot up front has some "old stuff" stored away and available in his brainpan.

Before going much further I should give you a picture of the state of air traffic control in those days as well as radio and weather flying. Before World War II, radio for both communication and navigation was crude. Communication was on frequencies from 3,000 to 8,000 kilocycles, for those interested—and we didn't call 'em kilohertz as they do today, Heinrich Hertz being the German who discovered all this business and in his honor *hertz* is tagged on all frequency designations, and so much for Heinrich. But whatever you called it, the frequencies were loud with background noise that tore at your eardrums because you had to turn up the volume to hear the message, which raised the level of the crackling in your ears. The frequencies were sensitive to atmospheric conditions, and were mysteriously aggravated by sunspots. This caused what we called skipping. It was a lot like listening to an old AM radio at night while thunderstorms raged outside—lots of noise that made hearing an intermittent thing, with skips so that you in New York, trying to tune a local station, would get programs from Cincinnati or Chicago.

This was exasperating. You could be near Harrisburg attempting to give a position report to Newark, but unable to raise Newark. However, Kansas City might be coming in strong and be able to read Newark, too, so Kansas City would take the message from you and then repeat it to Newark. We called it relaying.

During periods of bad reception, the ground only received bits and pieces of what was said, so we'd repeat each word twice. The person trying to untangle the garbled message was a TWA radio operator who understood code. Some of the ex-navy pilots were sharp with Morse code—Don Terry in particular—and would whistle dots and dashes into the mike and get their message across that way.

Sometimes one flight was able to reach a ground station that another flight couldn't, and could hear them both, so it would serve as a relay station. Certain pilots enjoyed this relaying, as it gave them a do-gooder feeling. Our VP of operations, who frequently flew line trips, was that type, and on one occasion as copilot I picked up the mike to tell him I could read his flight and would relay a message—but my captain, a hard type who held no love for the VP, interrupted me: "Don't call the sumbitch—he'll have us relaying all night."

The navigation radio was a low-frequency system called a radio range, and it created the beam you followed—a name that sticks today when laypeople talk about airplanes coming in on the "beam" even though it no longer exists.

This was the primary means of navigation. There weren't any dials on the instrument panel to tell you if the airplane was right or left of course; you listened to signals that told if you were on or off course. One side of the course was the letter N (–.), and the other side was an A (.–). When you were on course, the two signals merged into a steady tone. The range stations broadcast on frequencies between 200 and 400 kilocycles, which were bad in static conditions.

The As and Ns weren't a crisp thing with fine lines of demarcation, but changed from the on-course steady tone, to the .– of an A, or –. of an N, in a subtle variation of the steady tone; your ear would pick up a slight interruption of the steady tone, almost just a suggestion of it, as the aircraft began to go off course. With a well-tuned ear, a sensitive pilot could cut this edge closely—that is, if static wasn't making a mess of reception with noise that made hearing any signal difficult to impossible. The further one got off the beam—we called it a "leg"—the more pronounced the A or N became.

Thunderstorms in the area made reception almost impossible; snow and some rain raised hell with it, too, because the friction of the snow on the airplane gave it an electrical charge. This excess charge wanted to bleed off, and did so on the radio antenna, making a great noise that cut out any radio range reception. Then you had to try to hold a compass heading and wait for the signal to come back. We called it P static—P for precipitation, because that's what caused it.

These beam legs were not straight-edge true but by their nature wandered, and also had multiples and false beams with bends, so there could be more than one "on course" signal. One might follow a false signal thinking everything was peachy keen, only to have it disappear and hear an off-course A or N—then it was a fast scramble to find the true beam.

This same beam was used for a low approach: you followed it and descended through the clouds to find the airport when the weather was bad. The actual station that sent out the signals was a mile or so from the airport. The procedure was to follow an on-course beam to the station and then, when you were over it, cut the power and shove the nose toward the minimum altitude it was safe to descend to. Some installations had another beam from the station to the runway, but some didn't and you just held a gyro heading descending, hoping something would show up.

A typical approach at Newark meant following a beam leg up from the direction of Princeton—southwest—toward the radio station located at the southwest end of the Newark meadows about two miles from the airport. We'd grind along listening with great care for the slightest break in the on-course steady signal to tell us we were slipping off course, and making quick corrections. It might be raining, the water dripping annoyingly on your lap, the lights turned low so your eyes would adjust to the dark and pick up the ground when and if it came in view, the altitude being maintained at 800 feet. The beam would increase in strength dramatically near the station, so it was necessary to turn the volume lower when you neared the station, and it was normal practice to have one hand on the volume control, constantly changing it. As you got closer to the station you'd hear a confusion of As and Ns; then, at the peak of sound, as you crossed the station, the signal would disappear completely, only to come back on the other side, loud again, as you passed and flew away from it. This was known as the cone of silence; pilots referred to it as the cone of confusion. But whatever you called it, it meant you had passed over or close to the radio range station.

As soon as you crossed it, you pulled back the throttles and descended to 300 feet and hoped the ground would come into view. The ground around Newark Airport meant the meadows—more swamp than meadow—with no lights. The airport surface was black cinders and appeared as a void—in the trade it was called a black hole. The lead-in lights were not the brilliant row of today with flicking "rabbit"—condenser discharge lights that streak toward the runway like tracer bullets from a machine gun; rather they were bars of red neon stuck out into the swamp, with an empty black beginning and another black emptiness at the end where the dark airport began. If they came into view, streaky and wavy through the rain-covered windshield, we flew down them and tried to land on the black cinder surface in a graceful fashion. There was a big luck element, as it was almost impossible to tell where the surface was. This made it easy to fly into the ground without a graceful flare; the result might be a bounce back into the air—high enough, as one pilot put it, "to circle down from!" Or you might flare, thinking the ground was close by when really it was still a considerable distance away—then the airplane "fell" onto the runway with a heavy crunch. The black hole caused many bad landings but little damage except to the pilot's ego—which, in the case of good versus bad landings, is very sensitive.

If there was freezing rain or such, you might have the front sliding window open in an attempt to see better, inching sideways from it, trying to protect your face from the sting of little pieces of ice coming at you around 90 miles an hour. If the lights didn't come into view or you couldn't make out the ground at 300 feet, we pulled up and went back toward Princeton for another attempt, or gave up and flew to an alternate.

Even worse was a thing called the circling approach, when we'd break out of the clouds low and then had to circle in poor visibility and low ceiling to find the landing runway because the beam wasn't oriented toward it or the wind was too strong across it. The trick was to keep under the clouds, but at the same time not get so low as to risk hitting the ground. The space we were working in, flying and seeing poorly, sandwiched between cloud and ground, was only 400 or 500 feet. This was a dicey business calling for a unique technique of half instruments and half looking out the window. Because of the reduced visibility and the closeness to the ground, especially at night, reference to a horizon didn't exist and optical illusions could easily give the feeling of being higher than the airplane really was. It was a shock of no small size to be circling, looking at the ground and trying to get lined up with the runway, and to look back inside at the altimeter and discover you'd lost 200 feet! So the method was to fly mostly by instruments, checking altitude, airspeed, and heading, with brief looks out at the airport to make sure you were flying the proper course and to line the aircraft up with the runway. It took experience to understand that this was the only safe way to do a circling approach, and a lot of crackups occurred during this maneuver for those who hadn't gotten the word. Today few circling approaches are made because instrument landing systems lead you right to the runway; if circling is required the minimums are high, at least 1,000-foot ceiling and three miles visibility, or it isn't done.

All this made it important to know the vicinity of the airport very well: road intersections, hot dog stands, a gin factory with a brightly lighted sign on it, the bend in a river. You picked out items that would line up with a runway, like the slag pile near the runway's west end at Pittsburgh's old Allegheny County Airport that was especially useful when they dumped hot slag that put a red glow on the bottom of the low-hanging clouds and indicated where the runway was. There were points we knew so intimately that we'd begin to pull power off for landing even though the runway wasn't yet in view, because we knew it would show up in a few seconds.

The business of how low to go when trying to find the ground was where the final piece of a pilot's judgment came into play. All the maneuvering around in the clouds—rain or snow—flying the beam, finding the station, and then descending, came together in that last 400 feet of descent. Still blind, the altimeter reading 300 feet, we'd know that the ground, hills, trees, poles, electric lines, whatever, were not thousands of safe feet beneath but very close, almost scraping the belly. If 300 feet was the minimum but nothing came in view, it was tempting to descend further, closer to the hidden obstructions, counting on missing them because there was always a safety margin that you could slice into, hoping the field would come into view before you hit something. Some days it was okay to sneak lower: the approach was good, the air smooth, making it easy to fly delicately with small, precise corrections. But other times the air was rough, the rain or snow heavy, and it just didn't feel smart to sneak lower, so you didn't.

The sacred minimum was the altitude below which you were not allowed to go. Minimums varied with each airport, depending on its location, obstructions, and so on. The lowest were 300 feet, and they went up to 800 in some cases. Arriving over an airport, you might not see the airport or the lights clearly, but you could catch tantalizing little glimpses of the ground, making you feel that another 100 feet down would get you under the ceiling. This cheating wasn't a safe procedure, of course, and accidents occurred because of it, but not many, because it was a pilot's judgment call, and pilots don't like to get killed either.

This was a time when we had what was called a look-see, meaning we could make an approach even when the ceiling was reported below the legal minimum of 300 feet. The official concept was that you descended to 300 feet, took a look, and if the ground didn't show you pulled up. But, of course, this gave free rein to sneaking down that extra 100 feet or so.

This came to a halt and look-see was taken away when a regulation was put into effect that if a U.S. weather report showed the ceiling less than the legal minimums—300 feet in the case of Newark—one couldn't even make an approach, but had to go to an alternate or hold to wait for improvement. Previously, if Newark was reporting below legal minimums, say 200 feet, you could make an approach, and if it came into view at 300 feet, you'd land. Of course, if the ceiling really was 200 feet, we still might cheat down to it and land anyway. The legal cover was to radio the tower as soon as you were on the ground and falsely announce, "I broke out at 300 feet." Other pilots, waiting to make their approach, would hear you report breaking out at exactly the legal minimum, and could translate the

message as, "Watch it, fellows—the ceiling isn't really 300; expect lower."
It was a subtle signal we all understood.

✳

THE INTRICATE SYSTEM of air traffic control was just coming into
being in the late 1930s, and it covered less than half the airways. At
best it was crude; the basic things missing were radar and communications.

Because there wasn't any radar, the ground couldn't "see" the airplanes
and had to rely on their own position reports. That's what made accurate
position reporting necessary, a careful checking and reporting that was
mostly the copilot's job—watched over with a steely eye by the captain.

Your communication was not directly to an air traffic controller, but was
radioed from the airplane to your company radio operator, who then took
the position report and telephoned or teletyped it to air traffic control. If
they had a return message for the airplane, the route was reversed—to
radio operator and then to the airplane. It all took time, so quick changes
in plans were impossible.

Since the ground couldn't "see" the airplanes, everything was a matter
of timing, and when more than one airplane arrived at a field, the first was
cleared to make an approach while the other held over the radio range or
some point until the airplane making an approach was on the ground or in
sight of the tower—if there was a tower. This made for long spacing
between approaches; an airport was lucky if it could accept five approaches
an hour, which is how stacking and holding came into being. Today, a
good control system can get in forty an hour because they have aircraft following closely behind one another, knowing the spacing is safe because
ground control sees with radar.

The only limitation now is how many airplanes can be squeezed onto a
runway in an hour, forty being about the limit. So if forty-one show up,
stacking and holding, even today, has to be used. The runway is the limiting factor; some airports use two—O'Hare, Atlanta, and others. But this
still is the controlling factor, because when more airplanes show up than
runways can take, delays begin. Adding more controllers, radar, or whatever doesn't reduce delays beyond a certain point; in the final analysis, it's
pavement that counts.

Way back in the early days of air traffic control, someone suggested getting a railroad traffic expert to look over the situation and make suggestions. The railroad guy studied it and then almost laughed himself silly as he explained that the aviation industry did it ass-backward, with many "tracks" en route, but only one—the runway—at the terminal. Railroads, he pointed out, have few tracks en route, but spread out to many in the terminal. He shook his head and declared it hopeless—and he may have been right.

The no-radar days caused some cheating and some artful maneuvers to get in first. At La Guardia, flights coming in from the southwest reported at Coney Island, and the tower would generally clear the first one past Coney as number one to land. Eager wheeling and dealing types called over Coney when actually they hadn't yet reached it, just to get the jump on another airplane—which caused an immediate response from the others and radio calls of "liar" or stronger terms. There was a lot of rivalry between airlines, and racing to get there first was a part of it.

When international operations began, some of the foreign pilots didn't understand the business of holding and waiting your turn. One approached La Guardia on a stormy night and was told to hold at 7,000 feet over New Rochelle—that meant there were six airplanes under him, and they'd be cleared to land from off the bottom of the pile and the pile would move down 1,000 feet after each landing. So this chap was required to circle and wait patiently as he was lowered, after each airplane ahead landed, down to 6,000 feet, then 5,000—4,000—3,000—2,000, and finally number one to approach. But to everyone's amazement, with six airplanes still in the stack, through the gloomy, rainy night this foreign aircraft appeared on the runway taxiing in! He had ignored the holding request and descended through the pile, made his approach, and landed. Stern action followed, and all of this airline's pilots had to come to the United States and go to school on our air traffic control system.

Clever timing of descents, and asking for descent early, could get the thinking pilot under an airplane ahead of him so you could land first. Cutting corners could do the same, and there was a lot of finagling and strategy involved.

Years later they still came into play—but legally, because radar, Big Brother, is watching. Flying New York to London, our rival was Pan Am, a fine bunch of pilots, but raised in the protected world of Pan Am's routes in the Caribbean and South America where they were the only kids on the block. They didn't have the same rough-and-tumble instincts of those of us who grew up in the tough competition of Chicago and La Guardia's heavy traffic—especially Chicago.

Pan Am's London flight departed New York the same time as ours, but if they got out first for some reason, we still could give them a fifteen-minute start and beat them into London, with both of us flying the same type of airplane. It was all done between the west coast of England and London by asking for lower altitude before they did. Having studied their ways, you knew where they'd start descending, and you'd get the jump on them by requesting permission to descend before that point. We also knew they descended at a slow airspeed, so by getting an early descent and letting our speed build up we'd slip by and be first on the ground in London. We'd laugh about it, saying they were staying up there longer getting more of the experience that their ad, "The World's Most Experienced Airline," bragged about. But they eventually got up to speed, especially after Pan Am acquired National Airlines, whose pilots were part of the gang that grew up learning the tricks of push and shove on domestic routes.

En route, over much of the country, traffic control was up for grabs, and off-airways flights and uncontrolled airports were the norm. At some airports you knew the other airline's schedule and would be on the lookout for any arrival close to yours, frequently sorting it out by radio contact with the other airplane.

There was a lot of looking and watching for the other guy, but, of course, when flying blind, you couldn't see them. On one of my copilot flights the captain had me flying the airplane; we were in clouds and I was following the beam toward the station at Goshen, Indiana, en route to Chicago. I was pleased with the way I was doing it and I went smack over the cone of silence—and an outburst followed. "Jeeesus Kee-rist! Don't ever fly right over the station—that's where everybody else goes! Miss it to one side so you won't collide with some bastard."

Control gradually covered the country, but progress was in short steps: first at airports where airplanes merged dangerously; then came control over short-haul airways, the busy ones between key cities, but the long-range en route part was not covered for a long time, and flying "out there" you had to count on luck for separation. Congress and the nation were warned by the pilots through ALPA, and by various individuals with aviation know-how, that pilots were playing a form of Russian roulette in the big expanses of uncontrolled sky. But progress, typically, was slow, with congressional bickering about budgets deserving much of the blame. The needs of air traffic control were, and are, always two steps ahead of the political system, and it seemed to require a major disaster to get attention. In the case of air traffic control it was a TWA Constellation and a United DC-7 running into each other over the Grand Canyon, killing 128 people on June 30, 1956. That accident is looked on as the time air traffic control started moving ahead—although today, after deregulation, the problems have again outpaced development, facilities, and governmental will. At the time of the Grand Canyon crash, Dave Thomas was the Civil Aeronautics Authority's most knowledgeable man on air traffic control—the best. In a hearing following the crash, he was asked why there wasn't a direct, controlled transcontinental route. His crisp, quick answer: "Funds, personnel, and equipment." Unfortunately, that same answer would fit the air traffic ills today.

But back there in 1937, control covered only a part of our flying; luck and looking out the windshield, when it was clear, was usually enough to keep us apart. Whatever you want to say about flying in those days, those of us up front weren't being pampered. And, to a great extent, we didn't know what we were missing.

CHAPTER 7

Way Out West

A SUDDEN TRANSFER TO Los Angeles, to fly vacation relief; junior copilots were sent wherever needed to cover the empty spots created by pilots' vacations during the slack times of the year.

Sunny California was a lonely place. My pay, $180 per month, didn't allow for fancy quarters, and I was trying to save money looking toward becoming a married man. My rented room in Glendale was barren and cold; it was in a typical low-cost California cottage made, as Dave Kuhn, our pilot humorist put it, "Of chicken wire and marshmallow." It had a pathetic gas heater, no basement, and no insulation, so the cold was free to creep in and make life miserable.

To escape the lonesome hours I gravitated toward the airport, to hang around the dispatch office. Unlike today's computer-decorated expanses filled with people, desks, and fluorescent lights, the dispatch center consisted of one dispatcher and a clerk who gathered teletype messages, made phone calls, and did gofer chores. Off to one side a meteorologist quietly and methodically went about the business of keeping up with the weather, trying to fathom its capricious acts and peeling off teletype reports that gave the conditions all over the land on an hourly basis.

The center of his forecasting witchcraft was the weather map that he plotted and created. The meteorologist was the dispatcher's right arm; the airline couldn't run without his weather information and forecasts.

I was drawn to the beauty and mystery of the weather map; in the day of the individual meteorologist, the weather map was a piece of art, a map of the United States covered with sweeping lines of isobars and the color of fronts—blue for cold and red for warm. Each station had data entered next to it telling the clouds, wind, temperature, relative humidity, pressure, and other things. There was a romance to visualizing the weather across the land: 10 below zero in Burlington, Vermont, with a brisk northwest wind—people wrapped up, heads low as they struggled in the harsh wind; 75 in Key West—shirtsleeves, rustling palms, and the sea breaking on a beach; 48 and rain in Seattle, chill, dismal, and depressing. I hadn't had much reason to think about these places before; prior to the age of the airplane, only the rich did much traveling, so distant places even within the country didn't mean much to me. Now, I could imagine them as places I'd likely be going sometime along the line.

The meteorologist entered all this data with fine steel pens in different colors for different things—three pens, red, blue, and black, held tightly together with a rubber band to make them like one pen with three points. He was adept at twisting the bundle to bring the color needed into use.

When all the data was entered, each little circle represented a different place, town, city, airport, or perhaps just a reporting point on a lonely mountaintop. It was all there in letters and numbers, along with an arrow coming out of the circle to show what direction the wind was coming from—the feathers, black lines on only one side of the shaft, represented wind velocity, each feather meaning 10 knots velocity. And then the meteorologist became an artist as he drew black lines that connected the points of equal barometric pressure—the isobars. Their sweep showed the flow of air, the north and south isobars in the northeast depicting the flow of Arctic air that had Burlington at 10 below; a westerly flow from the North Pacific, pulling in that wet, raw air that covered Seattle; languid southeasterly winds at Key West.

Then he put in the blue cold fronts and red warm fronts, the boundaries between the air masses—a blue line across southern Virginia showing where the cold air ended and the warmer air of the South began—

although the front would keep moving down, being pushed by cold air to invade deeper south—by tomorrow the Carolinas would shiver.

Completed, he would stand back and look at the map, making an appraisal of how the air was moving and circulating across the country—he seemed to do this before going into the details of specific places and routes the airplanes would be flying. I think the meteorologist received joy and satisfaction from having created a work of art. The sweep of the isobars and the color of the fronts cutting across the map creates an abstract piece of art in concert with nature—is it possible that a force not known or understood creates wind flows that result in design? The patterns, the symmetry or lack of it, differ almost as moods differ; some days the map is graceful and smooth, one flow blending with another to make an easy forecast, while on others the winds change direction abruptly, cold and warm fronts overlap, become confused, so the map looks cantankerous and the forecast is difficult. All this makes one ponder questions of grand design and purpose.

The weather people at Burbank were kind, pleased to see my interest. I was enraptured with the discovery of weather, and that sense of being lonely in Glendale went away. I spent much time with the met (meteorologist) men; they encouraged me to fill in station data, taught me the codes, explained what they were doing as they drew in isobars and fronts, and then spoke about forecasting, almost as an aside, as they considered what was there and what was going to happen. The forecast is scientific, but it is also an art; there were enough times when the actual weather turned out different from the scientific prognostication to make them aware of local effects that can trip science flat on its face. You develop great respect for a good meteorologist; sadly, today they seem to be a dying breed. The computer draws the map and even makes forecasts, so a pilot rarely if ever comes face-to-face with a weatherman, never gets the chance to watch him at work and learn the how and why of weather, which can be an enormous help once you're up in the air facing something you didn't expect. This is one place that the computer and modern communications have done flying a disservice.

Years later I learned the value of local knowledge at Gander, Newfoundland—a tricky place that can close with fog, have its ceilings lower in rain or snow, encounter high winds, all within hours. The forecasts coming from Gander were excellent for years—then they abruptly went to pieces, the forecasts were wrong and our confidence plunged. What had happened? It turned out that the Gander chief forecaster had been transferred to Toronto and a new man brought in—the valuable local knowledge of the old forecaster had been lost, and with it the good forecasts.

The meteorologists loaned me books: one was *Synoptic and Aeronautical Meteorology* by Horace Robert Byers. A part of the preface tells where we were in the state of the art: "students who wish to begin study based on the newer methods of synoptic meteorology, called, in general, the air mass system." In other words, the consideration of fronts and air mass movement was new stuff in 1937, although the Norwegians had been working on it for many years.

This air mass business means, in a simple way, that a hot humid day is caused by the invasion of air that originated over languid tropic water and was heavy with heat and humidity as it flowed around palm trees and frangipani bushes—but atmospheric pressure, strong winds blowing seven miles above the earth, and other factors combined to move it northward. Air masses from the north in winter—cold, dry air from continental Canada that comes south to cross the Midwest—could bring below-zero temperatures with strong winds, while in the summer they bring cool relief.

When warm, humid air from the south crawls northward, and cold air from the north comes south, the two eventually meet, and it's this confrontation that creates our weather—large areas of rain or snow if the warm air crawls up over the cold, or bombastic thunderstorms and tornadoes if the cold air slams into the warm.

I eventually learned that the American Midwest is a unique weather factory because there are no mountains north or south of it, so the warm air comes north unimpeded from the Gulf of Mexico while cold winds whip freely southward from the far north. This special area makes for some of the world's worst weather as the warm and cold air have at each other. After searching the globe for the world's worst thunderstorms on a research project during World War II, I found them in Kansas City's backyard.

These air-mass movements reflect the atmosphere's efforts to equalize the earth's temperatures, to smooth out the differences between the Arctic and the tropics. It's an impossible chore the earth has set up for itself, and the struggle never ends, so weather is always in motion—and man, trying to outguess these great and capricious forces, finds the task difficult, the science still inexact, and forecasts frequently in error simply because that's the way it is. When a pilot learns that he cannot always count on what weather will do, and is prepared to accept and deal with it as a fact of flying life, then that pilot has matured and become wise in ways that create a high standard of safety.

My L.A. period proved to be a lucky one, sparking an interest that was to make for a second career that fitted perfectly with flying. I discovered, quickly, that weather isn't simply what we see on the earth, where we walk and live; there is weather above in the atmosphere—in the troposphere, stratosphere, and higher where winds flow in many wandering paths at a range of velocities, where turbulence tears at the sky, where clouds form that contain ice or thunderstorms with severe turbulence. Often this great area aloft is clear of clouds with only a placid blue sky—the action's invisible, but it's still up there, wind and weather, and your task is to visualize, to create a picture and to wed that to where you have to go with the airplane.

Working with the weathermen made my flights more interesting. I carefully plotted on the log sheet the temperature at each level as we climbed or descended, sketched in the base and tops of clouds, the location of turbulence or ice, and any phenomena that seemed pertinent. I'd then bring the log to the weatherman and we'd talk it over, figure out why things were. Sometimes the forecasts didn't work out and the weather was different than expected, and we'd discuss why—it was a wonderful education that has never ended, even though my time in L.A. soon did, as I got transferred to San Francisco. I had gained a source of endless fascination and mystery, and developed enormous respect for weatherpeople and their craft.

✳

SAN FRANCISCO was a small base, an offshoot from the main line, which ran from Los Angeles to New York. The terminal was modest, and for a time there was only one TWA flight outbound and one inbound a day. The flying time to cover those flights was too much per month for two captains but not enough for three, so two captains were assigned and the dispatcher did the excess flying. There was no such solution for copilots, so they assigned three, which meant we flew less than normal and had a pretty easy time. The flight was a round-trip to Boulder City, Nevada, which we did in one day, and after that we had two days off. Alternatively, we could fly two or three trips in a row and then take four or six days off. Flying trips one day after another is called flying back to back, and we could do as many as seven in a row and still be legal—which meant fourteen days off. The company didn't care how we did it and left the copilot scheduling to us, so we worked it out together and had some nice times off. The company just said to be sure there was a warm body at the airport every morning to take out Flight 26, and we never missed.

Three hostesses, a few mechanics and passenger agents, and a small office in town to sell tickets with a salesman who beat the bushes for commercial accounts—that was the airline's total complement and organization. We all knew one another, and it was a big family that worked and socialized together.

San Francisco was a different place from L.A. Quieter, sedate, aristocratic, and solid compared to Tinsel Town down south. The era of expressways hadn't arrived yet; the north-south road was El Camino Real, lined with eucalyptus trees that formed a canopy overhead and perfumed the air with an exotic fragrance. The towns down the peninsula were separated by open country: San Bruno, Burlingame, San Mateo, Palo Alto—distinct and individual places, not the homogenized mass of today. Almond and apricot orchards scattered across the countryside, and the surrounding hills were round and smooth except for dark patches of live oak trees. The hills were a rich green from the winter rains, but turned gold in summer. The markets were a cornucopia of fresh fruits and vegetables.

There was a fog from the cold sea that draped over the hills west of the airport like a white blanket—it hung there quietly all day and then, toward evening, it awakened and crawled slowly down the hills toward the airport, becoming an ominous creature that could cover the airport and close it for the arrival of our Flight 25 from the east. It was a race between the fog and the flight. If the fog won our airplane stayed in Oakland for the night, and passengers and crew were driven over the long San Mateo Bridge to the San Francisco airport.

Flight 26 was a DC-2 that departed early in the morning to Oakland, Fresno, Las Vegas, and Boulder City, where passengers connected with the flight from Los Angeles to continue east. Flight 26's airplane and crew sat in Boulder City for a few hours and then originated Flight 25 back to San Francisco, making the same stops, if the fog didn't stop it at Oakland.

The station was too small for a meteorologist, so the dispatcher worked alone. He was Andy Andrews, an early airmail pilot who had bailed out over the Allegheny Mountains one foul winter night when his single engine Northrop Alpha was so loaded with ice it wouldn't stay in the air.

Andy was tall and Western-looking, with a lined face and a stiff walk like a cowboy. When he laughed his eyes almost disappeared into the wrinkles carved in his face from long hours squinting and searching the sky.

Each evening Andy would sit in his small office, leaning back in a swivel chair, feet on the desk, watching the fog on the hills to see if it would behave or would sneak down and interrupt Flight 25. I hung out with him frequently watching the fog, too, and listening to him talk about the airline and the other pilots. I tried to drag out of him the story about bailing out in the snowy dark over Pennsylvania, but the kind of details you wanted never seemed to surface.

"It was a hell of a night—couldn't get under the stuff or over it—about Chestnut Ridge I had it wide open and it was still goin' down. I shut everything off, trimmed her nose up, and went over the side." He laughed. "Dean Burford was out there goin' the other way—he bailed out, too." He laughed again. "We found the airplanes, got the mail out, and wound up in the same little post office with our mail."

But I wanted the feeling: how scared was he, what was it like going off in the black void, wind, snow, and clouds, knowing you were thousands of feet over forest and mountains, not knowing where you'd wind up—miles from habitation or near a town? But it didn't come out, and his answer to my question was a simple, "You're goddamn right I was scared!"

Aside from being dispatcher, he was also supervisor of the base and, of course, flew his trips. I flew many with him—another link with the past, as I at least brushed against the era of helmet and goggles, flying suits, heavy boots, and parachute.

Andy didn't let you fly, but he expected you to look after details like setting the power and mixtures. "Guess I'll put the gear down—seem okay?" was his request rather than a crisp command. He also seemed to want some assurance that you agreed with what he was doing; he knew how to fly, but he was a bit rough on controls—I suspect because he'd spent all those hours alone being able to do it his way and not worrying about passengers, since mail sacks don't get sick. He understood our service to people and all that, but he was an airmail pilot and always would be.

You could see this when you flew weather. Most of the airmail flying was down under the clouds so they wouldn't lose sight of the terrain. By the time of the DC-2s they'd learned instrument flying, but in weather these pilots retained a strong interest in the ground and where they were over it. Modern instrument pilots are in the sky; their connection with the earth is time remaining to destination, the degrees from a station, what the ground speed is, drift, and such numerical things. The airmail old-timers watched the ground, recognized where they were from seeing it, knew which way to head for the next piece of known terrain and about how long it would take to get there. Their flying had not been released from the earth; it was the airplane flying over ground instead of through the sky. The old-timers knew each hill, river, mountain, pass, and railroad, and they could navigate by such reference even when visibility was almost zero. While the beam took them where they were going, their interest would heighten with a glimpse of the earth—even a small piece through a meager break in the cloud layers. You could see it on an instrument approach; they'd descend and finally break out of the clouds, perhaps low in poor visibility, but they then set the instrument guidance aside and let the eyeball take over until they were lined up with the runway. Today, properly, we criticize pilots for doing that—stick with instruments to the runway is the rule—but these men were different; few pilots exist in modern times who understand contact flying like they did, and with radio aids hampered by poor reception and scraggly imprecision, their knowledge fit the conditions and saved our necks more than once.

In the end it must have been difficult for them to recognize that this intimate knowledge wasn't going to be needed anymore, that instruments and radios were taking its place—but maybe they never did, and when they retired their concept of flying was probably still bound by that attachment of airplane and earth.

✶

MY INTRODUCTION TO the San Francisco operation wasn't pleasant. I met the chief pilot, actually the Western Region chief pilot, who reminded me of a bulldog; big jaw, tough-looking, no smile. We talked on a chill, rainy day in the terminal.

"Buck," he started, which always ticked me off. My father used to say, "Call me Doctor or Byje"—his nickname, his full name was Abijah Orange Buck—"but don't call me Buck," and I'd picked up the antipathy. So I didn't like this chief pilot from the start.

"We want all copilots to have their 3B rating." This was a CAA rating that qualified you as a big-airplane copilot, and it meant being checked by a government inspector, demonstrating your ability to fly the aircraft. "I notice you haven't had much big-ship time, so we're going to give you some practice. Be out here eight o'clock tomorrow and I'll fly with you."

"Yes, sir."

Not much big-airplane time—hell, I'd only landed one once. But the next morning I was there promptly at 8:00—and I waited until 10:30 and then was told the captain couldn't make it, I should come out three days hence for my practice time.

Three days later he was on time, but there was another man with him; I've forgotten his name, and maybe I never knew it because when he was introduced all I got was the fact that this was the CAA inspector and I was getting my official rating ride—no practice, no nothing!

Check ride! How often those words send flashes of anxiety across a pilot's mind. You live with checks all your life: instrument checks, line checks, FAA rating checks, simulator checks, physical checks—each one with a potential for ending your career, and you take three or four a year all your flying life; screw up a line check and you immediately slide behind the curve and a tough process starts to get back to where you were. You do get another chance, but now you're less than level, you're minus, since you failed before and are therefore suspect—to pass now it's necessary to do better than a normal check. Your attitude is different, nervous, apprehensive, more apt to make a mistake, you're in a hole and have to climb up and out to regain your past status and confidence.

Some pilots seem to take check rides in stride, their wonderful egos let them swashbuckle through, but even they have a nervous undercurrent in their bravado. Give enough checks and you realize all pilots being checked are a little up-tight in there somewhere.

The pilots who really get checkitis are visibly nervous, and that makes their flying unsure and ragged; instead of thinking how best to fly, they think more about the check pilot; how he wants it, are they pleasing him or her, and these distracting thoughts affect flying and techniques, keeping you from flying at your best.

The longer you've been in the business and the more checks you've taken, the less checkitis is a bother; it becomes just another check, with a feeling akin to going to the dentist. But no matter how many you've taken in the past, how free and easy you are, there's still a certain seriousness in your manner as you approach the test.

So here I was developing checkitis before we even got to the airplane. This was a big one, a CAA and company check rolled into one—and I was vulnerable because my probation wasn't finished, which made me as easy to fire as tossing a piece of paper in the wastebasket.

At least I knew the airplane. I'd studied the manual until the gadgets, oil pressure and temperature limits, voltage required, and systems were pat in my mind. When we climbed aboard and I settled in the left seat, it was familiar and that was worth something. The chief pilot got in the right seat and the CAA inspector stood in the aisle between us.

"Start 'er up and we'll go up for some air work," the chief growled—at least it came across as a growl to me.

I was a bit clumsy starting, but I got the engines going and we taxied out and took off. It wasn't bad as I climbed to altitude.

"Steep left turn," was the first order.

This I'd never done in the big airplane. I turned the wheel, banked 45 degrees—the nose dropped and I pulled back to get it up and hold altitude, but it wasn't holding, so I pushed in some top rudder, which never seems to work but the book at that time said it was the way, but the book was wrong, and it only made the airplane skid.

"Watch your altitude! What are you doing with the rudder?"

I forgot all about flying—I was moving the controls trying to get organized, but I was thinking about his shouting: Was this the way he wanted it? Was I pleasing him? In the meantime the steep turn was scalloped, climbing, then descending—not terrible, but not good.

"Try a right turn."

I unbanked the left turn and rolled into a right one. It wasn't great by any means and I was clumsy, upset by the chief pilot yelling critical comments, thinking that if he wasn't there, if I were alone, I could do it well.

The steep turns over, we did stalls, slowed until it didn't want to fly and shook in protest. I pushed the nose down, a little abruptly—I'd never stalled a big airplane before.

"Easy, easy!"

Well, hell, I knew that to unstall you got the nose down, and that's what I was doing, just like in a Monocoupe.

After the ordeal of a few stalls he told me to land. I was sweating, upset, sure I was being judged badly, sure I was failing.

The first landing approach: "You're too high on base leg."

Base leg? I'd never heard the expression before, but guessed what he meant because we were on a line perpendicular to the landing direction and I was high. I knew it and I was working to correct it. I lost the excess altitude, clumped it onto the ground, and got the airplane stopped. Was this it? No.

"Now take off, get over the field at fifteen hundred feet, and do a power-off one-eighty—touch down there," he said, pointing to a spot on the runway.

I taxied to the end of the runway, my hands felt unsteady on the controls, I was wringing wet, my mind wasn't on flying but on the implications of failing, my career over. But then a wonderful transformation took place; I started to think about all the flying I had done, and I realized that I knew I could fly. I was convinced they'd never pass me, but what the hell, it was over and suddenly I didn't care about the chief pilot or the CAA inspector—screw 'em, I was going to fly my way and have some fun and let him shout.

I did the 180 degree turn rather well, the airplane felt natural, I was feeling flying. I made some more landings, one with an engine pulled back. He said that was enough. We taxied in and shut down. I waited for the axe.

The government inspector spoke first.

"It wasn't the greatest ride I ever had, but you're okay—let's go inside and do the paperwork."

It was an exhausting relief, a wrung-out but reborn feeling—I'd come from the depths to the heights. Most important, too, was the fact I'd gotten a handle on checkitis; in the future I might be apprehensive over a check, but I knew I'd fly first and worry second.

The chief pilot never did smile, congratulate me, or say anything except a sort of acknowledgment that I was okay. I never felt comfortable around him after that—I always felt he didn't think much of me as a pilot. If I had only gotten over the checkitis in time to show him some good steep turns—or if I'd actually gotten in a practice session . . . oh well.

But this wasn't the end of my checking—the company decided all copilots should get their SATR, the sacred Schedule Air Transport Rating, the highest license a pilot could hold; with that you were legal to transport mail, people, and goods.

The 3B rating I'd suffered through with the chief pilot was only one phase of it—now came the instrument part, which meant showing a Department of Commerce inspector I could fly blind. I knew I could do the flying by instruments, but I'd never had any radio experience and there were certain hoops you had to jump through to show the inspector you could follow a beam, make an instrument approach, and, in case you got lost, find where you were. This meant practice.

The company wasn't about to have us churn around the sky in a DC-2 learning this, so they provided a biplane—a Stearman—about the size and shape of my Mailwing with one cockpit out in the open and the other covered with a hood. That's where the student lived, in the hot black world under the hood, nothing to see except the instruments grinning from the panel.

The instructor was Roscoe Dunahoo, one of our most senior copilots. A nice guy, but serious—square in today's parlance, and toughened by years of flying with the military. His instruction methods were in the fashion of the times: shout and intimidate.

But this wasn't anything like the DC-2 check. First of all, I knew how to fly instruments; the 1-2-3 system I'd taught myself was up to date. The radio was something else and although Roscoe would shout at my wanderings, it didn't get to me—sometimes it was funny. Besides, Roscoe was a copilot himself, a nice person, actually harmless, so it was a lot different flying with him than with the chief pilot.

Radio range stations possessed an ambiguity that was known to cause trouble, and a big part of the sessions with Roscoe was learning how to cope with this—it was called radio range orientation. The four on-course signals formed a cross with the station at the center, and outside the legs of the cross are pure As or Ns—two sectors of A and two of N. Suppose we're lost because static has obliterated all radio reception for a long time, the static stops and our eager ears grasp the first signal—it's an N. But which N? Are you approaching the station or past it? Ah, there's the problem. There are orientation procedures to solve the problem, and they were important to know, although I only needed one once, for real, in my entire time flying radio ranges.

So I practiced these, with Roscoe setting the airplane in a position to make all the bad, doubtful things come into play and then giving me hell if I didn't grasp it right away. It was hot and bothersome under that hood. We also did low approaches, simulating a letdown to the minimum altitude under the clouds during bad weather. At minimum Roscoe would say, "Okay, pull up and go back out for another one," meaning fly away from the station on a leg of the beam for ten miles, make a turn, and come back for another approach.

We churned up the California sky for seven and a half hours like that, an hour's session at a time. Finally Roscoe said I was ready for the test and a CAA inspector came to the field, looked at my paperwork and climbed in the airplane and away we went. He was a slim, gray-haired man who said little and didn't display any change in expression for any detectable reason. For an hour and a half we did air work and then a couple of low approaches. That was it; he signed me off and now I held an SATR—today it's called an ATP, air transport pilot.

I was now at the zenith of licenses, but still had a lot to learn. The company showed its appreciation by raising my pay $15 a month—so now I was in the big money of $195 per month total. They took the bloom off their munificence, however, by charging me $15 per hour for the time in the Stearman—a little over nine hours including the flight test. The $15 was taken from my pay a month at a time, so it was nine months before that raise actually reached my pocket.

With the license ordeal behind me, flying became a joy. My education as an airline pilot reached the graduate level, and I was getting a firm foundation under the tutelage of the great pioneer pilots. I was fortunate enough to fly with Alexis Klotz, Lex; aristocratic, opinionated, genteel, thoughtful—a tall, slender man—a superb airman from open cockpit days with Western Air Express; and with Bill Dowling, quiet, sweet, and gentle with a deep knowledge of what made it all work. His hobby was pistol shooting and he won impressive championships—he was also an ace at sleeping on a flight if the weather and sky were easy. You'd no sooner get the gear up than Bill was sound asleep, but well awake when he should be.

Flight 26 started early in the day, with the San Francisco sky generally cloudy, the air wet and chill. The first leg was to Oakland, just an up and almost immediately down to land; Oakland is only twelve miles across the Bay from San Francisco, and we'd sneak over under the low cloud deck. It seemed absurd to pump that landing gear up for a couple of minutes of flight and then pump it down again, but we did it because the airplane flew badly in case of an engine failure with the gear sticking down in the airstream. We discussed it a number of times, but the smart thing was to get it up, even for those few minutes. Discussion may not be the right description, it was more like the copilot trying to con the captain into leaving the gear down to avoid the manual labor of raising it.

Out of Oakland we climbed through the clouds, which were never very thick, and broke out on top around 2,000 feet into bright and cheerful sunshine with the blue sky above. As soon as we got away from the Bay Area the clouds below would dissipate and we'd see the rolling hills that in spring were covered with blue lupins and orange poppies. We'd slip down and fly low enough that the beauty was clear to see. The early morning air was calm because the sun hadn't had time to heat it and create turbulence. We could wander up and down following the hills' contours, change course to see something or cut a corner and save time. Traffic wasn't a problem and radar wasn't in use—they were just inventing it.

It was less than an hour to Fresno, an agricultural town set in the San Joaquin Valley rich with grapevines and all manner of bounty.

The terminal was a small building behind an iron wire fence. The fence was almost removed by one of our flights when the captain cut both engines right at landing to show how he could roll the DC-2 all the way to the gate and swing in and park perfectly with both props stopped, the airplane quiet and coasting gently. He did a beautiful job, but the brake cylinder was weak and he had to pump the brakes to get stopping action—

something he only realized as he approached the terminal, turning in toward the wire fence with brakes that didn't work. His pumping action became fast and frantic, and the airplane had to be ground-looped to miss the fence, which it did successfully. It came to rest a short distance away and cockeyed, so, in embarrassment, the pilot had to start the engines and repark the airplane. That was the end of that pilot's show-off tactics.

The San Francisco pilots were generous in giving takeoffs and landings, and the copilot flew at least two of the eight legs on the trip—often more. We also flew from the left seat. Today copilots never climb into the left seat, that's the captain's place and where he remains by order, so a copilot's first experience with left-side flying is when he's checked out to captain—he or she, because there are lots of shes flying now.

Lex and Bill taught me as I flew, showing me ways of doing it better—"Never use full flaps, they don't help that much and they make the tail more difficult to get down—use three-quarters." Much of the learning was in observing their methods; learning to get propeller alcohol onto the props to keep ice off well before it developed not only taught you something about propeller icing, but taught you to anticipate, to think ahead so trouble is seldom a surprise and you can prevent it. Pumping the gear up on that short twelve-mile flight to Oakland taught you something, too: that there is nothing trivial in this business, and that a twelve-mile flight has to be flown as carefully and thoughtfully as a 1,000-mile one.

From Fresno the flight went to Las Vegas. The distance direct was 257 miles, but we didn't go direct because of the Sierra Nevada mountains with their high, rough country—Mt. Whitney, the highest in the Lower 48 at 14,495 feet, was within five miles of the direct course. So we went down the Valley to Delano and then cut east through Walker Pass—5,250 feet—to Inyokern and Vegas. This was 315 miles—longer by fifty-eight miles or about twenty minutes. Of course, on very nice days, and perhaps if we were running a bit late, we'd cut the corner and go direct even though it wasn't legal.

Coming through Walker Pass, the course departed the fertile land of California and flew out over desert. Ahead left were the Panamint Mountains with Telescope Peak at 11,049 feet, and just beyond it the ground dropped into Death Valley, 282 feet below sea level. The visibility was generally unlimited and you could pick out peaks and cuts in the mountain ranges and look down on the endless arid, inhospitable country where little grew except cactus, sage, and mean critters like scorpions and rattlesnakes.

Frequently, landing at Las Vegas on a hot day, we'd see dust devils whirl across the airport—miniature tornadoes picking up and swirling sand in a gossamer, almost invisible fashion. "Don't fly near one of those," the wise old heads told you, "they're rougher than hell—you might even lose control." Admonition noted.

Las Vegas was a pleasant, quiet place, with a few resort spots, and slot machines in most places—that seemed to be the major gambling method except for a few casinos. The airport runways were sand and dirt, and the terminal was one large room in a building constructed in Old West style. There was a counter for ticket purchase, and some slot machines on tables; we'd always "sacrifice" a dime or two, but mostly shunned the action because we quickly learned that you can't win. There weren't all the lights or all the people crowding in yet; it had more the feel of a town in the Old West.

After a short ground stop, then the last leg to Boulder City, twenty-four miles away, to an airport built on a slope that was interesting to land on especially if the wind was cross and nasty. At Boulder we lay over for three hours—had lunch in town, sometimes swam in Lake Mead. Boulder Dam had been finished in 1935, but Lake Mead was only about half full early in 1938 and we watched its progress each trip, seeing water crawl up the bottom of the brown hills, finally surrounding them, making islands that eventually disappeared below the water's surface. In 1947 the name Boulder Dam was changed to Hoover Dam.

In the afternoon we originated Flight 25 and retraced our hops back to San Francisco, if we could get there before the fog settled in. Most times we made it. The days could be hot, but the descent into the Bay Area was a sudden return to cool weather. Where the cloud tops had been in the morning—2,000 feet or so—we'd hit a sharp bump, just one, and the temperature would drop 20 degrees—the Bay's inversion. The coolness came into the airplane and quickly changed the feeling from languid heat to exhilarating cool.

The airplanes were not air-conditioned, and operating in hot desert areas called for many tricks to try to get cool and stay cool. The air came in through that nose valve we could open or close. It was wide open on takeoff and during climb. The temperature on the ground would approach

95°F, but the air at 7,000 or 8,000 feet would be roughly 67°F. The airplane, sitting on the ground in the hot sun, would soak up heat like a closed car in a sun-drenched parking lot and become unbearably hot. In the cockpit, sweat covered our faces, soaked our shirts, and made life miserable. As we climbed, nose valve wide open, the air temperature decreased and the cabin began to cool down some; after half an hour at cruising altitude the outside 67 replaced the torrid cabin air, and by the time we reached our next stop the airplane was cool inside, people's sweat had dried off and most likely they were asleep in the pleasant atmosphere.

But then we had to descend into the furnace heat again. We'd hold off descent until the last minute; the company wanted us to descend at 300 feet per minute, which meant starting down perhaps twenty-five or more minutes from destination. But as you descended, the air was warmer by almost 4 degrees for each 1,000 feet, heating up that cabin again.

So the trick was to stay aloft as long as possible. We tossed the 300-feet-per-minute rate out the window and went for 500 feet or more, so the descent was only fifteen minutes rather than twenty-five. Of course this was a little hard on passengers' ears, especially if they had a cold, but most never complained, and we decided without consultation what was best for them. We closed the nose valve tight to prevent any hot air from coming in and replacing the cool air as we descended. With such tricks, if the station stop was quick, we could get out, off, and up again before the cabin became a furnace itself. The air might get a little stale, so nonsmoking pilots would leave the "No Smoking" sign on until the outside air was cool enough to open the nose valve again. There was a lot to flying aside from flying.

Another pair of flights was added, Flight 8 eastbound and Flight 7 westbound. This was a sleeper DC-3 from San Francisco to Winslow, Arizona, and then express to Newark, with few stops—we flew the San Francisco–Winslow portion. This was in considerable contrast to our local Flights 25 and 26, a luxurious DC-3 cruising uninterrupted to Winslow, a hop of about 650 miles that took a little over four hours.

This new route enlarged the base and more captains came in, but only a few. They were of the same mold, youngish, pleasant, willing to give you flying time. The personalities of the new pilots covered a wide range: Ted Hereford was one of them: young, single, athletic, boisterous, and a great individualist—contrary to company orders he never wore his uniform hat—he was trying to hold on to his golden locks, which showed signs of thinning, and he thought hats made one go bald. He disdained signing a clearance and rarely did it, but had the copilot go to the office, sign it, and bring it out to the airplane. On layovers you were his playmate: tennis, swimming, wrestling, anything strenuously athletic. The swimming hole was a considerable distance from Winslow—this was long before the era of hotel swimming pools—so for transportation Ted went to Sailor Davis, the radio operator, and borrowed his motorcycle, and I climbed on behind for a snappy ride to the swimming hole, a wide place in a rare river of the West that didn't go dry. Learning of a girls' normal [teachers'] school in Flagstaff, Ted decided we ought to go there and have a look. How to get there? Easy, because the railroad grade was uphill from Winslow toward Flagstaff and the freights pulled long and slow—we hopped one and rode it to Flagstaff!

He was a superb pilot who flew the airmail as a minor; the Post Office Department discovered Ted's age and realized the rules didn't allow minors to haul the mail, and a brouhaha developed over the issue, but Ted went on flying and finally was exempted from the rule. His competitive nature carried to the airplane, and he'd bet with you on almost every landing whether you or he made it. The bet was on smoothness, on touchdown spot with power off from heights 2,000 feet or so over the airport, on checkpoint accuracy, what the cloud tops would be, or the bases. The motive wasn't gambling because the bets were for a nickel or maybe a beer and were rarely paid off, but the bets tested skill and they sharpened you, especially because of their ease and joviality.

Lawrence Chiappino was from an old California Italian family: tall, dark, neat, and precise, a gentleman with a warm smile. An excellent pilot who demanded perfection and sticking to the rules. On my first trip with Chip he showed me what his precision meant. First checkpoint we flew over Fresno, he signaled passage by wiggling his thumb back and forth as he looked down at the station. The clock said three minutes past the hour and I wrote :03 in the log.

"That is not correct," Chip said, looking down at me with his strong Italian eyes.

I checked my clock again, looked over at his, and both read the same. "Sure it was zero-three—look, our clocks are the same."

"No," he said. "It was zero-three and twenty seconds."

Gad! He wanted minutes split—I'd never had anyone ask for that.

Later I was filling out the maintenance log—aside from the date and times off and on, there were various mechanical readings to record. I put down 14 volts after checking the voltmeter. Chip corrected me.

"Look closely at the marks on the instrument face, the divisions, the 14 is a little further over, it's actually 14.2—put that down." No one else did that, either.

At first his persnicketiness annoyed me, but gradually as I flew more with Chip it became a game, and fun. I realized, too, that his method prevented sloppiness from ever creeping into his flying. It created a quicker awareness of things being right or starting to go wrong; the tenths of minutes made estimates and knowledge of winds a little bit better; the exact reading of the voltmeter created a base to work from with any instrument so you caught the first sign of irregularity developing. Chip's way worked into my flying character, a way that would pay dividends many times over.

There was Dan Medler; we called him Senator because he always wanted to talk, argue preferably, about events, politics, and union matters. He was an intellectual and it almost surprised you to realize this philosophical aesthete, who didn't look or act like an airline pilot, was a very good one who could tough out the worst weather. His manner was gentle and quiet; I always felt good when I saw on the schedule that my trip would be with Dan.

Johnny Graves, auburn hair, polite, strong character, medium size, who somehow gave the impression he looked like an airline pilot should look. His judgment and method gave you confidence, made you feel you were with a good solid pilot. His was another name you were always happy to see on the schedule.

These were the men I flew with in the golden days of San Francisco. A wonderful experience of men with different character, all good to fly with, teaching, showing, and giving much of that valuable left-seat time. The hostesses were part of the family, too; Ida, Mac, Stevie, and others. Mac and Stevie eventually married pilots; Ida went on flying, and long years later I attended her retirement party—age sixty and still a great gal.

San Francisco and the West weren't as busy as Chicago and New York, so it wasn't as necessary to fly the straight and narrow. The smallness of the base created a sense of informality and a relaxed feeling. Although we had rules and the "book" to fly by, neither was intimidating—the rules most obeyed were the ones of common sense and good solid flying. Many times in the future I yearned for that San Francisco aura, especially as the industry grew and bureaucracy took over—only to restrict, rarely to improve.

CHAPTER 8

Copilot Days and Nights

ER NAME WAS JEAN PEARSALL, a beautiful blond young lady from my hometown of Westfield, New Jersey. Her family was a reserved, dignified group with roots going back to the Revolution, in contrast to my Swiss-French-German background only one and two generations removed from the Old Country—but the Pearsalls never looked askance at me because of it.

The company gave me two weeks off to go back east and fetch my bride—a copilot, Hervey M. Salisbury, was flown in from Kansas City to take my place for the period.

A day after the wedding we departed for San Francisco. Jean had never had anything to do with airplanes until we met; I took her for rides in small airplanes, once to the end of Long Island for a fashion show she was taking part in. She bravely accepted the presence of airplanes in her life, though turbulent air brought on queasiness that she fought—not always successfully.

The flight west was smooth, and I regaled her with tales of wonderful California and the fine people I was associated with. She met the first of them at Boulder City when we changed from the stolid main line to the San Francisco offshoot, Flight 25, and our more relaxed way of doing things. The captain was Lex Klotz, and he turned on his most genteel and gracious manner to welcome Jean. On the leg from Vegas to Fresno, Lex went all out: flying low over the desert country and then down into Death Valley for a view of the lowest place in the U.S.A. The airplane bounced and heaved, tail swinging. Jean's color faded toward white. As we left Death Valley, Lex put the DC-2 in low pitch, poured on the power, and climbed to go over the top of Mt. Whitney—all this within eighty miles, from the hot, dry, sandy desert to the beautiful Sierras of pines and snow in minutes. The rough air and the turns to provide better views were too much—her smooth composure degraded to active, let-the-world-end airsickness and intense concentration on the quart ice cream carton carried for such action. It was a tough trip for her into Fresno.

But the day was slipping toward evening and the air was smoothing out. The hop from Fresno to San Francisco droned peacefully in mild, calm air. Jean gathered herself, resumed her normal color and beauty, and graciously thanked Lex for his special "treat."

And so we were home in our small apartment in Burlingame, California, on the last day of February. But March was ill-fated.

On March 2, the field telephoned early in the morning—last night's Flight 8 was missing; I was to come to the airport immediately and stand by for a possible search flight.

"Who was flying?" It's always the first question.

"Graves, Wallace, hostess Wilson—Salisbury was dead-heading to Kansas City."

The news hit me like a blow to the solar plexus: the idea of people you know, a flight you fly, crashing in a region of mountains wrapped in bad weather leaves an empty confused feeling cloaked in the mystery of death—it's difficult to understand and sort out. Salisbury's presence on the flight magnified those feelings and added an element of guilt, because he was the copilot filling in for me during my time off; now, with me back in California, he was returning on Flight 8 to his regular base at Kansas City. If I hadn't requested leave he'd never have been on the missing airplane—it seemed my fault, and the thought ground into me.

Of course the airplane had not been found and was only listed as missing, but you knew the unspoken fact that an airplane that doesn't show up after a night of struggling with bad weather isn't likely to be found in a remote field with all aboard safe.

An air and ground search continued intensively for two weeks, during which time a heavy snow covered the area where the flight had last been heard from, and undoubtedly had covered the wreckage as well. TWA posted a $1,000 reward for finding the aircraft and officially reduced the search effort. We crews didn't stop looking, however, and on our own we frequently cut the Las Vegas route corner if the weather was clear, and spent the twenty minutes we'd gained flying over the Sierras and looking for signs of the aircraft. Mostly we saw trees, rocks, and snow. Lord knows what the passengers thought we were doing; to pacify them we called it a scenic tour. Finally we gave up these "diversions" because the snow had covered everything and it was obvious the wreckage lay buried out of sight beneath it.

The accident occurred on March 1, but we didn't know exactly where it had crashed until June 12, when H. O. Collier III found the airplane as he searched the area on the ground. When news came that the wreckage had been found, TWA immediately sent Lex and me to fly over the site to verify it. We flew low over the wild mountain country and spotted the airplane on a piece of open ground where the snow had begun its spring melt—an area we had flown over many times during our scheduled-flight searching.

The tail, half twisted over on its side, was sticking up the most. The other wreckage, a mess of debris, was strewn across the sloping terrain. A bright splash of red caught and focused my eye; it seemed to be someone's garment, and it was in bright contrast to the green trees, white snow, and gray-black of the aircraft's pieces. We circled a few times and made a low pass—all was still and quiet, and a melancholy seemed to come up from the earth; nothing could be done, nothing renewed, no chance to move time and events back. We flew to Fresno in silence.

Ground parties went to the wreckage on horseback at considerable hardship, battling rushing streams filled by the melting snow and water, ignoring the sore rear ends of normally deskbound company people and government investigators whose job descriptions didn't usually include riding horses up and down mountains. For some reason I was asked to stay in Fresno and help where needed.

I did little until the pieces of baggage and personal effects came into town. The baggage was laid out on sample tables in a hotel room: broken open, damaged by water and the elements as well as the crash, sobering to look at—a link between the dead victims and the lives they'd led. I helped sort it out and set it up properly for relatives who would come claim it. Personal things—clothes damaged by wet and hard-creased from three months of compression in one spot, toilet articles so personal I felt as though I were intruding just to handle them. Among the toothbrush, razor, and shaving cream tube of one broken-open toilet kit were condoms—would they upset the person who picked up the kit? Perhaps I could do a favor to the deceased; I removed and discarded them.

What caused the accident? Visualize the cockpit, dark, snow falling, ice quickly forming on the wings and zinging off the propeller blades to whack against the fuselage, static making radio beam signals irrational and blurry. Then, quickly, comes a positive, overwhelming feeling that the situation is getting unsafe, too much to cope with—a feeling that brings on a quick and positive decision: turn back, get out, and return to where it had been safe and manageable. Once turned around, the situation was different and a number of questions and new decisions confronted Graves: where to go—where did the company want the airplane? To San Francisco, or land in Fresno? Get some more weather information and perhaps give it another try? Air traffic control had requested that the flight stay on the right side of the beam—the beam that was coming in poorly in snow static—and that was surely an added heckling factor.

Unknown to Graves and crew, the 28-mile-per-hour wind had now become 50 to 60 mph and the storm had intensified and moved quickly toward the coast.

The investigators appointed by the Department of Commerce spoke to people on the ground who heard an aircraft and, in one case, saw it circle and then climb away rapidly. In all probability Graves was descending to try and see the ground, learn his position, and get out of the clouds, ice, and static to proceed toward Fresno. He heard the beam's N signal and thought he was approaching the south leg when actually it was the northeast leg—the classic ambiguity and disorientation of a radio range. Today it wouldn't happen, as the static-free omni navigation aid would give him his exact bearing and distance from the station, Fresno in this case.

In the days of radio ranges and their beams you listened for the signals, but when the signal was confused by static you simply flew a compass course based on the wind forecast, holding tight to it like a sailing ship captain, until the beam came back in hearing. Graves probably was doing this, holding a course based on the forecast winds of moderate velocity; the increased wind of the deepening storm, however, made his actual path over the ground different from the planned one.

California is generally visualized as a sun-kissed land of fair weather, but there are times when it can become tempestuous with heavy rains and high winds. Slam such weather against the hodgepodge topography of California's mountains and all hell can break loose. The storms coming from the Pacific, where reports were scarce in 1938, can deepen, speed up, arrive before the time anticipated with strong winds and rain that is snow and ice up where we flew. Flight 8 was victim of such events.

These things you tuck away to remember, to learn from, but not to wear outside. The matter of Salisbury was difficult to shake—I felt a certain responsibility, but gradually reason mollified my feelings. I will always be saddened by his untimely death, and the thought of the accident still makes me uneasy, but that's the way the dice come up.

Accidents in the early days were not any more on a pilot's mind than they are now. There were more of them, but really not enough to be a constant thought. When one did occur, everyone was interested in what had happened, but most pilots felt it couldn't happen to them. This has always been a protective device: "I'd never do that dumb thing" or "It wouldn't happen to me."

The passenger count was lower than today; twenty-one for a DC-3 and fourteen for a DC-2, and generally the loads weren't full. Some accidents were blamed on pilot error, but not as much as today; more were caused by engine failure or some mechanical problem. Today's engines almost never fail and they rarely develop mechanical problems, so there's more room to call "pilot error" the culprit.

But I don't think we worried about being in an accident any more than now. It would always happen to the other person.

*

THE ACCIDENT RECEDED in our minds and we ceased living with it day to day—it was there somewhere, but life moved along.

I spent a great summer flying with fine people, feeling less like an apprentice and more like a knowledgeable pilot.

Jean and I enjoyed the golden land: excursions to Muir Woods and the redwood forests, days spent at Searsville Lake behind Stanford University, picnics with fellow workers, visits to Fisherman's Wharf in San Francisco, which was still mostly a real fisherman's wharf and not yet spoiled by the tawdry chase for tourist dollars.

One evening, as we drove across the new Golden Gate Bridge coming home from Muir Woods, a Pan American Clipper flying boat droned overhead on a westerly heading across the bridge—steady, majestic, flying in the lingering twilight that trailed behind the setting sun. It was bound for Hawaii and the far islands of the Pacific—a deeply thrilling sight, and one that sent a twinge of regret through me because I yearned to be doing that kind of flying, but I'd wedded myself to an airline that would have me flying coast to coast for a lifetime. How little I knew.

The summer weather was generally excellent, a few bouts with fog in the Bay Area, but not much else. When thunderstorms came they were widely scattered and visible from many miles away in the clear Western air, which made them easy to anticipate and fly around. Low ceilings were almost nonexistent except for an occasional flight into Los Angeles that required getting under the low stratus that slips over the Los Angeles basin from late afternoon to early morning.

It was evident that the airline was growing and my chances of moving up to captain soon were good. I realized I should be getting flying experience in the East, where the weather made for tougher flying that required many judgment calls. Without that seasoning, the difficult and important process of checking out to captain would be even more demanding. Aside from all that, we were missing our family and friends.

There weren't any openings in Newark, but I found a California-born copilot there who yearned for the West, so with company approval Art Nelson and I swapped. The approval stipulated that no trips were to be missed, so Art flew a flight into Kansas City, as did I, then he picked up my San Francisco return and I took his Newark return—it went off as smoothly as an exchange of spies, and we were each where we wanted to be. Our wives came on passes, and our meager household goods were shipped COMAT, company material. This was allowed, but on a space-available basis only, meaning it was put on an airplane if there was room; the boxes with our belongings dribbled in for a month.

That was toward fall, and with fall comes the chance of a hurricane. On September 21, 1938, one roared across Connecticut, Massachusetts, and through Vermont to enter history books as the worst single meteorological event ever in that region. With roads and railroads blocked, it paralyzed the Northeast and stopped all travel.

Airlines were called on to supply the missing transportation. The sudden cutoff of normal land routes revealed the tremendous amount of traffic between Boston and New York. The New York–Boston route was American's, but no one airline could handle the demand during the hurricane emergency, so the rules were cast aside and all airlines pitched in.

TWA's little round terminal at Newark was jammed with people. There wasn't any ticketing; the passengers just plunked down their money and went outside to stand by the iron fence. When he was ready to load the airplane, an agent opened the gate and people pushed through toward the DC-3. The agent counted heads, and at twenty-one—the DC-3's full load—the gate was closed in number twenty-two's face, to wait for the next airplane. Eastern, United, and American were doing the same sort of thing. It was barely an hour's flight, the weather good after the hurricane had passed, and we flew load after load.

Today flying a different route is routine, but back then, Newark-Boston seemed foreign territory. Charlie Kratovil and I were set up for a trip. "I—have—never—been—to—Boston. Where's—the—airport? How—about—maps—and—all—that?" Kratovil bellowed.

"Just follow the guy in front of you," the dispatcher half seriously replied.

In a couple of days the crush was over, but the Newark-Boston passenger business had increased, and from then on it never fell to pre-hurricane levels. The people who used to travel back and forth between the two cities by train, bus, or car had seen what flying was like, and the time and effort it saved. I've often thought that the hurricane of September 1938 was the real beginning of mass air transportation.

Fall worked its way toward winter, and the gentle weather gradually got more serious. Low pressure areas spun their way up the East Coast bringing rain, fog, and the first snow. Our flying changed from quiet days in summer skies to flying blind with all its problems of ice, turbulence, and low ceilings.

There were a lot of early morning flights, when you'd slip into an airport near dawn as the population was just stirring—but you'd been up all night and were tired and sandy-eyed. You often had to deal with fog, ground fog, which either meant you'd go somewhere else or, if the fog was thin, try to land through it, which was a tricky thing to do. From aloft, looking down through fifty feet of fog, the runway is visible and outlined by lights. But as you descend at a shallow angle approaching the airport, you encounter the top of the fog, but then you're looking through it horizontally, which makes the fog not simply fifty feet thick but more like a blanket thrown over your head so you can't see anything but whiteness. Sometimes, if the fog was very thin, we'd touch the ground at about this time, and quickly get her stopped before we went off the runway; but if the fog was thicker and you had a brain in your head, you'd pour on the coal and get up out of there, because feeling your way down through fog for the ground was and is a dumb maneuver. Norm tried it at Dayton and the airplane stalled and fell off to one side, which broke the wingtip and the stabilizer. There was no harm to anyone except to Norm's pride.

Fall grew colder with shorter days and longer nights, the leaves of red, gold, and brown gradually fell from the trees to leave sculptures of dark bare branches, the fields brown except for coverings of white frost in the early hours after dawn and you realized it was winter. Now the rain changed to snow and the clouds held super-cooled water that, when the wing flew into it, changed into ice that built into a white ridge on the wing's leading edge and propeller blades. It was a fight to change altitude and get out of the ice layer—or, if you were on approach, to descend quickly to get through the ice before too much collected on the airplane. If you were on departure, you had to climb as fast as she'd climb to get on top of the clouds, up out of the ice—provided the tops weren't too high.

There were tricks for all this weather that I learned as I flew with a group of captains who were younger than the West Coast crew. I was learning to think logically and make judgment calls about when it was okay to press on, or best to retreat; when to climb and try to get on top, or to stay down low. Judgment said when to have extra fuel and a certain alternate in mind beyond the one the dispatcher was using, simply because you felt squeamish about the alternate's weather.

With each captain there would be some special trip or incident to remember and forever after associate with that particular captain.

With Eddy Boqua, it was the nonstop from Chicago in a DC-2 when our fuel reserves were low—because nonstop from Chicago to Newark in a DC-2 was always tight for fuel. The coast was clobbered with rain, but the ceiling was expected to stay well above limits; our alternate was Philadelphia, just within legal fuel range. But as we approached Newark, Philadelphia folded to zero-zero (no ceiling, no visibility) in fog, and Newark was 300 feet with half a mile visibility. By the time all that happened we didn't have enough fuel to get back to the good weather at Pittsburgh, so it became a simple proposition: we had to get to Newark.

Eddy flew it well, stayed tight to the beam and clipped through the cone over the Newark swamps. The final crossing was 800 feet, and when we'd crossed he pulled back the throttles and shoved the nose down, staying tight on instruments, but having clearly instructed me to stare into the wet darkness and sound off when the lights showed up.

This I did with very serious intent, but I could not resist a quick scan back to the altimeter for a glance to see how low we were getting. At 300 feet, there was nothing, Eddy continued the descent knowing there was nothing between the range station and the airport that stuck up any higher than swamp grass—the trick was not to be too low too far along, because you might go past the airport where there were things to hit. At 200 feet I saw something and called out, "I think the lights are coming in." He delicately and carefully eased down a little more. We were slightly below 200 feet when the red neon lights came solidly in view, showing up in the black void—just the row of red lights in a sphere of nothing.

"I've got the lights!"

Eddy looked up, away from the instruments, and flew right over the lights, descending with care, knowing that beyond them would be the airport, which was ill-lighted and dark. He held a steady descent, and past the lights he let the wheels touch and we were home safe. A big feeling of relief and pointless chatter as we taxied in, but we both knew we had been testing limits, had been in a tight bind, and we wouldn't want one any tighter.

It was an adventure, not particularly dramatic, but threatening in the slow way that peril can keep you sweating for long periods—the condition that created that most expressive of expressions, "sweating it out." I remember that night well, and it comes back to me vividly and fresh even now.

Looking through my logbook for that period I notice the entry "L.S." scattered throughout. It signified when I got left-seat flying time. The entries showed how far I was progressing, because I was getting left-seat time from the conservative old-maid types who rarely gave flying time to copilots.

A simple occurrence during that period brought on some serious cogitation. We had just taken off from Newark on Flight 17 for Chicago and were crossing the first checkpoint, New Brunswick. As we crossed, in fine weather, Flight 16 went by us on the left in the opposite direction—he'd be on the ground at Newark within fifteen minutes, the end of his day's work.

It struck me that tomorrow I'd be flying that Flight 16—the return of this trip. So we'd go to Chicago and then turn around to come back to Newark, and approaching Newark we'd probably go by that day's Flight 17 outbound on the same sequence. Wasn't this a useless repetition? Nothing accomplished in the sense of creating something one could feel, touch, or offer—just herding an airplane to Chicago and another one back; same route, same kind of airplane. Would the years ahead be years of back-and-forth boredom? It was a frightening thought, the possibility of a life without explicit goals.

I tried to sort it out, to rationalize it. Gradually, not that day but many days and months further along, I came to an understanding: the task wasn't repetitious back and forth with nothing more, because each flight was an entity to itself. All flights were not the same; the weather was different, the winds, conditions, judgment required. Many trips might appear the same, but dig into the details and there was a difference: the passengers were different although you didn't get to know them well; the hostess was different and that was interesting; then there was the challenge to be safe, comfortable, and on schedule. There was a challenge to do it better; to practice skills, make each flight as perfect as possible. On the drive home from the airport I began a practice of mentally reflying the flight I'd just finished, picking out things that could have been done better, places where judgment was questionable, the technique sloppy or obtuse—all things to note and to do better next time. This practice has stayed with me even to this day.

I also realized there was the opportunity to experiment, to learn, and always the mystery of weather. Careful notes on weather conditions, temperatures, winds, movement of highs and lows against forecasts and why they did or didn't work, little signs to tell if an airport would stay clear or go bad; study of charts versus an airplane's actual performance to see if the charts were accurate. Different methods of cruising power that saved fuel but still got us there on time. Learn each airport, its terrain, runways, nearby obstructions, the winds off certain runways and how they affected the landing, and how to be cautious under certain conditions. These were some of the things that made each flight unique, and more developed as time went by, as one point investigated suggested another, and that one yet another. The art of flying is constantly changing, new things being discovered and developed, and part of its enchantment is in these discoveries, recognizing them, passing them on to become part of the operation.

So I became aware that hauling passengers and goods for commerce or pleasure was a service of useful and honest mien that contained, in addition, the exciting challenges to do everything better and keep alert to the quest for discovery. Through all the years these elements made each flight an experience I looked forward to with pleasure.

The seasoning and the left-side flying made the airplanes familiar, and soon I was at home with the DC-2 and 3 just as I'd been with the Monocoupe and Pitcairn. There were adventures and close ones, but despite the tight wire we often flew there were few accidents, but as if to prove it was serious stuff they did happen, perhaps far enough apart to find you relaxed, only to be jerked up out of comfortable complacency by the occurrence—like a TWA crash at St. Louis, just before Christmas, when the pilot was doing a circle to land under a very low ceiling and crashed, killing everyone aboard.

My winter was interrupted by chance on a Kansas City layover. I was walking down the hall from the front door toward Dispatch. This hall took me past a row of glass-fronted offices that contained such lofty personages as Chief Pilot Harlan Hull. I always took a quick glance to see who was in, and as I looked into Hull's office, he looked up and saw me.

"Buck, come on in."

Greetings over, he said he'd like me to come to Kansas City and work with the Link trainer the company had gotten, and later teach a class of new copilots. It was a flattering offer, but I wasn't enthusiastic about moving to Kansas City. The decision, however, was easy, because it was either that or be furloughed for a couple of months during the slack winter schedules.

I've often wondered why I was chosen to do this work, and I decided it wasn't because of any special skill or ability, but probably because Hull was thinking about who to get for this job, and looking up to ponder the question, he saw me walking down the hall—a warm body who'd been around enough to know something. Luck and being in the right place at the right time play a big part in our fortunes.

✳

THE LINK TRAINER was the forerunner of today's simulators: a small airplane likeness made of wood and mounted on a pedestal; the fuselage was painted blue while little stubby wings, rudder, and elevator, put on for effect, were yellow. The pilot mounted a hanging step to get in, and the wood structure creaked and wobbled unsteadily as you did. The cockpit was just large enough for a single person. The controls were like an airplane, with rudder pedals and a control wheel.

The pilots came in for sessions, some very skeptical and critical: "Hell, it doesn't fly like an airplane!" We knew that, and we explained that the trainer was for teaching improved ways to navigate on instruments and to handle the radio range, not to learn to fly—heck, they knew how to fly. We didn't mention that we were trying to institute procedures, too, to get everyone flying airplanes on the line the same way.

Before this, each pilot flew his own way; some took off and held the airplane close to the ground to build up speed before climbing, while others climbed right out at maximum angle; some landed from a high approach, power off, while others dragged in low with much power on. There was a best way to do these things, and that's what conformity and procedure would assure, once we'd worked out what was best.

The commands for the copilot differed from pilot to pilot; the command to retract the landing gear after takeoff, "Up gear!," was one, while a flick of the thumb with no words was another, and "Get 'em up" was a third way. Putting the landing gear down was equally variable. "Down gear!" was the most direct, while some might say as we approached the airport, "Well, let's have the rollers," meaning the wheels to land on.

The airline was trying to get everyone to do things the same; one standard command for all pilots—"Gear down"; "Gear up"—carefully thought out so the wording would be the least ambiguous, easiest to say and understand. With such standardization, crews could be changed and a copilot starting a trip with a captain he'd never seen before would know what commands and signals to expect. Such procedures created a safer environment, but they didn't come into being overnight; the opposition of the individualists was strong, never completely overcome with some old-timers.

In the Link we were establishing navigation procedures; if you were lost and you heard an N, immediately pick up a heading that bisected the quadrant to start an orientation—that was a procedure and we drilled it into people. It wasn't difficult in this case, because pilots knew a range could trick you—and the pilots weren't dumb, they looked eagerly at things that could help them fly safer and better.

The atmosphere in our Link room was relaxed. The first thing we did was to make certain the student pilot knew this was for learning and not for checking or examining. That created a free flow of information and ideas. The old-timers weren't hard to get along with, and the flying sessions became interesting to all except a few diehards.

I'd only been at this a few months when Hull told me a copilot class would start within a week and I'd better get ready to teach it.

There were nineteen new hires, as I remember, mostly civilians—I don't know why—maybe at the time there weren't military people available. Qualifications for hire as an airline pilot change with demand. I've seen times when an applicant had to be a college graduate with 3,000 hours flying time, good teeth and personality. Then I've seen days when we hired high school graduates, or equivalent, with a leather jacket and 200 hours in a Piper Cub. In the long run, after those who made it checked out as captain and flew a dozen years, you couldn't tell if they were the 3,000-hour superman or the 200-hour Cub pilot. The ones who didn't make it to captain included both civilian and military, superman and Cub.

But the group I had was a typical bunch of pilots, and thirteen of them flew to age sixty and compulsory retirement without accident or unmanageable adventures. Those who didn't make it were let go before becoming captains—they just didn't cut the mustard—except for one who decided he didn't like airline flying and went off to the world of corporate aviation.

Then a second class was dumped on me. The first day, en route to the airport, I picked up my copy of the *Kansas City Times* and on the front page was the story of Harlan Hull being killed in Seattle on a test flight at Boeing—that empty feeling in the pit of my stomach again, and anger.

He was flying a prototype of the Stratoliner. They had gone aloft with some KLM pilots to try the airplane, see how it flew, how the design was coming along. Someone wanted to try stalls, deep stalls, which means not just slowing up an airplane until it quivers a little and then sticking the nose down, but to keep pulling back the control wheel until the quiver becomes a wild shaking, the airplane trying to dig a wing under and spin. This one did, and in the spin the structure failed; it gyrated and floundered to earth, killing all.

It seemed in those times you could periodically count on someone being killed, but it was a troubling loss to me. I didn't know him well, but I admired his ability to fly, his technical approach that aimed at bringing flying out of barnstorming toward being a science, something more precise and predictable. His personality was warm with a bright smile. I had wanted to know him better, hoped to work with him, but all this was denied. Never quite knowing him gave him an idol-like aura whenever I think of Hull—he became an example of what a pilot should be, and forever influenced my goals and mores. His picture is over my desk even now, and a small-scale ruler he used that I obtained from his estate has always been among the paraphernalia of my workplace.

Otis Bryan became the new chief pilot—a pleasant, competent man I'd known before. But after I'd finished with the second class I asked to go back east to the line; the luster had dulled, and captain checkout was getting closer for me and I wanted to be out there flying.

CHAPTER 9

Checkout

C HECKING OUT TO CAPTAIN was the consuming thing. That step toward the left-side seat usually came about two years after you started with an airline back then (today it takes more like eight years to get up to checkout); it was still about a year off, but the shadow of the event made me use every flight for exacting practice.

I tried to observe the captain's decisions, wondering if I would have done the same or something different, and why. During the checkout process I'd be flying as captain, the check pilot acting as my copilot and asking questions ranging from what the weather ahead was to making me explain the hydraulic system of the airplane. They scrutinized your every move and decision, ready to criticize you to judge how firm you were, if you might vacillate and show uncertainty. And while assuming the copilot's duties, they'd play dumb so I'd have to watch all their actions the way one would with an inexperienced, new copilot.

Checking out to captain meant laying it all on the line; if you failed you were fired, your chances of getting another airline job nil. An entire career rested on the checkout, making it important enough to lose sleep over.

Spring blossomed into summer, and thunderstorms grew to towering heights. The spring storms are worrisome; cold air has not completely retreated to the Arctic, yet hot, humid air has begun to crawl northward.

Your spring flying goal is to stay clear of the conflict; duck every thunderstorm, wander all over the sky to avoid them, which isn't easy when they line up into a solid line stacked to the stratosphere, spitting lightning bolts, rain, hail, and wind.

Thunderstorms are more docile in midsummer; the cells are scattered and great lineups less frequent. But flying Flight 7 between Chicago and Kansas City, even in summer, could be difficult. The flight originated in Newark and went to Chicago. Approaching Chicago at night, we'd study the sky beyond Chicago toward the southwest, where we'd be going after our stop, searching for distant flashes of lightning to get a hint of what was in store. We called the route the "Great White Way" because thunderstorms hung there most of the time.

The storms often had high bases, so if we flew low, 2,000 to 4,000 feet, we'd be under the turbulence. Lightning bombarded the sky and rain poured down furiously, but the flight path would be smooth though nervous, because we never knew when a storm might have a lower base we'd run into and catch hell.

So we wanted high-base storms, high-level storms they're called. We'd scan the weather reports along the course looking for clues: Joliet, Illinois, overcast; Galesburg, Illinois, overcast, lightning southwest; Burlington, Iowa, overcast, ceiling 3,000 feet, light rain; Kirksville, Missouri, thunderstorm, ceiling 800 feet, visibility half a mile in moderate rain, wind southwest 10 miles an hour—there was the key you were looking for, because a light wind meant the storm's base was high. If the wind had been 30 with gusts to 50, it was a sure bet the storm's violence extended to the ground and blocked the sky we'd have to fly through.

It seemed so soon that shadows began to spread across the land earlier each day, the air chilled at twilight and the sun came up later each morning, the grasses browned, leaves turned to fall color and captains frequently said, "Guess I'll put the hood up and practice an approach," their bones telling them it was time to sharpen up for the serious flying of winter.

In November 1939, with some sadness, we moved the New York operations to La Guardia Airport—New York City flights would land in New York and not the New Jersey swamps. La Guardia had spacious new hangars, paved runways, and up-to-date lighting; the modern age was creeping in.

In February, a break in my routine duties: I had orders to fly copilot with Jack Zimmerman in Indianapolis, where he was to observe and critique new runway lights designed to help land in bad weather. Indianapolis was the CAA's experimental station, where research was done on a variety of things aeronautic from testing runway lights to firing dead chickens from a cannon toward a built-up windshield at a couple hundred miles an hour to see if the windshield could withstand the crunch of a bird hit in flight. The result was lots of blood and it was hard on the chicken carcass. (Bird strikes are not uncommon during the fall southward migration of ducks and geese, sometimes with disastrous results when the windshield glass and duck parts smash into a pilot's face. I hit a duck once over Columbus, Ohio, at 10,000 feet. It was night, and we were flying along in a half-sleepy state only to be jerked awake by a very loud bang. On the ground we found a foot-sized hole in the leading edge of the right wing, and lots of duck parts and feathers—a mallard.)

I got to Indianapolis a day ahead. The day of the tests, fog blanketed the area. It was zero-zero and, ironically, Jack's flight couldn't land at Indianapolis. I had to take over. The inventor, engineers, and observers were stuck with the fact that it was too bad to fly, so how could anyone get up in the air to see the lights? Ah, a brilliant idea and a call to the Army Air Corps at Wright Field, Dayton, Ohio, for a balloon that they shipped over by truck.

It is night, dense fog, and the balloon sits quietly above the ground; tied under it is a metal bucket seat, no cover except for the balloon overhead. A long rope is attached to the seat's bottom and down through a pulley held to the ground by sandbags, then the rope extends to a truck. I sit in the seat while an army sergeant explains a few things.

"If anything happens, like the rope breaks, just pull this." He places a small rope in my hand. "The gas will come out and you'll come down."

"Gently, I hope?"

"Oh, you wouldn't get hurt."

The truck backs toward the pulley, feeding rope, allowing the balloon to rise. I elevate into the darkness. The heavy fog makes everything wet and covers the balloon with moisture that runs down its sides to collect at the bottom and cascade on my head. The ground disappears and I'm hoisted 300 feet into the darkness while asking myself what in hell I'm doing in a foggy night, under a balloon, very alone, over Indiana, with a stream of cold water falling on my head.

I look toward the runway and see the lights outlining it. They do a pretty good job, and I think that I could land an airplane in this fog with their help. Bartow lights they were called, named after the inventor, but they never caught on as standard; I don't know why.

After a reasonable time of study I shouted to the ground, "Okay, I see 'em, pull me down."

The truck drove away from the pulley, slowly pulling down the rope, the balloon, and me. I had grimly held the rope for dumping gas through all this. Back on the ground I struggled out of the seat, cold and soaking wet.

The next day was clear. The CAA took me aloft in their four-place-cabin Waco N to show me the navigation equipment they had been developing. It was impressive stuff. One instrument constantly read off the airplane's distance from the airport; it made me think about how Johnny Graves would have known how far he was from Fresno and instantly seen that he had to get away from the mountains. This distance measuring equipment, DME as it became known, could handle routine navigation like computing ground speed for exact estimates, and you could tell well in advance if a head wind was slowing you down and fuel might become critical. This was in February 1940, yet it wasn't until 1950 that the CAA contracted for the equipment to be installed around the country, and 1961 before air traffic control included DME in traffic clearance procedures and airlines put it in their jets—twenty-one years to get the job done. On one hand it showed the ability and skill of government people to develop good things like DME; on the other it showed how bureaucracy and economics are slow to put it in position for the benefits of safety and efficiency.

Then Jack arrived, and we flew the latest experimental ILS, instrument landing system—my first experience with it. This was a sharp, high-frequency beam that led you right down the runway—not just horizontally, but a second beam, laid on its side, gave you a descending path to follow to the ground. The two beams were brought together in one instrument that showed the pilot side to side and up and down; no more listening through static for a vague A or N signal—simply keep the two needles centered. That wasn't exactly easy and it took a while to learn the tricks.

The earliest attempt at such a system was in 1931, but the first beams wandered and had bends; the glide slope—the vertical beam—was scalloped and it bounced off hillsides, buildings, and other obstructions, but constant experimentation and development had made it accurate though not yet perfect by the time I flew it in 1940. Weather minimums could be lowered to a 200-foot ceiling, but more importantly the airplane would be led right down the runway rather than looking for a road, stream, or chicken coop to help find it. The end of barnstorming around airports was in sight.

With World War II civilian development of the ILS stopped, but the military installed it in a few special places, and its accuracy made operation along Alaska's Aleutian chain of islands possible in the foul weather they're famous for.

After the war, the airline industry was anxious to get ILS installed nationwide. By 1947 twelve airlines were using ILS, though it wasn't until 1965 that real low ceilings—down to 100 feet—were permitted with ILS. Today, with the best and latest system plus sophisticated automatic pilots, airlines can go all the way to the ground and land in zero-zero conditions if the airport has the latest ILS transmitters and the runway length and obstructions meet certain standards, as most major international airports do.

This may be a lot of wandering from my approaching checkout, but changing technology weaves through any tale of aviation, even though it comes in fits and starts as funding and politics make the path of progress a rocky one. It's all as much a part of aviation as wings.

✷

LATE WINTER my time came, and with it a letter on brown stationery—always known as a "Brown Letter," a company communication. It said I was to be checked out as captain. It was a sobering thought, and I worried about the tests ahead, although I also had a bright feeling of elation skirting around the edges.

The start was an equipment check. A check pilot in Kansas City would take me aloft in either a DC-2 or DC-3, just the two of us, and have me do a series of maneuvers to prove I could fly the airplane.

The first concern was who the check pilot would be; the possibility of drawing certain ones could create a nervous tic or cold sweat. But I was lucky, I got Mo Bowen, one of the finest people to ever grace an airplane. Mo was an ex-marine, medium height, with his most distinguishing feature a warm smile that revealed a set of the most perfect white teeth a human ever had—he chewed gum constantly. He was gentle, spoke softly and so infrequently you thought he was rationing words.

A cold Kansas City night, clear, the airplane a DC-2. We settled in the cockpit, me on the left like a captain, Mo in the copilot's seat, a clipboard on his lap that held TWA Form 0-275, "Pilot Check on Equipment."

"Well," Mo said, "I guess we'll just go down the list—get her started and take off."

The list was impressive, twenty-five items.

Item 1. "Starting and stopping engines." That was easy, but I did it carefully.

Item 2. "Taxiing, operation of brakes, handling of throttles, tailwheel lock control." Brakes I could handle smoothly and well from the tutelage of Lex Klotz when I flew out of San Francisco.

Item 3. "Proper use of checklist." These were just coming into use, but this was a simple bookkeeping job—as long as you really did check the object.

Item 4. "Takeoffs, observing engine operating limits: Day_____ Night_____Crosswind_____Single-engine_____." It was night, so the day part didn't count and anyway night was considered more difficult than day, so this would cover both.

We made numerous takeoffs, and on one Mo cut back an engine and I had to struggle around the field and land. It wasn't all that difficult, although the single-engine performance was limited. With just Mo and me in the airplane it was light in weight and that helped me in the struggle.

The check went along smoothly, there wasn't any tension and Mo didn't yell or carry on about little variances or clumsiness at maneuvers I'd never had a chance to practice like the single-engine work. If the maneuver wasn't just right Mo would say, "Let's do another one."

When a maneuver was completed Mo would check it off the sheet and look at the next item.

"It says do some figure-eights—just get over the river and do 'em up- and downstream."

I never was an ace at figure-eights but I did them well enough to satisfy Mo—they had to be done with both engines and with one engine shut down.

The dreaded check ride was turning into a pleasant experience—a chance to really work over the airplane and do things one usually never had a chance to do. Mo turned the mood from a scrutinizing examination to my having a chance to try some abnormal maneuvers with his little hints to help.

The list went on: "Skill and technique steep turns, 45 or over, unusual maneuvers, recoveries, stalls."

Unusual maneuvers were done under the hood. For unusual maneuvers, Mo took the airplane and I covered my eyes with one hand so as not to see what he was doing—that was the ritual. He'd go into a steep turn, cross the controls, and pull the nose up or put it into some other weird attitude, and then call out, "Okay, you've got it."

You'd put hands and feet on the controls and, by instruments, right the airplane and get it back flying straight and level. Unusual maneuvers were fun to do.

Item: "Approach technique, airspeed, glide angle, use of power, trimming plane, adjustment of all controls, lowering landing gear, setting propeller pitch."

Routine stuff, but I worked to do it smoothly and precisely—not to undershoot or overshoot an airspeed or altitude—to keep airspeed constant and not have wide variations during approach.

Item: "Handling of plane normal instrument flight. Handling of plane single-engine instrument flight."

Here we did a simulated low approach using the Kansas City radio range—two approaches, actually, one of them single-engine.

Some of these items overlapped others, so they were checked off without repeating.

Item: "Handling of engines and accessories, correct interpretation of manifold press, RPM, indicated airspeed, knowledge of engine operating limits, takeoff, climb, cruise, knowledge of power and cruising charts."

We didn't fool with much of this except for keeping within limits on all the maneuvers. The other things would be picked up on line checks. I would spend about forty hours flying the line with a check pilot—more than one—and the check form would be completed through a stream of questions during the empty time of cruising between stops. The same was true of items such as: "Knowledge of landing gear, hydraulic system and operation."

These questions would cover the autopilot, heating system—on which any experienced copilot was an expert—radio and electrical system, emergency flares, dump valves, fire extinguishers; knowledge of loading charts, correct loading and weight distribution; lashing down, tie-down cables and fittings (in case of a forced landing and overnight stay at a remote field so the airplane would be secure).

Lots of these items are history now; engine management is very different with a jet engine, which is much less complicated. Landing flares are only found in museums, and tying down a jet airliner of today a laughable fantasy.

"Well," Mo finally said. "That's the end of the list—let's go home." There wasn't any ceremony or congratulations or even saying I'd passed; it was all taken for granted as we shook hands, then parted in the dispatch office.

The first check was over. Back to La Guardia and the line checks.

∗

LINE CHECKS are done on actual line flights, hence the name. Pilots receive them at least once a year. The check pilot—now called by a fancier name, line check airman—sits in the copilot's position while you fly as captain, making decisions, giving orders.

These are dreaded flights for someone advancing to captain, because the line check pilot sits there, stone-faced or jovial, deciding whether or not you're good enough to be a captain, but gives no indication by word, action, or expression what that decision might be.

Days and nights before the check flights you studied the airplane and operation manuals, memorizing things from the takeoff minimums at Pittsburgh to the maximum allowable oil temperature of the engines. There were calls to the weather office during the night to see what kind of weather you face on the trip; if the forecast called for thunderstorms or ice, low ceilings and fog, anything bad, you'd toss and turn, visualizing how to fly the weather. It's a fretful, stressful time.

Playing captain on line checks, I was at the dispatch office early study-ing weather, deciding on fuel and cruise altitude and all the things a cap-tain does. The check pilot stood aside, silent, accepting my analysis and judgment that later would either turn out well or show up badly in a humiliating fashion. But I still had to make out the flight plan—no check pilot was going to carry the make-believe that far!

In the airplane I gave the orders: "Read the checklist, please." I'd deter-mined to add *please* because most times as copilot I'd hear a simple, perhaps rough, and borderline impolite, "Check list!," which meant to read it. I wanted to be explicit and to inject a suggestion of gentleness.

The check pilot picked it up and did as he was told, with me carefully checking each item visually and placing a hand to feel if it was set cor-rectly.

The check pilot didn't say much, just did what he was told. If I made a gross error or omission he'd point it out, and my embarrassment was deep and a tug of fear slipped through my stomach.

My check flights were done by three different pilots I'm going to call Numbers 1, 2, and 3, because they were different and maybe did some irregular things. Their names wouldn't help the telling, and they're all dead anyway—they died in bed, incidentally.

After flying forty-six hours on different flights with them I'd get a semifinal and then a final line check with the chief pilot or his assistant. These were the big ones; after the final line check you were either a captain or headed for a black fate.

Check pilot Number 1: this was informal stuff with a man I'd flown with many times, one who laughed easily.

Despite the frivolity, Number 1 flew well and expected you to as well. If the landing was a bit firm he'd flip a humbling remark: "Trying to lower the airport?"

A question like "Suppose an engine quit right now, where would you go?" was generally asked when you were wrapped in weather, in zero visi-bility with snow and most airports below close to limits or closed. But I had the answer ready, because during checks I expected a question like that.

I flew a round-trip to Chicago with Number 1: ten hours and twenty minutes under the check pilot magnifying glass.

Then a respite before my second check, a ritual known as "making the fields."

The fields were emergency fields, you wouldn't really call them airports, that had been established for the airmail service and their single-engine airplanes; they were small grass strips a pilot could duck into and wait out a storm or fix an ailing engine. None had runways much over 2,500 feet and they were almost all grass-covered.

The idea was that a pilot preparing to be captain should know these fields more intimately than just flying by at 6,000 feet or so as one did on the airline. The CAA, Civil Aeronautics Authority—forerunner of the FAA—said the pilot should land in each one to qualify as captain. We had advanced to the point that this seemed a silly idea; we flew by instruments, had two engines and radio navigation guidance; no one of my era ever used one of these fields in an emergency to my knowledge. So why did we have the regulation? Simply because, at that time, we weren't very far removed from the old airmail days and clung to old ways.

The company provided a single-engine, four-place biplane for this, a Waco; no wasting of big airplane time, and beside, many of the fields would be marginal in size for a DC-2 or 3. Another pilot also going through checkout went along. The two of us scraped in and out of fifty-two different airports; the chore took three and a half days of hard flying, but it was fun and we had a new appreciation for the country below, an intimate feel for the airports. As I passed over places like Hayesville, Ohio, now, I could visualize the grass strip with trees on one end and the feel of the Ohio countryside. I never expected to use a field like that and I never did, but it was a good experience. This is no longer part of the requirements—and modern captains don't know what they're missing.

Number 2 check pilot was a different situation. His reputation said he failed more pilots than he passed. I'd flown copilot with him and knew his demands for perfection and detail; nothing went unnoticed and all was serious. I didn't look forward to the round-trip to Chicago and back.

But I knew this man and he had an ego, felt his aviation knowledge and ability was better than most—which was true. He liked to talk, and I played on this without compunction or subtlety; I asked him questions like, "I've noticed how tight you hold the range on an approach—any hints on how you do this?"

That would be good for twenty minutes of talk—not without gain to me because he knew his stuff, but when he'd finish I had another question ready and then another. The time was used up, so there was little remaining before landing to question me—just the way I'd planned it.

There's a strange occurrence in sessions like that: the person being asked, having the opportunity to pontificate to an attentive listener, develops the subconscious impression that you're smart, too, and an admiration evolves. It's based on a false premise, of course, but it was handy at the time.

I had to think up a lot of questions because the flight coming back from Chicago got canceled at Pittsburgh on account of weather, and we turned around for an extra lap to Chicago. Sixteen hours and fourteen landings. One of them astounded me.

Inbound to Pittsburgh, snowing, ceiling and visibility poor. A Chicago nonflying dispatcher was on board and check pilot Number 2 invited him up front. "Go ahead, sit in the copilot seat—I've got to go back for a bit."

So he disappeared into the cabin and I flew through the snow, swapping gossip with the dispatcher, John Dungan. We approached Pittsburgh, but no sign of the check pilot. We crossed the last checkpoint, still no check pilot; I lowered the landing gear, we got closer to the field, landing was at hand. Should I pull up and hold until the check pilot came back? Nuts to that.

"Fasten your belt and let me know when you see runway lights," I told the wide-eyed dispatcher. Lights came in view through the snow; I put down the flaps, crossed the boundary, landed, and taxied to the gate.

The check pilot appeared. "Somebody I got to talking with back there," was his total and unconcerned comment—not a word about the landing— and this from the most persnickety check pilot we had.

Number 3 was an old friend who asked little; just a routine flight to Kansas City, Chicago, Pittsburgh, and New York, nineteen and one half hours.

So I'd had forty-six hours of checking and thirty-four landings. I was ready for the two big ones: the semifinal and final rides. The semi was a flight to Chicago and Kansas City with Jack Zimmerman, New York's chief pilot. We'd flown many times together, he knew me and demanded little except a hooded approach into Chicago. No sweat.

The final was back to New York: Kansas City, St. Louis, Columbus, Pittsburgh, Camden, and La Guardia. Swede Golien, assistant system chief pilot: quiet, gentlemanly Swede. It was a routine flight with conversation that revealed my flight philosophies, and few direct questions. Swede was a pleasure to fly with, someone you looked up to in the hope you'd be half as good some day.

At Camden, Swede said he'd fly it to La Guardia. He offered his hand.

"Congratulations, Bob, you are now a TWA captain." Oh, those sweet words, and especially from one I so much admired.

Next day, in the hall at the La Guardia hangar, I passed Ray Wells, New York's assistant chief pilot. He said it a little differently.

"I hear you passed your final—congratulations. Remember, now you're one of the highest-paid pilots in the world. For Christ's sake fly like it!"

CHAPTER 10

Captain Buck

✳

BEING ONE OF THE world's best paid pilots equated to about $600 a month, which in 1940 was a pretty fair bit of money and a dramatic jump from the $210 I was making as copilot.

True to form, Jean and I purchased our first new automobile and awaited the birth of our first child. This was almost a routine procedure for newly checked out captains. The new automobile was a Studebaker Opera Coupe with all the extras possible—radio and whitewall tires among them. It cost $990.

My first flight as captain was Flight 59, a DC-2 La Guardia to Pittsburgh. I spent an awkward, nervous, and serious moment standing in the dispatch office, looking over the weather and telling the copilot to make the flight plan for a chosen altitude. The chore of making out flight plans was over—I could stand and gossip with other captains while the copilot twisted the calculator and filled in the form's boxes. No one came up and said, "Your first flight, eh?" which was some sort of discipline much appreciated. The copilot knew, but he didn't remark on it either.

There is a difference sitting on the left; I realized that as copilot you're conscious of the flight management, weather, and all those things, but the real decisions are up to the captain and you, as copilot, really don't have the load on your shoulders—you're relieved of the final responsibility.

On that first captain trip you realize—and it's almost a shock—that there's no one behind you to fall back on; nothing relieves you of the final responsibility, it stops right in your lap and says, "Boy, what are you going to do?" The idea that being captain can be a lonely spot explains itself right quickly.

But there's a heady feeling, too: "It's all mine and I'm in charge to call the shots, make the decisions." You like that, but you realize there's a price to pay—you have to be ready to answer for your actions, not only to the VP of flight operations, but if it's a first-class error maybe to that chief pilot up beyond the pearly gates.

Still, I had flown plenty before I joined the airline, went many places alone, in charge, responsible for my own outcomes; thinking back to those days helped me accept the responsibility of being captain.

The flight proved to be routine, weather fairly good, and nothing untoward happening except seeing a run-back of oil on the right engine nacelle. This was nothing unusual, but enough to get my attention and to fret about to a small degree. The copilot, Miles, wasn't very senior and this was good because I felt more in command than if I had had a very senior copilot, ready for checkout, who might have acted as though he was watching me for any mistakes.

The return from Pittsburgh—an immediate turnaround—seemed quite natural. I felt it was my airplane and I was running the show. I liked being captain.

The second trip was something else. Another trip to Pittsburgh, but this time weather; warmish in New York, then a cold front to pass through just west of Allentown. Behind the front would be clouds with tops around 10,000 feet. Pittsburgh weather looked okay for landing, with good ceilings and only the possibility of a snow shower. This wasn't a difficult setup and didn't inject even a smitch of anxiety.

Off we went into a gray sky. We entered clouds around 3,000 feet, and before we flew very far west rain commenced. I leveled off at 9,000, as I recall, on instruments. The Allentown range was coming in okay. I pulled on carburetor heat and leaned out the engines. We flew on, relaxed, in the gray, wet world.

The rain mixed with snow, wet snow as expected when we approached the front. A little turbulence bounced us; suspecting ice, I had the propeller alcohol on.

The wet snow became dry—moderate at first, and then heavy. A line of white built on the wing's leading edge; some of it was ice, but mostly snow pelted the surface. There was no special concern; in a moment we'd come out the other side and after cutting in and out of various cloud layers, with light ice, we'd emerge between cloud layers and gradually the upper clouds would dissipate and we'd be on top of a white blanket, up in the sunshine. All this I knew from study fortified by experience.

The sense of being responsible for the passengers did not weigh heavily on my shoulders—nor would it ever, from a few passengers to 400 in a 747. My interest in a safe flight was personal: I most certainly didn't want to risk my neck, and if I got there safely so would all those folks behind me. I never felt any different flying a cargo flight full of boxes or a passenger flight full of people as far as responsibility was concerned. I did stew, fret, and go to every length possible to make the flight as smooth as possible for the passengers' comfort, but once I'd done everything possible for that my next priority was to get there on schedule.

That was how I felt about flying even in my early stages of being in command, and this flight felt good despite the weather. But in the midst of the heaviest snow, when the outside air temperature had dropped well below freezing, the engines lost power—I sensed it by the reduction in noise and could feel the airplane slowing, and the engine instruments told it, too. It was disturbing, but obviously caused by carburetor ice. I pulled on more heat, readjusted the mixtures. "There, that should fix it."

But it didn't, and the power fell back more. I pulled on more carburetor heat—finally had it all on, all I could get, but the engines continued to lose power, to the point where we couldn't hold altitude, we were slowly descending! Now I was disturbed, tense, my mouth dry. The prospect of a forced landing was frightening, the terrain below was mountains with small valley fields obscured by falling snow, the visibility poor, probably less than half a mile; how could I dead-stick down through that, see a field, and land? What in hell was wrong with the engines, why didn't they respond to the heat?

I tried to reason: heat wasn't getting it done, it was all on; what would happen if I removed it? I took heat off the right engine, pulled the mixture back and forth between rich and lean; for an instant, nothing. Then a loud backfire, wham, and the engine surged, coming back to power. I adjusted the throttle and mixture, left the heat off. It ran. I took the heat off the left engine, repeated the mixture shuffle and whamo, a backfire and surge. Throttle and mixture adjusted, it ran—with the heat off. We continued that way, against all rules and principles, nervous because here I was on instruments, in snow, cold, and running without carburetor heat. It was a squirmy situation, but as long as the engines ran I wasn't going to touch them; it seemed as though touching anything might break a spell and bring trouble.

We finally flew out between layers, then on top and routine into Pittsburgh—never touching the carburetor heat.

The copilot had been suffering in silence.

"What do you think?" I asked him.

"Beats the hell outta me," was his reply.

By the time we flew back, the front had passed off the East Coast and the weather had cleared.

The next day I was at the field telling the chief pilot about the incident. Did he know the answer, had he experienced anything like it?

"No, that's a new one on me—maybe full heat was too much."

It had been, of course, but why? I thought I had a reason. In the front of the front—in rain—we needed heat, but as we passed the cold front and the temperature dropped, the heat wasn't necessary because the snow was dry and would zip through the engine without sticking. But still, having the heat on, even in the dry snow, shouldn't have made the power go down.

Well, the reason finally dawned on me: the heat was raising the temperature at the carburetor enough to soften the dry snow into slush, which refroze farther down in the carburetor where the air gets colder. By putting on heat, in this condition, we were making ice!

Now I wanted to learn more, so I wrote to carburetor manufacturers, talked to power plant engineers and anyone I could—there were lots of ideas, but nothing solid. It was obvious there was an empty area in our knowledge of carburetor icing.

The carburetor air temperature gauge had registered above freezing— so why the ice? It turned out that the answer was the temperature bulb's location; if it was located in the front part of the carburetor, the reading would be higher than farther down in the carburetor where the curved throat lowered the temperature further. It stayed warm on the gauge, but that didn't reflect what was going on down in the cold action spot.

So I learned where all the temperature bulbs were located on the different aircraft, and how much temperature drop there was between the top deck of the carburetor, as we called the first part, and the throat, as we called the coldest area. With that knowledge, one could tell what was what, if heat was needed and how much.

Later, so-called nonicing carburetors were developed, but they really weren't; then came fuel injection, and that was supposed to be the ultimate cure, but it wasn't. An engine needs air, and that comes in from the outside, bringing along snow, rain, freezing rain, or whatever else is out there. The carburetor might not ice, but the induction system—all the passageways the inbound air flows through—will.

A new model Constellation came with injection and consequently was announced as "nonicing," but we still had trouble because the induction system would collect snow that made the engines run erratically. What we needed was a way of shutting off the air coming from outside and taking it instead from under the cowling where it was warm and snow-free. The problem was that the airplanes didn't have this option, known as Alternate-A (A for air). We pilots urged the company to modify the airplanes, but they didn't want to—it cost money.

Every time we encountered snow as we flew across the ocean the engines acted up. The flight engineer played with different power settings, leaned or enriched the mixtures, anything. We flew on with the engines surging—running irregularly, but running. But it was damned disturbing to feel the rough-running engines, on instruments, with the cold, stormy North Atlantic 17,000 feet below. No one ever had a complete failure because of it, but there were no guarantees, and each time it occurred you squirmed, hoping this wasn't the one.

The solution was simple, and it came about on a flight I happened to be flying, New York to Shannon, Iceland, and Paris. One passenger was John Collings, our VP of operations, a thin-lipped old-time pilot who demanded perfection. International operations had recently been combined with domestic, which had been his bailiwick, so now he was boss of it all. Ocean flying was relatively new to him, and I think he may have had that uptight feeling people are apt to suffer when first heading out to sea.

We were about 100 miles off the coast of Nova Scotia, flying through light snow when I drifted back to the cabin for my smile-and-nod session with the passengers and to look in on John. I knew the snow would become heavier as we approached a low-pressure area. He was eating dinner.

He asked me, "How's it going?"

I kneeled down in the aisle and responded, "It's going fine, right on flight plan, a little snow outside—we're 100 miles off the Nova Scotia coast."

Just then the engines decided they weren't happy with the snow and started to run rough.

"What's that?" John nervously asked.

"Oh, just snow making the engines act up—can't help it." I didn't feel comfortable and wanted to go back to the cockpit, but I decided to grind this into John a bit.

We chatted some more, as the engines' normal rhythm was disturbed by roughness.

"Don't you think you ought to be up front?"

"It won't do any good—I've got a good flight engineer, he's doing his best; without that Alternate-A we can't do a hell of a lot to help." He was well aware of our demands for this modification.

The engines continued their slight surging—Collings looked nervous.

"Bob, I want you to go back up front!" It was an order.

"Okay—see you later." And I sauntered back to the cockpit—glad to be there.

We finally flew out of the snow and the engines settled down to their smooth pounding. But not long after that trip the order went out for Alternate-A to be installed on the fleet.

✶

IN THAT FIRST YEAR as captain I flew 256 flights, most of them between La Guardia, Pittsburgh, and Chicago—mostly La Guardia–Pittsburgh shuttles, frequently with stops at Harrisburg and Camden until a new Philadelphia airport put an end to Camden and New Jersey acting as aircraft carrier for New York and Philadelphia. The first TWA flight to land there happened on my schedule, so I had the honor—that was June 20, 1940.

About half the trips were in DC-2s and half in DC-3s—occasionally I managed to get to a country airport and fly a small airplane to remember what it was like, do some aerobatics, and keep in touch with what was called private flying.

On my fifth trip I gave my first landing to a copilot, but it was Dean Officer, who was almost as senior as me and about to get checked out as captain.

I made an instrument approach into Chicago in a DC-2 equipped with the new Curtiss electric propellers. Their pitch was made constant by an electric motor driving gears and such to change the propeller blade angle as power and speed required. It worked fine, but the DC-2 electrical system wasn't powerful enough to handle the extra electrical load—the result was my battery got lower and lower and finally the lights dimmed and the radio weakened to a faint signal that really wasn't useful. It was raining and the ceiling was about 400 feet. Fortunately we had a standby radio powered with a dry-cell battery for emergencies. Well, this was one, so I broke the safety wire that was there to make sure it couldn't be turned on accidentally. It worked fine and the approach went well, but we'd slowed up Chicago traffic because we didn't have the power to transmit and tell the ground where we were and what was going on, so they held everyone at various points above the Chicago area until we landed.

One early April night, when the ground still had snow cover that melted in the warm daytime and added moisture to the air, the cool darkness brought on fog and Chicago went zero-zero—no ceiling, no visibility. Other close-by fields promised to do the same thing, so I chased across Lake Michigan for South Bend, Indiana, which was still open because of an overcast that slowed the nighttime cooling and made it the best bet of airport choices. But it wasn't going to last, and South Bend would fold, too; my chore was to get there before the fog. I poured on the coal and rushed down the west leg of the radio range. As I did, the visibility went from two miles to one, and I slid farther forward on the seat and started that nervous, anxious period when time goes very slowly and one sweats it out.

The procedure was to go over the range station at a prescribed minimum altitude certain to be above all terrain and obstructions. Passing over the station established a positive position, but it was too high to descend and land directly ahead, so you made a turn to fly away from the station for ten miles, then turned back—called a procedure turn—and now you could descend to a lower altitude on the beam and cross the station again, this time low enough to descend to the 400-foot minimum before reaching the airport, then hopefully see it and land. All this messing around took time—too much time. The new report had visibility three quarters of a mile. It was going down and I didn't have enough fuel to get away from this unpredicted bad weather area.

I wasn't about to use all that time—I knew the terrain between Lake Michigan and the airport, knew how low I could safely sneak. I descended below the legal prescribed altitude so I'd arrive over the station low enough the first time to get down and land.

We did just that, and as the volume built up telling me the station was close, I let down some more—then, at the cone of silence, I pulled back the throttles and went for minimums. We broke out of the skimpy overcast into a gloomy world with a misty light or two directly below—and then the runway lights came into view, fuzzy, dim, and close, but we had it made. The visibility when we landed was half a mile, and before we got shut down and out of the airplane it went zero.

Of course what I did was irregular. On my next trip into Chicago the chief pilot, Phares McFerren, grabbed me.

"The CAA is in my office and wants to talk to you about your South Bend landing."

A sinking feeling—now I had a good chance for a violation and Lord knew what penalties.

"It seems you didn't do a procedure turn at South Bend, but landed straight in. What's your explanation?" the inspector asked.

"Well, I did a fan marker approach." This was a type of approach found at some airports where a high frequency radio on the beam leg activated a light and beeped as you passed through its fan-shaped signal announcing you were ten miles from the field and could let down to final altitude without the procedure turn.

"There's no fan marker at South Bend!"

"There was the other night." Mac and the inspector laughed and I felt there was hope.

"No," I said. "I used my emergency authority. Everything was folding and I had to hurry. I descended to an altitude I knew was safe and went straight in."

He accepted it, a pleasing surprise.

Later Mac said, "You did the right thing. It was your best judgment for the condition. That's what emergency authority is for—don't be afraid to use it." Lesson learned.

Before that first year was over I'd flown with fifty-two different copilots—an astounding number, but the company was hiring pilots in big chunks. Some of them were pilots I'd put through school in Kansas City. Of the fifty-two, fifteen never made it to captain and drifted off to other places—one was killed in a training accident.

I was twenty-six, slender and still holding my mop of hair. I looked young. A lady passenger saw me get on the airplane at Pittsburgh. "Is that the copilot?" she asked the passenger agent.

"No, ma'am, that's the captain."

"That youngster! I'm getting off!" And she did.

On November 15 our daughter, Ferris, was born. It was quite a year.

✳

I HAD A FULL YEAR of flying as captain before World War II came, going back and forth between the East Coast and Kansas City, confronting the eastern mountains that start at Pittsburgh and become a barrier between it and Harrisburg before sliding downhill to Philly and New York. While the Alleghenies are mere hills compared to the Rockies, they can produce king-size weather that is tough to combat when flying low-level airplanes like our DC-2s and DC-3s.

It was a time of learning, not just for me, but for all of us. There was still a lot we didn't know about airline flying. The basic rule that was the foundation for all the rest, simple but paramount, was: avoid the terrain! This meant knowing how high any ground, hills, or mountains below you were, so you'd have enough altitude to stay above them. We didn't always know exactly where we were, but we knew within an area, a certain range of flight we had to be in considering our speed, winds, and time flown. This knowledge extended through the flight: during climb, cruise, and descent, with particular attention to the obstructions around an airport when we were looking for a runway. Today it's called situational awareness.

The three basic differences then from now were how we flew low ceilings, ice, and thunderstorms. Descending through the clouds while listening to the As and Ns of the beam was inexact; the beam got you in the vicinity and headed for the airport, but once the ground came into view, the pilot found the runway by searching. It wasn't all that easy to see, because the runway lighting wasn't sophisticated and varied airport to airport.

Thunderstorms were another matter simply because we didn't have radar to see their dangerous cells and, as I've described, missing or flying smack into them was more luck than skill.

The technique of flying ice was simple: as soon as you encounter it, work like the devil to get out of it. Climb or descend if you knew where the cloud tops or bottoms were or where temperatures were above freezing. On a winter day going from Pittsburgh to the East Coast we frequently climbed through a thick deck of clouds that created ice on an airplane in scary amounts. The object was to get on top of the clouds before the airplane became loaded with enough ice to stop its climb, make it sluggish so it couldn't climb anymore. These tops, east of Pittsburgh, would often be 12,000 feet; getting through 12,000 feet of ice-producing cloud flirted with the limits of the airplane's ability.

We developed tricks. The clouds west of Pittsburgh, where the hills are lower, had lower tops, around 7,000 feet. So when the tops were high east, and the icing severe, we'd take off and climb to the west, getting on top at 7,000 feet or so. Once on top, up in the sunshine or star-studded sky, we'd turn around and head east, climbing as we did, so when we got back to the area where the cloud tops were 12,000 feet we'd already be on top, in clear air looking down at the woolly clouds below.

During that first year as captain I flew more DC-2s than DC-3s. Seniority had something to do with this; the old-timers with gray beards and lots of seniority were able to fly the plush flights, like Flight 7, a DC-3 sleeper from La Guardia to Chicago and Kansas City, where other crews took it on to L.A. Low-seniority pilots, like me, flew the local DC-2 flights—down there rootin' with the hogs, as we called it.

There were a lot of landings and takeoffs, like Flight 17 from La Guardia to Camden, Harrisburg, Pittsburgh, Columbus, Dayton, Fort Wayne, and then Chicago, an all-day affair. At each stop we'd climb off the airplane and go into the little office where the radio operator worked and the paperwork was sorted out for loading the airplane. This is where I'd pick up the clearance, the collection of papers with formal language saying I accepted the flight. There would be some language such as, "Cleared HX to PT 400 gal, CO alternate, SCD," and it would have the dispatcher's name. Translated it means: cleared Harrisburg to Pittsburgh with 400 gallons of gasoline with Columbus, Ohio, as alternate. The SCD meant "subject captain's discretion"; these were mighty important words because they signified who was in final command, who could say we'd go or not, who'd say how much gasoline was acceptable and if the alternate was, too. The dispatcher could clear a flight or cancel one, but he couldn't order the pilot to go. The manual says a flight must be agreed on by dispatcher and pilot working in concert, but the final say-so was right there in those letters SCD.

Attached to the clearance were pages with the latest weather and forecasts, which we studied carefully to see what was in store for us on the next leg. A teletype circuit ran from Kansas City to La Guardia, listing each station in its geographical order: Kansas City; Kirksville, Missouri; Columbia, Missouri; St. Louis, and right on down the line to La Guardia. It was easy to study this lineup and see exactly where a cold front was located and how it had been moving in the last hour. We developed bits of local knowledge, and checking the wind, precipitation, and visibility gave a picture of what you might be up against. You studied all this carefully before signing the clearance.

The clearance was and is holy, and you cannot legally move without it. The fuel given was subject to argument after we studied the weather; if the load was heavy, the fuel load might be light and not enough to satisfy you, considering that you might be fighting ice to Pittsburgh, which would use up more, and then if Pittsburgh was below landing limits you had to continue to Columbus. So I might demand more fuel. Sometimes this was a tough decision, because to get more fuel the load would have to be reduced.

We stayed overnight at the end of a flight—Chicago, Kansas City, Pittsburgh, and now and then Columbus. The Columbus layover was in a large, barrackslike room upstairs on the side of the hangar. In Chicago we stayed at the Del Prado on the South Side—after we'd given up on the Hyde Park. We seldom ate in the hotel, but had our favorite small restaurants around the corner, so to speak; we were interested in food at a price, except for occasional forays downtown where we'd eat at Jack Diamond's, which had the biggest martinis and steaks. Another favorite was a German hofbrauhaus, Berghoff, and Barney's Market Club, which served steaks and lobsters in gigantic proportions. In those days we ate mostly "heart attack food."

We knew the hotel people and locals in the hotels. These less-expensive hotels were great examples of decayed elegance. Big-league baseball players stayed there, too, and while I don't remember names I do recall they were sort of set apart from the rest of the inhabitants. They had an athletic look and were different from the other guests: big, strong, dressed more casually, and clannish.

In Kansas City we stayed at the Kansas City Club, where not-yet-President Truman played poker with his buddies in their private club on one of the upper floors.

In Pittsburgh we stayed in a big old house called the Flyer's Club, which was across a road from the airport. It also had the kitchen where a TWA chef prepared the food for flights. I got stuck there for five days when a snowstorm closed the airport and the city snow removal equipment was too busy taking care of roads to worry about the runways; no flights operated, so the chef devoted his time to preparing food for the stuck crew members. There were three crews—six pilots and three hostesses. It was quite a five-day party, and the food was excellent. Talking to the chef, a big, chunky man, I learned things about food and especially remember his admonition never to eat anything with curry in a questionable restaurant, because curry can hide any bad food. He told stories of his days as a student chef when the restaurant owner, burdened with spoiled chicken, would tell them to curry it.

At each station you knew the station personnel, and there was more banter than serious discussion. At small stations there were few employees and even the bigger ones, like Pittsburgh, had a minuscule number of people compared to the mobs and confusion of today's airline terminals. The feeling was intimate; from coast to coast we knew all the people, worked together, argued at times, and laughed a lot.

We knew the passengers, too. There was time, on good weather days, to go back into the cabin and visit. There were businesspeople who flew some sectors frequently. We knew their names and family status, gave them the straight dope on weather and how the flight would work out. There was nothing impersonal about the experience of flying; it was a wonderful time.

CHAPTER 11

The Battle of Presque Isle

WAR CAME, and conservative concepts flew away like autumn leaves in the wind. We stretched our wings and found out what the airplane could really do—and what we could do, too. Before the war, rules regulated where and how we flew—down airways, along beam courses, to specific airports we'd been qualified by inspection to use. The airplane's performance was closely governed and the permitted gross weights carefully spelled out. We'd just finished a battle royal with the company about raising the DC-3 gross weight from 24,400 pounds to 25,200; this 800-pound increase, we feared, would degrade safety, making its performance marginal if an engine failed. Little did we know that, with the airplane adopted for military transport, we'd soon be carrying nearly 7,000 pounds more!

The change came suddenly. One innocent afternoon in June 1942, I sauntered past the chief pilot's office. "Hey, Buck, I've been looking for you." In the quiet of the office behind a closed door he explained that I was to take one of our airplanes, with nine crew members as passengers, and fly to Presque Isle, Maine, for a hush-hush military mission.

"What then? What's it all about?"

"Beats the hell outta me. When you find out let me know."

Presque Isle? Until then it was a vague name of some place in Maine where they grew potatoes. But, quietly, a large army airport had been created, with hangars, barracks, service buildings, trucks, Jeeps—a new world. We were a befuddled group that climbed down from the airplane, lugging bags and gawking at the surroundings. Other airline crews came from United, American, Eastern, and Pennsylvania Central—they were as perplexed as we were.

Questions from everyone, mostly directed at me because the chief pilot had appointed me den mother. I didn't have any answers. Everything was army, and with a war in progress our imaginations went off in irrational directions—could they keep us? Were we in this for the duration? Where would we be going? To the fighting areas?

The basic dope sifted through. There were airports under construction in Canada, Greenland, and Iceland, stepping-stones of a bridge to Europe for moving fighters, cargo, and whatever was needed. They had to be supplied with construction materials and priority items, and we were going to lug them.

Now we started to learn about the army. Confusion, typically, had taken over. Our mission was under three different commands, which made trying to get answers more difficult. There was the Ferry Command, which governed the airways and operations over the North Atlantic, and the Air Service Command, which was in charge of moving supplies. But neither command had any airplanes, so the 60th Transport Group of the Army Air Forces was told to get up there with their forty-four airplanes and crews to do the job. Enter Colonel A. J. K. Malone, a short, crisp guy with fierce pride in his group.

The Air Service Command thought it would be a great idea to have airline crews fly trips from Presque Isle north, come back and, while they rested, an army crew would take the airplane and fly a trip—back and forth, swapping duty, making maximum use of the airplanes that would be flying around the clock except for maintenance. Not a bad idea.

Bullshit—or words of that sort, from Colonel Malone. Airline crews weren't going to fly *his* airplanes! A call to Washington and a general who, I guess, humbled Malone a bit as he ordered that airline crews were indeed going to fly and be part of the 60th Transport Group.

After dinner—excuse me, mess, a much more apt description—there was a briefing; an auditorium full of airline crews waited for it to start, slouching back or twisting sideways to talk to their neighbor, but always with questions. All the war years, we learned, the dominant conversation consisted of questions: When and where do we go? When do we get home? The answers were often vague—orders changed quickly and drastically, it was hurry up and wait amid much confusion, but that's the way war is. The symbol for war ought to be a question mark.

The meeting started with Major Zimmerman of the Ferry Command—Jack Zimmerman, TWA's Atlantic Division chief pilot, now on active duty for the duration—who told us where we'd be flying: Goose, Gander, BW-1, Meeks, all names without meaning. Zimmerman chuckled at our ignorance and then said these places were in Labrador, Newfoundland, Greenland, and Iceland, for gawd's sake!

Then Malone took over, standing on the stage, legs spread apart, rock solid, cocky, tough. He gave a football coach speech about getting the job done, how we'd have to cooperate. Then he read an order cut by the mystical, but potent, general from Washington that, among other things, attached us to the 60th. Malone put the clincher on it: "You're all in the army now!"

Nine pilots turned to me and said almost in unison, "Those sonsabitches can't do that to us!" Then a more subdued, "Can they?"

Hell, I didn't know, but I didn't think so. It took orders, a draft, volunteering, something more than a cocky colonel's pronouncement. After the meeting I wormed my way through the crowd to the colonel.

"You weren't being literal about us being in the army?"

"Well, you're not officially, but as long as you're flying my airplanes and on this mission you're under my orders and my command!"

I got the picture and there wasn't any point in arguing, but I knew if push came to shove we could tell him where to head.

Then more shocks: after the colonel's briefing, Zimmerman told us to go to the hangar for maps and field data. The walls of a big room were papered with maps marked, boldly, with course lines going off to Gander in Newfoundland, Goose Bay in Labrador, and BW-1, across the Davis Strait, to Greenland. Then on to Meeks in Iceland. Unknown lands, stuff you only looked at in *National Geographic*—a big, cold, lonesome area we were going to fly across hoping to find the tiny places with strange names surrounded by miles and miles of nothing—without navigators, either. Do it yourself with anything that experience and stormy nights had taught you—and then hope luck would overcome ignorance.

We sat at tables and plotted courses on maps, sparse maps with few towns, no emergency airports en route, and some areas were blank white spaces devoid of topographical information—no mountains, rivers, lakes, roads, or railroads. None of the friendly things that tell you where you are and how high you have to fly to avoid collision with the hard dispassionate ground.

"What's the safe minimum altitude between Presque Isle and Goose?"

"We're not really sure, but don't think there's anything higher than 4,000 feet between here and there." That wasn't very comforting. And Greenland was worse—the height of the mountains sticking up out of the ice cap was uncertain; one army man said, "I'd never cross there under 12,000." Mentally we all noted to make that 14,000. The navigation facilities were slim—a radio range at Presque Isle and one at Goose run on an engine-powered generator subject to failure—and it's 600 miles between the two, which is further than you can hear a squeaky loop-type range. The task, after the signal from the Presque Isle radio range faded from hearing, was to hold a compass heading until the signal from the range at Goose became audible. Over to Greenland it was the same, but with longer distances of vagueness.

We double-checked the course lines and noticed with some awe the big magnetic variation numbers that came from being way north and not too far from the magnetic pole that the compass points to, although you navigate by reference to the geographic north pole—the one on top. The variation in degrees is a part of your course computation. You know, too, that being close to the magnetic pole makes the compass flighty; the errors it naturally has—running ahead, holding back, northerly turning—are all magnified.

The airplanes were basically DC-3s, but they were called C-47s by the army and lots of other names by the troops, like Gooney Bird and Dakota (British). The cabin was empty to leave room for cargo. Hard, fold-down metal bucket seats were along the sides for soldiers, maybe parachutists. There was no real soundproofing. The bleak interior was painted GI green or whatever you call it—the light was dim and the atmosphere depressing.

The ones of the 60th carried extra fuel with a 200-gallon tank in the cabin (good for two extra hours), but be careful how you use the valves because set improperly you could create a vapor lock and no fuel would flow from the tank. The gross weight to be used was calmly announced as

32,000 pounds! Good God, and we'd argued over 25,200. How would it fly that heavy? You knew damned well it wouldn't have any performance if you lost an engine.

The orders: first trip for me would be at 2:00 A.M. Someone shook me out of my sleep at one o'clock. It was raining, I could hear it on the roof. Russ Morris, my copilot, sleepily crawled out of his sack. The radio operator, Louie LaFrank, would be at operations—Ops.

I looked into the night: rain, visibility poor, certainly not much ceiling. To Russ: "Looks pretty low."

"Yup—wonder how that clunk will climb with 32,000?"

"Not snappy, for sure. You remember what the terrain is like around here? Weren't there some hills off to the east?"

"I think so."

I was thinking I'd have to study a local chart of some sort. Going off in this weather we'd be blind soon after takeoff, and I was interested in climbing swiftly away from the earth and any obstructions—knowing, too, that our climb rate at 32,000 pounds would resemble that of a ruptured duck.

We got lined up and ready to go. The landing lights poked ahead through the darkness, making the raindrops shine like bright streaks. It was misty, and the runway disappeared into blackness not far ahead. In the fuselage behind us was iron pipe and a mass of boxes; we weighed 30,800 pounds—not up to the 32,000, but two and a half tons more than the airline 25,200. It was cold comfort.

"Well, here goes nothin'."

The throttles came up and the snarl of the engines with them, and the small front door on the right rear of the cockpit buzzed. It connected us to something we knew, almost like hearing encouragement from a friend—all DC-3 front doors buzzed on takeoff. The runway moved in toward us and we accelerated.

The apprehension of weight, strange country, hills hidden out there in the darkness, and what in God's name you'd ever do if an engine quit—all that subsides and your attention turns to flying: airspeed, pulling gently back and feeling the airplane lift, eyes dropping from the windshield and the runway ahead to the instruments, the artificial horizon, and directional gyro—wings and nose position, direction. The big airplane was controlled via these two instruments about four inches across, just those with their spinning gyros inside, some gears and levers, the whole ball game depending on how they move and how two eyes, hands, and feet respond to them. There's no use looking out, because there's nothing: rain across the windshield, and blackness; all reference to the world is in the instruments, your connection with reality.

The rate of climb didn't seem too bad, we were gradually crawling our way up and away from the earth with its hills, trees, and man-made towers. We climbed through 2,000 feet, and as I settled back in the seat, relaxation flowed through my body and the wild snarl of engines calmed to a more tranquil beat as I pulled back the throttles and propellers to climb power.

"Not too bad," I said to Russ.

"Naw, but it wasn't sparkling, either."

We leveled off at 6,000 feet. Turning on the landing lights, the precipitation zinged at us in streaks—at the higher, colder altitude it was snow, but it wasn't sticking. With the light off we were back in our little capsule.

The capsule—the cockpit—is the same as it might be between St. Louis and Kansas City: instruments saying we're level, directional gyro showing where we're headed. That heading would be something like 278 degrees on the flight west across Missouri, but here it was 61 degrees because we were headed northeast. Was that the only difference? The sky was the same, the snow falling outside like any snow, the problems the same: did we have enough fuel to make Goose Bay from Presque Isle—or Kansas City from St. Louis—and fuel to go to an alternate? If we got ice, it would be ice—if we were heckled by thunderstorms somewhere, they'd be the same. The distances might be further, alternates less available, but you plan for all that every time you fly.

And that was what war did to spread our wings: we realized that flying was flying, and it wouldn't make any elemental difference where you flew. The differences were the unusual destinations, some of them exotic; the arithmetic was simply other numbers, longer distances mostly; climate and weather were more or less severe, but it was weather, just like in Kansas, California, or New York.

The airplane is a creature of the air, what's under it is of little importance, and this we learned during the war. Before the war, we thought a dream route was Albuquerque to Los Angeles, though Pan Am was flying

Clippers across the seas. But after the war we knew that you didn't need a flying boat to cross an ocean, land planes could do it, and better. It made the airplane's ability unlimited, unrestricted; it is why the globe today is crisscrossed with air routes, no spot on earth uncorrupted. Some of this started sinking in that night on the flight to Goose Bay.

The unusual part was navigation, because we wouldn't be pampered with radio beams and beacons; it would be dead reckoning and celestial if the stars were out. There would be hours of uncertainty, not knowing our position, how fast the airplane was going, all of which related to the fuel remaining and whether it would be enough to reach the destination—assuming you could find it. We'd have to reach back to pull up some old-style barnstorming tricks.

Dawn changed the world from black to gray, and we found we were between two layers of clouds. The snow had stopped and the visibility between the layers was good. The static ceased and the Goose range came in and we flew along it, just as you would going into Pittsburgh. The problem now was that Goose weather was reported as 200-foot ceiling, and the minimums the army had established were 800 feet.

The approach wasn't easy because the range didn't line up with the runway, so you had to let down, break out, and then make a turn to line up with the runway—a procedure considered only marginally safe. Well, we'd try it anyway; the rules weren't going to be enforced as they would be in the States on the airline. At 500 feet there were glimpses of the Hamilton River and a jack pine forest, so we gingerly poked on down some more—a nervous way to operate, but this was war, and you felt duty-bound to stick your neck out a bit further. Finally we were under the clouds, almost on the treetops, but visibility wasn't too bad; a steep turn, gear and flaps down, and we were rolling along the gravel runway.

Now it seemed like war, though we were thousands of miles from enemy fire: olive drab airplanes on the field in big numbers, people and equipment in hurried motion. A truck backs up, unloads us; we get gas and are off, back to Presque Isle for another load. That was the first trip, an introduction to wartime.

Then a flight to Gander, Newfoundland, over more water, with less radio navigation help. There was a navigation station built into the airplane, with a small table, celestial sight reduction books, an almanac, and an astrodome (a transparent dome sticking up through the airplane's fuselage where one could hold a sextant and see all the sky for a shot; in effect your head was outside the airplane, though protected inside the bubble). A sextant and astrocompass for use in the dome were secure in a small compartment; the problem was that I didn't know how to use them. While I'd always been fascinated by the science of navigation and studied it diligently, I didn't know celestial—why would I need it between Kansas City and Albuquerque? So all this wonderful paraphernalia sat mute and unused.

The world became the cockpit of a C-47 and the base at Presque Isle; fly, then come back to eat, sleep, or sit around and swap experiences. Red (Arthur) Foster had a scare at Goose Bay: when he got over Goose the ceiling was 100 feet, too low to land, but the copilot had misused the fuel valves so Red didn't have enough to get back to Presque Isle.

"What'd ya do, Red?"

"What do you think—I landed the son of a bitch—and get me a new copilot before I kill this one." He'd done a masterful, risky job with only a glimpse here and there of anything useful, but risk wasn't new to Red; he'd been an exhibition parachute jumper before joining the airline.

The problem of navigation was on everyone's mind. There were large, empty periods en route when we didn't know where we were, periods when we squirmed in the seat wishing for a glimpse of the earth, or a radio sound that told position or progress. During times like those, sweating it out, your imagination could conjure up all kinds of things. One such tense and nervous pilot was flying in clouds, blind; then a break came through the cloud layers and he could see the earth, but he didn't see land, only water. It seemed a large expanse through the break in the clouds, and then the clouds closed up again. What in hell expanse of water was between Goose and Presque Isle? None, God, we must be over the ocean, blown there by a freakish wind. A feeling of panic and fear—what to do? Reason says if you're over the ocean, head west toward land. So he took up a westerly heading and flew, blind and waiting for another glimpse of something. Finally the clouds broke and the sky cleared—he'd flown out of the weather. There was land below, but where? The fuel was almost gone, so landing was imminent and urgent. A big pasture stretched out below so he landed on it, successfully except for going down to the wheel hubs in wet ground.

Where was he? It turned out he was west-northwest of Montreal!

But what about that ocean seen through the cloud breaks? It wasn't the ocean, but the St. Lawrence River. On a direct flight from Goose to Presque Isle one crosses the river where it's seventy land miles wide. In poor visibility, looking straight down through broken, misty clouds, it can look like an ocean—especially when one is spooked by uncertainty, and your imagination's running wild. It took two weeks to get the airplane out of that soggy field and back in operation.

The Battle of Presque Isle, as we called it, lasted a couple of weeks. We were released from the duty and returned to airline flying—we had never officially been in the army.

Regular airline flying didn't feel the same anymore; I was thinking about the activity up north, east, and all over the world in olive drab. To own up to reality, I wanted to be part of it; there was a war going on where the flying was exciting and different. I knew damn well we'd somehow be called on to mix our airline experience with old tricks, and to develop ways to cope with a kind of flying we'd never dreamed of; we were being pushed into the future and didn't know it.

For sure, no matter what, I figured I'd better learn celestial navigation.

Celestial was a mystery: spherical trig, learning stars and planets, hour angles, a bundle of strange stuff.

There were no schools available so I found some books, purchased a very simple learner's sextant with a bubble on it, shut myself up, and went to work. Days later I surfaced with an understanding of celestial and an angry feeling, because when I finally broke through the mystery I found that all you needed was some common sense and the ability to do simple addition and subtraction. Why in hell had they made it so complicated? It wasn't Nathaniel Bowditch's classic tome on navigation that clued me in, but a simple slim book by Commander P. V. H. Weems. From it I learned that time and longitude are related, and a celestial fix is a backward way of saying you aren't where you thought you were, but a precise distance and direction from it; celestial isn't some magic way of always knowing where you're going, but an additional aid mixed in with other information you can study and digest. It boils down to using experience, judgment, and a bit of hunch—sometimes referred to as art—for the final run at your destination.

Now when flying the line on flights to Chicago, Kansas City, and other places I lugged my simple sextant and Drisenstock's thin little black book of navigation tables for sight reduction, as working out a celestial line is called. Of course we knew where we were, but I wanted to practice celestial. Up in the cockpit, much of the sky above was cut off from view by the airplane's structure—line DC-3s don't have an astrodome you can see the high sky through. I did have a solution: the DC-3's toilet, way in the back, had a tiny window up above the pot, a slice of glass perhaps six inches by a foot. Through it I could see the high sky. So periodically I would walk back through the cabin, sextant in hand with notebook and watch, to disappear into the lavatory. I imagine the passengers wondered what mysterious thing the captain was up to.

Standing on the cover of the toilet, I aimed the sextant at a star, and by moving the sextant's index arm I brought the star down, as the expression goes, next to the bubble, which substitutes for a horizon—and then read the degrees by a vernier. (Horizons are used for shots from surface vessels, but in an airplane the horizon doesn't give the needed level reference, so we use a bubble instead.) The bubble on my sextant was crude, and since the back end of a DC-3 has a natural swaying motion, it was damn difficult to get the celestial body centered next to the bubble while perched on the john, which was swinging back and forth. I'd mark the time and degrees, which are called the star's altitude, on my notepad, return to the cockpit, and work out the sight. At home I stood outside many nights, taking sights. I had to learn stars' locations and names; the bright easy ones first, Arcturus, Vega, Sirius, Rigel, and Betelgeuse in Orion and the less brilliant North Star, Polaris, the navigator's friend because it's perched almost directly over the North Pole. Glancing at Polaris tells you where north is, and if you know where north is you've got navigation well under control. Polaris became a talisman, a reassurance up there in the north sky, ready to help. Whenever I go out on a clear night I look up at it and silently salute an old friend. Whoever created the universe and put Polaris over the North Pole did a big favor for those who traverse the sea and sky.

I didn't know when I'd need my new celestial skills, but they gave me one more area of knowledge to fall back on the next time I had to cross a dark and empty region without the aids I'd grown accustomed to.

CHAPTER 12

Intercontinental

W HEN THE WAR STARTED TWA had five Boeing Stratoliners, the transport developed from the B-17 bomber; same tail, wings, and landing gear. The fuselage was a big, fat, round one that was pressurized and could seat thirty-three passengers; it was the first pressurized airliner, and the first wide body. Four engines, of course.

The army quickly commandeered the Stratoliners, seeing their long-range possibilities, but it told TWA to operate them. They had to be modified for long-range operations, and the normal CAA rules went out the window; this was war. Extra fuel tanks went in, and the pressurization equipment, which was heavy, was removed; the TWA markings came off, replaced by camouflage color. The gross weight was raised from 44,000 pounds to 55,000. These fat airplanes really were the beginning of the Air Transport Command.

The operation started with our most senior pilots and flight engineers. Navigators and radio operators were added; they bravely crossed the North Atlantic, without previous experience, making stops at Gander and on to Prestwick, Scotland, learning as they went. The flights went where fuel, weather, and whoever was on board commanded: Montreal for Canadians, Chungking for Madame Chiang Kai-shek, and lots of North Atlantic crossings between the British Isles and Washington.

Captain Stan Stanton was on a westbound flight across the Atlantic when he popped out of clouds and saw below a sight that scared him stiff: a mass of ships in convoy. The rules were to stay away from convoys, but how can you when you're in clouds and can't see? The convoy orders were to shoot any aircraft overhead. Stan took a 75mm shell right up the rudder post, but despite holes and damage, he limped into Gander. The Stratoliner had enough B-17 heritage to stand up under fire.

These were not easy flights; they were pioneering, in the sense that we didn't know all that much about long-range flying over oceans. Many of the navigators had come from the sea and were accustomed to slow ships, not fast airplanes—although ours weren't very fast; we used 144 miles an hour for our indicated long-range airspeed, which is about 170 mph at 10,000 feet. Note I say miles per hour, not knots; in knots it would be 125. So the flights were long, some up to twenty hours.

The passengers were mostly generals and admirals, diplomats, and, on one flight, President Roosevelt en route to the Casablanca conference—but that was later on.

Our base was Washington, where we had a hangar and complete maintenance, as well as training and operations. New Douglas C-54s were just starting to come out of the factory, a four-engine ancestor of the DC-6 and DC-7: unpressurized, but faster and with longer range than the Boeings. ICD, for Intercontinental Division, as our operation was called, got some of the first, and an expansion started. Early on I was asked to transfer to ICD and be assistant to Joe Carr, the director of training, and to fly as well.

Washington was a busy, crazy place: masses of people, all kinds of uniforms, housing impossible. The pilots for our operation lived all over the United States—New York, Kansas City, even Los Angeles. They commuted to Washington, then flew a flight overseas, which could take a few days, or weeks, even months because once you were out of Washington there was no telling where you would go or how many flights between, say, Natal, Brazil, and Accra, in Ghana, or even on to Cairo, Egypt, before finally heading back to Washington and home for a rest.

Pilots came to Washington a couple of days ahead of the flight to be briefed, to gather the crew together and go over the coming mission, check maps and emergency supplies, be certain shots were up to date, and get a preflight physical. It seemed that for two days before each flight one was constantly going to meetings. Most of them were hush-hush, with thick security.

We'd obtained a suite of rooms in the Hotel Cairo, up on 16th Street; it wasn't the Ritz by any means, but it was useful for our purposes, for pilots checking in before a flight, or coming back for a night's rest after a flight. It became something like a college dorm, closets jammed with clothes (both civilian and uniform), stuff scattered about, not the neatest place by any means but tolerable.

Pilots getting ready to go out would corner pilots who'd just returned, to try to get information ranging from routes, weather, and navigation to where the action was in Natal. Each arrival had more or different information, and the comings and goings were a constant swap of the latest gen— a useful term we picked up from the Brits. (It came from "general information," and it consisted of a mixture of observation and gossip. If one said, "Duff gen," it meant the information was unreliable, but if one said, "Pukka gen," then you could take it to the bank.)

Then one day we were told we'd have to find different quarters, that the military had taken over the hotel. This was a disastrous development because there just weren't any accommodations in Washington. We went to work, somebody did, and convinced the powers that be that we were part of the war effort, too, and deserved proper quarters. The result was that we could stay in the hotel, but all other civilians had to go, and they did. The military filled the remaining rooms of the hotel with WAVES, female sailors! This created some very interesting situations and liaisons, not unpleasant by any count. The WAVES didn't stay long before being moved out and replaced by marines—but not ordinary marines, these were BAMs, as the slang went, broad-ass marines, i.e., female. So the interesting atmosphere was maintained.

We were a bastard lot because we weren't in any service and were still civilians. It took a while to figure out how to outfit us; we were going into war zones, so wearing suits and ties wasn't quite right, and neither were airline uniforms, so someone created a uniform much like army garb, but our wings, bronze in color, had the letters ATC in their center—Air Transport Command. We had strange black and silver-rimmed bars for rank on our shoulders, plus black stripes on the jacket sleeves.

While still not in the army, we had privileges including the PX stores, army mess, quarters, and the rest. Because we were civilians there was the possibility that if captured we might be shot as spies; to blunt this I carried, as did the others, a letter saying I wasn't a civilian, but in the service of the army, and if captured I was to be given the same treatment as a U.S. Army major. To the best of my knowledge, no ATC pilot was ever captured and forced to see if this letter would have the desired effect.

It was time to go off and see what was out there. My first trip was actually as copilot, but acting as captain. It was a familiarization flight, with a pilot who'd been over the route a few times showing me the ropes—Earl Fleet, an old-timer I knew well. Today, on commercial airlines, such a flight is called IOE, for initial operating experience.

We did all the briefings and preparation, and finally on the morning of February 6, 1943, we gathered the crew together and marched into our airplane, a new C-54. The passengers were army men with ranks from private to general, the destination Africa via South America.

As we gathered and got aboard, we could feel that this wasn't any DC-3 Chicago-bound. The airplane was larger, the inside spartan, the floor uncarpeted and solid for cargo when carried. There wasn't the usual colorful array of passengers; everything seemed tan or brown. Faces were unsmiling and serious. I felt it, recognized my entry into a new domain with a mixed sense of unfamiliarity, a slight fear of the unknown ahead, and a small question about my competence for this different world of flight.

Our first leg was to Miami, and quickly the art of flying reasserted its most basic premise, that an airplane is an airplane, large or small. It was a routine flight with some instrument weather, but nothing serious. Miami felt warm, tropical, and good after gloomy Washington.

Then, in the dark, off at 3:30 A.M. for Trinidad, loaded to maximum, across Miami Beach and out to sea. The water wasn't visible, just the darkness. I knew the water was below, and that old nervousness instilled in my early flight to Cuba crept in; being over water with no place to land was always a little uncomfortable. I knew I was fortified by more reliable engines, and there were four of them out on the wings, pounding away reassuringly; if one stopped the other three would keep us airborne, and even if two failed we'd be okay. So why worry? Because old obsessions don't die easily; for many years, after hundreds of ocean crossings, that old apprehension still crept into my subconscious at stressful times. Although this grew less and less frequent with time, it was never completely subdued until I was flying the jet-powered airplane, with its almost perfect engine reliability.

The air that night was smooth, the temperature pleasant, stars above; a beautiful night. The worries did not consume my thoughts. With war upon us there would be a lot of oceans to cross, and logic said I might as well sit back, relax, and enjoy the ride because there was nothing I could do about it.

As dawn came I was flying when the dark form of Haiti grew ahead: green mountains, jungle, the excitement of seeing an exotic place that had only been an island on a map before. This was something else the war gave us: familiarity with distant places, terrains, climates, people of different races, colors, and creeds. We didn't realize it, but we were opening the door to one world.

Beyond Haiti the open ocean again, blue with whitecaps and swells that gave a breathing motion to the sea. I studied it, learning to read the direction of the wind not simply for navigation, but on the off chance we might have to ditch in the sea. It was a careful study, visualizing which way to land along the waves and swells, where best to touch down. There was no immediate problem, I was simply studying this to develop a plan in case we ever needed one.

Finally, mountains ahead, a dark form in the distance that broke the monotony of water and waves. Then land and our destination, Port of Spain, Trinidad.

As you descend to land, the ground and its features develop—a beach, palm trees, fields, jungle—but it's impersonal, still a picture. Then, on the ground, taxiing to a parking spot, more detail: people, buildings, the minutiae of the palm trees, but still a picture. You park and shut down the engines, secure the cockpit, and slide open a window. Suddenly it's no longer just a picture; the warm tropical breeze flows through the open window bringing its softness and perfume. In an instant you're pulled from the impersonal perch of the airplane to become part of the place you've landed, now Trinidad and the tropics. Airplanes do that: you spend hours looking at a picture and then, almost instantly, you enter the picture and become part of it.

Miami was ten hours behind us. We slept in Trinidad and then, at 3:30

A.M., took off, heading south to Belém, Brazil. Time of day means nothing, except it seems we fly more in the vacant hours of night than day. We settled down after takeoff, and the front end was quiet, the bunks full with off-duty crew members, including Captain Fleet. As this was a familiarization ride, not a proficiency check, it effectively was a two-captain crew, so one of us could rest without concern as to how things were going.

I flew because I was interested and wanted to see it all. In the dark there was nothing to see, just night much the same as between Kansas City and Albuquerque. But dawn came, rather quickly as it does in the tropics, and as dark receded below, long shadows became short and soon the earth was fully revealed: jungle, the trees from our altitude seeming all of the same height, giving a flat top to the miles of green; patches of eerie fog draped over trees, hanging down between them. The green canopy was vast, unbroken to the horizon.

As the sun rose higher and the earth heated, cumulus clouds developed, materializing like scattered popcorn. I flew at 9,000 feet, which at first topped the clouds, but soon they reached my altitude and I wove around them to avoid bumps.

I searched ahead for more clouds because I knew we would inevitably have to transit the Intertropical Front. This is the place where the southeast trade winds meet the northeast trade winds, shoving into each other, converging and lifting the hot, humid air so that thunderstorms form. Technically it's called the Intertropical Convergence Zone, but during the war that fancy appellation hadn't been created and it was the Intertropical Front, feared by all, and especially the newly trained army pilots ferrying their aircraft to South America, Africa, and the action. It wasn't tossed off lightly by experienced pilots, either.

I was not disappointed. The clouds built higher, scattered became broken, and finally before me was a solid line of cumulus clouds that towered to tremendous heights, far higher than our aircraft could climb; this front is known to create storms that reach 65,000 feet!

We were over unending jungle, facing a front as we had many times at home, but this one was far from any place to land or run to, thousands of miles from familiar territory, and I didn't know what was inside those massive boiling clouds. Such a front in the United States would be rife with severe turbulence, and I expected this one would, too. I explored right and left, trying to make an end run, looking for a break in the clouds, but there was none. Well, there comes a time and this was it: tighten belts, turn up cockpit lights to prevent a close bolt of lightning from blinding me, slow to the best turbulence speed, and wade in.

There wasn't the big feeling of lifting as we came close, as in a Kansas storm; a few jolts and then rain, rain so concentrated it inundated the aircraft, we felt more like a submarine than an airplane. Turbulence was, at worst, moderate—enough to have me toward the edge of the seat expecting something unpleasant to cut loose, but it never did. The rain finally slackened, breaks in the cloud mass appeared ahead, and before long we had shaken loose of the front.

But the Intertropical Front isn't like one in the United States, where the weather clears behind it; the Intertropical Front goes on for a few hundred miles dotted with thunderstorms to weave around, and they occasionally line up as a front. Although I had wilder rides through the Intertropical Front on other flights, none were as tough as what I found in the American Midwest. There's a reason: tropics don't have those contrasting air masses we have in our Midwest, the cold air from Canada flowing southward to confront warm air from the Gulf of Mexico. The meeting creates a violent battle of weather. But here, the tropic air on both sides of the front is much the same, with little contrast.

The Intertropical Front does terrify you visually because of its height and solidity. It claimed the life of many pilots, trained for war, new to the game, who tried to duck and weave away from the front and got lost over the jungle, or flew too low trying to go under it. I felt for them deeply and wished I could inject experience into their minds.

After the front we crossed the Amazon: jungle, water, islands in the river and miles of it, 200 miles where we traversed. The Mississippi seemed a creek compared to it.

Then landing at Belém, a fair-sized city, but to us only an airport cut out of the jungle. We had lunch while the airplane was being refueled. The place we ate had a low roof and screened sides so I almost felt outside, but this allowed a breeze to flow through and make the tropical air less pressing. Mostly I recall a few bowls of shelled Brazil nuts on the table—this is where they come from—the nuts warm with some sort of oil over them so they shone. They were very, very good.

Off Belém, the jungle gradually changed to a somewhat sandy coastline. It was boring and I was tired—I took to the bunk almost until we landed in Natal. Our flight times: six hours forty-five minutes Trinidad to Belém; five hours forty-five minutes to Natal.

✶

NATAL SITS on the tip where South America juts out toward Africa. We were in Brazil, but the wartime airport was all American: airplanes, tents, barracks, outdoor GI movies, mess building, and more. The landscape was stripped of verdure, a wasteland existing only so airplanes could come and go bound for war or supplying it; military vehicles from Jeeps to gas trucks scurried here and there kicking up dust. We might as well have been on the moon.

We civilians were lodged in a compound in town called the Staff House—someone's large home, with a central courtyard and surrounded by a high wall, Spanish style. A huge mango tree kept out the sun and gave a dark, cool feel to the place. There was a big cage next to the mango tree that housed a spider monkey, fox, armadillo, four marmoset monkeys, and five parrots. The big, mean spider monkey harassed and abused all the others; there was constant action and noise.

The house was big, with many rooms where we slept on cots under mosquito nets. One room was set aside for a poker game that always seemed in session; being a poor gambler I only observed the serious action except for one half-hour session of blackjack in which I lost $3. But there were high rollers around, and paychecks often lay on the table covering a bet.

The Staff House was filled with civilian crew members from various airlines, all doing the same thing we were: coming, going, or just waiting. We seemed to wait a lot. Airplanes frequently sat immobile getting mechanical repairs or waiting for a part from the States. Pilots came in whom you hadn't seen for years; one day my old friend Ernie Gann came through the screen door swinging his B-4 bag—a GI clothes bag we all had—calling out greetings and exclaiming with a laugh to anyone listening, "What the hell's this all about?"

A shuttle bus took us to the airport where we could eat in the army mess, go to a movie, or poke around trying to find out when your next flight would be and where.

There was a downtown Natal, a typical hot, tropical town. The center was a hotel and its veranda where we sat and watched the local action—people going by on foot, burro, or automobile, all very basic. Hawkers worked the street, their big item being handmade leather boots that they urged us to buy, and we did. The boots were about ten inches high, yellow, and made from buffalo hide. They squeaked, so we all squeaked walking around; mine never fit and squeezed my right foot, with its bunion, so excruciatingly that I threw them away.

The nightly diversion was a cabaret called the Wonder Bar. Tables, drinks, linoleum decor, a small noisy band, and hostesses thickly made up, dressed in shiny bright-colored dresses, an occasional flash of gold adding to their toothy smiles. They sat and drank with the customers and, if their lure worked, slipped with them behind curtains into a back room—pretty much a worldwide modus operandi. Crew members didn't respond, more scared stiff of disease than out of moral values. The activity was amusing to see, but the place was technically off limits—if MPs showed up there was a mad scramble to get out; one of my cohorts dove out a rear window not realizing he was on the second floor, but luckily the building was next to a river into which he splashed unharmed.

We were scheduled to continue east, to Africa. After false starts for five nights thanks to mechanical problems, we finally took off in a Boeing Stratoliner, the old airline aircraft. Pitch-black dark, a long run to get in the air, bumping down the runway, only the runway lights visible; then the smoothness of flight, a turn to the east and within minutes we're over the ocean pointed toward Ascension Island, a nine-mile-long dot in the South Atlantic 1,950 miles ahead. The island is about 700 miles northwest of St. Helena, where Napoleon finished out his days.

Ascension was a stopping point for fuel en route to Africa, and for a tiny island it was a busy place. The trick was to find it. Radio helped, but it took careful navigation just to get within hearing distance of the radio guidance.

We ground through the night, lights low, conversation almost nil until the navigator leaned forward and told us he was desperately ill. Bad food had gotten him, the illness severe enough that he couldn't function, and he slumped to the floor, lying there emitting foul odors, unable to work. At that moment my effort to train myself in navigation became useful; the flight engineer moved into my seat and I fell to the task of taking celestial sights, plotting our way until Ascension radio came in. It wasn't difficult because the night was clear, the air smooth. I felt pretty damn satisfied.

Dawn broke over the sea, the surface light shining blue. Ascension's signals came in loud and clear and close to our estimate; a dark lump appeared dead ahead on the horizon and grew into an island, one that poked up out of the sea like an inverted cone, its highest elevation about 2,800 feet. Man and dynamite had blasted a runway through the cone, and we landed with rock cliffs on either side of the airplane. In the parking area the usual gas trucks and vehicles moved about; a fuel truck pulled up and, with help from Harry Young, our flight engineer, started pouring in fuel. The idea was to get out as fast as possible and head for Accra in Ghana, in order to get there before dark—why it had to be daylight is lost in time, but we had to go.

The navigator revived after the local medic gave him some pills. We rolled down the runway with its hills on each side, lifted off, and immediately were out to sea, bound for Africa. It seemed as though we'd only glimpsed Ascension, but we weren't there to sightsee, and we were in a race with the sun.

A few built-up cumulus clouds dropped rain, but we wandered easily between them. Sextant sights on the sun helped our navigation. One passenger, a major who flew pursuits, visited the cockpit and we talked airplanes. He was bright-eyed, quick, smart.

"Would you like to fly this thing?"

"Sure would."

He slipped into Fleet's seat, took the wheel, and seemed right at home, flying well. The blue sea below, smooth air, sun beating in the windows, the cockpit warm; it was difficult to stay awake, and we dozed like old dogs in the sun while the major flew.

The hours ground away, and finally a line of cumulus clouds ahead announced we were approaching land; then the dark form of terrain, hills, a coastline, beach, and the airport not far inland. We had beaten the sun by a good margin.

The runways were black asphalt laid across red soil, not unlike Georgia. Tall anthills—maybe ten feet high—dotted the meager grass area off the runway's side. Then we parked at the ramp, more GIs and parked airplanes, natives helping with the heavy work, loading, unloading, the eternal gas truck pulling up as we gathered our bags and climbed down a ladder to the ground.

So this was Africa, not Pittsburgh or Chicago; our set ideas of what we might experience in a lifetime had changed, differences between places and people were less surprising, the unique was becoming normal, and flying would never be the same again.

Looking around I didn't see Tarzan, or Stanley and Livingstone; but it was Africa all right: black people dressed in cloth slung around their upper bodies like shawls, on the move over red dirt roads, on bare feet or riding burros, perhaps a scrawny horse-drawn cart overflowing with possessions; dilapidated automobiles, and a few good ones; a tangle of high-pitched voices using a language unknown to us, not one word comprehensible; dust, and an alien smell from strange burning wood.

This was where the slave trade had ignominiously flourished, with European nations vying for rights and territory. The Danes were here and built Christiansborg Castle, but the British finally won out; we could feel an overtone from the British colonial days.

We were billeted in British-built barracks, a room for each crew member and a boy to take care of us. Mine was a smiling youth with big white teeth and an infectious laugh. I paid him a pound a day, which brought serious admonitions from the Brits for being far too much, but I didn't change the amount, and I had a gleeful feeling that I was upsetting the colonials, whose day wasn't that far past.

It seemed we'd be here for a few days, and Earl announced he wanted to search for native dolls to bring home to his daughters in Kansas City—one of the rituals of his travels.

Earl appropriated a small Ford automobile, a native driver, and an extra can of gasoline probably drained from the gas tank sump of some airplane. The driver spoke English, but not in sentences, just one word at a time for the entire communication, embellished with gestures to fill out the meaning.

We went to two or three villages before we found the dolls; they were not on display for tourists, but they appeared after much talk and running about by the residents, and they were finally offered by women who came from one of the huts. They were chunks of wood carved in primitive fashion to resemble a child; Earl brought two and I one. Later on I learned these dolls were for mothers who had lost a child, an image to cuddle until the sorrow subsided. That spooked me, and I always had an unpleasant feeling when I saw it on the bookshelf at home. A friend, enthusiastic about primitive art, raved about my possession; I shoved it toward him, saying, "It's yours," relieved to have it gone.

We waited three days, then back to Natal in one of the old Boeings; a light load made it possible to go nonstop. Off Accra, we skinned the coast for a while and then out to sea, a wide sea that would not end until we crossed the beach at Natal. The cockpit was dull, sleepy, grinding through the sky hour after hour, fourteen and a half of them, with little demand for nervous alertness except for a few rain showers; a bump or two, a splatter of rain on the windshield, then out the other side into a peaceful sky. We landed in Natal at mid-morning.

Natal felt familiar now, the busy airport, Staff House, people we knew, the routine known. Breakfast, then into bed under a mosquito-netting canopy and quickly into deep sleep.

We settled down to waiting, and with idleness came rumors: we were going back to Accra, to shuttle back and forth for three months, or we were going to Accra and then across Africa to Cairo, but suddenly orders came to return to Washington—so much for the rumors.

Off Natal at midnight in a C-54 headed for Georgetown, British Guinea (now Guyana), on the north coast of South America. I flew because Earl was ill with some bug that had knocked him flat—he crawled into a bunk, not caring about anything except getting home.

Our course was inland because of reported German submarine activity along the coast; one of our C-54s had disappeared, never arriving in Natal. We flew into dark nothingness until we came face-to-face with our old adversary, the Intertropical Front. I approached cautiously looking for an easy way through as lightning illuminated the sky, but blocking our path was a cloud mass impossible to go around, get under, or fly over, so we plowed in at 10,000 feet. Instantly we were pelted with rain so heavy I wondered how the engines could continue running and swallow such a torrent of water. The turbulence was moderate, not severe enough to scare anyone, but enough to keep me on the edge of my seat. The action was constant; moving controls, maintaining heading and altitude, but not fighting up- and downdrafts enough to strain the airplane—let it go with the flow, gaining or losing 500 to 1,000 feet in undulating flight.

Where the airplane can take us is not just impressive, but frightening as well—so small a vehicle compared with the forces of nature around you and the vast unfriendly terrain below. Only a few feet below my chair is the thin skin of the airplane; on one side are wires, tubes, and the airplane's innards, but a fraction of an inch away is the outside, a rush of wind and rain tearing across the smooth metal skin. The darkness, the rain, the bombardment by lightning, the turbulent air in this cloud mass—this was truly a place man was not born to. But we think little about this, since too much thought would create useless anxiety. Earl certainly didn't think about it; he stayed in the bunk with his illness, never coming forward to see how we were doing.

Three hours after dawn we landed at Georgetown, an interesting airport hacked out of the jungle. The taxiways were paths through the jungle, and the airplane seemed to be taxiing among the trees that towered higher than the airplane. Tropical plants hung from the trees and flashes of color flew through the tangled growth—exotic birds, disturbed by our passage.

Our stay was short—breakfast and off to Miami. The feeling of heading home lightened our thoughts: past Trinidad, over the Caribbean, Haiti again, the Bahamas and then Miami, the U.S.A.; nine and a half hours from Georgetown, nineteen hours flying time from Natal, all in one day. The airline limit of eight hours in any one day had been blitzed by war, as were many old conservative ideas and rules, most to become the norm again after the war as international commercial flying grew. The next day it was back to Washington; my indoctrination was over.

CHAPTER 13

Across the North Atlantic

URING THE WINTER the North Atlantic was closed to us because, the story goes, a general flying a cargo version B-24 had run into severe icing and almost spun into the sea. He said no more North Atlantic flights until spring—everything would have to go via South America and Africa.

Joe Carr was back running training and I was available for flight. Swede Golien, the chief pilot, called me into the office.

"They're opening the North Atlantic. How do you feel about being the first one?"

"Hell, I've never flown the North Atlantic."

"I know, but I'd like you to take the trip."

"Well, if you're willing to send me I'm willing to go."

That was it, except he added that I'd be checking a new captain. So not only was I making my first command North Atlantic flight I was also to check another pilot. War makes for strange situations.

We did all the preflight routines and I met the pilot I was to check, Bud Russell, a bush pilot from Maine who decided he wanted to get into the war effort and signed on with us. A rugged, gentle man with good flying skills—when the war ended he went right back to Maine and the bush.

I was a little spooked about the flight, mostly because April isn't summer or even spring on the North Atlantic; and as we confirmed in later years, April is one of the worst weather months out there.

I went to a movie the night before departing to sort of relax and get away from thinking about the coming flight, but I wasn't let off that easy: the newsreel's lead story was about violent storms on the North Atlantic. I squirmed in my seat looking at pictures of tremendous seas, wind, and rain taken from a heaving boat. My concerns went up about three levels.

Washington to Gander, with a stop at Presque Isle, was easy, little weather. After landing at Gander we headed for the weather office; me, copilot, and navigator, all quiet, each with his thoughts about the deep mysterious ocean out there beyond the rocky shore. The meteorologist pointed with the stem of a vile-smelling pipe at what was out there. The data had big empty spaces, places where little was known about the present conditions. Because of the lack of actual reports, the met man had to do some educated guessing: yes, there was a front out there, probably some ice in it, whether light or severe not known. The forecast for our destination, Prestwick, Scotland, was good; that was the only solid fact.

We were airborne at 2330 Greenwich time—everything was Greenwich time, or Z time as it was called. In the black night we climbed to 7,000 feet, weather clear except for some high thin cirrus clouds well above us as we crossed the coast and headed out. We settled into a peaceful weather-free flight. The stars were bright and a celestial fix showed our speed as 240 knots, temperature outside 38°F, a pleasant no-ice surprise. Light rain showers fell from a cloud deck above us, but mostly we were between layers of clouds with a temperature of 40 degrees—lots warmer than expected; 400 miles off Ireland the upper cloud deck cleared out and the lower deck became scattered. It remained benign the rest of the way to Prestwick, where we landed at 9:30 A.M. in sunshine. The trip had been a piece of cake, except for the disquieting periodic rough running of engines Numbers 2 and 3 that was chronic in the early C-54s. Later, when I'd had much more experience crossing the North Atlantic, I would learn what an exceptional trip this had been, the ease of it; others to come would be much different.

Scotland meant soft coal fires, the air raw, cold stone buildings, nice people. We were billeted in a small hotel, the St. Nick, a stone structure, small rooms furnished with solid chairs and rockers, rugs, bric-a-brac on a small circular table with a lace doily in the reception room, a coal-burning fireplace, a kind of musty smell. My room: cold, with a single bed, thick pillow, wool blankets heavy on one's body but friendly. I snuggled down and fell asleep immediately; in that solid bed, the North Atlantic behind me, responsibility removed, I slept for fourteen hours.

So ended my first trip across the North Atlantic, one I'd desired since age sixteen when I dreamed of flying nonstop from New York to Geneva, the city where my grandmother was born. That never came to pass. Could I have made it? On a night like we just had, I surely could have.

Another wait, this time four days, but Scotland was different; despite the war, food rationing, blackouts, and people on the move, there were things to see—we made a pilgrimage to Ayr, to the Robert Burns museum and a look at the Bridge—Brig o' Doon—only they say it differently; flowers, holly hedges, lovely country.

When do I go back to Washington? You don't, you go to Marrakech in Morocco! We were fighting Rommel in North Africa; people and supplies were going in, and action, action everywhere. We carried cargo and personnel.

Europe was still in German hands, so our trip from Scotland to Africa was heavy with security and a devious route: from Prestwick southwest, out to sea, to longitude 15 W, which put us about 400 miles off Brest, France; after passing Portugal the course came back southeast to Africa.

I checked weather at 1800. The weather office was located in a country home, down a lane, past a pretty garden—very unwarlike, but the house was filled with phones, radio equipment, weather maps, people, activity. All sense of a peaceful country home was gone, but I could still see the lovely interior woodwork, the window that looked out on a garden, and behind it a hedgerow and field with grazing sheep.

I received my security briefing; there was a sheet with codes for various times of the day, so if challenged we could flash our Aldis lamp with the proper dots and dashes for that time period or fire a Very pistol through a hole rigged into the floor of the airplane for that purpose. The pistol fired flares with balls of different colors and sequence: midnight until 3:00 A.M., for example, might require a flare with balls of green, green, then red; another time might be red-green-red; a different sequence for each time period. We were very careful to have this correct for obvious reasons. On the same night we flew to Marrakech, the actor Leslie Howard was lost on a flight to Lisbon—the story we heard was that his pilot had codes for the wrong day and when challenged, he replied inaccurately and was shot down. That's the story that went the rounds, true or not.

We took off at 2110—9:10 P.M. I saw a few boats and a flare go off below in the Firth of Clyde, so we flashed our Aldis lamp showing the dots and dashes of the code for that time so we wouldn't be mistaken for a German bomber.

Full moon, a beautiful night as we flew down the 15th meridian. The sea was dark below. All the cabin windows were blacked out. The radio operator wasn't transmitting, but he listened, searching the frequencies for something useful such as a weather report. The crew seemed to become part of the dark; we didn't quite whisper, but our conversation seemed lower pitch and less than normal. Cockpit lights dimmed, we searched below, and suddenly a flare from the surface was followed by a burst of tracer bullets in an arc toward some unseen target—then darkness again, nothing more, all very eerie.

Then a ship, brilliantly lit and standing out in this piece of the sea active with war. As we got closer the reason stood out: it was a hospital ship, the red cross on its side visible from our altitude.

We ran into showers at about the point where we turned to head toward Africa, but despite some roughness in the Number 3 engine we got to Marrakech without incident. During the flight, Drew Middleton of the *New York Times* spent the last few hours with us in the cockpit. We had an interesting conversation about the war, rumors, mutual friends—the kind of thing that can happen far from home.

The hotel, the Mamounia, was big and first-class: brown-colored like the land around it, arches of Arab design, and a huge bougainvillea vine covering the front in full purple bloom. Over breakfast in a cool large room, I sat with Colonel Julius Holmes, an ex-diplomat who had been one of our passengers. He'd been in this land before and introduced me to yogurt, white in a small brown ceramic vessel.

This was my first experience in Arab lands. The strange sights of men dressed in caftans, flowing white cloth like a nightgown, walking with little donkeys that carried big loads of things; the market filled with noise, dirt, baskets, voices loud and high-pitched in throaty Arabic. I wandered through all this, looking, and having a fright when a cobra rose in swaying motion out of a basket right in front of me, mesmerized by the man with a flute. I backed up a few paces.

There's a big wall around the city, and everything has a feeling of antiquity that's very different from what you feel at George Washington's quarters in Morristown, New Jersey. This was really old. There was a garden at the hotel, the dominant growth tall bamboo, a maze of it to stroll through, a fountain, and after a curve in the path a secluded alcove and bench; quiet, cool, and restful, a place to sit and think about it all. I realized I was privileged, the feeling of antiquity strong, of a connection, a bridge to this very different world from the United States, one that commanded attention, thought, and study.

The trip back to Prestwick was delayed because of weather. The problem was a lack of weather reports over the Atlantic and Bay of Biscay; the met people took information from North Africa and the British Isles, along with reports from flights that had just come in from the north, and with that skimpy mishmash of information they drew weather maps and tried to make forecasts. That night a big low was centered over the ocean on our course—Operations said to cancel, and again the next night.

The third night wasn't much better, but there was an indication, perhaps an educated guess, that the low might be moving from the sea to France; another day's delay could assure a better situation, but I was anxious to go. The shaky forecast seemed worth a chance, and I talked them into releasing the flight.

But the low hadn't moved, my guess and theirs was bad. We ran into heavy cloud mass with rain, a long period of it. Navigation was by dead reckoning, which requires a combination of skill, guesswork, and luck. We had no star sights, hours went by, and dawn was approaching. In a desperation move I climbed, trying to get on top where we might see stars and get a fix. At 12,000 feet, the height at which oxygen was required, the top still wasn't in sight. The crew went on oxygen, but we lacked provisions for passenger oxygen; well, a little higher wouldn't hurt anyone if we didn't stay there too long.

At 17,000 feet we broke out, the stars visible but fading in the early dawn. The navigator quickly shot three of them. Another cloud deck filled the sky ahead, and in moments we slid into the grayness; ice started forming, and I descended, interested in finding the bottom of this mess. At 4,000 feet when we broke out of the steel gray stratus clouds, daylight was well on its way. As I searched sky and sea, trying to size up cloud formations and inferring the wind from the wave action below, the navigator came forward.

"I worked out the sight—you might be able to see Brest." We were way off course, and in the wrong direction, toward danger. I looked east for land, but instead I saw, flying just under the overcast a long way off but recognizable, a German Junkers JU-88! Fast reflex action: a firm tug and twist on the wheel to zoom us into the clouds and head west. We held that course away from France for thirty minutes and then we carefully sneaked down, slowly descending, staying in the ragged edge of the cloud's bottom, looking—nothing—then a sneaky further descent into the clear, all eyes searching for that Junkers. He was gone, the horizon clear in all directions. He probably never saw us.

From the star sight we knew our location, and after our thirty-minute westerly deviation we set a new course for Prestwick, landing early morning.

Where next? Back to the U.S.A.—not in one hop, but via Iceland—Meeks Field—Goose Bay, Labrador, then Washington. We're all ready, crew on board, and I stand at the bottom of the passenger steps to see who's coming along and I guess to greet them. I was startled to see Major General Ira C. Eaker approaching the airplane. Eaker was a hero to me, one I'd followed since childhood: he was a captain on the world record endurance flight in 1929, refueling to stay aloft 150 hours. The crew included Major Carl Spaatz and Lieutenant Elwood Quesada, all close friends working to create what would become the air force; their crude refueling, grasping a hose dangling from an aircraft close above, would evolve into the sophisticated probe poking into bombers and fighters enabling them to span the world in later years. Eaker was also a pilot on the Pan American goodwill flight in 1927, the first to circle Central and South America, landing at almost all the capitals; he was now major general and leader of our first daylight bomb effort to Europe, commander of the famous Eighth Air Force. Good Lord, here I was about to have this hero of my youth as a passenger! I was overwhelmed by the circumstance; I straightened up and saluted, and he returned the salute and stopped to chat for a moment.

"How's it look, Captain?"

"Fine, sir, we should have a good trip."

"You made many crossings?"

Well, what should I tell him? Might as well level.

"This will be my second crossing."

He never flinched. "I'm in good hands, I'm sure."

He climbed on and took one of the passenger seats—I went forward to the cockpit and settled in my seat. "We've got General Eaker on board," I announced to the crew. "He's one of the great ones."

The flight to Iceland was a breeze; little weather, on top most of the way, an easy approach and landing.

We got out of Iceland three hours late because the engines wouldn't start. Gasoline engines were temperamental at times when it was damp or cold. We had to change all the front spark plugs before they came to life.

On top of the clouds, but in daylight, so no star sights; we descended to 1,500 feet, under the clouds so the navigator could get a drift sight on the sea.

Flying under gray overcast with good visibility was fortunate, because south of Greenland we sighted a convoy, a big convoy—if we'd come upon it suddenly in poor visibility we would have caught hell, but we could see far enough ahead to go well around it. After another 100 miles we sighted a big oil slick on the surface and a large piece of wood floating. What had happened? Something desperate and tragic, the turmoil of war.

The ceiling lowered, and the sky structure of clouds reached above to regions where the temperature would cause icing. We stayed down low, really low, 500 feet above the angry, heaving sea; a strong south wind ahead of a front kept the temperature above freezing. It seemed crazy to be down at 500 feet, but there wasn't any icing, and the beauty of flying over an ocean is that there's nothing to run into, no mountains, and the highest thing is probably an iceberg.

Finally we faced the front and plowed into clouds and heavier precipitation; the temperature lowered and flying low was no longer so clever, so we climbed and hoped the ice above wouldn't be too bad. There was light rime ice at 4,500 feet; about 7,000 feet we clipped through the tops of ragged clouds, in and out of them with some ice, but they became orderly as we flew away from the front, finally becoming flat on top and well below us.

We stayed on top until about eighty miles from Goose Bay, when a big break in the clouds appeared. I could see down and the visibility was good with a reasonably high cloud base. We descended through the break and flew by visual contact through light showers to Goose. All during the flight the radio reception was a hashy, scratchy mess, impossible to read until about sixty miles from Goose. An hour and a half before Goose the Number 4 fuel pump failed and we continued on the standby electric, which we hoped would keep working because if it didn't the engine quits running. But it held to the task.

During all this General Eaker stayed in his seat in the back, even though I'd sent word that he was welcome in the cockpit anytime he wanted to come up.

On the ground he was busy with the Goose commanding officer, evidently an old friend. They disappeared in jovial fashion. He showed up when we were finally ready to go.

The engines acted up again in the cold of Goose Bay and didn't want to start. But Goose had equipment, so we put heaters on the engines, big gasoline-burning units that stood in front of each engine, a canvas hood leading from the heater to the engine. An hour of that and the engines started without balking.

The weather was fair between Goose and Presque Isle, and we flew in view of the earth. General Eaker wandered up front and stood awhile watching us; he remarked on the better weather, and said we'd done well in all the slop between Iceland and Goose. We didn't know then that our weather troubles weren't over.

Though not originally scheduled, we were ordered to make a short stop at Presque Isle to drop off a passenger. This we did in hasty fashion and without shutting down the engines to avoid the difficult starting business again.

We cleared Presque Isle for Washington. We'd been on duty a long time and we were tired, but pepped up with the fact we were on the last leg of this unusually miserable trip.

Shortly after takeoff we encountered snow, which hadn't been forecast. I tried to get weather information through our radios, but reception was nil. We were flying blind, in snow, not knowing what was ahead, without good radio reception for navigation.

There comes a decision moment in flying, when one suddenly knows what should be done and does it. When we had flown past Bangor, Maine, the snow hadn't started there yet and visibility was good; I decided to turn around and run back to Bangor, hoping to get there before any snow. We did and we landed.

The met office showed a warm front to the south that had the East Coast well socked in. As I stood over the weather map, studying the situation, Eaker stood by my side observing. I turned to him and said I was sorry, but the weather was really poor—not unflyable, but a tough outlook, and we were very tired; I felt it wise to hold until morning, get some rest, and hope this had all moved off by then.

"It's a good decision—you boys have had a long, hard flight—best we rested."

Relieved by his understanding, we held.

In the morning, daylight showed Bangor fogged in, almost zero-zero as I again stood in the weather office looking at reports and listening to the met lieutenant. His outlook was gloomy. Eaker stood behind me, silent but observing. Clouds above would be very high with ice in them, according to the met officer. Studying the map, I couldn't see his reasoning; it seemed obvious the warm front had gone through and we were in the warm sector— the fog outside was from nighttime cooling, and there was probably little cloud above the fog.

I turned to Eaker and the crew members with me and, trying not to insult the young lieutenant, said I thought we'd be okay, that in daylight we could cope with any ice—of course, I didn't really think there'd be any. The lieutenant shook his head and was doubtful about my intentions.

When I said we'd go, Eaker simply nodded.

At the end of the runway, ready for takeoff, we could only see a few hundred yards. Eaker had decided to watch the action and stood in the cockpit right behind me. I lined up carefully, made certain all the instruments were up to speed and reading correctly compared to the runway heading. Concentrating on the directional gyro to keep straight and on the runway, we raced into the fog—at liftoff speed I pulled back the wheel and we climbed, immediately becoming blind in the fog. At 1,000 feet the sky looked brighter, and at 1,500 feet we popped out on top of a white cloud blanket, no other clouds. The sun reflected brilliantly from the fog top below, above was only blue sky. I turned and smiled at Eaker, he patted my shoulder, turned around, and went back to his seat in the cabin. In a few hours we landed at Washington. It had been a rough trip, one of the worst I was ever to have. The good part was the time with General Eaker, even more now a man I admired and looked up to.

I spent the next seven months flying across the North Atlantic, to Marrakech, and once more to Natal, all under the Air Transport Command.

We were mostly carrying personnel, from civilians to generals and everyone in between. On our return flights, as the war progressed, our passengers were often battle veterans bearing physical or psychological wounds.

At Goose Bay we saw B-17s in great numbers headed for Europe and battle. The crews were fresh out of school, concerned about flying the ocean, and if they could corner you they'd ask about ocean flying. One nervous second lieutenant pushed up to me, nose-to-nose, scared, almost confrontational, "What's it like over the ocean, how do you fly it?" I tried to explain a few things, calm his fears, all I could do in twenty minutes.

One morning at Prestwick I stood outside, the day gray, visibility low, misty and cold. A B-17 group was arriving from Goose and I was out there to see the action. The action was wild, B-17s going in all directions like a covey of frightened birds in disarray, flying at treetop height. Prestwick's ground control, trying to show where the airport was, fired flares into the sky. It was an exciting, frightening time, but one by one they found the runway and landed; a few missed and landed at Ayr, an airport close by. These were the 200-hour kids fresh out of school, the ones who'd asked me at Goose Bay how to fly the ocean. They'd done it, and I was misty-eyed proud of them all.

I look through my logbook of the time, now fifty-five years later, and the terse scribbling brings back those periods of stress, action, and excitement:

May 6: Went to Goose, then off to BW-1 [in Greenland] between layers and on top; clouds broke up off Greenland, saw pack ice and icebergs and beautiful mountains with icecaps behind them. Went up fjord to field. Some fjord! [BW-1 was at the end of a fjord one had to fly up almost forty miles; near the end it forked, and it was crucial to pick the correct fork because the wrong one came smack up against a glacier with no room to turn around. Going up the fjord with low visibility was dicey; there was a small boat anchored off the end of the runway to help identify the airport, which started right at the water's edge.] Took off from BW-1 for Meeks, landed in good weather. Got set to leave for Prestwick, but engines would not start. Poor flight engineer changed three sets of plugs.

Army said Prestwick weather was bad and desired we wait. Hung out. Watched Tom Ward, one of our pilots, and crew play poker in the afternoon—impressive stakes. Bumped into Fred Koupal, old friend who told me about rescuing a B-17 crew who had landed on the icecap; they were flying on instruments in snow and mysteriously began to slow down, finally coming to a stop—they had flown, in flat cruise flight, onto the snow field, which looked just like the white snow they'd been flying in! Little damage, and none to the crew. They huddled in the airplane for a month with little food; finally a PBY amphibian landed in the snow with its wheels retracted in its flying boat mode, picked up the B-17 crew and took off. One crew member broke down in tears when they were picked up. What a story!

A later entry: Prestwick: Found big patch on right deicer boot that lifted up in a balloon fashion that was unacceptable for an ocean crossing; decided to fly, at reduced power, over to Langford Lodge in Ireland and have Goodrich company men at Lockheed plant fix it properly.

Weather was poor, but took off flying low under clouds in rain. Over the Irish Sea saw big splashes in water right below us, a moment later flew over a stripped float that was being towed; a target! The splashes were shells. I did a quick turn back to Prestwick. Irate, I went to the briefing room and asked what in hell was going on. Very calmly briefer said, "Oh yes, guess we didn't mention naval gunfire practice in that area."

May 26: Return flight from Natal: have some wounded men from North African campaign. Two gunners from a B-24; one had a 20mm shell explode next to his neck, spun him over, he remembers his feet going over. Wound in neck, and thought his arm was off, too; decided to end it all by not using oxygen—at 23,000 feet. A buddy pulled his arm, so he knew it was still there; got oxygen mask back on, blood froze and he stopped bleeding.

July 5: To Prestwick via La Guardia and Gander. Over Philadelphia Number 3 engine did not want to run. Landed at PG [Philadelphia] after feathering; checked plugs, rocker arms, and vent line, fixed vent line, and took off just ahead of a thunderstorm. In LG [La Guardia], short stop and out. Weather lousy through New England. Was guaranteed Gander would stay open, but had to make instrument approach down to 350-foot ceiling—didn't like it because nearest alternate was 1,000 miles away.

Passenger was Dick DuPont, an old friend from gliding. We talked gliders. He talked about glider towing for war; in bad weather they keep reference with the airplane by an indicator on the towline. [He was killed in a wartime glider.]

Talked with B-17 boys who had finished their missions, twenty-five raids. Major Martini of San Francisco in his B-17, *Dry Martini.* Prettiest thing is Focke-Wulf 190 slow roll into you for head-on shots. Talked of weird shots, like a headphone being knocked off an ear but no physical damage. Two hundred fighters at a time; bomber pilot has nothing to do on a bomb run when someone comes head-on but sit and take it, wishing he had a cannon or something to shoot with.

Out of Meeks for Goose, but right deicer boot lifting up and vibrating, returned to Meeks and took the boot off.

Talked to some of the combat crews we're taking back—they had fifty missions! Mostly in Sicily area. Even gunners were throwing bombs out the window, no air opposition at the end. A kick seeing bombs, guns from boats, and troops landing as the island gave up.

Test-hopped ship to see effect of one boot off—made ship slightly wing heavy, three on trim tab. Went to bed and slept twelve hours, but while sleeping Earl Fleet landed, blew a tire, and took one of mine. Looks like two days before I can get a replacement.

July 14: Back to Prestwick via Goose Bay. Landed at Goose and found hydraulic line leak. It had been temporarily fixed by welding on July 5 and returned to Washington where permanent repairs were to be made. They never were. Now the weld has parted and can't be welded again—so we wait for a new line from Washington. How do we win a war?

July 21: Prestwick westbound. Made low approach at Meeks to 500-foot ceiling. Off Meeks and through front in Denmark Strait. Another front south of Greenland; snow and light rime ice. Had Colonel Pennington for passenger—old army pilot; made first pickup from airplane by tight circle with dangling rope used to pick up a pail! Also a lieutenant who'd been a B-17 pilot in North Africa; last two raids had his ship on fire. He was a nervous wreck and almost had a fit every time we went on instruments in cloud. He paced up and down the entire flight. Felt sorry for him. When we crossed the Labrador coast he said, "Is that North America? Are we home?" When assured we were, he collapsed in a seat and slept the rest of the way.

August 13: From Meeks to Goose, the Northern Lights were very bright as we approached Goose. They seemed to be in a band that was directly overhead and ran WNW–ESE. Sort of a brilliant haze that shimmered and changed in intensity. The long band wove back and forth like a large serpent. It seemed to lower over the airplane and looked as though it would envelop us. It was greenish, but broke out in spots of purple. The band was over us and almost looked on top of us, but I could see stars through it—spooky but beautiful.

September 2: Prestwick westbound with quite a passenger load—Bob Hope and his entire group; Frances Langford, Jack Pepper, and Tony Romano. On top of that some old friends: Major Crocker Snow, a Bostonian and Mr. Aviation in Massachusetts; plus Lieutenant Colonel Beirne Lay, once editor of *The Sportsman Pilot,* a magazine I'd written pieces for—I learned a lot from him about writing as he cruelly tore my stuff apart and criticized it. Now he was on General Eaker's staff and had recently flown a B-17 on the famous and bloody Regensburg raid. He wasn't a mental case by any means, but it was obvious the hard bombing raids had put him on edge; the big raid had only been two weeks before. He was anxious to see home and family; real, touchable, and secure. [Later he co-authored the bestselling book and movie *Twelve O'Clock High*.]

We also carried a private with a brain tumor, accompanied by a surgeon, and another private going blind. Quite a mixture.

✳

Hope was friendly and spent a lot of time in the cockpit. It wasn't an easy trip to Meeks; climbed to 15,000 to top some ice in a front, then at Meeks the weather was low, ceiling less than 500 feet, Hope stood behind me during the approach and when we broke out and landed he remarked, "Man, what you needed was roller skates!"

The weather beyond was bad and Meeks didn't have any radio reception with Goose or Presque Isle to update reports, so we held at Meeks. It wasn't scheduled, but the local commander asked Hope to put on a show. Hope quickly agreed, although he was tired and worn from having done 212 shows in eleven weeks throughout army camps in Europe.

"Buck," he asked me, "is this a put-up job, are you delaying just to get us to do a show?" I assured him that this wasn't the case, but I don't think he really believed me, although he kept a good spirit about it.

Naturally we attended the show and it was wonderful; a great surprise present for the troops on Iceland and they hooted and hollered at Hope's jokes and roared with approval when Langford, in slacks and a tight sweater that showed off her ample chest, sang "Gimmie, gimmie what I crave for." The exact lyrics escape me except for the "Gimmie, gimmie" part when the GIs came right out of their seats with a roar. (In his postwar book Hope mentioned the Iceland stop. We kept in touch after this and I visited him on sets a few times. He has been a loyal friend and every year since—and even now in his nineties he sends me a Christmas card.)

The next day we flew on to Presque Isle and then La Guardia, where Hope and company got off. Beirne Lay stayed on, headed for Washington, but this wasn't easy. The weather was poor and traffic at Washington backed up because of a lost army plane. We held over Baltimore, were told we'd be number six to land at Washington; I decided to land at Baltimore, get more fuel and wait for the situation to settle down.

On the ground at Baltimore, Beirne said he'd had enough, the trip was jinxed and he wanted to get home safely. He got off and took a cab. I didn't blame him.

CHAPTER 14

Two Kind Words

✳

A NOTICE MADE THE ROUNDS, saying anyone interested in doing weather research flying a B-17 should send in a bid. A bid is your indication you'd like the assignment; the most senior person gets it. It was my kind of thing and I bid immediately. On November 11, 1943, they said I was it, and so began the most interesting, happy, and rewarding time of my flying life.

The director of the technical part of the project was Ralph Ayers, an engineer in TWA's radio department; I was the director of operations. Ralph was quiet, pleasant, cooperative, and very, very intelligent.

"What we're doing is precipitation static research," he told me. "We need to fly into areas of snow and weather, to make measurements and try various kinds of experimental equipment."

This was a big problem at the time: an airplane, flying in snow, certain types of rain, and thunderstorms accumulates an electrical charge, so much that the airplane cannot contain it. So the charge bleeds off, and it wants to go via the easiest route such as a radio antenna; once this bleeding starts the radio signal becomes hash, like a radio near a diathermy machine. We were losing airplanes because of it; the frequencies for navigation beam reception were knocked out by this P static.

To be a little technical, the electrical charge that builds up on the airplane comes in two varieties: one is the kind that spreads on the airplane from friction, like the crackling noise a plastic comb may produce when combing one's hair on a dry day, or the spark from a hotel key when you insert it after walking along a dry, thick carpet. Snow is the perfect thing to rub across an airplane's skin to build up a charge. Some say rain does, too, but that's a more complicated story as will be obvious later on—in a non-technical way.

The other way a charge builds up is when the airplane flies through an electrical field, generally found around or in thunderstorms. These fields are big, with tremendous voltage—it's like flying through an electrical waterfall. The fields do strange things around thunderstorms: change polarity, attract or repulse, create lightning and other weird phenomena.

The first kind, what we'll call snow static, doesn't have anything close to the amount of charge as the other kind, which we'll refer to as field static. The project was aimed at the two different problems.

None of this was new to me, as I'd experienced it many times on the line. TWA had a group of brilliant people in the engineering department in those days; Jack Franklin was its head, assisted by Ralph Ayers and Howard Morgan. I realize now what an exceptional group they were, intelligent and informed well above the norm, a pleasure to work with and learn from. They had developed the antistatic loop antenna that was on all TWA airplanes; it helped when riding the beam in snow, and to take bearings, but had certain inadequacies they were trying to overcome while also trying to find ways to combat the static for communication as well as navigation. The army knew of their efforts, and I suppose that's how TWA received this contract. Also, an army general later told me, they thought a civilian group doing the job could cut through army red tape and accomplish the task quicker. He was right and we did some fancy maneuvering along the way to prove his point.

To find the snow and weather was my task, along with seeing that the airplane and crew were capable and ready. Our meteorological department suggested we base the operation in the Northwest somewhere; sit and wait for those coastal storms to arrive with snow over the Cascades. I thought about that and somehow didn't like the idea of sitting and waiting, we ought to be mobile, ready to head for weather wherever it might be. The B-17 with its long range could fly where weather was, even track along with it. It was easy to get agreement from Ayres, and the army liked the idea because we could sample static problems in different parts of the world where the war was going on.

But first we had to get the airplane and gather together the people who'd fly it and fold them into a unit. So we were off to Wright Field, Dayton, where our B-17 awaited us.

The copilot was C. O. Johnson, a Forth Worth Texan, raised in the world of general aviation, flying anything available. His father struggled to start an airplane factory and built a sleek, fast airplane that seated four and was called the Johnson Rocket. It was a fine airplane, but the factory never got off the ground. C.O., as we called him, or Del, was blond, blue-eyed, quiet, and an excellent pilot, smooth at handling controls, and wary of flying's pitfalls.

The crew chief, the important man who keeps the airplane maintained and running, was B. J. Dowd, Barney. A man of small but rugged stature, black hair, a swaggering gait, and a smile that radiated the humor with which he was blessed. Irish way back, but a Kansas City native who had been with TWA in maintenance since his nineteenth year; he came to be the operation's backbone.

Guy Arnold was the navigator; dark hair, broad smile, precise to the persnickety point, superbly able in his craft.

Dowd had an assistant, a mechanic from TWA's overhaul shop named Bill Foley; able, full of fun, ready for anything. These two were magnificent, seldom bitching except for bitchable things by quick oath, ready to work under all conditions and some of them were miserable. Their pride at keeping *Two Kind Words,* the name we eventually gave the B-17, was fierce and they wheeled, dealed, even stole to get parts, preference, and whatever it took to keep us flying.

During the three years of the project many people took part, but the real core, the basic gang, was Dowd, Foley, and a civilian engineer from Wright Field who also doubled as our radio operator; his name was Phil Couch, a quiet, intelligent man whose humor and dedication fit right in with ours. It was a bit of banter between Foley and Couch that named our airplane. Foley had said something to Couch, who wanted to reply, "Fuck you," but being in polite company it wouldn't do; he floundered for words genteel enough for the gathering, and in frustration blurted out, "Two kind words to you, Foley." We all understood what Couch meant, and in spontaneous discovery knew it was the name we'd been searching for; *Two Kind Words* was painted on the airplane's nose, and B-17 Number 42-31294 became a personality, one of the gang.

Ayres was with us much of the time and was also part of the inner circle. We changed copilots after a year when C. O. Johnson returned to the line for upgrading to captain; in his place came Garth Sharp, a tall, slender farm boy from Missouri with all the fine attributes farm-born pilots have: serious, skeptical, and skillful, with a deep sense of humor he displayed with a chuckle rather than loud laughter. That was the crew, the team; close knit by loyalty, dedication, and love. I was fortunate to have such people.

✻

WE FLEW TO WRIGHT FIELD, which was the center of army aviation research and development—an exciting place. It was November 13, 1943, and my diary notes, "Saw my first helicopter fly—very impressive. Captain Vavarina, who's flown it, says it's quite difficult to fly."

The army insisted that we go through a high-altitude indoctrination to prepare for flying in a B-17, which could go very high. This involved our going into a chamber where the pressure would be reduced, reducing the oxygen, simulating the effect of high altitudes. We were briefed about the chamber, how we'd be sitting in it with an instructor beside us, all of us wearing oxygen masks, and then we'd remove our masks; without supplemental oxygen, you were supposed to keep writing your name until the writing became a scrawl and then, when you were on the verge of passing out, the instructor would slap the mask back on you and you'd be revived. At 35,000 feet it took fifty-six seconds for me to reach that point.

We were strongly advised to signal the instructor if we developed any pain in joints such as the knees, shoulders, and knuckles. This would indicate that a person was subject to the bends—much as a diver can suffer when coming up from water depths. Having such pain would disqualify you from flying.

They also raised the chamber atmosphere above 40,000 feet and demonstrated pressure breathing. This is when oxygen is forced, via the mask, into your mouth and nose because there isn't enough pressure above

40,000 feet for the lungs to absorb it, so it has to be forced in. This is tricky breathing, as you have to be conscious of every breath.

During the tests I noticed Lawton grimacing, and Dowd's eyes, which showed over the top of his mask, were telling me he wasn't happy. The altitude was finally lowered and the tests were completed. We all passed. But later, away from any army people, Dowd let out a whistle: "Man, my finger joints were killing me, I couldn't have taken much more of that." Lawton joined him, saying a knee was causing him severe pain, but he'd held on. They were too eager to be a part of the program to show any pain and be disqualified.

Even with that out of the way, the army did not simply hand me a B-17, but insisted I first be checked out in the airplane. So off I went with Captain Vavarina, did the usual stalls, steep turns, cutting an engine, then another, making landings. It felt a lot like the Stratoliner, which, of course, was its first cousin. My notes remind me, "It has to be manhandled when two engines are out on one side." After two hours Vavarina said I was okay.

Now the army and its red tape stepped in, as Vavarina's boss said I was required to have ten hours "instruction" before being officially checked out. Vavarina argued with him, said it was silly and that I was okay to go, and he carried his argument up higher, to a colonel, who said a two-engine landing would be enough. So up we went, cut two engines, circled and landed—all in twenty minutes rather than ten hours.

I signed a slip of paper and now had a B-17 of my very own—in a sense. We all piled on board and at 8:35 A.M. headed for Kansas City, which would be our home base—a proper location with TWA's maintenance headquarters and engineering department.

Right out of Wright Field we christened the airplane with snow as air traffic control held us for forty-five minutes on the east leg of the radio range in snow showers. Finally we were turned loose, climbed to 10,000 feet, and headed west. I was pleased to see the airspeed settle on 175 mph indicated.

We were like kids with a new toy, people wandering around looking at the gadgets; it was a G model with all turrets and armor plate installed. We worked the turrets, but only Foley was slim enough—and gutsy enough—to crawl into the tiny ball turret that hung beneath the belly.

The airplane had turbo-supercharged engines, and an automatic pilot, which was intended for the bombardier to use to steer the airplane over a target, but worked for us as an autopilot as long as we kept one eye on it; it kept the airplane level and headed on course as long as we made periodic adjustments. There was a Bendix fluxgate compass; this was a new and exciting instrument that wedded the compass and gyro so we always had the precise compass heading without all the irregularities of a compass such as hold-back and run-ahead. Prior to this, gyros had to be set periodically to agree with the compass heading because the gyro alone precessed and wandered from the compass heading; this was an annoying job and difficult to do if the air was rough. We also had a VHF, very high frequency, radio transmitter and receiver, another innovation; it was limited to a few frequencies, mostly for use by combat aircraft.

The instrument panel had an ILS, instrument landing system, with its two needles, one for the glide path and the other for the runway center line. This was in the earliest days of ILS, which was barely out of the experimental stage.

These new instruments and gadgets were my toys en route to Kansas City, and I tried them all as best I could. The turbo-superchargers were new to us. Electronic controls gave you command over their action, but they were "electronics" in their most embryonic stage—we had more to learn about these, but my first quick experimental toying raised furrowed eyebrows because the turbos were the source of carburetor heat, and from what I saw they didn't provide enough. This was a serious detail, because we'd be flying in weather, our basic task, getting ice; the carburetors could easily collect enough to stop the engines. This had to be cleared up before we started our work.

I landed at Kansas City and taxied to our hangar, off to one side of the airport and known as the Gobel Hangar; offices on the side and storage space, this would be our base—the same offices from which I'd taught copilot school just five years before.

So we had the airplane, but we were a long way from being ready to fly. A B-17 comes equipped for war, not research; we had to add the necessary equipment and gadgets, test them, and be certain they all worked before we took off on our search for bad weather.

We began by hanging on to the tail a contraption with horizontal tubes about seven feet long that sprayed alcohol and acted like a condenser to build up a charge on the airplane and then discharge it to create a higher current. Mechanics around the hangar called it our manure spreader. Dowd placed a 55-gallon tank in the bomb bay to supply it with alcohol.

Two GVMs, generator voltmeters, round gadgets about eighteen inches in diameter, were mounted on top and bottom of the fuselage—outside—to measure electrical field strengths.

On Number 3 engine's propeller we glued strips of cloth, made conductive, to read static discharge from propellers.

The airplane had only one pitot mast; this stuck out from the fuselage in the airstream and held two tubes, one facing forward, to collect air for the purpose of measuring airspeed. (Pitot was a French scientist who wanted to measure the water flow in the Seine River at the top and bottom to see if the water on top flowed faster than the water near the bottom—it does; that was in 1732. Some smart person from the Royal Aircraft Establishment in England, about 1911, figured the principle might work on an airplane, and voilà, the airspeed indicator.) Knowing we'd fly in ice and that the mast might get carried away if ice built up on it, I decided we ought to have an extra one, and Dowd installed it.

In the cockpit I wanted a radar-type altimeter that would tell me within a few feet how high I was. I wanted this for the low, bad-weather approaches. I also wanted a high-level radio altimeter for navigation purposes, so two electronic altimeters were installed. One could not do both jobs because of display and other technical matters. The high-altitude one was mounted at the navigator's station.

Two fold-down bunks were installed just ahead of the waist gunner positions—very basic canvas-covered frames. Two airline seats went in by the waist gun windows. A big box Dowd and Foley constructed for spare parts and "stuff" went in the bomb bay next to the alcohol tank. Near it was our toilet, which consisted of a tube with a funnel on our end; the tube wound down to a small opening near the bomb bay doors where the liquid sprayed out into the atmosphere. It never worked well, because it was generally frozen closed. Cold was part of the B-17; the heating system put out a mere suggestion of heat, and the bare walls were only slight protection from the subzero outside air.

Little things accumulated; a light put here or there, a pencil holder, map case, hooks for personal things; it grew like a lived-in house and became very personal to all of us.

Forward of the cockpit and below it, on a sort of lower floor, was the bombardier station and the controls for the chin turret; we removed the bombardier equipment and this became the navigator's place. It included a table and chair facing the side, and above, in the center, an astrodome the navigator could stand in and take celestial sights. This bubble stuck up out of the airplane just ahead of the cockpit, and we could see the navigator's head and sextant when he was taking a shot; it gave the impression his head was outside the airplane as it stuck up above the fuselage skin. I was going to spend a lot of time in that dome as things turned out.

The nose of the navigator station was mostly glass and made a great observation place; we eventually put some flooring way forward and a mattress where a crew member on long flights could stretch out, looking down through the glass at ground or sky. It became a favorite hangout.

We fitted the propellers with grooved rubber boots on their leading edges, down which alcohol would flow on demand to keep the props ice-free. The long-range fuel tanks in the bomb bay, known in slang as Tokyo tanks, were removed to give us extra room for our alcohol tank and storage. There would be times when we wished those tanks were still on board.

While Dowd and Foley were doing the installations I decided to learn more about B-17 engines; they were Wright 1820s, essentially the same as we had in DC-3s except for the turbo-superchargers that ran off the exhaust gas and gave high-altitude capability. In other words, the engines would put out power up high where normal engines, without superchargers, were running out of air. To learn more about the engines, how best to operate them, and what the cautions were, I went to the Wright factory in Paterson, New Jersey, and talked with engineers and operations people; it filled a gap in my knowledge and I returned to Kansas City ready to go.

Our first test flight included stalls with results between 76 and 96 mph depending on deicer boots on or off; I noticed a wing wanted to drop when stalled with the deicer boots operating. I tried the turbos for carburetor heat at low altitude—6,000 feet—and could only get a 10°C temperature rise; this wasn't enough and worried me.

Guy Arnold, the navigator, checked airspeed indicators as I ran over a measured course at 150, 180, and 205 mph, 300 feet above the ground. We tried to get ILS—instrument landing system—to work, but it didn't. Fuel consumption was about forty-four gallons per hour per engine, except the Number 3 engine burned 51 gph—this was a rough cut, but Number 3 engine was to become a troublesome child. The alcohol flow to the props for deicing checked out to be a pint in four and a half minutes at half flow; full on they used a pint in 2.3 minutes.

We were interested in all this because we'd be flying in the weather, and much of the time down low. Normally, on the line, the object is to get out of weather, to climb on top where it's clear and duck around thunderstorms, but with the B-17 we'd be looking for weather and trying to stay in it for data. So the task of deicing the propellers, engines, and wings was mighty important, and the data stuck in our minds.

We decided to test the low-level radar altimeter by flying low over a smooth surface. Where to find such? Easy: the Missouri River, which winds through and beyond Kansas City. So we flew down the river at a very low altitude—fifty feet or so—to see how the altimeter reacted. It was very good: small gains or losses in altitude showed immediately.

Winding down the river, almost on it, Dowd exclaimed, "I hope we don't get shot."

"What are you talking about?"

"Hell, it's duck season and we're scaring them all off. Maybe the guys in those blinds won't like that and might shoot at us instead of the ducks."

We laughed about it, but we later got some flak from the hangar boys, saying they'd heard we'd made a lot of duck hunters mad.

Before we departed our home base I decided we should make a high-altitude flight to make sure everything worked at altitude and that the crew and the people on board could handle oxygen, cold, and everything else that goes with high flight.

We all dressed in gear the army had issued us: parka, fleece-lined pants and boots, fur-lined helmet, headphones, and throat microphone. We looked ready for the moon; awkward in all this rig plus a parachute harness, we waddled to the airplane, a bunch of amateurs showing off their lack of seasoning.

We talked things over before the flight and I made rule 1: whenever we were high enough to use oxygen—above 12,000 feet—everyone had to be on the interphone with mikes and headsets hooked up and working, and every ten minutes I'd do a roster check to see if all were conscious and doing well.

We took off and climbed toward Columbia, Missouri. Checking with crew members periodically, I found the throat mikes produced a mushy-sounding voice that was difficult to understand—we'd have to do something about that. At 23,000 feet I noticed clouds to the southeast, so I headed for them. About then I began feeling hot chills and the engines seemed quieter; the Number 1 engine head temperature had been running 200°C and I didn't like it, but I really didn't care much—then suddenly it dawned on me that I was suffering from oxygen deprivation, so I turned the regulator selector to emergency, which pours oxygen at you. A few breaths of that and the engines became louder and my concern about Number 1 head temperature returned.

We had some trouble with the supercharger regulators, which were an early example of electronic gadgetry and not very reliable. The Number 3 engine manifold pressure kept dropping off, but I couldn't turn the regulator to bring it back because I'd overboost the other engines. Then the Number 2 oil pressure dropped to 50 pounds.

None of this was anything dramatic, but rather annoying and obviously would need fixing. But we discovered, as time passed and we gained experience, that there frequently were little problems and gadgets that didn't work for a time and then mysteriously cured themselves. Dowd and Foley, of course, worked to cure problems, but it was like stomping out grass fires—as one problem disappeared another appeared. We operated through all this, and looking back I realize these were just the growing pains of aviation.

Arnold called when we were at 29,000 feet and said he had a problem, but I couldn't understand what it was because of the mushy throat mike; he didn't sound desperate, but to be safe I descended and we landed back at Kansas City.

My notes say, "The time to 28,000 feet was 53 minutes, turbo regulator never higher than #6 [that was a setting index], carb temperature +10 degrees C to top, outside air −40 degrees at 29,000—used 608 gallons."

There were more local flights, getting things to work, feeling them out, looking for problems that we wouldn't want in some remote place. After a few weeks of these we felt ready to go. The idea of a base in some North-west place such as Spokane had pretty well fallen away, and we decided to go to Alaska and see what winter weather up there had to offer.

During the war each theater of operations was like a forbidden land, impenetrable unless you'd been inspected and cleared at some point, rather like a war-oriented customs and immigration. To go to Alaska we had to clear in Great Falls, Montana, so on the ninth of February 1944, we departed Kansas City and headed north. En route, near Custer, Montana, I climbed to a high deck of cirrus clouds hoping for static from the ice crystals that cirrus clouds are made of. It was there at 25,000 feet, temperature minus 30°C.

What was this hunt for static about? Well, the object was to come up with something to prevent precipitation static from making radios useless, but before tackling the problem it was necessary to know what the static was: how strong the electrical fields and the charging that built up on and came off of the airplane were. We also needed to know if the instruments we'd developed for the hunt were adequate and working. Instruments like that don't come ready-made; you have to devise and build them. That's part of all scientific research, the unglamorous part perhaps and sometimes the toughest, but occasionally those instruments turn out to be the best thing a project comes up with. So we were out there trying to find static and prove all the gadgets that we'd put on the airplane.

On one crew oxygen check on our way to Great Falls, Dowd just mumbled in reply. He was standing right behind us, and when I turned to check on him he had a faint bluish tint, which says lack of oxygen. I turned on the emergency flow and searched down his oxygen hose and found it kinked. That was easily fixed and in a few moments Dowd's blue face turned to pink and he exclaimed loudly, "Man! That feels good!"

We descended through various cloud decks with light ice and landed at Great Falls, Gore Field, only to be told it wasn't the correct spot, everything had been moved to East Base, so we took off and went to the other field, perhaps our shortest flight: twenty minutes.

Our pre-Alaska entry examination said we had to have tires that would help braking on icy runways, and we needed a survival kit.

The tires were changed from ordinary rubber to rubber with lateral steel strips sort of like a coil spring embedded in the tire surface. They made an awful howling noise when taking off or landing on a hard-surfaced runway. The steel soon wore away and I doubted their usefulness after a few landings. We took them off and installed another experimental type; these were weird-looking, with dozens, maybe hundreds, of upside-down soda bottle caps stuck in the tire's surface. They grasped the runway ice pretty well, but they, too, only lasted a few landings before the caps popped out of the rubber or wore off. It wasn't long before we were back to regular tires.

The survival kit was a big box loaded with all kinds of goodies such as stoves, a gun, ropes, first-aid gear, tent, and more. The gun was a neat over-and-under; .410 shotgun under and a .22 rifle on top to be used for small game if we were down and hungry in a remote place. I always regretted my honesty in turning it back when the project ended; in the giddy period at the war's end lots of things never got returned to Uncle Sam, and I sure hankered for that gun.

We got out of Great Falls and headed north, across the Canadian border toward Alaska. My diary notes that we flew at 7,000 feet through heavy cumulus cloud and a cold front south of Edmonton, Alberta; the air was turbulent with much snow bringing the static we wanted. Two men in the back, technicians, got airsick. We stopped at Fort Nelson, British Columbia, then on for Watson Lake, Yukon Territory—a lovely place, lots of pines and verdure. It was possible in the mind to shut out the army atmosphere with its barracks, vehicles, and activity, shut it out of your consciousness and make believe we were in pristine wilds, camping, hunting, fishing. The pine smell of the north woods overpowered the army aura, and a little imagination put me at another time.

I'd flown this area a year or so back in a DC-3. Here was Teslin Lake, seventy miles long but barely two miles wide, looking like a skinny blue worm on the map; you fly over it low between the mountains that rise 4,000 feet above it. I'd skimmed that long, slim body of water in the DC-3, and here I was again in the B-17. The mountains were snow-covered, majestic, and as big mountains always are, mysterious and a little frightening.

We flew through snow going to Whitehorse, the snow all occurring with a temperature of 20 degrees below zero C—there was very little cloud, with the snow forming directly from water vapor, sublimation we call it. Because there wasn't any cloud there wasn't any ice.

Off Whitehorse and across those majestic, mysterious mountains: looking down into the rock valleys, peaks, and snow fields, the four engines reassuring, I felt more comfortable than I had in the DC-3 with its limited performance, which required knowledge of the mountain passes to fly through; in the B-17 we could go high, power our way over the big mountains.

On to the coast and a landing at Juneau; my diary notes, "One of the most beautiful spots I've ever seen." After a steak dinner we flew back over the glacier and the mountains that seemed to sneer at our passage.

Into Watson Lake again, where we held a day because the weather was too good. Holding with us were pilots ferrying Bell P-39 Airacobras to Nome, where Russians would pick them up and fly across the Bering Sea to the Russian-German front. The ferry pilots were holding at Watson Lake because the weather was too bad, but for us it wasn't bad enough.

Holding meant sitting around a room close to operations—a place to hang out. Chairs both hard and soft, a beat-up sofa, tables for magazines, ashtrays. Worldwide, pilots hung out for hours and days in rooms like that, waiting for weather or orders. The bored pilots founded the Nose Pickers Association—all there was to do. In keeping with the association's charter, some pilots drew pictures of devices designed to aid one in the task, and some went so far as to create gadgets, mostly carved from wood, to help out: a slender four-inch-long screw that tapered to a point; a shaft of wood ending in a sharp-edged cup; delicate wood pincers to insert and capture. There were others, all displayed but never used—at least I never saw any in action, for which I am grateful.

The weather cleared with no prospects for our bad weather; we flew to Fairbanks in CAVU (ceiling and visibility unlimited) conditions.

Because we were always on the search for weather, and we never knew when or where it might turn up, I established as a procedure that the airplane should always be ready to go. This meant that when we landed after a flight, no matter the length or time, the airplane had to have any maintenance items corrected, oil and fluid levels topped off, and as much fuel taken aboard as possible.

Sometimes this was a trying rule, as on a night we arrived at Fairbanks after a long flight from Great Falls, Montana, with a broken oil radiator. This was a bitch to change, but despite fatigue, below-zero temperatures, and no hangar, Dowd and Foley tore into it. We helped where we could, mostly in gofer roles, getting tools, stands, or whatever they needed. The job finally done, we got warm, nourished, and slept.

On another arrival at Fairbanks the oil radiator was leaking; this time it was 40 degrees below and impossible to work outside. The army was very tight with hangar space, especially for an unattached bastard operation like ours, but we were quietly towed into a heated hangar, thanks to a bottle of Scotch we slipped to the sergeant in charge.

We learned how to wheel and deal to get things done. Our status was strange: a B-17 manned by civilians, in all theaters of operation, not attached to any official unit. Our calling card was one thin sheet of paper that said that Captain Robert N. Buck (Civilian) was in charge of B-17 Number 42-31294, engaged in research, and it would be appreciated if he was allowed to operate in any weather he desired (or words to that effect). The "allowed" phrase was necessary because the general at Wright Field couldn't dictate to a general in another field of operations. This never caused us any trouble.

There were times when we didn't rest very long before some weather would show up and we'd get right back in the air. I note in my diary another night when we landed at Fairbanks at 10:05 P.M. and were airborne again two hours later. We went to Ruby, over it, and then back to Fairbanks at 7,000 feet in snow with light to occasionally heavy static; there were clouds with the snow, so we collected ice that was quite tenacious. One army pilot that night found the static so bad he turned around.

While examining P static was our primary goal, I was thrilled to be in a position to study weather, especially icing and turbulence. This opportunity to go directly into weather, hunting out its most hostile form, was a chance to confirm old theories—or to destroy them and develop new ones. Weather had become my main interest. I love airplanes, but to me they were increasingly a means of getting into weather, seeking out its mysteries, its meanness, and sometimes its helpful friendliness. I felt a strong link across time to the ancient explorers and navigators, they with their sailboats, me with my airplane, both of us headed out to navigate through and do battle with whatever weather lay on our course.

Despite all the decisions to be made, the planning and responsibility, I was having a great time. I'd long believed that there is no ice in snow, that

ice requires cloud, and that theory was holding up. Ice building up on propellers was the paramount ice problem; if the props couldn't pull, the airplane wouldn't have enough airspeed to fly. I spent a lot of time, when in
ice, down in the navigator's station staring at the props through a strobo-
scope, a device that enabled me to view the propeller as if it were stopped
even while it kept on spinning. I learned that the props often iced up
before the wings did; what this told me right away was that you should
turn on propeller alcohol whenever you were in a condition of possible
icing even if the wings didn't show any. For safety's sake, you should get
the alcohol flowing, and do it early.

Our flights must have seemed crazy to anyone who didn't know what
we were up to: we'd go north, turn around and go south; land, but take off
again and head another way; nothing was planned, all our movements dictated by where the weather was. Our wandering paths took us from Barrow on the top of Alaska to the Panama Canal and a host of places in
between, and finally around the world.

I studied a lot of weather maps and reports as I tried to anticipate where
bad weather might show up; I was learning more about weather prognostication, seeing what I could glean from the reports and maps. It seemed
there was more good weather than bad; we waited more and ventured farther to find bad weather than I ever had to for good weather.

The instrumentation was pretty well checked out and we had learned
the vagaries of our task. The crew cohered into a fine group that worked
and played well together; we liked one another. And we'd learned the airplane, its good traits and bad. The world, to an almost unprecedented
extent, was ours to roam.

CHAPTER 15

Flights of Fancy
with a Purpose

✳

ELLIOT LAWTON OF General Electric, a fine gentleman who flew on many of our far north trips (often shaking his head at our rough profanity), wanted snowflake samples. The method for catching snowflakes was to use a tube in the nose, its forward end out in the airstream, the inside exhaust end in the navigator compartment where Foley stood poised with a soft plastic plate about six inches square. As snow rushed in through the tube and impinged on the plate, Foley quickly covered it with a plastic sheet the same size, sealing it; the shape of the snowflake was "etched" on the plastic plate, and when it melted the water was captured to be analyzed later in a laboratory. Flying in snow, it wasn't unusual to hear Foley on the interphone: "Elliot! I caught ya another goddamn snowflake!"

The real scientific brain behind our P static work was Ralph Ayres, who flew on many flights and was constantly coming up with new ways to accomplish what we wanted to do.

Ralph experimented with various antenna sizes and materials. The idea was to have a large-diameter antenna wire so the electrical charge wouldn't bleed off it, causing noise and ruining radio reception. Copper, aluminum, polyethylene-covered copper wire—we tried these, as well as smooth hardware fittings to attach the antennas; the hardware was specially designed so it would not go into corona. (When the electrical charge builds up on an airplane or a ship, and it reaches a point where the airplane can't hold it all, the charge bleeds off from sharp objects like a small-diameter antenna in visible form—it creates a bluish aura called corona. It's never very big, but it can form a band on the tips of the propellers, or the tip of any antenna with points on the end; this causes radio noise—static. Reaching back into history, there are accounts of corona—then called St. Elmo's fire—visible from the rigging on clipper ships when they were sailing in thunderstorms or heavy snow. St. Elmo comes from St. Erasmus, who was patron saint of Mediterranean sailors in very old days.) Frequently Ralph would ask if I could land somewhere so they might change antennas, or other test equipment. It made life interesting because I'd try for the nearest field, which often was in the harsh weather we were working, so it meant a bad-weather approach to some field I'd never seen before. We startled a few ground people who'd see a B-17 appear, ghostlike, from the snow, landing where no B-17 had been or had reason to be.

Along with the large-diameter wire antenna—about the thickness of a pencil—we added wicks to the wingtips and tail. These were half an inch in diameter and about ten inches long, a plastic tube filled with woolen yarn that had been impregnated with graphite or something that made it able to conduct electricity. The idea was that the large-diameter wire would prevent the antenna from going into corona, but the electricity had to discharge from the airplane somewhere: so Ralph gave it a path through the discharge wicks, where it bled off noiselessly from the thousands of tiny threads that were exposed at the wick's end. You can see these today on the wingtips of an airliner; they've been improved, the yarn done away with, but follow the same principle and do the job.

Our wandering took us to Florida for about a week, but the Florida thunderstorms never seemed to have the clout or action that those in Kansas did. It was a little like the Intertropical Front, I suspect because the freezing level is so much higher. Normally rain forms at a level aloft that's below freezing, and there's a release of heat from the condensation process that gives more vigor to the storms. In the tropics, rain often forms at above-freezing temperatures and doesn't have that same characteristic. (I can hear some Ph.D. types yowling at my theory, and perhaps I'm wrong, but I've been inside all that stuff, and this theory goes along with my observations and perhaps takes some form of priority over computer-generated theory.)

Florida was very uncomfortable because it was so warm. Thunderstorms build best in the afternoon, so we didn't get things going until after lunch. The airplane, sitting in the sun, was hot all over, inside and out; touching the metal sides as we got it ready for flight would burn one's hands. B-17s didn't enjoy any luxuries like air-conditioning; in flight it was uncomfortable even at the altitudes where we were penetrating thunderstorms, and we flew most of the time in our underwear shorts. We were not unhappy when it came time to head back north.

We roamed far and wide, and a full listing of our travels would be long and probably boring. But certain times stood out, and with the help of my diary and letters from Dowd, now retired in Kansas City—we're the only ones remaining from the project—it's possible to show what the time was like and what we accomplished:

"Had Captain Holman, a B-17 replacement, on board so he could get his time in. [We often did this—helped pilots sitting and waiting for orders somewhere get the monthly flying time they needed for flight pay.] A nice little guy who'd finished his missions. Let him fly and he did a good job."

"Flew via Tulsa and Springfield, Missouri. Some high-level showers, circled in one, started at 8,000 feet and after an hour got down to 6,500. Seems to be a strong downdraft whenever the static occurs. This not definitely established as yet. Static always seems to be on north side of storm."

"Flew through a small shower near Mt. Pocono, Pennsylvania, top estimated at 15,000 feet—innocent-looking, but very high fields and very, very rough." (This was probably a thunderstorm in the process of creation. This, we found, is the time the turbulence is often strongest, the primary stage of a thunderstorm. Lesson: don't think a pretty, white cumulus cloud building is innocent; it may pack a very hard punch. As we wrestled around in it, trying to soften the bumps, Phil Couch came in on the interphone happy as could be: "Boy, that's really hot stuff!" Meaning the static he was recording. It was his expression, frequently used.)

"Thunderstorms began vicinity Burlington, Iowa. Base high, only light rain. Moderate to severe cloud-to-cloud lightning and moderate cloud-to-ground lightning, occasional moderate turbulence. Very bad atmospheric static and when over Kirksville, Missouri, unable to read the radio range—but loop and ADF worked well. Worst cross-field static in downdrafts, which generally are where the heavy rain falls."

The deicer boots of wartime were made of inferior rubber and we had trouble with them tearing or ballooning on the wing; some spots looked like big black boils. Changing deicer boots was a laborious job, and I had never thought them effective anyway. In Miami, a wing boot ballooned and tore; we removed the boot from that wing, so one wing had a boot and the other didn't, which would cause an aerodynamic imbalance. We were in Miami, it was hot, and I didn't want to face at least another day down while Dowd and Foley changed the boot. So I told them, "Take the other one off, too, the hell with boots." So they did and we finished the project, including going around the world, without deicer boots; a few times this required serious action to avoid severe ice, but that was rare, and it seemed to prove that having no boots wasn't any worse than having them.

Working in thunderstorms we were getting strong electrical fields. These had tremendous strength and went off the scale, pegging the voltage-measuring instruments to where they couldn't read any further. The large-diameter wire antenna and discharge wicks didn't faze the cross fields and they knocked out all radios; the exception was our VHF radio, a communication set for talking to other aircraft and the ground assuming both had VHF. It was new, an advance that worked in the 120 megahertz range. Its drawback is that it's line of sight only—you can only receive across a distance you can see, meaning you won't receive transmissions from a station that's beyond the horizon. (TV sets are the same, hence cable, satellites, and such.) Today, except for long-range flights, VHF is the paramount radio, used for all air traffic control, interplane, and plane-to-ground communication when within range. VHF isn't affected by the big fields around thunderstorms (except for unusual conditions when the radio will squeal, but that only lasts for a limited time).

These electrical charges were so immense they swamped the airplane, and that's when a discharge happened, actually a lightning strike as the charge on the airplane twitched out toward a cloud with opposite charge, and *whammy*, a brilliant light and loud snap of the nearby lightning. We had it happen often—six times on one flight—but it seldom caused any appreciable damage: a hole about the size of a silver dollar off a wingtip, or tail; one discharge went out through Number 3 propeller and made a small hole, about an eighth of an inch in diameter. We became accustomed to these discharges, but they always created a brief surge of fright when the noise and light went off.

The Naval Research Lab out of Minneapolis was anxious to try a new antenna, a polyethylene-coated wire, but of a small diameter they felt could handle strong fields—we didn't think so. Their problem was finding thunderstorms in midwinter with the limited range of their B-25; we agreed to fly south and hunt some out for them. A technician arrived in Kansas City with the antenna and off we went. The B-17's range came into play: we turned tail on the cold and flew south, after a fuel stop at Miami, until it was warm enough for thunderstorms, which came off the coast of Colombia about 170 miles north of the equator. My old friend, the Intertropical Front, provided the action: rain, moderate turbulence, and pretty good fields. It didn't take long to punch holes in the antenna and prove it wasn't any good.

We turned back and landed at Albrook Field, Canal Zone. During our overnight stay we discovered certain scarce goods were easily available; a case of Johnnie Walker Scotch and three cases of Chesterfield cigarettes nestled, when we took off, in a compartment Foley had created under the floor where the ball turret had once been, a compartment difficult to detect for anyone outside the immediate crew. We called this loot our trade goods, and in all honesty we never used it except as material to grease the way for parts, favors, or whatever was needed to advance the project. Such delightful goods caused paperwork to disappear, along with bureaucratic befuddlement.

We departed the Canal Zone, went nonstop to Miami—Arnold wasn't along so I did the navigating. A short stop for fuel in Miami and then non-stop to Kansas City; the technician sent to us by the navy was impressed with our mobility and our philosophy of keep going until you get there.

Our farthest trip north was to Barrow, Alaska. There had been snow in the vicinity of the Brooks Range and we went for it: very dry, light to moderate static. North of the Brooks Range it cleared, and being this close to Barrow we decided to land and look over the northernmost point of the United States.

Barrow was a group of buildings in the snow-covered land, to its north the Beaufort Sea. Looking down, offshore, the water appeared black; big ice floes floated in it, looking like sinister monsters, and ice fog rose and drifted as slowly as swirling curtains. The scene sent an uncomfortable, spooky feeling through my bones.

The airport demanded attention: no runways, all snow with markers to designate where to land, and so we did. The temperature was minus 40 degrees as we touched on the snow and slowed—but as we slowed and the airplane's weight went from wings to wheels, we started sinking into the snow.

"Let's get out of here!" I turned the airplane to get back for takeoff, but we kept sinking in, so I had to keep up speed. The engines wouldn't run below about half throttle in the desperate cold. As one stopped we primed it desperately and got it started again, only to have another quit, demanding immediate priming and attention. Dowd had taken over the copilot seat because that's where the engine primers and starters were located; as he fought to keep the engines running I raced to get to takeoff position, keeping up a fast taxi speed to stay on top of the snow surface. We well knew that if we sunk in and got stuck we'd be there forever. I swung wildly around into the wind and opened everything full; the blessed engines took, and in a breathless moment we were back in the air, shaking free of disaster. Back to Fairbanks and a solid runway.

"Out of El Paso: off into light rain, climbed and rain changed into snow, no actual cloud and could see the ground all the time; radio noisy at 19,000 feet, at 30,000 feet still in snow, but could see blue sky above, never in any cloud; snow forming directly from water vapor. Temperature at 29,000 feet, -20°C, but a warmer -15°C at 30,000 feet; an inversion." Rather than an inversion, I had probably stumbled upon the tropopause, whose level changes with weather patterns and can be at 25,000 feet or 50,000 feet—or more, or less. We didn't think much about it then, but with the jet age the tropopause became an important factor in flight planning and avoiding turbulence.

"September 6, 1944, local test flight to see what performance gain we'd get by the drag reduction"—this was necessary for future flight planning. We had removed the turrets, and found that without them sticking out in the airstream we gained 22 mph in airspeed, and a much smoother-feeling airplane.

"Deep low pressure vicinity of Boston. Departed Presque Isle; ceiling 300 feet and visibility one quarter of a mile at takeoff. Climbed to 8,000 in snow until at Augusta, Maine, temperature rose to 1°C; climbed to 25,000, not on top, but snow with static, not very strong so increased speed to make it worse." Snow static is a function of speed; the faster the louder, so I often increased speed in weak conditions to get better charging. Even knowing what our purpose was, it's kind of funny to see the actions I took to make our situation worse.

"October 14, 1944: special day as Dr. Irving Langmuir, Nobel Prize Laureate in chemistry, flew with us from Minneapolis to Lafayette, Indiana, where we had a conference with some people at Purdue doing snow research. They were frantic because of a power failure that threatened to melt the snow they had stored in deep freezers for research. Never did find out if they saved it. Later to Dayton, Ohio, with Langmuir still on board. He was a private pilot and I let him fly some, he did well."

"Out of Fairbanks, Alaska; wet snow at 6,000 feet, rime ice, not enough carburetor heat, alcohol cleared carb very slowly, landed Fort St. John."

The lack of good carburetor heat at low altitudes continued to plague us. On one flight at 7,000 feet in heavy wet snow we were getting some very useful data, so I wanted to stay there. The engines surged and ran rough from carburetor ice. Our only way to keep them going was to pour alcohol down the carburetor throat. We were getting propeller ice, too, and that also required alcohol; luckily Dowd had installed that 55-gallon tank we used for alcohol in the bomb bay. The controls for both props and carburetors were more convenient from the copilot's seat; I had Dowd sit there playing the alcohol controls like a pipe organ so we could stay in the weather. The unquiet feeling of this strange world was aggravated by loud bangs as the Number 2 and 3 propellers threw off chunks of ice that slammed against the fuselage. At least we knew the alcohol was doing its job. Finally a call from Ayres that he had enough data, and as soon as air traffic control approved higher altitude we poured on the power, twisted the supercharger controls as much as possible, and started up; the surge of power felt very good. At about 15,000 feet the temperature lowered, the wet snow became dry and nonsticking, we were in business and I slid back in the seat and relaxed.

Dowd worked on the carburetor heat and made an experimental muff to direct hot air across the intercooler on Number 4 engine; it helped, but it was late in the project and we didn't do any further development before we turned back the airplane. I tried to tell the army they had a very serious carburetor heat problem and probably were losing airplanes because of it; yes, I was told, they knew about it, but the problem wasn't high enough on the wartime priority list for attention. We seldom think of war's casualties from such subtle omissions or distant side effects, but they happen. I'm sure lives were lost because of the inadequate carburetor heat in the B-17.

CHAPTER 16

Distractions and Adventure

J UST WHEN I WAS ENJOYING LIFE, TWA offered me the job of
chief pilot. It was tempting, an opportunity to improve and advance
flight operations, but my loyalty to Dowd, Foley, and the gang, along
with my deep interest in the P static project, tugged the other way. I
told them I'd take the chief pilot job provided the B-17 research was under
my direct supervision, and I'd have a chance to fly it now and then. This
also would mean a chance to live with my wife and daughter again; Jean
and Ferris were back in New Jersey at Jean's mother's house while I was
roaming the skies in the B-17. The chief pilot job meant I'd be stationary
long enough for them to join me in Kansas City.

TWA agreed, and the pilot who replaced me was an old friend, John
Charles Hagins; everyone called him Buddy, and he called everyone Slick.
Buddy came from Texas, where he'd been a crop duster; he was a naturally
good stick and rudder pilot whose skills had been honed flying a few feet
above the ground spraying cotton fields, pulling up at the last moment to
miss trees, barns, or whatever, landing in outrageously small pieces of
ground to refuel and reload. Anyone who lived through a few years of that
had skills beyond the norm.

I wanted him to see the operation and learn how things were done before he went off on his own, so we did an Alaskan trip. We prowled around without much luck, mostly because it was the dead of winter and very cold, which made dry, crystal-like snow that didn't produce the strong static needed.

We flew to the Aleutian Islands where I hoped it would be warmer, causing snow with moisture and higher charging rates; Adak was the central command field for the Aleutians. We almost came a cropper on our first landing. Buddy was flying, and the ceiling reported as 800 feet. We received the altimeter setting via a code, to prevent the enemy from getting barometric pressure to use for meteorological information, or tactically if they decided to attack Adak. Buddy made an excellent approach, and at 800 feet we broke out of the clouds with the runway right ahead, but not very far below; it was a matter of cutting the power and landing.

"Jesus, that's no 800 feet," Buddy shouted and I had to agree; it did seem the ILS and altimeters hadn't compared very well. It turned out the code had been wrong, actually we'd had about a 100 foot ceiling! No harm done, however.

We also landed on Attu and Shemya. Attu was not much except a field covered with glare ice that was hazardous to our landings and taxiing, so we discarded it. But Shemya was different; an island more like an aircraft carrier, a flat piece of terrain sticking up out of the Bering Sea, the runway 500 feet wide and the weather often vile. It is the only place I've ever seen dense fog while the wind blew 60 knots! The fog actually came off the Bering Sea and was blown across the island; the effect was weird as the fog raced in front of you in a dreamlike fashion, leaving you little or no forward vision; it was disorienting and very strange.

But the Aleutian weather was disappointing; most of the cloud mass had low tops, 7,000 feet or so, without the kind of stuff we needed. I stared at weather maps, trying to decipher where we should explore. It didn't take long to realize the weather we wanted was south of the Aleutians. Low pressure areas tracked across below the Aleutians—a perfect area for a mix of cold northern air and warm wet air moderated by the Japanese Current, which flows north of the Hawaiian Islands.

The lows were far enough south that we couldn't fly in them and then return to Adak; and anyway, how dumb would it be to use the Aleutians and their poor weather as a place of refuge? The only way seemed to be a flight from Adak to Midway through some of those lows.

One major problem was that Guy Arnold, our navigator, was not with us, but we did have an extra pilot, Garth Sharp, our copilot; I'd act as navigator. But I had qualms; I was a self-taught navigator, never had any formal schooling. Making it more nerve-wracking was the fact that we'd be aiming at a speck almost 1,700 miles away.

Trying to dig out information on Midway, I quickly learned that the Alaskan theater of operations wasn't tuned in to the Pacific theater of operations. No data on Midway's radio aids, if any. One GI at the operations desk thought Midway had a loop radio range, but no facts or frequencies, even for communication. In the operations office a big board covered the wall, and posted on it were aircraft arrivals, expected departure times, and destinations.

"Where you going next?" the GI manning the board asked me when we checked in.

"Midway."

He shook his head. "Never had anybody goin' that way before."

I was a little concerned that the commanding officer might nix our flight. The bold writing, Midway, on the Ops board made me squeamish, but I'd learned along the way that you never ask for permission, just act as though you have it. Even so, I was nervous over the posting until we got out of Adak. (I later learned that the commanding officer, coincidentally a Colonel Buck, hadn't seen this until we'd departed, and then he raised some hell about us going without approval. Our don't-ask procedure worked.)

I planned a departure just after sundown because I wanted stars along the way for celestial navigation. The boys busied themselves double-checking the airplane, topping off fuel and doing many small chores. I checked the navigation gear, charts, and chronometer. It was late afternoon with the sun hanging low above the horizon; the sky was clear and the air crisp with unlimited visibility, a beautiful late afternoon. As I looked over the navigation chart and folded it to fit on the desk, the immense area of blue caused an unsettled feeling; on one end was Adak, then miles and miles of empty ocean, and at the bottom the tiny islands that make up Midway, less than five miles across. Was I taking on more than I could do? Was I being fair to the others, who were blindly following me thinking I was an ace navigator? But hell, I'd read the books, did a lot of navigating, practiced in the air and on the ground; still, the bad feeling didn't leave.

I needed to calm myself, and I picked up the sextant, which felt familiar in my hand, and climbed out of the airplane. The sun was still above the horizon. I raised the instrument to my eye, centered the bubble, got the sun in it and noted the time. Back in the airplane at the navigator's desk I pulled down the *Air Almanac* and the sight book and ran the numbers, then plotted it; the sun line went right smack through Adak. Hell, we were in business—and a sun low toward the horizon like that is often a difficult shot. I went off with the gang for some food and a short nap.

When we got up it was dark and snowing lightly. I checked the weather, which seemed fairly good except for the possibility of a low along the way. As I've always done, I asked the meteorologist how good the data was from which he'd made the forecast. He smiled and shook his head. "Not much from down that way."

Bad weather wasn't the problem, after all that's what we wanted, but I needed reasonable wind information to use making a flight plan and to have an idea of how we'd be blown about while I navigated. It was obvious the Alaskan theater didn't know or care much about what was going on south of there—we were on our own. I took the best estimates and made out a flight plan that called for a time of eight hours and ten minutes to Midway.

Buddy made the takeoff with me in the copilot seat. We ran down the lighted runway, sharp streamers of snow tearing by in the landing light beam, then lifted off. Once the end of the runway passed under our wing the world became black, nothing. We carefully climbed to avoid hills, and I gave Buddy a heading of 170 degrees to start with, climbed out of the seat, and went below to the navigator's station—Garth got in the copilot seat.

I sat at the small desk, the blue chart taped to it, log there, too, and I wrote the time off. At 10,000 feet we leveled off, it was 0923 Greenwich time—Z time—actually the next day because of the International Date Line. We were 8:23 P.M. local time, almost twelve hours from Greenwich. The snow had lightened a bit.

There were a few radio stations on islands behind us so I took bearings on them that showed us a little east of track at 9:43. Too early to get excited about that. I dimmed the lights until it was dark and then stood up in the astrodome. My head level was outside the airplane and it made me feel detached and right out in the sky; it was almost like standing outside and looking back at the airplane strung out behind. I looked back toward the windshield and could see Buddy's and Garth's dark forms glowing slightly from the cockpit fluorescent light.

I looked up and slowly turned to sweep in the complete sky; the moon was shining through the last of the clouds and snow. The moon was not an advantage; its brightness dims the stars and makes it difficult to see the small ones like Polaris, the North Star. I looked ahead and through a hole in the clouds I could see the brilliance of Sirius, one of the biggest that even the moon glow couldn't diminish. Its brightness gave me a good feeling, a friend to call on.

The radio bearing putting us a little east nagged at me; it could be from a number of things—the forecast winds wrong, the bearings a little suspect because bearings taken from stations behind are never very good, or it might be compass deviation. I decided to check that and got to work putting the astrocompass in its mount in the dome. I got the hour angle and declination for Sirius and set it up on the astrocompass. The clouds were well broken and I could see Sirius well as I squinted through the little magnifying glass and saw the two radium-painted lines that point out into space; I swung the instrument until the bright star was right above them. I quickly looked inside at the airplane's master compass and noted its heading, then looked at the heading on the astrocompass, applied the variation, and it came out right on with both compasses—no deviation. That was good, but just to be certain I did it again, this time on Polaris, and it came out the same; the compass was right on the money, our being east must have been a poor radio bearing and the winds not as forecast.

I got out the sextant to take a fix. I checked my wristwatch against the chronometer on the desk and they agreed, so I got up in the dome again and looked the sky over. There in the east was Jupiter, big and bright for a good course line. I lifted the octant to my eye and there was the dimly lit bubble that takes the place of a horizon. (It's impractical to use the horizon from an airplane unless you're flying very, very low—skimming the waves. The great Francis Chichester did that in his little Moth biplane on the first flight ever across the Tasmanian Sea, but he was a special person in pioneer times.)

I got the bubble centered and then twisted the altitude knob and brought Jupiter into the bubble, but it slid out. I worked it back in again, but it slid out again.

I got down out of the dome and put on earphones and picked up the mike.

"Buddy."

"Yeah?"

"You flyin' this thing or is it on the autopilot?"

"I'm flyin' it."

"Well put it on the autopilot, I'm trying to take some sights."

"Okay." He sounded a little hurt. Most pilots, myself included, hate to admit that for keeping the ship steady for sights, the autopilot's better than we are.

I had to take sights between bouts with cloud masses; the fronts and lows were out there and we plowed through many. These bouts with clouds reduced my chances for star sights, so I wasn't certain of our position, which was disquieting.

I bugged Phil, who was industriously working the radio, to try and get Midway, but his search through the ether only made contact with the Aleutian stations behind us. "Keep trying" was my plea.

Phil was also busy taking data because each cloud mass we penetrated produced the charging and static we were out there to find.

My navigation worries kept me close to the astrodome waiting for a break and some stars. The cloud mass often produced ice, and the front of the astrodome was frequently smeared with it so I couldn't sight a star there even if one came in view. The top and back half of the dome stayed clear, but that reduced my available sky by about 40 percent.

We bounced through the stuff and I stood, octant in hand, for long periods watching through the astrodome and hoping for a break. Fortunately Buddy was at the helm and I knew he could handle anything I could—maybe better—so I didn't have to fly, I could just be a navigator.

There was another method for learning which way the wind was drifting us, and it involved that high-altitude radar altimeter Dowd had installed for me when we got the airplane. At the time this was called pressure pattern flying; it was a new development and had some gray areas, but it was part of our research. During this night of uncertainty it was a point of reference as long as one understood it wasn't solid gold. Lots of things in flying are that way, but if there are enough pieces of information one can take the good from each, use it, and come closer to the truth.

The airplane's altimeter actually measures the pressure around the airplane and calls it altitude; if we're flying in a low pressure or high pressure area, the altimeter might indicate 10,000 feet, but the real altitude above the sea will probably be something else.

The radio altimeter Dowd installed bounced a signal off the sea surface that came back to the airplane and said exactly how high we were above it; we could get an idea of whether we were flying through lower or higher pressure by comparing the altimeter reading with the accurate radar altitude. By making these measurements some time apart, say thirty minutes, we could tell if we were flying toward lower or higher pressure. Now that's something to sink your teeth into, because if we're flying toward a lower pressure area, the winds will be blowing from left to right, and we'll drift that way, on account of the counterclockwise air circulation around a low that the TV weather people keep reminding us about when hurricanes are on the prowl. Of course, it's the other way when we're flying toward a higher pressure. I couldn't tell how fast we'd be drifting, but knowing which way we were going was a help, and I could make an educated guess on speed.

Star sights don't come all neatly packaged and exact; if the air is rough the sight has natural errors because of that little bubble bouncing around, and sometimes I'd only get a sight on one star before we hit a bump and cloud covered us, which resulted in one line of position, a line that says you're on this line, but you have to guess where.

So the art of navigation is taking bits and pieces of clues—a pressure line, one star line or a sloppy fix, maybe a poor radio bearing—and drawing them on the chart and then, like a Gypsy reading tea leaves, making an educated guess as to what's going on and what to do.

The weather we hunted was there and my pressure measurements during the night revealed five wind direction changes; we passed through five fronts.

At 1315 I got another fix and for the first time got a good chance to use the North Star, along with Arcturus and Procyon. The fix showed us on course, but only making 142 knots.

At 1401 I took a four-star fix using the same stars, but added Spica. It was the kind of shot you dream about and it put us right on course making 153 knots; we were at 40 degrees north latitude.

I was relaxing and had an idea that maybe I could catch a ten-minute nap when the smooth flight was broken by a bump—a quick jar and then it smoothed out. We were at 10,000 feet and ahead the clouds built up to unreachable heights. I called Buddy: "How's it look from where you are?"

"It's built way up. I don't think much about topping the stuff."

I called Phil: "Looks like some hot stuff up ahead. You set up for it?" I meant his test equipment and photo recorder.

"Yup, you bet. I got some hot stuff in that last weather we went through."

I grabbed the sextant to get a quick shot before it got rough. There were breaks and I set my sights on Sirius, but every time I'd get ready to shoot we'd run through clouds and it would ruin the shot.

We started going on instruments for longer periods. There was heavy snow and it was rough and some of the stuff stuck and formed ice. Our airspeed went down, but the ice wasn't too bad. "At least," I thought, "we can always go down to lower, warmer levels and melt the ice."

I got hold of Phil: "Have you talked to Midway?" The name seemed so far away when I said it, it seemed as far off mentally as when I sat in New York reading about the battle of Midway.

"Nope, I haven't got 'em yet."

I took the sextant and just stood up in the dome with all the lights turned down and waited for a break in the clouds, for a star to peek through. I was sure we'd eventually find and hear their radio, but in the middle of the ocean you don't depend on anything, so I operated as if we had no radio, to be ready to make it anyway in case there was some failure on our airplane or on the island or something.

I felt like a hunter waiting for game, except that I wasn't very patient. At 1605 I got a shot at three stars. It was choppy and I swore and got mad, but I got something on Vega, Pollux, and Polaris. But the Pollux shot was wild and I had to cast it out.

We were running in and out of the clouds pretty often now, but it was too rough to get a good shot. We were a lot farther south and the temperature was above freezing so the ice worry was gone; an occasional flash of lightning helped make up for the ice enough to keep you on your toes. I kept thinking how I'd like a good shot, and the lightning made me feel that even more because if the static got too bad to pick up Midway's radio—assuming we found it—we'd really want good celestial. I got another fix, but it was bad; it showed we were going along pretty well and gave us a good speed check, but the course information was off. All I could guess was that we were still east of our intended course. The stars were getting dimmer and the sky showed red in the east with the clouds breaking up.

Buddy called me: "The weather's lookin' better, I think I'll get some sleep. Okay?"

Garth and Foley took over. I tuned our radio loop over the frequency dial to see if I could get some signal. There seemed to be a faint one, but it wouldn't steady down. The automatic loop would settle down for a bit and then just when I thought it was going to tell me something it would spin a complete circle—useless.

I went back over my notes and chart, looked over all the shots—the bad ones, the good ones, the pressure lines—averaged them and made a course to Midway. It seemed about right because all the shots put us east. I figured an estimate and decided Midway at 1850—real optimism.

"Well," I thought, "I guess it will be a landfall using a sun line." It's a dicey procedure that's supposed to work, but I wasn't wild about it.

Phil called: "I've got Midway!"

Suddenly Midway became a part of my life, not just a name, not just a battle in the far-off Pacific, but something real out there ahead of me, connected by a tiny, tiny thread the radio made. "Ask them for a bearing."

I waited. I felt good now, we were at least back on earth connected with someone. It seemed a long time but Phil called: "C bearing zero two magnetic."

I quickly plotted it. It lay right on our course line, just where I thought we were. A class C is the poorest bearing and means the reception was bad, but it all fitted, it had to be right.

"Give him our ETA; 1850," I told Phil. Then I crawled up out of the nose to the cockpit. Garth was flying and Foley sitting next to him.

"How we doin'?" Foley wanted to know.

"Be in in fifty-five minutes," I said, and added, "Let me sit there."

As we flew along under those big fluffy cumulus clouds with the blue water below and the sun high enough to make the light sparkle, everyone in the airplane came awake, everyone knew we were getting close and like sailors on a long voyage everyone either came up front or searched out the windows for land. There was an element of tension. I dared to break it and picked up the mike, pushed the button and said, "Midway from Dog Baker one zero one, over." It didn't seem right to say Midway—I'd have felt more natural saying Pittsburgh.

Midway answered and I asked him for a bearing.

"Dog Baker one zero one—bearing zero two, distance fifty-five miles."

I mentally calculated. "I think we're only forty miles out," I said to Garth, "but I won't split hairs."

Everyone was elated over the contact, but the straight-ahead search and tension continued.

"Look! Over to the left," Barney shouted and I thought, "How in hell could it be on the left?" But then he added, "Two airplanes!"

"No, four," said Garth.

To our left were four small specks, and although they had to be friendlies it gave us an anxious moment as they swung toward us. As they came closer I made out that wonderful gull wing.

"They're Corsairs!" we all seemed to shout. They came in from about nine o'clock and slid under us, close, with that sudden smooth rush of a fast airplane. I lowered the landing gear to assure them we were friendly and not some enemy trick with a captured B-17, and we fired the Very pistol with the colors of the day. They were close enough to wave at, and Dowd threw kisses.

They throttled back and in two groups of two wove back and forth across our ship as we held course and flew on. I couldn't help but think of the picture it would be if one could stand off and watch from a vantage point.

Someone said, "There it is!" but it was only a cloud shadow. But a moment later it did show up, at first a slight shadow, and then there were the breakers and the little island stood sandy and green and warm. It was 1900.

I lined up on the runway and descended toward it; the world looked bright, with sunshine sparkling on sand and water. We were just ten minutes behind the original flight plan. We felt wonderful, all concerns tossed aside, we didn't even think about being dirty, tired, and hungry.

✲

W̲E HAD GATHERED ample data on the flight from Adak; it was time to go home and analyze it.

The route would be to Honolulu, San Francisco, and Kansas City. Midway is one of the Hawaiian Islands, but it's 1,360 miles west-northwest of Honolulu. We seldom realize the Hawaiian chain stretches more than 1,600 miles, with many small islands and shoals.

The flight to Honolulu was made in daylight, super clear weather. The winds were gentle, the islands positive fixes—it was an easy hop.

The city was full of military; army, navy, marines. Our civilian clothes stood out and caught the attention of uniformed men; a few loud remarks along the lines of, "They look healthy, why aren't they fighting?" made us uncomfortable. It wasn't always fun being bastards without attachment or uniforms. We decided to go on home without dawdling; next stop San Francisco.

It was a night flight for the sake of navigation. Diary: "CAVU, lots of star sights, one tropical light shower 300 east of Honolulu—twelve hours."

A night in San Francisco and then eight hours and ten minutes to Kansas City. I landed with a melancholy feeling; I was letting go of the most interesting flying of my life, and the finest people. We got our personal gear out, and put the airplane in its hangar.

There's a letdown after an airplane is in the hangar, sitting there quiet and inanimate. You walk away, but only a few steps before turning for a last look, a quiet look that feels more than it sees; the noise, the excitement, weather problems, decisions are all done and filed away, something has ended, died, but things that die leave a certain awareness inside you— that's the way it felt that day.

Dowd and I walked toward our parked cars, quiet, but I wanted to say something.

"I'll keep tabs on it, Barney," I told him, "and if anything isn't right, anything you need, you know where to find me—and thanks for everything." He nodded and we understood.

Where he would find me was in a circular office, ground floor, on one corner of the hangar. That's where the chief pilot grappled with the problems of the airline. Actually the title wasn't chief pilot, as tradition said it should be; some modernizing smartass management people had changed that noble title to system superintendent of flying.

Bill Mumford aloft in *Diving Dottie II*, our home-built glider.

My instructor, Pa Bowyer (*left*), poses with me at the Westfield Airport.

With my father, Dr. A. O. Buck, and my mother, Emilie, before I took off for my junior transcontinental record flight, September 1930.

At the helm of the *Yankee Clipper*, my Pitcairn Mailwing, 1930.

The *Yankee Clipper* in flight.

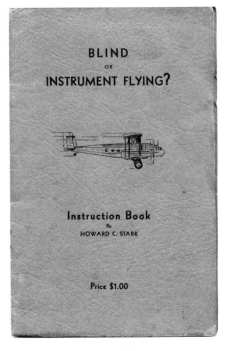

The most important dollar I ever spent: the original instruction book that taught "blind flying," or flying by instruments, to a generation of fliers.

In Los Angeles, at the turnaround point of my transcontinental round trip. With starlet Francis Dee, I looked very sixteen. I think I looked a little more mature at the Los Angeles Breakfast Club event honoring my flight: from left, golfer Harry Cooper, polo star Eric Pedley, golfer Glenna Collett, me, and boxer Jack Dempsey.

A brand-new copilot, so new I practically squeaked. Notice the over-packing that included a suitcase, my "brain bag," and the typewriter I never even opened.

The interior of a DC-2. While lacking in niceties like pressurization, the seating itself was downright luxurious compared to the cabins of today.

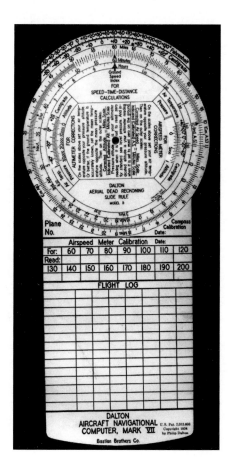

My original slide-rule computer, the one that able copilots could make "smoke" as we figured the flight plan.

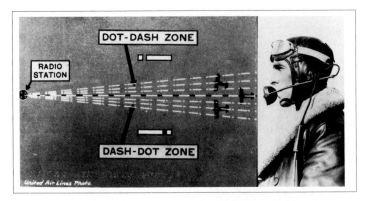

A demonstration of the radio-range system of navigation: in the Dot-Dash Zone, you were approaching on the right; Dash-Dot meant you were to the left.

A typical instrument panel from the 1930s. Contrast this with the multiplicity of controls in the 747 I flew in my last trip for the airline in 1974.

Aviation's last barrier: no matter how sophisticated our systems may get, we will always have to bow to the awesome power of the thunderstorm.

The crew of *Two Kind Words*, our noble B-17: Tucker, physicist; Guy Arnold, navigator; Barney Dowd, crew chief; Ernest Cleveland, Air Corps liaison; me; Garth Sharp, copilot; Bill Foley, assistant crew chief; Brunocardi, electrical engineer; Phil Couch, radio operator; Schechter, Air Corps scientist. The places we stopped are written on the fuselage.

Foley, Dowd, and me with the P-61 Black Widow we also used in our thunderstorm research.

The crew of *The Geek* at the start of its journey: from left, Bill Ritter, radio operator; Tyrone Power, captain; Lana Turner; me, copilot; Bob Stevens, navigator; Bill Agnew, flight engineer.

The Geek, with the flags of the countries and the cities we visited.

Ty Power and me in Kruger Park, South Africa. Ty is on the left.

With Jean and Ferris, upon delivering the first commercial Lockheed Constellation to TWA's headquarters in Kansas City, on Ferris's fifth birthday.

In Valdosta, Georgia, taking jet training. The smooth and reliable power of the jet engine took much of the worry out of commercial flying.

TWA Stratoliner Hostess

Women in aviation have come a long way. The image of the "TWA Stratoliner hostess" promises glamour and beauty, and belies the dedication and determination of those who "had the fire" to earn their seats inside the cockpit door. Three who have that fire (*clockwise from top right*): Vanda Crook, the vice president of operations for CommutAir; Debbie Gary, one of the finest aerobatics pilots I know; and Bonnie Tiburzi, who spent twenty-six years with American as flight engineer, copilot, and captain.

A TWA publicity shot, with
a hostess riding shotgun.
Life was as good as it looks.

Marie-Claude Fontaine, the French hostess
who opened my eyes to the world of art.

While I was in Hollywood, awaiting instructions from Howard Hughes, I got to visit Bob Hope over at his studio. (I'm the one with the shorter hair.)

Seeing the world meant I got to meet so many wonderful people, and so did playing golf—still does. At the Gezira Sporting Club in Cairo I played with Hassan Hassanein, the club pro (here with two caddies and the card of a 66 he had shot for the course record).

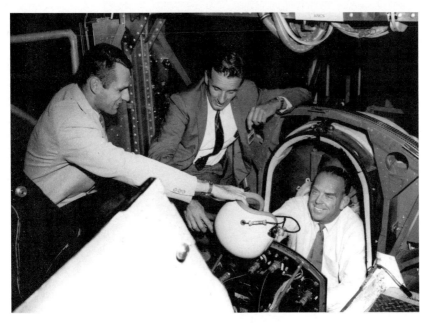

In the NASA simulator that rotated and tumbled as we worked on the problems of flying a supersonic transport. With me are NASA pilot Glenn Stinnett and Pan Am captain Charlie Blair.

Posing with Bernt Balchen, the great polar aviator with whom I was fortunate enough to fly on the round-the-world flight over both poles. Flanking us are Harrison Finch and Fred Austin, TWA captains who put the whole enterprise together.

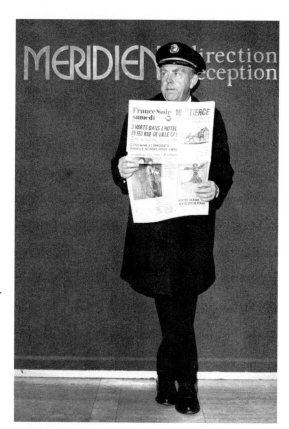

Waiting in front of my hotel in Paris for the crew of my final TWA flight across the Atlantic.

Going over the final flight plan with dispatcher Bill Wood. No matter how many trips you've taken, you never take anything for granted.

For all my years in all types of airplanes, my greatest love in flight was always soaring free in a glider, as I am here in an LS-4.

Captains Robert Buck (TWA, ret., and Delta Air Lines, active, respectively) in the beautiful mountains of Vermont in the fall of 2001.

CHAPTER 17

Chief

To THE LEFT OF my office entrance was a small office with a desk, files, a window, and a very fine lady named Helen Gunn. Middle-aged, dark hair, and almost always a cigarette balancing on her lips, or in hand; she was an even-tempered person, quiet, unruffable, with a pleasant smile and a subdued chuckle rather than an outright laugh.

Without her I would have been lost. She kept the seniority lists, checked most of the bulletins the chief pilot wrote for the troops, filtered my mail, and did other mysterious things with pilot records I never quite understood. Helen had been in this job from almost the first chief pilot; certainly she'd been there when Harlan Hull, the man who hired me, held the post.

Aside from being someone you liked and were glad to be around, she was a fount of knowledge, and I never made a serious decision without swinging around the corner to Helen's office and saying, "What do you think of this idea?" Perhaps I'd explain it, or hand her a bulletin I'd just written and expected to distribute.

Helen would listen, or read the bulletin, pause for a few moments and perhaps say, "It sounds okay to me." Or she'd look off into space for a bit and then say something like, "Otis tried that," meaning Otis Bryan, a previous chief pilot, or maybe George Rice, or Harlan, or whoever held the post, "and it didn't work." She'd tell me what had happened after the idea was put out into the field, and many times, as I walked back into my office, I'd say a quiet "Thank God for Helen" as I tossed a crumpled piece of paper in the wastebasket. She should have been chief pilot—although she didn't fly—with people like me as her assistants for technical matters (a facetious thought with a modicum of validity).

There was another office, on the second floor, that had a lot to do with my job. It was large with a circular window that faced the airport's north-south runway and terminal. A desk faced into the room, but the large swivel chair attending it swung around so the occupant could survey the action out on the airport. The man who sat in that chair was John Collings, my boss. He spent a lot of time looking out; even during meetings he'd frequently have his back to the room as he gazed out the window.

Any unusual action caught his eye; he'd reach for the phone and get the dispatch office to find who the crew was on the airplane, and the next call would be to me, with the pilot's name and the action John didn't like, passed on with the order, "Get him in and find out about it."

A great sigh from me and eventually a chat with the pilot and then a report to Collings; he always wanted to know what disciplinary action I'd taken, and if none, he sounded short. I don't think he ever thought I was tough enough.

One day he called to report that the treasurer of our company was riding the Chicago–Kansas City flight and our airplane had passed Braniff close enough to be frightening—Specht was the pilot, get him in.

I knew before I called Specht what it was all about: Braniff and TWA were rivals on that route, and we raced to get to Kansas City ahead of them. If you were able to pass, by tricks of the trade, the game was to go by close enough to let Braniff know you were there.

Specht came in and I got after him about it.

"I was never closer than 500 feet," he insisted. That was the legal minimum distance then in the regulations.

I admonished him not to get that close, it scared passengers, give any other airplane a wide berth. That was it; he hadn't broken any rules.

Collings called: "What did you do with Specht?"

"I had a talk with him, and said to give others a wide berth, but he was legal."

"That's all you did?" In a voice of astonishment.

"Yes, he told me he was outside 500 feet, he's my pilot and I have to have faith in him. Besides, that treasurer isn't a pilot, doesn't know what distance is from an airplane; who am I supposed to believe, a pilot or some bean counter?"

The phone slammed down and Collings didn't talk to me for a week, not even an acknowledgment when we passed in the hall.

So that was the other office I had to contend with, the VP of ops, as we called it. But Collings was actually a good pilot, very precise, demanding, with a piercing look that people tried to stay away from.

What does a chief pilot do? Well, many things: hire pilots, oversee training, worry about the pilot's union contract and infringements, develop new or better procedures. One that concerned me involved the navigational paperwork that included the time over checkpoints, fuel usage, and so on. The first block on the log sheet was time off the ground, and I noticed that as soon as flights were in the air, the copilot dug out the sheet and marked the time off the ground, as well as time away from the blocks; he had his head down, writing, when he should have been looking outside for traffic. So I set up a new procedure: no paperwork until the airplane had completed its climb and leveled off for cruising. Also, after a long squabble with the cabin service department, I established procedure so the hostess wouldn't come in the cockpit after the "No Smoking" sign went on unless she had an emergency, to avoid distracting pilots during approach and landing. There was a little grumbling from the troops, but it didn't seem unreasonable to ask pilots to remember what time they'd left the ground until they'd reached cruising altitude, or for the hostess to stay out of the cockpit at a busy time. That was the start of the "sterile cockpit," as it came to be known, and a sample of the kind of procedure a chief pilot's office can put in force.

Scheduling pilots was in your bailiwick, and that was a constant pain in the neck. We had five bases where pilots lived and flew from: Los Angeles, Kansas City, San Francisco, Chicago, and New York. They flew all over the airline, and certain flights were assigned to each base; which flights had a lot to do with money made and hours of work. The result was one base arguing that another base had flights the first base should have. This was a monthly problem, and the Air Line Pilots Association descended on me with arguments, threats, and pleading; sometimes these meetings got pretty intense and my patience wore to an edgy state. On one occasion I gaveled the group to silence and announced, "I'm going out of the room, you all get together and set the schedule up yourselves. Let me know when you're finished."

I knew what would happen, and after hours of wrangling they gave up and handed it back to me—with some humility.

Of course, I didn't sit there myself and draw out all the run patterns, or lines of time as we called them, but had expert schedule people do the job. My task was to be a moderator and pacifier, within the economics of an airline.

Keeping all the pilots under you proficient was part of it. Pilots took periodic instrument checks and line checks. For an instrument check we used an airplane; simulators as we know them today hadn't reached the level necessary for a complete check. This made checking expensive, somewhat dangerous, and subject to the vagaries of weather. If it was too bad the check was put off, and sometimes this affected schedules when there weren't enough pilots qualified to fly.

Line checks were done on the line with a check pilot. Choosing check pilots wasn't easy; you wanted pilots with good skills, temperament, and a personality that wasn't overbearing or cocky. There were many searches down the list of pilots to find the right one, only to have him turn down the job. Lots of people didn't want to be a check pilot, and some shouldn't have been.

A check pilot came into my office one morning to tell me he'd checked Captain X to Albuquerque.

"How was he?"

"He flew all right, but his instrument work was sloppy so I told him he'd need some additional training."

"Did you fly his flight back to Kansas City?"

"No, he flew it back, I had another pilot to check."

"Jesus! You let him fly a flight back after a down check? Do you realize what would happen if he'd had an incident on the way back? The CAA, lawyers, and everyone else would discover you'd down-checked him and then let him fly. They'd sue our ass off!"

That created check pilot meetings, to be sure all were clear on this point. It was the kind of thing you had to handle.

The war was winding down, but the airlines weren't; they were frantic to resume flights that had been cut. With soldiers coming home, increased economic activity, and a general feeling of excitement, they also wanted to expand.

In May the Germans surrendered and a lot of people were released from the military. Many of them were our line pilots who were in the reserves and had been called up when the war started. My world went chaotic as pilots showed up eager to know where they fitted in and what their status was, along with the happy greeting of people you knew but hadn't seen for a long time, weren't even sure they were alive.

The answer on their status was easy: right where they left it, their seniority number as it was and all the choices that went with it. This meant they could return to their previous bases able to fly whatever their seniority dictated.

This didn't sit well with all pilots, although most thought it fair and proper. The ones that didn't complained to me, and I had to give them the facts of life and send them off.

Of course, we had to put the returnees through training and updating, and while this didn't amount to much it did use up our training and check pilots.

To top it off, the company started hiring; Collings ordered me to hire seventy-two pilots every two weeks. So piled on was the problem of reviewing dossiers, doing interviews, and then sending the hired ones off to our school. It was a crush because we didn't have ground school facilities and had to scrounge for space, even renting motel rooms for classes. The weather didn't cooperate and training flights got canceled, which backed up everything. In the meantime the airline was scheduling more flights and Collings was demanding pilots.

What in hell had I gotten myself into? The idea of doing unique things to improve operation and all the other goals to make it better were shoved aside while trying to hold back the flood of problems.

I made Red Foster my assistant chief pilot and turned the hiring over to him. Red was an old friend from my early days in New Jersey; the first time

I ever saw him was as he dangled from a parachute after making an exhibition jump on Sunday afternoon at the Westfield Airport. I never did know how he joined TWA; I certainly had nothing to do with it, although I would have if necessary. But Red fit the job perfectly, and not only interviewed but filled in as a check pilot.

The pilots we were hiring came from the military, young men from B-17 bombers or other aircraft, navy pilots, marines, the lot. It was a great group to choose from, sharp young men, perhaps not with a lot of hours of flying; a typical pilot would have flown a B-17 on about thirty-one missions over Europe including some of the very tough ones, plus a bit of instruction after returning to the States, accumulating a total of only 760 hours flying time before coming to us; prewar we wouldn't even look at a pilot with less than 1,500 hours.

I look back now at these men who became captains and have retired after spotless careers, flying their runs, flying bad weather, changing airplanes as we progressed from DC-3 to Boeing 747—I have a warm, proud feeling toward them; TWA—despite Flight 800, an aberration—had a record of safety and service looked up to and envied by the industry. The pilots we hired during those confusing, hectic days accomplished it.

Seventy-two additional pilots every two weeks was a staggering amount, and I had serious concerns we were overdoing it. Among the pilots we'd hired was a Lieutenant Colonel W. Evans, called Pug, a very sharp young man who had been on General Curtis LeMay's planning staff in the Pacific. He had fancy ways of projecting things with flow charts and mumbo jumbo I didn't understand, but checking around I found his reputation solid.

"Pug, run out your charts, and tell me if we really need all these people."

It didn't take him long to cover my desk with a long sheet of paper that overflowed both ends. "We're way over hiring." And he showed me why.

"Let's go see Collings."

The paper was laid out on his desk, and Pug gave a careful and simple explanation. Collings looked it all over, listened, looked up at us and said, "Keep hiring."

Sad to say, Pug's work was correct; a year later we were furloughing pilots.

The backlog of untrained pilots built up because of bad weather, and Collings was on my neck. I had an idea, and after a bit of research I flew off to Arizona. There, empty, were a number of Air Corps fields used for wartime training, complete with sleeping quarters, kitchen facilities, even swimming pools. The Army Air Forces in the Phoenix area had lost only one day a year because of weather; I found we could lease one of these airports for $1 a year. I wanted to move the training to Arizona: airplanes, instructors, students, the lot.

Back to Kansas City, up to the second floor to Collings. I put it all out for him. "No, it wouldn't work." He squashed me flat. So we slogged on as best we could.

One day, a pilot came in to gripe about something, I think it was a layover time being too short so the crew didn't get proper rest. I added it up in my head and it didn't sound too bad to me; I was mentally impatient with this trivial matter compared with my other problems. But suddenly a little bell rang in my mind, and I realized I wasn't listening as a pilot, but a damned executive. Yes, that was a tight layover—I'd do something about it.

The incident made me realize I was losing touch with the real flying world; I hadn't flown a trip in a couple of months. I went to the dispatch office and looked over the schedules; there was one that went Kansas City, St. Louis, and Indianapolis, stayed overnight and returned the next morning, Saturday to Sunday. "Put me on that trip," I told Dispatch, "every Saturday until I tell you differently."

It was a lifesaver. I returned to the real world, where the action was, where you appreciated the problems. It sacrificed my weekends, but it was worth it.

Once, in the summer, I was returning from Indianapolis to Kansas City after an all-day meeting. There was a heavy sky with thunderstorms growling in late afternoon development. I wondered who the captain would be and I hoped for a skillful old-timer—but it wasn't, it was a brand-new captain whose papers had just cleared my office, out on his first trip. I thought about him, a quiet, humble man, and how he'd cope with the forming thunderstorm that had developed on all quadrants of the sky by the time we took off. He welcomed me aboard and went forward to the cockpit. I was a passenger and determined to stay in the back no matter what.

No sooner were we airborne than we were dodging storms and we finally plowed into the center of one with all its turbulence, rain, and lightning. As we tossed, heaved, and jolted through the angry sky my heart said to get up front, look over his shoulder, be ready to advise, but my job was to let this new captain know I had faith in him—I wouldn't dare go forward. Besides, we had checked him out, said he was skillful enough to cope, and I was duty-bound to accept this; I'd let my family ride with him. That was the pet way check pilots expressed their feeling about a pilot under scrutiny: "Would you let your family ride with him?"

After we landed I complimented him on the ride; I felt good about it, and I'm sure it made his day.

I was part of the team we sent to Boeing Aircraft to examine the Boeing 377, a possible purchase for our international routes. This was the commercial development from the B-29; I flew it quite extensively with Boeing test pilots and on one flight, as we were doing maneuvers at 18,000 feet, we had a radio call: "The Japs have surrendered!"

That was a wild night in Seattle, and a happy one, though perhaps not for Boeing because we turned down the airplane and headed south to Burbank to talk to Lockheed about its Constellation.

The overseas routes were about to be awarded by the government. A battle royal went on over the choice routes, and TWA was pulling out all the political stops. Our chief rival was Pan American Airways, who thought they should be the one airline representing the United States. The governing body was the Civil Aeronautics Board, and we all awaited their recommendations. The political undercurrents were strong; when the CAB's report came out, Pan Am got everything and TWA almost nothing.

But the battle wasn't over. The final awarding of international routes was up to President Truman. I happened to be in our Washington, D.C., executive offices when the CAB's recommendation came out; I saw our TWA president, Jack Frye, who had lived in Washington for the past few years working almost solely on the route awards.

"Jack, I'm so sorry about the report, I know how hard you've worked on this."

He smiled, in good spirits, nudged me with his elbow and said, "Don't worry, we'll get 'em."

The final awards, with presidential approval, gave TWA the crème de la crème: Paris, Rome, Athens, Cairo, Zurich, Geneva, Frankfurt, London, Tel

Aviv, Bombay, Lisbon, Madrid, and more. A lot of people had forgotten that TWA was a Missouri company and that Jack played poker and drank bourbon at the White House.

In Burbank, Lockheed was finishing up our first Constellations, the airplane we'd use on our international routes (and some domestic). This was a big advance: 300 mph cruising speed, pressurization so we could fly 20,000 feet if need be, four engines, and long range. It was a big leap from DC-3s, DC-4s, and our five old tired Stratoliners.

The Constellation had flight controls moved by hydraulics—a new thing—and flying at 300 mph burned a lot more fuel than anything we'd ever flown. As we inspected what this airplane could do, the North Atlantic came into consciousness as my mind drifted far from California to the coast of Newfoundland, the broad sea, the green of Ireland as the coast was crossed, the North Atlantic I'd flown, battled, nervously struggled with. It was an ocean I felt close to: an adversary, but a part of me, something not unlike a love. But with this new airplane and its altitude ability, much of the bad weather would be below us; we'd be above clouds and ice, looking smugly down on the problems of the past.

We walked out to the airplane. It seemed to tower above me. The landing gear legs were long, like the legs of a stork, except there were three; the wing stretched wide and the four engines were big and round, slinging large propellers. It was a bit dismaying to think a man could command this mass of wings, propellers, machinery. But those thoughts were cast aside as I approached a long metal set of steps that went from the ground to a small door just behind the cockpit; I placed one foot after the other, clanking on each step, lugging the black navigation case, thinking thoughts that mostly were pride and pleasant expectation. Through the small door, crouching, into the cockpit, past the flight engineer's station and slither sideways into the pilot's seat, settle in it, fasten the seat belt, look around: then all apprehension gone; it was another airplane with familiar wheel and rudder pedals, throttles, and other controls. Let's fire it up and get going.

Before accepting delivery, we had to be checked out on the airplane. First we satisfied the Lockheed pilots who took us up and put the Constellation through its paces; then we had to satisfy the government, the CAA. An inspector would fly with each of us, and if we passed his test we'd be given a rating for that airplane.

Early one morning I was standing by the airplane when the CAA inspector arrived. It was an embarrassing situation, because the inspector was a recently released TWA copilot who had failed in his test for captaincy and we had let him go—I had even signed him off. It wasn't unusual then for a pilot who couldn't make it with an airline to wind up a CAA inspector. Fortunately, this was a good chap who smiled sheepishly as we shook hands.

Once that process was done with and we were fully certified and schooled, it was time to turn over the airplane to us. This was not done simply; the procedure was for Lockheed to fly it to Las Vegas, where I'd give them a check for $690,000. Delivery in Las Vegas avoided the California sales tax.

Paul Frederickson, our West Coast regional chief pilot, flew it at my invitation because it was his region; I acted as copilot. The Lockheed pilots, who theoretically were supposed to fly, luxuriated in the cabin.

At Las Vegas there was a big to-do. We were met by a stagecoach, the senior Nevada senator, the president of Lockheed, TWA officials, a band, pretty girls, and all. It was a big event.

We stayed overnight, and the next day we headed for Kansas City. Now I was captain and Frederickson my copilot. TWA engineers rode along, as well as the Wright Engine Company's test engineer, Bob Johnson.

I had orders from Collings on exactly how to manage the flight: use only 65 percent power, fly down the airways and arrive at Kansas City at exactly four o'clock in the afternoon.

Off we went, but the 65 percent power idea went out the window. We used various power settings to check out performance data and a lot of other things. We carefully reported over each checkpoint, sending position, time, and altitude to Kansas City where Collings sat in his office, a log sheet on his desk, carefully marking our times and progress. Little did he know that the times weren't all that precise, as I juggled them a bit to cover the different power settings and speeds so he'd think we were right on his 65 percent.

Our time was good, and I realized we'd be a bit ahead of the 4:00 P.M. arrival, but an old trick cured that: about thirty miles south of Kansas City, not far from Olathe, I made a couple of lazy circles to kill time, then only eight minutes away we headed for Kansas City and made a low pass across the field at exactly four o'clock. John Collings was the first to greet us and allowed we'd done a good job. There were cameras and people including Jean and Ferris; it was her fifth birthday, November 15, 1945, the day of the first airline delivery of a Constellation, ever.

Being chief pilot meant constant worry and frustration, and had little to do with flying; I missed its freedom, its challenges, and the intimacy with the sky, clouds, and stars. Dowd wasn't much help as he'd drop by the office to say howdy and tell me stories of his flights; whenever he'd leave I could feel that B-17 rumbling its way through the sky and I missed it badly.

But there wasn't any way out. I couldn't walk in and quit; the Constellation program was in full swing and I had to do a host of things to obtain CAA approval of the operation. The first one was to write a pilot's manual, a book of explanations and procedures. I surrounded myself with fat Lockheed manuals and data, shuffled it, dug through, and tried to sift out the necessary things. It was tough going and I wasn't getting very far, but then it hit me: the purpose of the manual was for pilots to operate the airplane, so what was I doing plowing through all this stuff when I already knew how to do it? I told my secretary, "Dee, get your notebook and follow me." We went out to a parked Connie, climbed in, and sat down; I took the captain's seat, and Dee sat in the copilot's. I went through all the gadgets and how we'd use them: practical, hands-on action, a direct line from reality to paper. Except for some references, now better visualized from Lockheed's paperwork, that's how we created the manual.

"Here's the pilot operation manual," I said as I handed it to Collings. He glanced at it.

"Hell, it's not as thick as the DC-3 manual."

"John, that just proves the DC-3's manual is too damn big."

He bought it, but that didn't cure my problem. I wanted out of that office I increasingly felt trapped in.

But things can change quickly, and a phone call did it.

The Army Air Forces wanted our B-17, *Two Kind Words,* to fly around the world, visiting theaters of operation, assessing the weather in their area—and they asked for me to command it. It was a spark, a way out, but there were problems: what about the chief pilot job, the Connies going into service, and what about Hagins, who had been flying the 17 for almost a year?

The Hagins part was delicate but proved easy. Hagins had done a fine job, flying a lot of tough weather in the United States, but the army's request for me didn't have anything to do with Hagins: I had started the project, flown it for a couple of years, knew about the political ins and outs, and I had a lot of long-range, over-ocean experience. I talked it over with Hagins, who understood; he indicated he wasn't too excited about prowling around the world anyway. I never knew if he just said that for my sake or not, but he was gracious about it all.

But what about being chief pilot? Well, I'd done a lot of preparation for the Connie introduction, and there were lots of people who could handle the job. I explained it all to Collings, who was a bit tight-lipped about it, mostly because of the Connie problem, but there was a good man in the wings whom both Collings and I liked, Busch Voights. He took over the Connie project, and the chief pilot's job went to Phares McFerren, one of our senior pilots who had management experience—a real good choice and I'm sure a better man for the job than me. And suddenly, after some loose ends were tied up, I was free! It felt wonderful.

Dowd and the gang were in their old jovial form as we flew off to Wright Field together for briefing and plans. The B-17 felt good, cares dropped away, and the sky was blue again.

CHAPTER 18

Around the World

A T WRIGHT FIELD we received our orders. They were a bit unusual:

SPECIAL FLIGHT RESEARCH MISSION
PROPOSED ITINERARY:

Wright Field	Karachi
Washington	Calcutta
Miami	Chabua
Puerto Rico	Kunming
Trinidad	Hong Kong
Belém	Manila
Natal	Guam
Casablanca	Kwajalein
Dakar	Johnston Island
Tripoli	Oahu
Cairo	San Francisco
Khartoum	Kansas City
Aden	Wright Field

Local flights will be made from various stations and deviations from this schedule are expected.

PERSONNEL:

ARMY	TWA
Capt. E. L. Cleveland	Capt. R. N. Buck, IN FULL CHARGE
Mr. H. Schell	Mr. G. A. Sharp
Mr. P. W. Couch	Mr. G. Arnold
Tuc	Mr. B. J. Dowd
Mr. S. Bruno	Mr. W. A. Foley

So it said on January 11, 1946, except for a few names I have changed for reasons of propriety.

On the army side, E. L. Cleveland was our Wright Field liaison man, officer-in-charge. Couch had flown with us a lot, and in addition to his data-gathering work acted as radio operator. I never did understand what Schell and Bruno did other than some mysterious electronic stuff, as well as being world-class tourists everywhere we landed. Bruno, with his Italian ancestry, was anxious to see Rome and assured us he could speak the language and would interpret.

Tuc, not his real name, was special: a brilliant physicist who had created a device to gather, measure, and study atmospherics, the stuff of lightning and electrical fields. His gadget could collect this over vast distances. Only Tuc understood or could operate the device. Eventually he received a decoration for his work.

They were an interesting mix of personalities: Cleveland was a formal, proper professor, Tuc a quiet studious person with an engaging smile, inquisitive about all things, and attached to drink. Couch was our quiet, pleasant old buddy, Schell a busy person who wanted to see and know everything, but in his own sphere, which we never quite understood—the moment we landed he generally went right off to see the sights, but he was no trouble. Bruno was the youngest and lived in Schell's world, paddling along with him wherever Schell went.

Our side was the old gang: Sharp, copilot; Arnold, navigator; Dowd, crew chief; and Foley, his assistant.

And off we went. The sunny sky of the Caribbean gave us little challenge; the Intertropical Front of South America was lurking with its thunderstorms, but we'd been there before and our trip through it gave us nothing new.

I'd studied terrain and literature looking for likely thunderstorm areas, and found one northwest of Rio de Janeiro. It wasn't difficult to convince the others we ought to go to Rio—and they weren't thinking thunderstorms.

Theory was substantiated: the land northwest of Rio rises from sea level to about 6,000 feet some 300 miles inland, and warm, moist air from the South Atlantic flowing up this slope kicks off thunderstorms of impressive size. We poked around these enough to know they were right up there in the big league, with all the trimmings: rain, lightning, turbulence. Despite having flown a lot of thunderstorms we could never say they were old-hat and routine; in the dark clouds with all hell breaking loose we were never blasé, but not scared, either. I knew *Two Kind Words* would hang together, so my only concern was carburetor heat and keeping the engines going in the fierce downpours. But we knew there were superstorms lurking out there; the major violence occurs during the building stage, as our innocent but very turbulent cloud over Pennsylvania's Poconos had taught us. There's a specification of air masses called potential temperature, and you do not want to be there at the point in a thunderstorm's growth stage when potential temperature is reached, clouds grow, rain pours down, and the latent heat of condensation starts a perpetual motion of violent weather. We never hit one quite like that, though we thought we had during a couple of wild ones. Such monsters are out there, and the occasional incident of an airplane's structure failing—as TWA's DC-3 did in the San Joaquin Valley in the summer of 1944—makes it seem real enough to keep one alert when plowing into a dark, threatening mass.

After that exploration we took a couple of days R&R in Rio and Copacabana Beach with its fine landscape of barely covered femininity. There's a fierce undertow and the water is cold, but who cares about the swimming? Foley was the only casualty; after a few beers and a futile attempt at conversation with one of the beach's habitués who only spoke Portuguese and got bored and wandered off, Foley fell asleep lying on his stomach. He baked in the sun, and only the water lapping over him from an incoming tide woke him in time to prevent a serious burn. He still got pretty well cooked, and the back of his legs seared so badly we had to carry him in and out of the airplane and to meals and bed for a number of days.

From Rio north to Natal, and then across the South Atlantic to Dakar:

an easy flight, a few rain showers, but mostly clear. The soporific flight was jolted to alertness when the Number 3 engine had a fit of mild roughness. We fiddled with the mixture and power settings and it settled to smooth running, but in fifteen minutes or so it quivered again, making the brown cowling shudder back and forth—it smoothed out and ran properly, but all the way to Dakar it shivered with periodic chills and fever, or whatever it was.

After landing, Dowd and Foley tore into it but they couldn't find anything wrong, it ran beautifully on the ground. So off to Casablanca. This flight was especially interesting to me as we traversed the coast of Africa where Antoine de Saint-Exupéry had flown the mail in the 1920s, and over Cape Juby where he had been the chief. Behind the coastline is desert, miles and miles of it; in his time unfriendly tribes inhabited the area and made flying the route a nervous task.

I looked down on the lonely, barren land, thinking of him and the other pilots flying their ancient Breguet XIVs: square, ugly biplanes, 80 miles per hour cruising speed, engines that periodically failed and dropped them down on the lonely sandscape, and sometimes into unfriendly arms. They often flew two airplanes in formation so if one was forced down, the other could land, rescue the pilot, and get off before the natives showed up.

These were the real pioneers, not the pilots in DC-2s over the friendly U.S.A.—or even in machines like my open Pitcairn biplane with its strong 225-horsepower Wright engine and 120 mph cruise speed. The term *pioneer,* like *hero,* is overused and carelessly spread about in a way that dilutes the real ones. I looked down and was awed. I felt privileged to soar above these routes, to imagine what it was like, to put myself in the noisy, slow, uncertain aircraft, being beaten by prop wash, heat, and sun, flying low over windblown sand. It has been said that Saint-Exupéry was a great writer and philosopher, but a poor pilot; the sight of that rugged country and its lonely vastness, and the fact that he lived through those times in addition to his flying mail in South America, certainly settled for me any questions about his ability as a pilot. St. Ex, as they called him, was two different people, a pilot and a philosopher. Which do I appreciate more? It isn't a contest: any pilot who thinks of those early times realizes he was a good pilot who pushed into the unknown—Africa, South America, and so on, not thinking he was a heroic pioneer, but a man trying to use the airplane for transport. As for his philosophy, one can read *The Little Prince* and that's enough; I think he became more a philosopher than a pilot toward the end, and while he knew well how to fly, he may not have absorbed the gut mechanical stuff of the modern airplane, being preoccupied with other thoughts. He wanted to fly in the war effort, even though at age forty-three he was too old by regulations; he appealed up the line of command until he got approval. On July 31, 1944, he took off from a base in Corsica for a high-altitude photo recon mission. He never returned and was never found. I've always thought he got lost because the oxygen system didn't supply his needs at high altitude. Was that a system mechanical failure, or a pilot's? We'll never know.

As much respect as I have for the airmail pilots who first flew the skies over America, we cannot forget others, and especially not the French and Saint-Exupéry, flying over land with high mountains and little civilization, where if you were forced to land you faced tribes who were ready to hold you for ransom if not kill you outright. These, truly, were pioneers first-class.

My reverent thoughts were broken by the Number 3 engine having another fit; teasing, it settled down for a long period, and then did it again. Foley stuck his head into the cockpit, looked out at Number 3, and muttered, "Goddamn, there goes Old Shaky again." So that became its name.

At Casablanca they pulled the cowling and checked it over again: compression, valves, ignition; but nothing showed up and it again ran perfectly on the ground.

To Rome, with Old Shaky doing its intermittent rough act. In Rome further inspection and checking, same results.

Bruno, at last in his dreamt-of Italy, fell flat as interpreter, as his American Italian didn't fit with the real thing. This wasn't unusual; immigrants in the United States, living in their own close-knit communities, eventually change their old language. In future years when I flew to Rome, our Italian passenger agents would often ask me in a quandary, "Who are these Italians you bring from the States—we cannot understand them."

Aside from telling the local Army Air Forces people about static and our efforts, and how big-diameter wire antennas with wicks could cure it, we were finding no weather to combat, although Tuc always seemed to gather something on his equipment, atmospheric static from far away.

In Cairo, more of the same: sightseeing, spreading the word, gazing into cloudless skies. To Karachi, India; wind, sand blowing as in a storm, but no interesting weather to speak of. Old Shaky continued annoying and infuriating Dowd and Foley as they checked, tried, and cussed.

From Karachi to Calcutta, we swung a bit north to get a glimpse of the Himalayas and perhaps pick out Everest. In the distance the jagged snow-covered peaks stood in a long line. They were impressive but lacking in definition; it was difficult to discern one peak from another, as there are so many almost as high as Everest. McKinley in Alaska seemed more impressive, rising to 20,320 feet almost from sea level; it stands there, tremendous, mystical, eerie, reputed to be the highest mountain in the world from base to top.

Approaching Calcutta, Number 2 engine gave a real fit, enough to shut it down. This one was easy, a stuck valve that proved unstickable. The big box of spare parts in the bomb bay came into its own. Dowd had carefully decided what parts to carry, and he'd included a spare cylinder or two; they changed Number 8 cylinder, and Number 2 engine returned to its faithful, smooth performance. Old Shaky, however, retained its annoying ways despite constant pampering and futile diagnostics.

Calcutta was in a state of ferment. We spent our first night in a hotel in the city; it was a revelation—dirty, crowded, poor beyond imagination, beggars, smells, and crowds gathering to protest something, we weren't certain what. The next night we moved to tents at the airport—each with its own mongoose for protection from snakes.

But one crew member, Tuc, was missing, nowhere to be found. We went back to town, searching for him. Crowds milling, chanting—it was scary, and where was Tuc? Then, in the confusion of the crowd, in the midst of hundreds, we spied him, drunk and happy, a big grin on his face and a small monkey on his shoulder.

Tuc came back with us to our tents at the airport. Outside, a huge mob chanted, "Go home!" It didn't take a riot for us to agree with the idea.

Couch didn't seem himself; he stayed in his cot much of the day, wasn't interested in food, didn't want to talk. What was wrong? Some interrogation and prodding drew out the reason: he was lovesick! We knew he'd met a lovely lady in Kansas City, but we didn't know the depth of his affection. He revealed that they had gotten married just before we departed. We nursed him the rest of the way, and got him back among the living, at least in part.

Number 2 engine fixed, we flew to Bangkok. Now we were getting closer to where the war had so recently been. Japanese prisoners were at work around the airport. Dowd had one up on the wing helping him fuel the airplane.

"I feel like a giant! Finally, someone smaller than me!" Dowd called out over the prisoner's head.

En route to Bangkok from Calcutta, there were a few thunderstorms, but while they built to great heights, they had that lazy tropical feel. They produced heavy rain, but they were way down on our scale of toughness.

There were no official quarters in Bangkok, so we wound up in digs on the palace grounds, very nice. We traded a few cigarettes for Siamese jewelry, silver with black designs of dancers. We lugged the goods home as gifts, but it was chintzy stuff, and after the war it showed up in cheap costume jewelry stores. We thought we'd found something special in Bangkok, but the trade for the cigarettes was probably an even swap.

Then to Manila, across Cambodia and Vietnam. Impressive jungles and mountains, impenetrable; as we flew by I thought about Saigon and its French influences, the city it was then, and not the battleground it was to become.

In Manila, Dowd was determined to deal with Old Shaky. Stripped to the waist in the hot sun, he and Foley tore into it. The decision: hone the valve guides, clean them out so there wasn't any possibility of a valve hanging up. This isn't easy with proper tools, and they were doing it without them.

They carefully released the valve springs, dropped the valve to the top of the piston, honed out the guide using, as I recall, the cleaning tools for a .50-caliber machine gun. After that, they reached in through the spark plug hole with a tool they made—two pieces of metal, working as a pincers—to grasp the valve and get it back in the guide, then refasten its springs. This was repeated on nine cylinders, and on the last one a small piece of the tool broke off, perhaps one eighth of an inch by a quarter. It was inside, in the cylinder. What harm would it do? Should we remove the cylinder?

Foley: "Hell, I've seen bigger things than that left in engines at overhaul."

Dowd: "Damn, I don't know, maybe we ought to take that cylinder off?"

Me: "Hell, it's a tiny hunk, as soon as we fire the engine that's gonna go right out the exhaust. Let's go."

The issue was settled by the presence of a general we didn't even know. He was stuck in Manila because his B-17 had a badly failed engine; he needed a new one and there were none on base. One of us realized, "If that bastard finds out we're here he might take one of our engines, and there we'd be—and he outranks us."

All of us: "Let's get out of here!"

We gathered the gang, fired up, and departed for Guam. The broken piece didn't seem to harm anything and we were satisfied it had gone out the exhaust. But true to form, half an hour later, Old Shaky did its thing again.

"Son of a bitch!" was the unanimous cry. And I felt for the boys, they had really done a great job under very tough conditions for naught.

Guam: a huge base, B-29s for bombing Japan. Be careful, they told us, of wandering off to remote areas, there are still Japs hiding in the hills.

Of more interest, however, was the big storage depot of airplane parts. By now Dowd and company had done everything except change the carburetor.

To the office: You have any carburetors for our power plant? "Buddy, there's thousands of parts out there, here's a list of locations and stuff—if you can find one, go to it."

Dowd studied the list, finally got to carburetors. Yes, there was one with all the correct part numbers, except at the number's end there was a dash 53 or something that didn't match ours. Probably a small difference; let's try it. So we went down long lines of parts, dug out the carburetor with the wrong dash number. It fit when we took the old one off, and the engine ran beautifully on the ground. Let's test-hop it. It ran okay. Maybe, just maybe Old Shaky was cured. We'd find out on the next leg of our journey.

Guam had an airplane and parts graveyard, a big area where airplanes, parts, and equipment not worth the time to repair during the war were thrown away. Foley couldn't resist poking around. Later he approached me.

"There's a perfect B-29 APU, could I bring it back with us?"

An APU is a small engine used on the ground for power to start engines and do other things when the airplane isn't flying.

"Jesus, Foley, I wouldn't let Schell bring a rug [he'd found one in India but I told him we couldn't lug it along], how'm I gonna let you bring an APU?"

"I'll take it all apart and hide the pieces around the ship; no one will ever see it, I promise."

How could I turn Foley down? "Okay, but I never want to see a screw from it."

He got it home and used it to make a go-cart.

Tokyo weather was bad; low ceiling, rain and fog. To go there from Guam, not be able to land, and have to return to Iwo Jima as an alternate would stretch our fuel range beyond a safe number. So we decided to go to Iwo, gas there, and then on to Tokyo with plenty of fuel to get back to Iwo.

We landed, pulled into a revetment, and parked. The gray overcast matched the black sand, rocks, and empty landscape. Depressing, really depressing.

The beach was wide and black, sloping up from the water. There was no cover anywhere. I stood there trying to imagine charging, crawling over the black sand with the enemy behind bunkers laying down a horizontal rain of steel that came at you furiously. How could anyone live through that? Over 4,000 men—4,192 to be precise—were slaughtered right there, and that was just our side; Japan lost 20,000. It was impossible to grasp, beyond understanding; your mind was flooded with the horror, your heart felt nothing but sorrow for the poor bastards on that beach.

To come face-to-face with this black sand of death was humbling. What had I done for the war effort? Nothing of real danger, sacrifice, privation; nothing that filled me with the fear that my next moments would be my last. My heart wept for all these young men, and I felt a slacker.

We saw the Japanese network of underground tunnels, gun emplacements low to the earth or below it, the island a flat featureless place; it held no beauty, no tenderness, nothing forgiving, it was simply a place to kill and be killed. The only break in terrain was Mt. Suribachi, a 550-foot lump of rock without character that served as a perch for 200 enemy guns that fired down on our troops.

We stayed the night and the depression never left me.

The next morning we flew to Tokyo, into Atsugi Air Base, once Japan's busy hub, now America's. Old Shaky never missed a beat; it was cured at last.

It looked as though the Japanese had simply abandoned the air base in a hurry; airplanes sat unused, derelicts in patches of woods around the airport. There were small buildings that probably held parts and equipment for maintenance, but nothing seemed organized, the tail end of the war must have felt like a hopeless retreat.

It was tempting to poke around the sheds and see what was there that might be useful, but we knew there could be mines. Foley's curiosity had to be satisfied: walking lightly, he went into one. Meanwhile, Dowd had found a hammer outside on the ground; he flipped it up onto the corrugated metal roof of the building causing much noise and a loud crash. Foley came out as if shot from a cannon, almost levitating; we were laughing, and when he settled down a little he vowed, "I'll get you sonsabitches."

The mess was a hall on the second floor of the barracks, with passable food served by young Japanese girls, dressed in colorful clothes, smiling and giggling. But I wondered how much sorrow lived close to the smiling surface. We'd try conversation, and some of them understood a bit of English. I'll never forget the giggling girl who said, with hand and arm gestures, "Bombs, boom," and, "No mommie, no poppie after." Treating it as a funny story. It couldn't have been.

I wanted to talk to a Japanese meteorologist about thunderstorms, because lightning frequently lit their fragile houses and caused widespread damage; it was logical that they'd studied the subject.

I asked around, and that got me to the head man, Dr. Fugiwara. Escorted by a U.S. Navy lieutenant commander who would interpret, we found Dr. Fugiwara's office. It was on the second floor of a bombed-out building, temporary wall and roof, no heat. Fugiwara, a man in his seventies, walked three cold miles to work each day.

He was a pleasant man, his studies obviously interrupted by the war. His first questions: "How Dr. Byers, and Minser?" He asked about other of our top weathermen; he had great respect for them and it was easy to see he missed the worldwide connection of study and information, the people he probably knew from prewar papers read or conferences attended. Just part of the harsh interruption of life war brings.

We settled down to talk of thunderstorms, with Lieutenant Commander Kelly impressing us deeply with his command of Japanese. Yes, they had thunderstorms, lots of them, and plotted them carefully for trends of location and severity. He showed me maps with thunderstorm locations throughout Japan.

"How do you decide there is a thunderstorm?" I asked.

Fugiwara answered in his halting English, "Only mark," and he pointed to the map with his finger, "thundastorm when hear thun-da craps."

It was an interesting and worthwhile morning. We promised to give his warm wishes to those he knew back in America. I later learned he was a highly respected man in his field. The differences and bitterness of war faded away in that cold office in the company of a worldly man.

From Tokyo we went east to Wake Island—biting off a big 2,000-mile piece of the Pacific to wind up on the tiny island so beaten up during the war. We took off at night so Guy Arnold would have lots of stars to shoot as we aimed at that tiny target. We had good weather, a big sky full of stars; we leveled off at 11,000 feet, sat back, and relaxed. We droned on through the night until Guy called on the interphone: "This is hard to believe, but we're doing 300 miles an hour!" We'd caught a 110-mile-an-hour tailwind! The jet stream.

It wasn't known as widely back then as it is now, but there were tremendous winds blowing from west to east off Japan. The early B-29 raids had run into them, which fouled up their high-level bombing. Bad for them, good for us. It kept its speed almost halfway to Wake, and even after that we had a delightful boost. Wake showed up far earlier than our flight plan had called for.

And there it was, a dot in the ocean, the runway going from one end to the other. We were still over water when I started the flare and cut throttles for landing; we crossed the shoreline and the runway slipped under us. This was a brief stop only; we fueled up *Two Kind Words,* exchanged a few pleasantries, and were off, destination Johnston Island. We might have gone direct to Honolulu, but the 2,300 miles was marginal for our fuel capacity; the west winds we enjoyed out of Tokyo were now easterly trade winds, blowing against us, slowing our speed.

Between Wake and Johnston we crossed the International Date Line. There's nothing amazing about that except for the argument it caused later on over Foley's pay. He was the only crew member on an hourly pay basis, and he had to turn in daily work sheets to substantiate the hours he'd put in. Crossing the date line slipped him back into the day before, so there were two work sheets for the same day. The accountants promptly bounced those back, and it took some geographical training and a map to get the point across.

The flight was miles and miles of water.

Sharp said, "Look at all that water," as he surveyed from horizon to horizon seeing nothing but the blue ocean.

Dowd: "Yeah, and you're only looking at the top of it."

The sun slipped below the horizon quickly, as it does in the tropics, the eastern sky turned from blue to black, and then like a curtain being pulled upward, the line where blue changed to dark crept across the sky, over our head, and then down behind us; night took over, the sea below hidden by the darkness, a black void, the sky above alive with stars.

Peacefully, smoothly, we pounded through the night, motionless, an entity hanging in space. We gazed into the night ahead, glancing as necessary at instruments to assure our course and that all ran well. Little talk, no inside commotion; we were like a ship headed for port at twilight in calm seas, a time for meditation and peace.

An estimate from Arnold, we were getting close, time to descend. But Johnston shattered our peace, telling us they had a total electrical failure and were on emergency power. All runway lights were unserviceable. Now what?

"There's a Jeep on the end of the runway, headlights on, land over it."

The island appeared, a few lights in a building, the night vision of surf breaking, and then, dim and small and lighting only a hundred feet or so of runway, we saw the Jeep. It was like a pair of lights stuck out in space. As I banked to turn, the lights zoomed into the sky; a turn the other way and they dove into the sea, or so it seemed.

The problem was how to turn and line up over the Jeep's lights, which zoomed or dove with each turn. The answer: fly by instruments, concentrate on making a turn by instrument, then level the airplane and look out to see where the lights were, judging how much to turn to line up over the Jeep; inside again, watching only instruments, descend to 1,000 feet, then 800 feet, hold a heading steady, look out again for the lights. On the left, a beam; so make a 180-degree turn on instruments, let down to 500 feet as we completed the turn, and look out; there was the glow of the Jeep's lights, a bit off to the left; look inside for a moment, make a 10-degree turn left, then back to the runway heading, look up and out, yes, we were lined up; descend slowly, over the Jeep, a runway surface for a few hundred feet, then darkness, but we're almost on, keep the steady descent rate, pick up the ground in the landing lights, contact as the wheels touched; cut the power, wheel forward, brake down, and stop. Quite a landing.

A Jeep pulled in front of us and guided us to a parking spot. Fuel, guidance to the runway, which now had a few temporary oil lamps along its edges, enough for us to keep a straight path, and we were off to Honolulu.

That city was bustling with military personnel and activity, and getting a place to sleep and eat was difficult—no one was interested in our bastard operation. After an overnight for rest and food we were ready to head to San Francisco, but that was not so simple: the 2,400 miles to San Francisco was a marginal distance for our fuel. We could make it without a sweat if there weren't head winds, but it was a crap shoot; a big high-pressure area usually sits over the Pacific between the Hawaiian Islands and the mainland, with the winds circulating around it in a clockwise direction. The bottom of the high has east winds—head winds for us—and the top of the high has west winds—tailwinds. When the high is in its normal place, the route from Hawaii to the mainland goes through its middle and up to the top of the high into those happy west winds; at the start, coming out of Honolulu, you're crossing the bottom of the high in the head wind, but you expect to get out of them quickly and get up in those westerlies. Sometimes, though, due to weather in Alaska and the North Pacific, the high moves north, and if that happens we wouldn't get up into the westerlies until it's too late.

The night we took off was a little dicey; the high wasn't north of its usual position, but there were some little meteorological hints that suggested it might be on the move. Still, the forecast gave us good winds and a flight plan that made San Francisco with enough reserve fuel.

We hit the expected head winds, anxiously awaiting the point where we'd get those westerlies. We waited and waited. I slipped down in the nose to consult with Arnold and study the charts. The last three-star fix Guy had so neatly plotted put us not where we should be, in tailwinds, but well behind—we were slow on the flight plan and over on fuel use.

We both looked at the charts and our plots on the howgozit chart, which graphically shows the planned flight plotted as a line. Then in flight we'd plot our actual position and fuel against the flight plan. If the actual performance fell too far below the line we weren't going to make it. On the chart was a point of no return; once past that we were committed to going on, so the PNR, as we called it, was important. If the actual flight was below flight plan approaching the PNR we'd turn back. We looked at each other and said almost in unison, "We aren't gonna make it."

The only thing to do was to go back to Honolulu.

The next day Dowd and Foley removed the alcohol from our 55-gallon alcohol tank and reworked the plumbing so we could fill it with gasoline and get it to the engines if need be. That's not a big amount, but even fifteen minutes of fuel could make the difference.

Dowd and Foley waited until the sun had set and the air had cooled before gassing the airplane; when the fuel was cool we could get more in the tanks.

The high-pressure area had waffled a bit and looked as though it was behaving. We took off and flew through a beautiful night as scheduled, crossed the foggy California coast an hour or so after dawn, and landed at Hamilton Field.

One night in San Francisco and then nonstop to Dayton, where the government contingent got off and we spent a day debriefing before flying back to Kansas City.

What had the trip accomplished aside from reaffirming that the world was round? We'd flown some weather, but nothing compared to our previous activities. Tuc had gained some important atmospheric information; we'd briefed a lot of army aviation people on static and its cure; and we'd learned that the Japanese knew a lot about thunderstorms and how to forecast them.

Our project was finished, and it was time to return *Two Kind Words* to the army. Dowd, Foley, Sharp, Couch, and I flew to Dayton, landed and taxied to the ramp. The engines were shut down for the last time. No one said anything; we just sat there, trying to absorb that it was over, the end of our exploration and its freedoms.

I stared at the control wheel and its black aluminum hub cover with the Boeing insignia inscribed on it. I grasped the hub and pulled; it came off and I put it in my pocket. Dowd did the same from the copilot control wheel. I kept the airplane's keys, too, and later, at home, put them in the hub, filled it with plaster, covered the bottom with green felt and made a paperweight—it rests before me right now on my desk. From time to time I pick it up and run my hand over its oval form, thinking back to wonderful days and wonderful people. Dowd made a paperweight of his, too.

What happened to *Two Kind Words*? Sad to say, the army bulldozed it to scrap. A miserable ending for a great lady.

CHAPTER 19

A Brief Debriefing

THE DEMISE OF *Two Kind Words* didn't turn out to be the end of my involvement in thunderstorm research. I felt we'd learned a lot about the storms themselves, but I wanted to know more about how best to fly through them, whether the airplane could withstand the violence, and how to use radar to avoid thunderstorms, which was just beginning to come into use.

I discussed this with General Eaker, and he was willing and eager to loan TWA an airplane for the work, but he felt we should pay for the operation. I got a positive response from TWA's president, Jack Frye, and so we set up a thunderstorm research department with me as director. I wasn't surprised that TWA was willing to spring for such a project; it was always the leader in technical advances among all the airlines, and Jack Frye was a guy who'd gamble and push for something he thought was necessary. He was also a good pilot, and he understood.

Dowd and Foley joined me and we flew an army P-61, the Black Widow night fighter, big and strong and powerful with two 2,100-horse-power engines. General Eaker was instrumental in getting it delivered to us; he referred us over to General Curtis LeMay's office, where a single phone call from the general cut through weeks and weeks of red tape and delays. I later learned that the airplane had been in Portland, Oregon, and

I could imagine some commanding officer telling a poor lieutenant that LeMay had to have that airplane in Dayton tomorrow, so get it there. He probably flew all night, with fuel stops, to do it.

Eaker had again been helpful to us. In his presence I felt privileged, but always comfortable. He seemed a gentle man with great empathy for others. On one occasion, during a lunch, I learned that all was not always at peace inside, when he disclosed his disquiet at having been the one to give Saint-Exupéry permission to fly on the mission St. Ex never returned from. It was a high-altitude photo mission over southern France, flying a Lockheed P-38 fighter fixed for photo work, not fighting; St. Ex never returned, was never found, and there was no German report of an Allied plane being shot down in that locale on that day. "That always bothers me," Eaker told me.

The P-61 was a powerful machine, and it took some serious effort to keep it together in some of the conditions we were seeking. One such occasion took place in the skies over Kansas City—Kansas being such a first-class thunderstorm factory. I didn't know exactly where we were, just that it was a good storm to work. It was a wild ride; the artificial horizon had spilled, tumbling over in a steep bank, and was useless. We had to rely on the turn and bank indicator, but at the P-61's high speeds, a steep turn showed up on that instrument as only a slight deviation of the turn needle, maybe about a sixteenth of an inch. It took a moment to analyze this, and to realize we were in a spiral dive, going like hell. We dove out of the storm's bottom and got back to normal flight, and found ourselves right over downtown Kansas City. As it turned out, there was a TWA board meeting in Kansas City while I was having my tussle with the thunderstorm overhead. I learned later that one board member, after a discussion of the thunderstorm project, heard the storm and exclaimed, "Buck better be up there." Little did he know, I might have landed right in his lap.

The project carried on for a few months, but then a labor cloud brought our attention back to the regular line flights. The end of the war had brought on serious issues of pay and working conditions. The DC-3 was being replaced by bigger, four-engine aircraft; faster and able to carry more people and goods. Should pilots share in this productivity? They thought so, and also thought they deserved more pay for international flights over oceans. Another big item was copilot pay: before the war, copilots were apprentices, learning the ins and outs of airline flying. But now, in the big four-engine airplanes, they were a vital part of the crew, an aid to the captain for the safety of the flight. The copilot was better trained and informed than we were in the early DC-2 and DC-3 era; the new hires were mostly military, and most had been commanders of four-engine bombers. Copilots who hadn't gone to war were experienced by now, and checked out as captains.

So battle lines between the Air Line Pilots Association and TWA had been drawn, and as each day of negotiations passed it was evident neither side was giving.

I talked to John Collings, warning him, "This is serious, the men will strike."

"They'll never walk out," was his cocksure answer.

On the night of October 21, 1946, they did walk, and Collings saw pilots appear with picket signs as the airline came to a stop.

The company made no attempt to break the strike. Where would I have been if company executives and perhaps scab pilots had flown? I would have been with the pilots, on the picket line. While I enjoyed the so-called executive and special assignments, I never doubted my place was as a line pilot, where I wanted it to be.

The strike ended November 19, with an agreement to arbitrate. Gradually line flights came alive, but the company, which was gasping for financial air before the strike, became even more strapped. The thunderstorm project was put aside, with a suggestion that we'd look at it again next spring. Dowd and I flew the P-61 to Albuquerque where it was put in a hangar, in storage for the winter.

Unsurprisingly, when spring came TWA was interested in getting back to normal, not in projects that didn't apply directly to operating the airline. The P-61 was returned to the army and my research days were over.

What had we accomplished?

The basic B-17 project was on precipitation static, how to cure it. We learned what the electrical charging values are on an airplane, and we developed the large-diameter antenna wires to contain the static, and discharge wicks to have it bleed off the airplane harmlessly; this took care of the problem of radio reception in snow static. I don't know if anyone else arrived at the same conclusions at the same time, but TWA's Ralph Ayers and his assistants got it done and passed the information along to the army before anyone else I know of.

We also found that the electrical charging in and around thunderstorms was so strong that the large-antenna wire and wicks didn't even slow it up. Encountering the electrical fields that go with thunderstorms is like flying into a huge waterfall of electrical charge, with tremendous voltage. So reception in and near thunderstorms was not improved.

Interestingly, other technology soon solved most of that problem: the growth and use of very high frequencies, VHF, which acts like static-free FM radio and TV. Of course, reception is limited to line of sight, but that's apt to be quite distant from an airplane flying high. These frequencies came into general use for navigation and airplane ground communication after the war. If the B-17 project had never been born, the problem would have been solved by the new technology anyway. Life is like that.

Still, airplanes out over the oceans cannot use line-of-sight VHF and have to communicate by frequencies subject to static. So mark a plus there for the B-17. Also, one navigation method, Loran (for long-range navigation), still uses frequencies that are bothered by static—but Loran will eventually go out of use as GPS, global positioning system, becomes the worldwide norm.

Technology also caught up with navigation with the release of INS, the inertial navigation system, from the military secret list. Airlines first used it in the 747. INS doesn't use any radio; it's all self-contained, using gyros and computers.

So the only thing still in use as a result of our B-17 efforts is in long-range communications, and that will soon be passé once communication via VHF gets bounced off the satellites.

We worked hard to solve a problem and we essentially did, but now, over fifty years later, it isn't a problem. At first this fact is discouraging, but progress is a norm and it often obviates solutions of the past. We had had our moment.

We learned about weather, how it differs in various parts of the world, but most of what we learned was about thunderstorms. Flying through thunderstorms in either the B-17 or P-61 didn't reveal anything we hadn't experienced in DC-2s and 3s before there was radar and we were playing blindman's bluff trying to stay out of them. Frequently we lost the game and flew smack dab into one.

It wasn't news that thunderstorms are dangerously turbulent. That's their chief hazard; lightning is a minor thing, you can cope with rain, and hail is a danger that can damage an airplane, but an intelligent pilot can avoid hail—there's really very little excuse for flying into it. We did learn that there were thunderstorms of a super nature that can tear an airplane apart if you encounter them at a precise period in their development.

After lots of time flying in ice, I felt it wasn't a big hazard if one used good sense and worked to get out of it as soon as it starts to form. Ice gives you time to do this except for freezing rain, which collects at an alarming rate and commands immediate action. A pilot has to understand that ice on a wing affects the airflow over it, and thus affects the airplane's performance, so it's necessary to fly intelligently and delicately when ice forms.

As for snow, rain, fog, and low ceilings, we flew a lot of them, but basically in the same manner we did on the airline. With the B-17 there was the added advantage of range, so I generally had plenty of fuel to find an alternate good-weather airport when I needed one. Since the ILS, instrument landing system, was new and not widely installed, we gathered considerable experience on how best to fly an ILS because we were out there using one of the few around.

Considering all aspects of weather and aviation, the final tough one is the thunderstorm, which will continue to make air travel occasionally unreliable. Even if we reach a day when everyone lands blind automatically, and a modernized air traffic control system has traffic flowing smoothly and timely, all that will still come to a stop when thunderstorms move into a busy area such as New York. There's no way the traffic patterns could be maintained, because it will not be desirable—to put it mildly—to fly passengers through thunderstorms, or to land an airplane with one at or near the airport. There is research going on now that promises a better way than radar to view the precise area of a thunderstorm's greatest meanness, which will allow traffic to skin by closely, but the turbulence will still cover a wide area that airplanes cannot penetrate. Future airplane design may also allow safer flight through a thunderstorm, but the aircraft will still bounce alarmingly, lightning will flash, and passengers will be scared stiff. And that doesn't solve the problem of landing in a thunderstorm.

So I bow to the thunderstorm; I respect it, and in a way I enjoy the idea that it's there to show man that nature is still the boss.

We accomplished some things that are now out of date, but mostly we validated a lot in solid, scientific fashion. Maybe there were no surprises, but it was still an affirmation that nature demands respect and that airplanes must be operated understanding that demand, and flown with wisdom and skill.

In all honesty, the one that gained most was me. The experience broadened my knowledge of weather and flying it, and that's been of great benefit to all my flying. It confirmed that we are creatures of weather, beneficiaries of that great canvas, the sky; it is a constant delight to look at its ever-changing beauty, and to be challenged by the nagging question of why it's doing what it's doing.

CHAPTER 20

Chance of a Lifetime

*

R ETURNING TO THE LINE wasn't simply a matter of putting on my uniform, climbing in an airplane, and flying. First I had to prove I could do it after my layoff: it was check time once again. I had to make three landings in two different airplanes, a Connie and a DC-4; I also had to pass an instrument check and a line check. With all that done I was again a captain and could fly free without any pending scrutiny, at least until the next round of checks.

With the research finished, I opted for our international division. We moved back home to Westfield, New Jersey, and it was great to be back in the left seat, headed for Paris. Our airplanes hadn't advanced enough to go nonstop from New York, so every flight went from La Guardia Airport at New York, to Gander in Newfoundland, then Shannon, Ireland, where we always stopped for breakfast—all the passengers and crew would go to the airport restaurant for the standard breakfast of porridge, steak and eggs, Irish bread and wonderful strawberry jam. It was a happy hour, with the few passengers—thirty was a big load—and crew all jovial and in a good mood with the ocean behind and now only a couple of hours left to Paris.

Other airlines and crews did the same. I often saw a British Overseas Airways crew at breakfast without their captain; he sat all alone and aloof, very stiff and proper, Vandyke beard trimmed to perfection, at a separate table—the caste system at work.

One of our hostesses was known to sneak an Irish coffee or three during breakfast. They're laced, of course, with Irish whiskey. As a result, she wasn't much use on the trip to Paris, curling up in a seat to sleep under a blanket, her duties covered by an understanding purser. The duties weren't too difficult because, with breakfast tucked away as well as a few Irish whiskeys of their own, the passengers also slept, so there wasn't any meal service. I wonder what that Vandyke-bearded BOAC captain would have done if one of his gals had gotten snockered in Shannon. But we Yankees were a happy, cooperative, and loyal group, sharing and helping with both the joys and the difficulties.

I only flew three trips to Paris, two in Connies and one in a DC-4, before getting a note back in New York telling me to see Kemper Jacks, our director of operations. I don't remember his exact title because TWA was constantly reorganizing and the first thing each new group did was to change everyone's title, but I do know it was September 1947 and Jacks was the head man—a nice person with slick wavy gray hair, a florid complexion, and an infectious chuckle.

"Have I got an assignment for you." He grinned at the thought. "You're gonna love this."

"What?"

"You go to Hollywood, pick up an airplane, and fly Tyrone Power and a few friends to South Africa, Europe, and back." He grinned widely and waited for my happy response.

It was different from what he expected: "Oh no, not me—taking some movie star and wet-nursing him and company around Africa isn't my idea of fun."

"You must be out of your mind," Jacks said. "It's the chance of a lifetime. And besides, Our Father Who Art in Hollywood [meaning Howard Hughes, who essentially owned TWA] specifically requested you. I've got a navigator, radio operator, and flight engineer picked out, how about going out there with them, meet Power, see what he's like, and if you don't like the setup, I'll fix it so you can duck it."

That all seemed fair enough, and while I didn't like the idea of the flight, getting to peek inside Hollywood was a bit enticing.

The crew was Bill Agner, flight engineer; Bob Stevens, navigator; and Bill Ritter, radio operator. I'd flown with all of them on the line, I liked them and respected their ability, so that part was okay.

We went through the sacred, impassable studio gate like dignitaries—we were expected—and found our way to Power's dressing room. There he was, dark-looking with black hair and eyebrows, and no man had a right to be that handsome. He smiled broadly, stuck out his hand, gave a firm handshake.

"Captain Buck, I'm Tyrone Power—glad to meet you."

It wasn't put on, he always introduced himself that way. Who in hell didn't know who he was? But Power did it because it was the proper and polite thing to do; it was genuine. I liked him immediately; he was one of the men, regular, no airs.

We were introduced to the other men there: Jim Denton, number two man in the 20th Century Fox public relations department, and a tall gangling man, Bill Gallagher, who was Ty's secretary and man of all chores for many years. Gallagher was Canadian, from Moncton, New Brunswick. They would be the others in the party; there would be four of us and three of them.

As Power explained things I had my first chance to look around. The dressing room was a small bungalow: desk, chairs, couch, nicely furnished, but disheveled enough with things strewn here and there to make it a man's place.

The setup was this: Fox had purchased a DC-3 from Hughes—not exactly a DC-3, but an Army C-47, no fancy interior, still basic army brown, no frills. The army brown had been removed from the exterior and it was polished silver like an airliner. The only decoration was the airplane's name, *The Geek,* after Ty's last movie, about a guy who goes downhill, finally winding up as a carnival exhibit biting the heads off chickens. Ty liked the movie because it demanded real acting.

Two comfortable seats were installed back near the fuselage door for Gallagher and Denton. To have enough range to cross the ocean, extra fuel tanks were installed forward, with a bunk on top of each. The wartime navigator and radio operator stations were in their normal locations, and the cockpit had the usual instruments. The airplane was outfitted at the Hughes factory. Whenever movie people wanted information or service in aviation it was automatic to call Hughes; in their eyes he was the big aviation expert, and besides, he capriciously bought studios and you never knew when it might be yours—so staying on good terms with Hughes was an obvious career move.

The trip would be to South America, over to Africa, to Capetown, Johannesburg, and game country. Power wanted to meet Prime Minister Jan Christian Smuts, field marshal, a giant in South Africa's history and in World War II; there was talk of a picture about Smuts that Ty might be part of. I never knew, but I suppose that was the reason—read: excuse to the stockholders—for the trip.

After South Africa, we'd go to Nairobi, Addis Ababa, Cairo, Europe, and then home. It promised to be quite a journey.

Power motioned to me and quietly said he'd like to talk alone. We went into another room, I think it was the bedroom.

"Here's the way I see it, if you agree—I like to fly and I'd like to do most of it. If you don't like the way I'm doing it, sound off, or just take over if you think it's necessary—and I'd appreciate your teaching me the way you airline pilots fly."

I'd done a bit of checking about Power with marine friends and learned that he was a real marine—not a War Bond salesman, but someone who'd flown his C-46 as a command pilot across the Pacific, going in and out of Okinawa with cargo in, wounded marines out. He'd learned to fly before the war.

He continued, "I like to travel and that's why the trip—it's sort of part of my pay. We'll just be seven friends traveling together, no one is working for anyone, where I go you go, same accommodations, same fun." His voice was beautiful to listen to, deep, clear, and strong. "Do you have any questions?"

"Only one: when do we leave?"

Gallagher and Denton fitted right in. Gallagher was smart, perceptive, a champion bridge player, a whiz at math, keeper of Ty's details; quick to see the point, be it business or a joke, with a solid, hey-hey kind of laugh. Ty called him Fiddle, a nickname stemming from the size fourteen shoes he wore—like violin cases.

Denton was a charming man; good-looking, fair hair, infectious laugh, and a great intellect, an ex-newspaperman aware of events and current political gymnastics, knowledgeable about history and literature, all this with a wonderful sense of humor and a zest for life.

Tyrone was no upstart Hollywood pretty boy, but a person of the theater going back four generations. His great-great-grandfather was a famous actor in Ireland, his native land, and in England. Like Ty, he loved to travel and made two trips to the States, writing a book called *Travels in America*. Ty searched bookstores in many countries and finally found six copies of the book—actually two volumes. He gave me a set, and the writing is wonderful and revealing of the times. The original Tyrone Power, in the eighteenth century, set a city-to-city speed record traveling from New York to Philadelphia in one day. The start was from the New York City Battery by boat to "the lovely city on a hill, Perth Amboy, New Jersey." Then by stage to Trenton, where he embarked on a boat to sail down the Delaware River to Philadelphia.

Ty was the fourth Tyrone Power, all of them serious actors, including his father, a well-known Shakespearian actor. Tyrone's mother, Patia, was a drama coach in Cincinnati, where Ty was born. I met Patia and she was a charming lady. Ty's father died of a heart attack at an early age in Ty's arms at the Hollywood Athletic Club.

Ty, like many American young men, thought he should serve in the war and felt like a slacker for not doing it. He was brooding about this while walking down a street in Washington, D.C., when he passed a marine recruiting booth, pulled to a stop, and on impulse walked in and signed up. The studio had a fit because he was in the middle of a picture. He was permitted to finish the picture before he reported to boot camp, and he became a proud and loyal marine, staying on reserve status after the war. When he died, he was a major in the Marine Corps Reserve.

WHILE TY WAS FINISHING the last shots of a picture, we checked out the airplane. Agner looked over the nuts and bolts, I made a few local flights to prove out the fuel system and the extra tanks, while navigator Stevens swung the compasses and Ritter checked out the radio. We were ready.

There was a week or so delay, so Jean and Ferris flew out to be with me. Ty was gracious and concerned with their every need, saw to it they toured the studio and were taken out to see the airplane. We got pictures with Ty and Lana Turner, his lady friend at the time. Ty and Jean took to each other, a deep and sincere friendship that lasted through his life. In an interview in later years, Ty remarked that the only woman who didn't frighten him and he was comfortable with was Jean Buck.

Lana Turner, aside from her good looks and the sparkling aura such people seem to carry with them, was a delightful person; real, down-to-earth, friendly. She got me aside and said, "I love that guy, be sure you bring him back to me." I promised, but it didn't work out: he was safe and would return, but in Rome the affairs of the heart took a dramatic change.

*

I WAS CURIOUS TO SEE what kind of pilot Ty was. I've checked many pilots, maybe hundreds, and have developed a sense of what a good pilot is, and surprisingly that judgment is about 75 percent established before we ever get off the ground simply by the way the pilot handles the preflight routine: the checklist, checking necessary instruments and gadgets, starting the engines and taxiing the airplane. And then comes my big one, how the pilot stops the airplane for run-up before takeoff. If the stop is smooth, with the little trick of letting up on the brakes just before stopping, like good motormen once did with trolleys, so there isn't any jerk as the vehicle stops, then the pilot is well along to earning good grades.

So I watched Ty at work, and by the time we'd finished run-up and were ready for takeoff I knew he was a good pilot. Mentally I breathed a great sigh of relief. We took off west, made a large, smooth turn over the shoreline, and came back heading east for Dallas, our first stop. It was September 1, 1947.

So what's it like flying with a top-of-the-pile movie star? Well, it wasn't movies we talked about, it was flying: where we were, how we were doing, were we close to the chosen altitude, all the things pilots talk about. The Hollywood trio were like kids out of school, and the flight was free—no secure cockpit that didn't allow visitors, everyone could wander at will, ask questions, talk. It was a private airplane without airline restrictions, though the level of flying and operation was very professional.

As we approached San Juan, the downside of the movie idol business reared its head. Ty said, "Look, they'll probably mob us here. So I'll get out as soon as I can and get them away from the airplane so it won't get damaged."

"You mean," I said, "we throw you to the animals so we'll be okay?"

"That's about it. We'll meet at the hotel."

I couldn't believe it until we landed and taxied toward the terminal: there was the crowd, Lord knows how many, it seemed to be thousands, waving, jumping up and down, pressing forward. We tossed Ty and Jim Denton to the mob, where police and officials escorted them to the terminal—ran interference would be a better description, except they didn't run but shoved and worked through the crowd.

The adulation didn't seem to affect him; I asked him about it, and his answer was practical and simple: he reasoned the people weren't doing all this for him, Tyrone Power, but rather for the characters he played, people and romance that fitted the crowd's fantasies. This philosophy kept his head size normal, and it allowed him to lead a normal life when he wasn't out there in public.

This wouldn't be the first scene like that, and I got used to it, but I was always amazed.

From San Juan we pressed on, flying twelve hours and fifty minutes to Georgetown, Guyana, for a brief stop and then to Belém, Brazil.

As I'd learned, no one goes from the Northern Hemisphere to the Southern without facing that wall of turbulent, wet weather, the Intertropical Front; it doesn't back off for movie stars or VIPs. As we approached the front I noticed Ty glancing in my direction now and then, probably wondering what I was thinking about his way of flying the stuff. It dawned on me that I might be a distraction for him, flying under the critical eye of an airline pilot, wanting to do it right. Well, he did, and I never said a word as we wound through the unfriendly mass; he picked the same passages I would have, and when we got trapped in a tropical downpour with moderate turbulence, he flew it like an old pro, doing all the right things.

There were issues on my side of this relationship, too: how should I relate to someone so used to being fawned over, mobbed by crowds, someone who cut such a handsome figure on the big screen? Well, flying has a way of equalizing; our relationship, as we flew serious weather, long distance, over unfamiliar and often unfriendly terrain, quickly became that of two men, working together. With each hour Tyrone Power, the star, became Ty Power, a man flying an airplane, hair out of place, sweat on his forehead as turbulent air and rain shoved us from our desired path, a determined look on his face, hands strong but delicate on the control wheel, "Whoa, you bastard, come back here," uttered to no one except the elements.

The whole fame thing was a chore and a responsibility he had to respond to when required, like going to work; with that out of the way, in private and especially in flight, he was just a man like the rest of us, comfortable to be with, enthusiastically responsive to new scenes and experiences, quick with humor, earthy when appropriate.

We stayed overnight in Belém, then six and a half hours to Natal. How different Natal was from the war days—quiet, only a few aircraft, almost no activity, it was now a ghost airport.

We stayed an extra day, checking everything before taking on the South Atlantic. Each person tried on a life vest to see how it fitted; Gallagher looked storklike in his, his long pant legs pulled up above his ankles by the crotch straps. I described the cord that would inflate the vest. "Like this," I said, and pulled Gallagher's—instantly the air rushed in the tubes, pushed them out and hiked Gallagher up even farther. His startled look caused great laughter. Our takeoff was set for the next day, late afternoon, so as to arrive in Liberia, at Roberts Field, after dawn.

Someone recommended a pleasant café we should visit. We were driven into the country and came to an elegant house, sitting alone on a rise, with gardens, a patio, and a sign we couldn't understand. A lady greeted us at the door, big smile, a sweeping hand inviting us in. Four or five girls gazed at us, stupefied: it was obvious we were in a whorehouse! The madam gave some orders and then showed us to a patio for drinks. Her orders, I learned, were to close the house to all comers. Drinks were promptly served; girls in gaudy and suggestive dress stood around, silent, just staring, never making a move, mesmerized that this hero of their films and dreams should be there! Ty, gracious as ever, treated them all as though they were fine ladies. Our conversations were rather stilted in the awkward situation since we weren't going to be customers; we laughed a bit, remarked on the various attractions of form and beauty. No one understood us, nor we them, so it was a standoff between the nonplussed girls and our odd situation. Gallagher tried to pay for the drinks, but the madam would have none of it. We thanked them all and departed. The girls, smiling and giggling, escorted us out, but as we passed a bedroom off the hall one pulled me by my elbow toward the room. "No, no—*abregado,*" I yelped, but it wasn't business, she only wanted me to see the big framed picture on the wall over her bed: a larger-than-life-size photo of Ty, smiling down on her workplace.

Originally we'd planned to fly to Ascension Island, then to Accra on the Gold Coast, but Ascension was closed, so we had to go across the ocean in one hop to Roberts Field in Monrovia, the shortest way, but still about 2,000 miles. We'd need all the fuel possible, so with full fuel, us, and our stuff, we were near military gross weight, that old wartime 32,000 pounds.

There was a certain tenseness; we were heavy, the temperature was warm, which reduces performance, and a big wide ocean lay ahead. Ty asked me if I'd feel better making the takeoff myself.

"No," I told him. "You're the captain, you do it." Which he did perfectly. The reserved feeling between us was all gone now; we were friends, and that bond continued and grew for the rest of our lives.

Along the way, we took some star shots that gave us some very strange readings; we realized the sextant was bad, but we could average the bad shots and get our general trend. It wasn't ideal, but the winds in the South Atlantic weren't very strong at this time of year, so I suspected we'd be okay. Dawn slowly crawled up ahead of us, illuminating a mass of tall cumulus clouds, a line of storms and rain. That meant land, and it was showing up close to Stevens's original estimate. Down in the mess of clouds and rain somewhere was Roberts Field.

As we approached our estimated time of arrival the ADF (automatic direction finder) locked on the airport's beacon—at first indecisively, pointing for a bit and then swinging to one side or the other. But as we got close, the needle settled down to pointing straight ahead; Stevens's navigation had been good. We searched down through uneven cloud masses for the ground and suddenly there was a hole, enough to see it. We made a quick descent and found ourselves under a 300-foot ceiling in heavy rain. In a moment, through a blurry, rain-smeared windshield, the field came in view: power off, gear down, we called the tower and got no answer, but there was the field, close; tower be damned, we grasped the opportunity and landed.

As we taxied through the rain toward a main building, we expected to see some activity, but there was none: not a soul, not an airplane, just the lush backdrop of jungle, green and dark, and the pouring rain. At the ramp area we shut down the engines, and just then, from the emptiness, two figures appeared, natives, barefoot, ponchos over their shoulders, expressionless. We got out of the airplane and walked up to them. One of the natives pointed at Ty and said, "I know him." The long tentacles of film go everywhere.

There were only a handful of men on the post. We chatted with them, had some food, and turned in early. The rain poured on the temporary building that housed us. The damp, moldy, musty air of the wet tropics permeated everything. Nearby, a swollen jungle river, full to its banks, rushed by, the constant heavy rain adding to its fury. An occasional strange cry could be heard from somewhere deep in the thick mass of trees and vines. As my eyes closed, I stayed conscious long enough to thank the Lord for keeping those two engines running, and at the same time I felt Africa all around me, submerging me in its smells, sounds, and tastes. Here we were; now, what's next?

ON THE WAY TO ACCRA we hit tropical showers, the usual stuff for that part of the world. In certain areas of the globe one doesn't think about meteorology so much as climate: the Intertropical Front is one example; arid regions where you know the weather will be clear and hot, only now and then coming alive when a seasonal wind springs up and causes sandstorms, which are like fog to a pilot because the visibility goes to zero. And there are places like India, where the weather will generally be good, but monsoon season comes and then it rains like mad.

In the mid-latitude zones, like the United States and Europe, cold air mixes with warm air to make weather that's subject to constant change. That's where you pay attention to meteorology on a daily basis, because the airport you're headed for could be clear or foggy, dry or wet, placid or turbulent with thunderstorms. Good pilots are versed in both meteorology and climate, while maintaining a skeptical attitude that never completely trusts anything when it comes to weather.

So we were in the rain with Accra reporting 800-foot ceiling and rain.

That meant an instrument approach, so I got out the approach plate and Ty studied it.

It was at times like this that I learned about Ty's remarkable photographic memory and fast mind. He took in an approach plate almost at a glance, but in that glance memorized everything on it: compass headings, altitudes over the radio fixes, how low to descend safely, what to do if the approach was missed, and all the rest—which is a lot to take in from a piece of paper.

I discovered this ability when we were flying during a time of boredom over a lonesome, traffic-free piece of sky. I was tending the store while he looked over a movie script he'd been given before we departed. He turned the pages looking down each one, but at a speed that for me would be skimming. Finished, he tossed it over to me remarking he didn't particularly like it—how did it strike me?

"How do you know you didn't like it—you only skimmed it."

"No, I read it—go through it, ask me some questions."

I did, and amazingly he knew the script in impressive detail.

He was loaded with natural ability, terrific coordination. Ty and Basil Rathbone were known as the best fencers in the movie world. Each star at 20th Century Fox supported a softball team, providing uniforms and such. Ty was one of the few who played on his team and I watched him, playing first base, looking like a pro; talking it up, making difficult catches, batting, all of it. I played golf with him in later years. That's a game that requires practice, and we played in Coventry, England, when he was on tour with Shaw's *The Devil's Disciple*. He hadn't played golf in a year. His first few holes were slices, hooks, and fat shots, but by the fourth he was hitting it better, and by the back nine he was playing like a regular 70s shooter.

He was an all-American boy, but he could talk religion, philosophy, art, literature—most things except politics. He felt that fame shouldn't necessarily set someone up to run for office; politics, he believed, was a special game, if you wanted to play it, something you had to take on full-time if you wanted to accomplish anything. One topic we did talk about was the result of our seeing the racial politics at work in South Africa, especially one day when we were taken to a gold mine where black mineworkers lived in a state of what was essentially bondage. I remember Ty's simple and prescient comment, "They have a long way to go here—and there will be a hell of a lot of trouble getting there."

And while talking of Ty, I want to make this clear, and as loudly as I can: he was *not* a homosexual! I knew him too well, lived with him on the most intimate terms in the years after our trip, we nudged each other at the sight of a stunning woman, and I was close to and knew his wives intimately.

As I got to know Hollywood and its workings, I realized it was the land of gossip, and much of it was intended to hurt others for some kind of advantage. It seemed to me I heard almost everyone out there, at some time or other, called gay or lesbian. Tyrone Power most emphatically was not gay.

✳

WE NEVER HAD TO make the instrument approach to Accra; minutes before our estimated arrival there was a lull in the weather and below, through a big hole in the clouds, we could see the airport. We descended, made contact (visually), and landed.

Next was Léopoldville in the Belgian Congo, as it was known then. We were excited about getting to the Congo River and Léopoldville. It sounded more African, more fanciful and romantic. But when we flew over the city, what we saw was a shock: large and modern, big buildings, a huge dock area on the river with big steamers tied up, not the dugout canoes we were expecting. How naive and ignorant we were learning we could be.

The airport was a beautiful piece of pavement 5,000 feet long, which for a DC-3 is about twice what you need.

A crowd greeted us, but it was orderly and curious, not pushy and rude. Many stood watching us pass through customs. We rarely cleared quickly, as you might expect of a celebrity; the bags were picked over carefully, especially Ty's, since everyone wanted to see what a Hollywood star had for clothes, toiletries, and what-not. It was a joke among us that the crew whisked through with only a perfunctory inspection, while Ty got a complete going over—polite, but meticulous.

Our exposure to the steamy jungle of Africa turned out to be a pleasant ride up the Congo, in an excursion boat reserved exclusively for us, to a native village where the villagers displayed their crafts and their way of life—just as they would for any tourists, though the villagers all recognized Ty and put on extra smiles and efforts while performing their native dances.

The question we were most frequently asked at the receptions we attended at nearly every stop was, "Where are you going next?"

In Léopoldville, the answer was, "Cape Town."

"But first you go to Johannesburg."

"No, we go direct."

"But where will you land en route?"

"Windhoek."

"Windhoek?" They said it in a questioning manner because it was off the beaten path, out west in the part of Africa Germany once ruled. To go to Cape Town via Johannesburg is a big dogleg and it's about 510 miles farther than direct. Airplanes can fly straight, but Léopoldville to Cape Town was too far to go nonstop. With a little investigation we found Windhoek, right on course and handy. Johannesburg is the big trade center, so airlines tended to treat it as the necessary entry and exit point, a demonstration of how commerce and trade routes can dictate people's movements. Windhoek is in the sticks, but it was perfect for our purposes.

The flight crossed Angola—Portuguese West Africa then. We started out over jungle, but the land gradually became semi-arid, and approaching Windhoek the country looked like New Mexico.

"That must be the veldt," Ty said, pronouncing it with all letters so it came out *veldit*.

"Yup, the veldit," we answered with the same pronunciation.

No one knew we were coming, so there was no big crowd; it was comfortable to be there in the high, dry air and moderate temperature. We met one man who told us of the land and the country and the springbok, a deerlike animal that lived in huge numbers on the "felt." That's the way he pronounced it.

I looked at Ty, and in unison we said, "Ah yes, the *felt*." We could say the word years after, for a private laugh, in incongruous gatherings far from Windhoek.

Then off to Cape Town. This is like flying from Reno to San Francisco, because Cape Town has climate, flora, fauna, mountains, and sea. And, of course, fog.

Ritter's weather reports showed Cape Town overcast with 300-foot ceiling, five miles visibility; an instrument approach. We studied the approach plate and didn't particularly like it, because the radio aid for the approach wasn't a radio range, but a marine beacon requiring a loop procedure. Not the most precise way to do the job.

We called frequently for weather updates; the ceiling went up to 500 feet, which was better, but nothing to write home about.

A South African Airways pilot flying the Johannesburg–Cape Town route noticed our slightly anxious questions about weather. He gave us a call.

"If you don't mind a suggestion, chaps, we generally go in contact," he said. "About 100 miles north of Cape Town there's a big hole, you can circle down through and fly in along the coast contact."

"Thanks very much," I said, and then about half chucked the idea, because contact flying is dicey—and besides, he was coming from Jo-berg, how would he know about a hole on our route?

We flew along, expecting and preparing for a loop approach, but lo and behold, 100 miles out we came upon the nicest hole you ever laid eyes on. We looked at each other, nodded, and augured down through, sliding under the clouds at 500 feet with good visibility. From there in it was a piece of cake.

Later I met that captain, Rod Madley, the most senior of the South African airline pilots.

"Tell me, how'd you know there would be a hole up north?"

"Oh," he said, "you see, old chap, that hole's always there."

We stayed a week in Cape Town. Ty visited old friends from the Marine Corps stationed there, and Cape Town is so beautiful and relaxing no one was anxious to leave. We rode to the top of Table Mountain on a thrilling cable car and could see the Cape of Good Hope, the end of the great African continent, and beyond the Cape to sea where the South Atlantic meets the Indian Ocean. It was a noble sight. I could sense the continent behind me: its countless diverse people; jungles, desert, the Nile, and the Mediterranean's waves lapping on its shores over 4,000 miles to the north. The airplane had made it possible for me, in just a couple of years, to see all that, from Cairo to the Cape. I was a lucky man.

The relative peace ended when we got to Johannesburg; the airport was full of people, a big crowd to welcome Ty. He was the first top movie star to visit, and they turned out in droves to see him.

There was an open Cadillac touring car to take Ty to town. He sat on the folded-down top, his feet on the rear seat; Jim sat on one side and I was on the other, each of us holding one of Ty's legs to give him some support.

The crowd never ended, and by the time we got to the edge of town people were on roofs, sticking out of windows, and covering the streets. Our passage was slow because of the mob pressing against the car. Jim was admonishing the driver, "Keep moving, keep moving—if we stop we're dead."

I saw women, wild-eyed, look at Ty and virtually go into orgasm, and then they fainted, but they couldn't fall down because of the crush of the crowd. People shoved paper and pen toward him for autographs, which was impossible. I was jabbed once by a wild pen shoved at him.

Ty sat up there, waving and smiling and said to Jim and me, "Jesus, suppose they were mad at us."

The driver said, over and over, "They didn't do this for the king and queen."

Finally we got to the hotel, where the police pushed, shoved, and waved nightsticks to open the crowd enough for us to go through—Jim and me first, like football blockers, shoving people aside, making a path with Ty close behind. The hotel lobby was also full of people, but they were more orderly, leaving an open path for us to go through.

Outside Ty's room, which faced the front of the hotel, a large crowd assembled, all classes and colors, chanting, "Tyrone, Tyrone." The crowd, believe it or not, was there the entire week we spent in Johannesburg, day and night. After our arrival the Red Cross set up a field station on the lawn in front of the hotel to take care of the injured. The Cadillac, which had been new, had to be refinished after its battering from the crowd.

When we'd settled down a bit, Ty remarked, "Say, did you see that redhead in the lobby?"

Yes, we'd all seen her, even while we were running for the elevator. Later I went down to the desk to officially register. The redhead was still there, lovely to look at, and chewing gum at an impressive pace. Later, when I saw Ty, I told him, "Saw your redhead in the lobby—she's something."

Ty lit up. I added, "She was chewing gum—solidly."

"Damn." End of redhead.

Our whole stay was a constant whirl of receptions, dinners, visits to an orphanage, a hospital, schools. The city was Ty's, to the delight of almost everybody. One dissenter was a very British gentleman who entered one of the best restaurants and asked the maître d', "Is Tyrone Power dining here tonight?"

Informed that Mr. Power was not, he said, "Good! Then I shall."

The great side trip out of Johannesburg was by automobile to Pretoria, the capital of South Africa, for a meeting with Prime Minister Jan Smuts. When we went to his office, a very formal male secretary shook hands with Ty in the reception room outside, and then announced that only he would see the prime minister. Ty drew back and glanced at the rest of us with a look that seemed to say, "Screw it, if you can't go, I won't." But before he developed any such notions we pushed him ahead and said, "Go on, you silly bastard."

So he disappeared with the secretary through the magnificent wooden door into Smuts's chambers. He was there about five minutes when the door flew open and out stepped Smuts, military straight, white goatee, radiating charm, smiling. "What's all this silly business? Come in, gentlemen, come in." He ushered us into his chamber, a spacious room with large windows that took in the magnificent country and hills. He talked of the country, and nature, mentioned the baboons one could see, and enthusiastically exclaimed, "It's spring, can't you smell it, feel the excitement of it!" He was energetic, poetic, fascinating. The only cloud came when he found out we'd ridden the cable car to the top of Table Mountain.

"You cannot appreciate the mountain unless you walk to the top!" He emphasized *walk* almost as an admonition.

At his invitation, we visited his home in the country, Irene, that afternoon; we met Mrs. Smuts and took tea with her, a lady as charming as her husband.

An exciting day. Being spring, the jacaranda trees were in bloom, the countryside alive with blue blossoms. It was the time of the jacaranda festival, and we went to some of the festivities; Ty met the jacaranda queen, a beautiful, shapely brunette whom all insisted Ty kiss. His comment, later: "Wow, that was some kiss!"

We finished with a visit to the lord mayor's office, where Ty was presented with a memento whose details I've forgotten, maybe the keys to Pretoria. As we departed the lord mayor's office he graciously escorted Ty toward the door; he was a big man, dressed formally, the chain and keys of office hanging from his neck.

Ty thanked him and then suggested that he dispense with escorting us to the car: "You see, there's a big crowd out there we'll have to bulldoze our way through, I don't think it would be wise for you to be involved."

"Oh, goodness no, they will stand aside for us."

And off we went, with the crowd pressing in. The last we saw of the dignified lord mayor, he was being passed horizontally over the heads of the crowd back toward his office.

But this wasn't the Africa of animals and the wild. When asked about this, the locals always referred to Kruger National Park, told us we must go to Kruger. So off we went, flying to a small town called Barberton, which had an unattended grass airport that was big enough for *The Geek*. Two cars and gamekeepers from Kruger picked us up. I gained respect for the Ford automobiles they used; the roads were severely washboarded, yet they drove 60 miles an hour, the shocks and wheels bouncing up and down furiously—"Ah yes, we junk the cars after 60,000 miles," they told us. I was amazed they lasted that long.

Kruger was wonderful, a tremendous area about the size of Connecticut; no people, comfortable thatched-roof cabins to sleep in, lots of animals, and special treatment from the director of the park, Colonel J. H. "Sandy" Sanderson, a flinty ex–South African Air Force fighter pilot and big-game hunter.

We were ensconced inside a compound where the gates closed at night to keep the animals out; it was a zoo in reverse, with us in the cage and the animals wandering around outside.

Dinner at Sanderson's with his family; he told us stories of Africa and of foolish tourists who got out of their automobiles and were attacked. The following days, with Sanderson showing us around, we were constantly out of the Jeep-like vehicle, wandering along paths to get a better look at the animals—we were nervous after the dinner stories, but not Sanderson, he pushed into paths by streams and into grass areas for us to have a look at a lion!

The landscape at Kruger is beautiful, a savanna, but also considerable forest. It's high, 3,000 feet or so, and dry, the days warm, the nights cool, a wonderful invigorating atmosphere. We saw all the animals as Sandy took us around. His relaxed attitude made them almost seem pets, although they damn well were not. In a large open field we came upon a herd of African buffalo quietly grazing, but Sandy and the natives became quiet, lowered their bodies, and motioned for us to do the same; we kept a fair distance, ready to escape any charge. These animals, powerful and unpredictable, commanded respect even from the pros.

Today, of course, seeing wild animals is old-hat; TV has put them right in our laps, but in 1947 there was still a sense of awe. The most exciting sight, to me, was a sable buck we saw in a forest we were walking through. It stood on a slight rise, its horns curving gracefully back, a white patch in front and a russet-colored body, standing there, lord of all. And the elephants weren't like the elephants I'd seen in circuses, these were huge and dark; the giraffes were unforgettable, especially when they ran through a wooded area, their heads up above or in the trees, going fast, but never hitting a tree.

It was a wonderful respite, no crowds, just nature and an exceptional, relaxed time.

But it was time to go on, our eventual destination Nairobi, 2,000 miles north, across mountains and arid country. The very name thrilled me, as it had since childhood, bringing up images of exotic adventure. But Nairobi was a bit disappointing; it still had an African feel, big open lands around, 5,000 feet above sea level, but the city had gone commercial: we saw advertisements for white hunters and safaris, a lion guaranteed. We were taken to see the animals in the game preserve just out of town; riding in cars, we chased ostrich, looked at wildebeest, impala, lions, and the African mixture you'd expect. After the natural feel of Kruger, Nairobi was a depressing letdown.

But exciting things were to come at our next stop, Addis Ababa, Ethiopia, after a flight of almost 700 miles over mountainous terrain that looked like the Rockies, little habitation except for tiny villages nestled in a valley, one road leading off to Lord knows where. Our old friend the Intertropical Front was between Nairobi and Addis; it wasn't as widespread as over wet lowlands, but there was a solid enough line with thunderstorms that looked like the serious kind we knew from the American Midwest. We wove and ducked, climbed and descended, cut back looking for a lower pass to sneak through, all the time looking below at the rough, lonesome terrain. We had no navigation aids, either, going strictly by dead reckoning of compass and map; Stevens couldn't get any reasonable celestial reading because there was only the sun, and the ride was too rough and bouncy anyway. We were hedge-hopping, weaving and ducking.

But finally we got through the front, flying in a clear sky except for scattered friendly fair-weather cumulus clouds. The country changed to lovely hills, green and abundant with eucalyptus trees; the city sparkled in the late afternoon sun with some modern buildings and many native-style dwellings.

It's high country, the airport 7,750 above sea level, the runway not overly long and with a pesky crosswind. Ty decided on partial flaps because of it, and the decision was a good one; we approached and landed in serious, concentrated fashion.

A large crowd greeted us, Europeans in European dress, and an equal number of natives not wearing much more than a few covering cloths. Our greeting included royal officials who informed us we were the guests of Emperor Haile Selassie, and off we went to our accommodations in guest houses on the palace grounds.

We were treated like crowned heads: cars and drivers showed us the country and places of interest. On one occasion Ty and I were being driven to the city post office, the only place we could send telegrams. A mile from the post, Ty decided it would be more interesting to walk the rest of the way and see the sights: "Hell, no one knows me here." We stopped the driver, got directions, and started walking; in no time a crowd gathered, closing in; we finished the last 200 yards running, and were barricaded inside against the mass of people outside.

To cap our stay, the emperor threw a state dinner for Ty and party; it was one for the book. I had lugged formal attire on the trip, but this was the only time I used it.

It was a bizarre evening that started in an anteroom off the throne room, where we were briefed on correct protocol when meeting the emperor: enter the room, bow once, proceed toward the throne and emperor across fifty feet of floor, but halfway to him stop and bow again, then proceed to the emperor, who sat on an ornate throne raised above you, and bow again. We exchanged a few pleasant words I don't remember, then I bowed and moved off to one side.

The emperor sat, surrounded by wives, princesses, and princes, all dolled up; the dominant impression was of gold and jewels.

Ty was presented last, and the emperor had him sit for a chat in French, which Ty spoke fluently—he had learned it from his first wife, Annabella, a charming French lady.

Then off to dinner: a big table, waiters—I suppose there's a fancier name for them, they were dressed as in the court of Louis XIV, in silk coats and knee-length trousers with gold brocade, white stockings. As they hovered over us, balancing the big heavy trays piled with food, the emperor's pet little Spitz dog ran about, nipping at their heels. I picked up a soup spoon and it seemed very heavy; it was pure gold, as was the rest of the service. The meal was a typical American turkey dinner; the emperor's cook was American and did this in honor of Ty.

The emperor gave Ty a beautiful and impressive gold cigarette case, engraved and adorned with jewels. Back in our rooms, relaxed and laughing over the evening, Jim broke us all up when he said that the cigarette case should have been engraved, "To Ty from Hi." Years later, Ty's apartment in London was robbed, the case lost to the thieves.

✳

FROM ETHIOPIA we set out for Khartoum and Cairo. The first half of the flight to the Sudanese capital took us over mountains as high as 13,000 feet, deep valleys, craggy cliffs, little habitation. Beneath us, way below, was the Blue Nile, and in the distance Lake Tana, 6,000 feet above sea level, the source of the river. The White Nile starts from Lake Albert, 1,000 miles south of Khartoum in the highlands of Uganda; the White and Blue meet at Khartoum to form the mighty Nile.

The romance of it is overwhelming: Khartoum; General Gordon and his loss of life to the Mahdi in 1885, Kitchener recapturing the land in 1898; those two great rivers flowing as one for another thousand miles through the desert to Cairo. The river's annual flooding has supported people for thousands of years; looking down on the vast desert below with the ribbon of river cutting through the arid terrain as we droned effortlessly through the sky was a dreamlike experience.

Khartoum was a busy city, filled with Arabs in their traditional dress, black Africans, conveyances ranging from modern automobiles to donkeys; there were lovely government buildings and a fine hotel. I slept well in my room, with the door locked and bolted; yet at 6:00 A.M. someone was shaking me awake and I looked up into a black, smiling face that said, "Your tea, sir." How in hell did he get in, and why waken me at 6:00 A.M.?

We toured the city, but the highlight was a boat trip out on the river, actually sailing over the confluence of the Blue and White Nile. They weren't blue or white but brown, mud-colored, dirt and silt from Africa's heart heading north to fertilize the land and eventually flow into the Mediterranean.

Our visit to Cairo was derailed by a devastating cholera epidemic. Officials felt it unwise to have Ty come there, causing crowds that might worsen the problem, and we weren't overly anxious to settle in the midst of the outbreak even though we'd been inoculated against the disease.

So our next destination was Athens, with an overnight refueling stop at Wadi Halfa on the Nile. Wadi Halfa had long been a village where agricultural goods were brought and transferred to boats for transport up the Nile; in later years it would be on the southern shore of Lake Nasser, which was created by the Aswan Dam.

We flew over the desert about 180 miles west of Cairo, and finally crossed the Mediterranean coast, the last of Africa behind us. The sea stretched below, then across Crete and toward Athens, passing over Greek islands with fetching names: Milos, Sérifos, Kithnos, all looking inviting with little towns spread across hillsides, harbors, blue water.

Then Athens and we were back in the crowd business; the airport was jammed with people. Twentieth Century Fox, Ty's studio, was then owned by Spiros Skouras, who had many Greek relatives to take care of us, and they did. We saw it all, from the Parthenon to Corinth and its canal; a wild party and Greek dancing at Piraeus; formal receptions, a swim in the sea; after six days of Greek hospitality we were ready to move on to Rome, where things came to a pleasant halt.

Flying from Athens to Rome is a journey through time and history: off Athens and over Corinth, Peloponnisos and Sparta on our left, across the Ionian Sea to the toe of Italy at Catanzaro, Mt. Etna and Sicily in the distance, Stromboli sticking up out of the sea, smoking; Naples, Capri,

Cassino, Castel Gondolfo, and then Rome; a flight from ancient Greece to World War II, covering in a few hours the small piece of this earth where western philosophy was born along with bloody wars and all kinds of culture in between.

Rome and crowds again; the Italian crowds the worst of all, rude, pushing, shoving, shouting. I was caught in a crowd with Ty and they tore the sleeve right off his jacket.

But Rome also had charm; it was late October, the season of warm clear days and cool nights that energize and put a bounce in one's walk. And Hollywood was there in full force: a number of pictures were being made with cheap postwar dollars, movie people blanketed the town, and being in Ty's entourage we got to know many of them, not just stars but cameramen, directors, and assistants. The famous corner of town on Via Veneto near the Excelsior Hotel, the U.S. embassy, and Doney's café, where men sat watching the girls pass and girls watched men, became known as the corner of Hollywood and Vino.

Gregory Ratoff was directing a picture and threw a big party on the set in Ty's honor. We arrived and were greeted by Ratoff in his most flamboyant manner: a huge table, covered with a great feast of goodies occupied part of the set. The large group of people—any visiting Americans and Romans even faintly connected with the movie world—eyed the food with drooling anticipation. This wasn't too long after the war and things were still scarce. Ratoff held everyone back until he'd made his welcome speech to Ty, then announced, with his heavy Russian accent, "Let the party begin." Whoosh, the people descended on the layout of food, and before we could get near it, it was all gone, picked clean like a Thanksgiving turkey.

We stayed in Rome for twenty-three days. Why so long? Because Ty met Linda Christian, an attractive, intelligent, sexy woman, fluent in about four languages. It must have been love at first sight, and it eventually wound up in marriage.

As they were taking in Rome, so were we, seeing the sights, visiting movie sets, getting to know the people, even a private audience at Castel Gondolfo with Pope Pius XII. I made one flight to Bari with Bob Webb, an assistant director who wanted to look over the American cemetery there as a possible location sight. And there was one trip, with Ty, to Torino to visit Ty's good friend Tino Rossi of the Martini and Rossi clan—a very charming man who showed us the proper way to make a martini, though for the life of me I cannot remember how much vermouth he said to use, probably because I don't drink martinis.

Sitting at Doney's sidewalk café, lazily ogling the sights, I was suddenly jolted to consciousness by a female voice calling, "Bob, Bob Buck!" I looked up to see an attractive blonde coming toward me, arms outstretched. She was a former TWA employee from Kansas City named Eve; she was married and staying in Rome while her husband, a naval officer, was at sea with the Mediterranean fleet. She became my companion and I swept her into our movie world, we saw the sights, dinner, dancing; a wonderful time with a great lady, and all very proper, a platonic, buddy relationship. I became very fond of Eve; alas, I never saw her again after Rome.

As our stay in Rome dragged on, the studio was getting anxious: Ty was scheduled to make a picture set in Ireland, so it was suggested we go there for location shots on the way home.

"You going to shoot outdoors?" I asked the assistant director.

"Yup."

"Need good weather?"

"Yup."

"I think you're wasting your time—it's November and the weather will not be pleasant; lots of rain and wind."

"Oh, we'll be okay."

So off we went, first to Paris, but only for a fuel stop. Then London for two days while deicer boots were installed on *The Geek*'s wings. It was getting toward winter and we planned to return via the North Atlantic, and *The Geek* didn't have deicer boots. "We'd better have 'em," I said, and Ty agreed.

Then on to Dublin, a great city, great people, wonderful times—and rain. We sat for six days watching it rain. Finally Bob Webb, the location director, said, "Screw this, we'll build Ireland in L.A., on the back lot. Let's get out of here." So off he went to London, and we began the trek back home.

The days of flights in sun and blue skies were over; now it was the often unfriendly North Atlantic. We had some nervous times in the crossing; the weather forced us to go nonstop from Reykjavik to Goose Bay, twelve hours and forty minutes, some seven hours of it in snow on instruments. While we knew we had plenty of fuel for the planned flight, there was always the possibility that the head winds were stronger than forecast, and as we were flying on instruments Stevens could not get any celestial, even a sun line. This would make the fuel calculations inexact and nervous—all we could do was to keep going and find out at the end.

Those hours of apprehension are so long. To be in a spot that gives cause for concern and then to have to wait hours for the answer is one of flying's most difficult phases. Generally something with a bit of danger goes quickly, like ducking a too close taxi cab; in an instant of fright one misses or gets hit, but in flying, some of it, like the position we were in, one sits and nervously waits, sweating it out.

Two hours from our estimated arrival the snow started to have cloud mass in it, and that meant ice. It formed quickly and we knew a front was close; the question was, could we get through the front before we got too much ice?

The propellers were icing fast; as the alcohol flow dislodged the bigger pieces, they banged against the fuselage with a shock and noise like a .45 going off six feet away. The chunks of ice didn't come off evenly, but rather from one propeller blade and then another, which unbalanced the prop and made the airplane shake hard. I thought of all the pipes and wires and hoped they'd stay together.

"Willie," I asked Agner, "you think the plumbing will hold?"

"I hope so," was his unconvincing reply, but he went on. "I checked every connection in Dublin and they looked good—she ought to hold." God bless good flight engineers like Willie.

We had run out of propeller alcohol and the situation looked serious, when a ray of sunlight flicked across the windshield—hope sending a message. And then we saw a patch of blue sky through a break in the cloud tops. Do you really know how beautiful a little patch of blue sky can look? There was elation in the cockpit, believe me. The clouds broke up and it cleared quickly; in the blaze of a setting sun we landed at Goose Bay.

In those days Goose had two sets of command: one side of the field was Canadian and the other American. As we stood in the operations office after arrival, a gentlemanly but firm argument developed as to which side of the field Ty would stay at, Canadian or American. It was an uncomfortable situation that demanded diplomacy from Ty when I'm sure he wasn't in a fawning mode. I stood off to one side, next to a display of weather maps. Ty glanced at me with a glance that said, "Roberto, get us out of this."

Our next stop was going to be Moncton, New Brunswick, Gallagher's hometown, a flight of about three hours from Goose Bay. Gallagher had talked throughout the trip of the party his sister and brother-in-law would throw when we stopped there, with much bragging about the lobsters and oysters of Northumberland Strait and the Gulf of St. Lawrence. I looked at the weather maps I was leaning on and noted a low pressure area to the west of Moncton that would be moving that way bringing snow and foul weather; from its location I guessed it would hit the Moncton area tomorrow. A scenario quickly formed in my mind and I walked over to Ty.

"Ty, I've been looking at the weather, and it doesn't look good for tomorrow in Moncton—I know how much you want to stay here, but if we only have a day for Moncton we'd better go now."

Being a good actor he put on the proper disappointed appearance and reluctantly went along with my suggestion.

The weather map had actually painted the weather as I'd told Ty, but en route we learned that it was snowing in Moncton, the visibility had gone down and the ceiling with it—the damn low had moved faster than forecast, surprising everyone.

We kept going, trying to be optimistic, but the next report was worse. And then Trans Canada's dispatcher called us on the radio: their Moncton flight had just made a pass, couldn't get in, and proceeded to Stephenville on Newfoundland, and he suggested we proceed there also.

We were close to Moncton by then, and Ty looked at me and asked, "What do you think we ought to do?"

"You're the captain, you make the decision," I answered, well knowing what I would have done, but he had been a good commander all this way and the call should be his.

"Well, hell," he responded. "We're damn near there, I'm for making an approach and see if we can get in, and if not then we'll go to Stephenville."

"You get an A plus for that one," was my response.

Moncton was not an easy approach. The radio range was east of the airport and the wind was east, so it meant making an approach, then making a half-circle to get into the wind for landing—and making a circle in reduced visibility with snow is tough stuff. One had better be good and know how.

Well, Ty made the nicest approach you ever saw, laid *The Geek* on its ear, circled, and landed perfectly. The next day's paper and radio said, "Tyrone Power lands when Trans Canada could not."

We had a party to remember; the lobsters and oysters were as good as Gallagher said they'd be, and Ty and I took on the Curling Club's champions and beat them. It was our first attempt ever, a triumph of two men not knowing what they were doing, going for broke against two opponents who, to put it mildly, had tipped a glass or two. Moncton remains a favorite and warmly remembered place.

From Moncton we made a stop at Bangor, to clear customs and reenter the United States, and then on back to California. We landed back at Hughes three months, almost to the day, from our departure. As Kemper Jacks had accurately said the day he talked me into going, "Chance of a lifetime." It was, but it wasn't that alone; more important was the warm close friendships we had all gained. It would be a little dull settling down to our various routines, but as Ty put it, "What the heck—we only have to work eight months and we're off again." That never happened, but the friendship and association continued, growing with every year.

CHAPTER 21

Back on the Line

RETURNING TO THE AIRLINE was like a homecoming. I got my instrument checks and three landings in both a Connie and DC-4; the Connie instrument check was with Eddie Wells, a great little pilot and a real New Yorker who would have fit in perfectly in the driver's seat of a Manhattan taxicab. He smoked cigars and puffed one all during the check, as did the flight engineer. The smoke and odor almost made me sick, but when I complained they only laughed and puffed some more.

Those days preceded the antismoking era and cockpits were often blue with smoke, as were the passenger cabins. The Connies were especially bad because the air was recirculated and got pretty foul. On one visit to Kansas City I went through our instrument repair and overhaul shop; a technician working there told me his major problem was removing tobacco tars from air-driven instruments, tar that collected from the circulating smoke in the cabin. That got me thinking about quitting smoking, and one Europe-bound passenger's story clinched it for me: he had recently had a son, and when he leaned over the bed with his wife and new baby, he stretched to kiss the baby, and his wife pushed him away: "You're not going to kiss that beautiful child with your foul-smelling cigar breath!" It so impressed him that he stopped smoking. And so did I.

One day, at lunch with DeWitt Wallace, founder of *Reader's Digest,* I told this story. DeWitt, a charming man, a cigarette smoker himself, thought it a great story and asked me to write it up. The *Digest* published it as "Why an Airline Pilot Quit Smoking." I understand he periodically tried to give up cigarettes and never did, and so he was always willing to publish an article against smoking.

It felt good to be back on the line; the interest, excitement, and anticipation of every trip made for a stimulating life. The flights were not one hop to Paris, but rather a long saga: La Guardia to Gander, to Shannon, to Paris. We had longer, brutal ones; on some we served Chicago, so I'd fly out there from the East Coast as a passenger and then work Chicago, Detroit, Gander, Shannon, and Paris. In an unpressurized DC-4 that trip could be tough.

The DC-4 was slim on gasoline, and sometimes we couldn't make Shannon to Gander; then we'd have to go Shannon, Santa Maria in the Azores, then Gander, perhaps Boston, then New York, and finally fly empty La Guardia to Wilmington, Delaware, which at the time was our international headquarters. My old logbook lists one trip like that where the flying time was twenty-five hours and thirty-four minutes.

We had bunks for naps in the airplanes, but with the number of crew members—three pilots, two flight engineers, one radio operator, one navigator, a hostess, and a purser—and just two bunks, a single and a double, no one got much over two hours sleep. Making up the bunk schedule, which was the captain's task, was a job I always hated. At the start of the flight everyone was reasonably rested, so no one wanted to crawl in the bunk except for the occasional crew member who had overdone it in Paris and was suffering from lack of sleep and hungover. This wasn't a routine occurrence, so the first bunk periods weren't very useful. Making the schedule, I always had to work around the fact that the hostess insisted on the single bunk. So a twenty-four-hour flight was a hard flight, and generally the captain got the poorest rest. I'd crawl in a bunk, shut my eyes, and go off to sleep, but a few minutes later the airplane might bounce, and I'd lie there wondering what we were running through; in winter the airplane might be getting into clouds with ice. So I'd crawl out of the bunk and go forward to see what was going on. The two copilots probably had it under control, so back to sleep. Next I might feel the engines out of synchronization, why was that? Stick your head out of the bunk, not too far from the flight engineer. "What's going on—why are they out of sync?"

"Oh, just readjusting the mixtures."

Back to sleep again, but it seemed the captain always got the least sleep. Oh, there were times when it went well and the nap was a solid two hours, perhaps even three on some flights. But three hours sleep in twenty-four isn't enough.

Many nights we'd leave Shannon for Gander with a flight plan that was nip and tuck as to fuel. Only once did our actual flight fall below flight plan approaching the PNR. It was in a DC-4, on a tough night with terrific head winds. We plowed into these winds, anxiously watching speed and fuel. Red Miller was behind me in another DC-4 on the London flight and we compared notes via radio. As we approached the weather ship, stationed almost in the middle for rescue and navigation aid, my howgozit line was in bad shape. I studied it carefully. Shocked, I turned to the copilot and said, "Goddamn it, we can't make it—we have to turn around!"

I called Red: "Red, I can't make it, I'm going back to Shannon."

Red: "I just decided the same thing. See you later."

Heading back, the wind was on our tail and in no time we were in Shannon.

The airplane had forty-three seats for passengers, a lot further apart and roomier than what you find today. In front of the passenger cabin was the galley where the food and drink came from; generally some crew member would be in the galley, getting a coffee, or just talking with the hostess. Forward of the galley you entered the business end of the airplane; the bunks were a double right on the floor, and above it a single, both across from the navigator. At the start of a flight the bunks were all neatly made up by ground personnel; folded white sheets showed at the top of the army blankets, white pillows were clean and in place. By the end of the second bunk period this had changed to a shambles of blankets, pillows, and sheets. But when we were ready for the bunk we were too tired to give a damn.

Crawling into the lower bunk you'd find another body in there, but no one cared who. On one long flight an exhausted hostess came forward and said she just had to sleep; the upper bunk was full, but she didn't care and crawled in the lower with another crew member who probably never knew he'd been sleeping with the hostess. I had this happen to me and I half awakened as she crawled in. I didn't know who it was, but she cuddled up to me in a half-sleep state, and then I knew the body was female. But that was it—we went off to sleep, all proper.

All the space up front was tight, and we had to pass each other sideways in the aisle. The aroma was unpleasant and the smell permeated my uniform. Often when I returned from a trip my wife would exclaim, "Phew—hang that uniform outside." When smoking ended in the air the odor improved, but any cockpit has a special odor, not really unpleasant, but not nice either.

Aside from odor, the piston engine airplanes had vibration, a constant shake that went through the structure from the force of seventy-two cylinders with explosions and pistons slamming up and down thousands of times an hour. It wasn't violent, but it was always there, a part of flying's character, and any interruption or change in its pace got everyone's attention. The vibration added to crew member fatigue, its relentless annoyance not consciously thought about but under the skin, gnawing away at your psyche. The jet of today is different; the engine doesn't have explosions, or things banging up and down, but simply a bunch of vanes, carefully balanced and spinning, always in one direction, smooth and without vibration.

The longer the flight, the more grubby and casual the front end became. Coffee cups here and there, pieces of paper, men needing a shave, the whiff of a foul breath. It didn't look very efficient. But an hour from landing things would tighten up: coffee cups disappeared, papers collected and tossed in the rubbish bin; the wandering crew members settled down to their proper positions, no one in the galley, and the hostess and purser getting their cabin organized and handing coats to passengers.

The passenger of that time was tougher, more resigned to the fact that it would take many hours and stops to reach a destination; on good days it could be twenty hours of flying from Paris to New York with stops at Shannon and Gander. Each flight seemed to be an affair of friends, new and old. The passengers, especially in the night, would tell you intimate things about their lives.

On one flight Irving Berlin was a passenger and I had a long chat with him. He was concerned about not having a smallpox vaccination—in those days one was required.

"I don't believe in those things, so I've refused to be vaccinated—what'll they do about that in New York?"

"Easy, they'll vaccinate you."

"I'll resist it."

We landed in New York, La Guardia, where international arrivals was the old Marine Terminal, a small round building. We passed Immigration and Health, then on to Customs. As we passed the health room I looked in to see Berlin, shirtsleeve rolled up, getting vaccinated. He smiled when I waved to him.

Later on I had him on another flight from London to New York. He remembered me and was pleasant and friendly.

"I see you have another great hit, congratulations," I told him, referring to *Call Me Madam* with Ethel Merman.

"Have you seen it?"

"Gosh no, it's impossible to get seats."

"When do you want to go?"

Sensing an opportunity I said, "Tomorrow night."

"There'll be tickets for you and your wife at the box office."

And there were: orchestra, fifth-row center. We noticed people looking us over, perhaps wondering who the two un–New York people were—and fifth-row center! It was a wonderful evening.

I frequently had as passengers some of the Kennedy sisters, before their brother was president, going to or from London. I got to know them fairly well in an airplane passenger sense, and we joked a bit about so often being on the same flights.

Much later, in the jet age, after Kennedy's assassination, I was en route to London when a hostess came up and said two Kennedy sisters were on board. "Oh, I know them, I'll be back later."

After we were cruising and settled down I went aft, saw the women in first class, took off my hat, and said something about, "It's like old times, nice to have you on board again."

They turned, looked out the window, and snubbed me cold. Oh well.

Some passengers leave a great impression, and while their names are long forgotten, they aren't: like the man who influenced me to quit smoking; or the archaeologist going to Greece who said that every leader, dictator, or top figure wants to leave a monument to himself—the Pyramids at

Giza, the Arc de Triomphe, and now I think of France's Mitterrand and the new opera house near the location of the Bastille, and the Mitterrand Bibliothéque Nationale. The list is long.

One day I came out of the cockpit and stood up near the galley and did a couple of deep knee bends to loosen up after sitting a long time. A man rushed up to me from first class: "Don't do that! It'll ruin your knees. I'm an orthopedic surgeon—believe me, don't do deep knee bends."

I thanked him and have never done one since.

I had a quiet talk with Ralph Bunche, Nobel Peace Prize winner for mediating the settlement of the 1947–48 Arab-Israeli war. I remember his soft, gentle way—I felt privileged to have met him, and even now, many years later, I often think of him as an example of grace and intelligence, one of the exceptional and great people I was lucky enough to cross paths with.

Another day the hostess came up and said Admiral Halsey was on board. "I'll be back, I want to talk to him."

I approached him, and he looked up and nodded.

"Glad you are with us, sir," I said, and went on. "We have something in common." His bushy eyebrow raised a bit in questioning fashion.

"We both attended Pingry." This is a prep school in Elizabeth, New Jersey.

He looked a bit astounded, then uttered, "Well, I'll be goddamned!"

We chatted a bit and I went back to the cockpit, a memorable moment.

There was a man in first class I talked with one night, obviously an intelligent and worldly person. We got into a discussion of nations and people; he apparently had traveled widely and knew the international scene. What bothered him about America, he said, was our intense zeal for competition; it put into shadow the decency of man, made one less thoughtful of others, brought out the ruthless. He was far more eloquent than I am here, but his message stuck and it put in place something I think about, am disturbed about: we've come a long and nasty way from friendly games of one sort or other to riots after big contests; contact sports such as hockey and football have grown more vicious, and yet the crowd yells for more like the Romans in the Colosseum. The merciless business world is guilty, too. Competition, it is said, builds character; it also builds insolence.

Not all the memorable passengers were quite so illuminating. On one flight to Europe, a little Italian man went wild en route, tearing up his traveler's checks, spitting in other passengers' faces, trying get a door open, and accusing us of trying to kill him. When we landed at Shannon I told our Irish station manager that this crazy man had to get off; he looked into the situation, and after a bit he informed me that this man could not be put off the flight—because he didn't have an Irish visa!

I thought for a minute and then said, "Jim, I have a solution. The flight is canceled."

"Jaysus, you wouldn't be doin' that to me, Captain."

"I just did it. It ends here in Shannon," I told him.

"Wait a minute, I'll be back."

He returned soon. "Okay, I've worked it out with the authorities, he comes off."

"Okay, the flight is resumed."

I later learned that this poor old guy had been drugged up by his family who wanted to send him off to Italy to get him out of their hair. The drugs wore off about halfway across the Atlantic, and his unstable mind took over.

Those were the relaxed days of flying. What a contrast with today: after I finished my rating ride with the FAA in the 747, the inspector informed me, "You did a good job, but I want you to remember, never leave that cockpit except to go to the toilet, and be as quick as possible about that." Progress, I guess.

In these early international days we floundered a bit learning how best to manage things. TWA was a Kansas City–based company with Middle-American concepts and values. Then, suddenly, we were trying to run an airline in Europe, the Near East, and Asia—and as one pilot put it, "How you gonna run an international airline with corn belt philosophy?" Basically we were naive to the ways of the European world. It was rumored, for example, although it was never confirmed to me, that we'd unknowingly hired a number of prostitutes for the hostess position. They disappeared as management became more sophisticated; there's great solidity in "corn belt philosophy," and once our folks got into the European swing it made for a nice combination and a great operation.

But in the beginning there were elements of confusion. We had pilot crew bases in New York, Rome, and Cairo—all manned by U.S. pilots. We

New York pilots flew to Shannon, then a Rome crew took it to Cairo, and the Cairo crew flew on to Bombay.

Flying only to Shannon was not what I wanted out of international. My flights ended in cold, wet Ireland—beautiful on a few days, but not many. We stayed right on the airport in low barrackslike structures with tiny single rooms we called rabbit hutches. They had little if any heat, and minimum bath facilities that consisted of a communal room with a line of wash basins and a shower with a tiny showerhead that squirted a few small streams of icy water in various directions, rarely on the showeree. We took few showers—BO be damned.

The rooms were so small it was necessary to store your suitcase under the bed, pull it out and put it on the bed when needed, then shove it back under the bed to have enough space to move about the room. A small washbasin with two faucets was stuck in one corner near the door; this was used mostly to pee in rather than go down a cold hallway to the bathroom.

The beds were singles with heavy woolen blankets, and by heavy I mean they felt heavy on one's body—and you needed a lot of them because it was always cold. Sliding into the bed, flinching as you slid down between the cold sheets, your foot would suddenly hit something hard and warm; this was a ceramic water bottle some kind soul had filled with hot water and placed in the bed, down at the foot. I never knew how this kindness occurred, but it was appreciated. Sleep meant snuggling down under the heavy blankets as far as possible, keeping everything warm except your head; I eventually got hold of a nightcap to wear.

To eat we bundled up and trudged to the terminal and its restaurant. The food was hearty Irish fare, and with this food and the heat in the restaurant you finally felt warm. The strawberry jam was sold in brown ceramic crocks that held about a quart; I carried many of these home and the crocks are still around, used as flower vases.

On some layovers, when the weather turned nice, those interested would go to Limerick and play golf. From the air the Limerick golf course looked boring, with one hole alongside another without much character. But it was deceiving and it proved interesting with subtle hills, gorse, and bushes to avoid. It cost in those days about $1 for greens fees; the caddie, always a small Irish lad with a cap and ragged-looking clothes, got 75 cents. One day I hooked a ball into a stand of bushes and went in to find it. The little caddie stood out on the fairway with the bag of clubs, not moving.

"Come on, help me find the ball," I called to him.

"Oh no, sir, I'll not be going in there."

"Why not?" I asked, fearing some unknown danger.

It wasn't a danger to me, but it was to him: "I'm not going in there—that's where the little people live."

So that was Shannon: fly from New York, cross the Atlantic toward Europe, stay in cold, uncomfortable Shannon, and then turn around after a few days and go back across the Atlantic, turning your back on Europe and its wonders, especially Paris, where I badly wanted to go. My mother's side of the family was French, Huguenots who fled to Switzerland, and my grandmother was born in Geneva; she tried to teach me French and some stuck, but more important were her stories of Switzerland and France and their history. I was stewing to get to Paris.

Then one day, a miracle, a company message the flight dispatcher in Shannon handed to me, saying, "You might be interested in this."

The message announced that starting March 1 the New York crews would continue to, and lay over in . . . PARIS! I was giddy with delight.

CHAPTER 22

Paris and Beyond

✳

GERTRUDE STEIN SAID, "America is my country, and Paris is my hometown."

Paris became my hometown, too. It didn't happen overnight, although I liked what I saw right from the start: the expanse of the Champs-Elysées as seen from the Arc de Triomphe du Carrousel, through the Tuileries, across the Place de la Concorde with its obelisk, up the sweep of the Champs ending at the Arc de Triomphe. There's no sight more grand; the Seine and its bridges, the Eiffel Tower, Invalides, Notre Dame, Madeleine. I took them all in, walking until my feet felt like stumps.

But there's much more to it than the sights; it takes time to learn Paris, and I got to do that over the years. Paris wasn't simply another stop on our routes, but rather a junction point, the key spot. It's where we stopped for a day or so before going south to Rome, Athens, Cairo, or Tel Aviv, where we stayed overnight before flying home to New York.

Coming east, our U.S.-based cabin attendants turned around at Paris after an overnight and returned to New York, and when we continued south our European cabin attendants climbed on board and took over. They were selected for their ability with languages, and were a mixture of French, German, Dutch, Swedish, Italian, and two Egyptians, with French and German predominating. There were pursers, too, mostly French and

Paris-based, but the women outnumbered them since there was only one
purser on each flight, but two hostesses, and as the airplanes grew more
hostesses were added until the 747 arrived and required twelve mostly
young women. They were attractive, especially with their European flair
and pleasant accents; I learned quickly that these hostesses had an appreciation for culture as well as fun, and they helped steer me to things and
places that were an education.

We'd fly to Cairo, which was a long day with stops at Geneva, Rome,
and Athens, getting to Cairo late at night, checking into the hotel (the
Heliopolis then), and quickly scattering to our rooms for sleep.

Cairo layovers were often two days, so there was time to relax and do
whatever one wished; visiting the Cairo Museum with its great collection
was interesting, but one can only spend so much time in a museum. There
was a swimming pool, named the Airline Club, where crew members hung
out—not just TWA crews, but other European airlines such as KLM,
British, and SAS. I got to know a lot of people from a lot of places. The
decorations at the pool were titillating to say the least, as the collection of
European hostesses, all young, attractive, and shapely, wore their skimpy
bikinis, which had recently come into fashion.

Some crew members played tennis or golf. Golf was at the Ghizira
Sporting Club, a colonial leftover. Farouk was king and Nasser hadn't yet
come along to revolutionize Egypt, so conditions reflected the age when
the white man of England was dominant. The era was almost over, but I
was among those who reaped its benefits, and I enjoyed them even as it
rubbed me the wrong way.

The Ghizira Club had polo fields, golf, and servants everywhere kow-
towing to one's every wish; pull out a cigarette—I smoked then—and
instantly there would be a hand holding a match to it.

At the golf club the caddies cost about 75 cents a round. They were
small youths, barefoot; we always had two of them, one for the bag and the
other, a forecaddie, to be out where the ball landed to protect it from vul-
tures that would swoop down, pick up the ball, and fly a couple of hundred yards with it before discovering it wasn't edible and dropping it.

The club was on an island in the Nile right in town. The traffic noise was
a constant din interspersed with horns and such strange sounds as an ass
baying; periodically it was time for prayers and high-pitched Arabic blasted

from loudspeakers mounted on various minarets. Late in the day, as the sun set and the shadows lengthened, a calm seemed to come over the land; it cooled down from the hot midday and the air was pleasant with a slight breeze. We often sat on the hotel roof, having a sundowner drink, watching the Nile close by below. Twilight slowly changed the day's brassy colors to subtle dark shades, the colors discernible but muted before turning into night; the dhows, with their triangular lateen sails, quietly plied the river as they had for a thousand years. It was a tranquil, romantic interlude.

We visited the Muski market, shopping. For a while the big item was a camel saddle, and many were lugged back to the States for household ornaments. When that craze subsided the item became large brass trays with designs hammered into them. My only purchase over the years was a small wood stool with ivory inlays, made with care and craftsmanship, an exact copy of one from ancient Egypt; the original is in the Cairo Museum.

I got to know some of the shopkeepers, sat and talked with them, and drank coffee—the heavy syrupy kind found all over the Middle East. These were fine people who forged my respect and fondness for Arabs and their many tribes. In the thirty years or so that I flew into Arab lands I never had anything stolen, and I was pretty sloppy about leaving things open in my rooms; I never had a promise broken, and all my contacts were pleasant. This admiration led me to read up on Arab history, and I came to recognize their tremendous gifts to mathematics, art, and science.

The flight from Cairo to Paris just reversed the order: Athens, Rome, Geneva, then Paris. In those days most stops were an hour and the passengers were given some sort of refreshment on the ground. Geneva was my favorite because of the delicious pastries and coffee. Crew and passengers would mix and chat during these stops.

So it was an intimate trip both ways, and a chance to get acquainted with the cabin attendants. They periodically came to the cockpit with our meals and any extra goodies that had been put on for passengers, asking where we were and what that interesting mountain or island was. It was a light, happy atmosphere. On the ground we frequently ate together and explored the city, talking, talking about everything. They told me about things to do in Paris, where to find the good and inexpensive restaurants, how to get around on the Métro, what concerts were on—and it was only polite, when someone recommended a restaurant in Paris, to ask her to go along.

The women I knew showed me Paris; I went to the Opera House and saw the ballet *Giselle* for the first time, listened to my first piano concert in the Théâtre des Champs-Elysées, a host of things.

One winter a strike in France shut down our operation; the strike dragged on for over a month, and service to Orly Field, Paris, was stopped. To keep things going we moved everything to Basel, Switzerland, flying into the Basel-Mulhouse airport, which, as I recall, was part in France and part in Switzerland. It was a relaxed place without much traffic. One foggy night as I approached, the tower gave me the surface wind as 15 knots. Landing straight in, as I was on an instrument approach, regulations only allowed a tailwind of 10 knots; otherwise a circle was necessary, and there wasn't enough ceiling for that.

I called the tower: "I can only land straight in with a maximum wind of 10 knots."

Immediately the tower responded, "The wind has just gone to 10 knots."

That was cooperation—and I landed.

Passengers were taken from Basel to Paris by rail, and the crews stayed in Basel, at a wonderful hotel called the Switzerhoff, the restaurant and food superb. It was an invasion of crew members, with the American and foreign crews all bunched in the hotel, going and coming, from the United States, Cairo, and even Bombay.

Marie Claude, a very beautiful French hostess, urged me to visit the Basel museum with her because it held some excellent Holbeins. My art education was slim; I'd never heard of Holbein, but the chance to spend the afternoon with Marie Claude was worth any museum drag.

Walking the hushed corridors in a desultory manner, I glanced at various paintings, until suddenly my eyes landed on an abstract work, a couple of rectangles in red and black, a few straight lines. It grabbed me, sent a thrill through my mind. I stood and stared for a long time, with Marie Claude standing beside me.

"I think it's a Mondrian, a Dutch painter," she told me.

That single experience opened me to art, a wonderful world I studied, haunting museums, walking the Left Bank looking in galleries. It has never stopped, and I pursue art, seeing it, appreciating it, searching it out, and it enriches my life. Thank you, Marie Claude, thank you, Piet Mondrian.

In Paris I entered a gallery on the Avenue de l'Opéra where paintings were sold, really a tourists' kind of store. An enthusiastic elderly lady was the salesperson and she showed me various paintings. A cottage in Normandy was one, and a dockside scene was another. They were only $35 each and she said to me, "The artist, Lecomte, is very old, he will die soon and the paintings will increase in value, you should buy them." I did, not on the inducement of the artist's demise, but because I liked them.

Through the years I purchased other paintings in other galleries and became good friends with one proprietor. A few years ago I asked if he'd ever heard of my Lecomte. He pulled down a reference book and looked him up. My paintings now were worth about $2,500 each—that old girl knew her stuff.

The center of activity in Paris was the Celtic Hotel, 6 rue Balzac. That's where we stayed, where crew members came and went, our home in Paris. (The Celtic has since been taken over, remodeled, and renamed the Balzac—a snobby, expensive hotel very far removed from our Celtic.)

Six rue Balzac is a block in from the Champs-Elysées; mount a few stone steps, open a typical large glass door with heavy metal sill and frame, enter the lobby, notice a sort of glow about the place, gold-yellow in tone. On the right a counter and there, smiling, head slightly cocked, eyeglasses and slicked-down hair, was the concierge, the room boxes and keys forming a backdrop behind him. He always greeted us warmly.

Further along, a recessed area with a counter and behind it a person to assign rooms and settle accounts. Often the person would be Max or Jean Percepied, the owners with another brother, Jacques, of the hotel and two others in Paris. Max and Jean always dressed in a blue suit, blue shirt, blue tie. Pleasant and warm people.

To the right a passageway; on its right a door to a storage room where my golf clubs rested, to the left a large sitting area with tapestries, comfortable seats and couches, and a glass-domed ceiling with decorations. Go through the room, turn right through a doorway, and one entered the bar. The bar was on the right, across from it a banquette, plush-covered, small tables in front; then beyond that more chairs and small tables, only a few because the bar was not large. To its left an archway led to the dining room—a few steps down into the pleasant, well-lighted room. Good food served by attractive girls: Gabby, Yvonne, Josette, and others dressed in black with white aprons and headpieces. It was a congenial place that radiated pleasant times.

One day I was having lunch with Max, and in the middle of it he leaped to his feet, slammed down his napkin, and rushed to a nearby table full of loud Americans.

"Leave this dining room! You owe nothing, just get out."

An American looked up, nonplussed. "What's this all about?"

Max: "You are impolite—no one whistles at our waitresses. Go." He pointed, and the party got up and departed. The waitresses were dear to us all, and, of course, whistling at them for attention was rude—the ugly American in action. I was on Max's side.

But back to the bar where, ready to serve, stood Jean Pierre Victor Maretheu, better known as Jackie: a small man, pleasant smile, father confessor to all, moneylender, patient listener, and discreet to the decimal point. He had been there a long time, bidding goodbye to the Germans who occupied the Celtic until they were chased out by the Americans, who took over the hotel with Jackie to welcome them. We all had great fondness for Jackie. For a time Jackie and I worked the lottery together: it's a small-denomination game with tickets purchased at a tabac. The rewards were modest, but it was fun. When all this ended, after a couple of years, our winnings had been about $20.

We had one flight that arrived in Paris in the evening. The crew bus taking us to town pulled up in front of the hotel at about 10:30, with tired crew members anxious to change clothes and go down to the bar for a beer. Sometimes, as the bus pulled up, Jackie would be standing in front waiting for us. This was a signal that said, without words, "The FAA is in the bar." The FAA periodically visited crew hotels to see how the crews behaved. So that night there would be no visiting the Celtic bar, and we'd go off to various places known to us, but not to the FAA.

When Jeeb Halaby was FAA administrator, I was loaned to him for a few months on special assignment. Jeeb was going to Europe on an inspection trip and asked me what hotel he could use in Paris in order to meet and talk with crews about flight safety and their problems. I suggested he stay at the Celtic. On his return he admonished me, "I stayed in the Celtic, but never saw a crew member, there weren't any around." Jackie had done his job. I should have done something about that before Jeeb went over.

There were occasional wild times in the bar, generally when crews were held over because of a winter fog. In those days we weren't supposed to land with lower than a 300-foot ceiling, although we often cheated to 200 feet. These restrictions meant no flights could come in, hence there were no airplanes to go out, and sometimes we waited for days—five was my record; since it was Paris I didn't consider it a hardship, but some got pretty bored and a bit testy waiting, and arguments could develop in the bar. In one instance a fight started that broke a few things. It so happened that the next day some FAA people cornered Max to ask him, in confidence, how TWA crew members behaved. Max looked them straight in the eye: "The most perfect gentlemen I have ever known, always courteous and sober, we don't make money from them at our bar."

I don't want to give the impression that crew members were party-loving, hard-drinking people. Not so. Certainly we had a few who liked to imbibe, but they were a minority, and even then they knew when to quit. A few alcoholics appeared in the ranks, a very few, but they were soon found and released. This was in a more ignorant time; airlines now will pay for treatment and attempt to get them back on track. But it wasn't a worry then, nor is it now as far as safety is concerned.

Max Percepied and I became close friends, and I remember our first encounter. When we moved to the hotel I was anxious to know how to get to St. Cloud golf course, and on a layover I approached the lobby desk. Max, in his blue suit, was busy writing in a large ledger. He looked up, with a big smile that made him look a bit like the French actor Fernandel: "May I help you?"

"Yes, I would like to know how best to get from here to the St. Cloud golf club."

"You want to play golf?"

"Why, yes."

"When?"

"I was thinking today—now."

"Good, we'll go." He put down his pen, got up and said to follow him, we went to his car, then to the club for a pleasant round of golf, with Max playing very well.

I hadn't merely run into a golf enthusiast; the Celtic was the golf center of Paris, where golfers came for long, warm, amusing dinners, especially after Sunday rounds. I was quickly welcomed into the society; before long I had joined the Lys Chantilly golf club as a nonresident member, kept clubs and clothes in Paris, met many wonderful people. Max's daughter, France, came and lived with us for a school year in New Jersey. She didn't speak a word of English on arrival, but within three months she was rattling it off, and had made many friends in our local high school, from which she graduated at the year's end. Max and Susane had a son, Lulu, who spent a summer with us; a wonderful, quiet, intelligent young man. Fate was mean, and we were shaken when Lulu, in the army at the time of the Algerian war, was killed; Max never recovered from that, and it left a sad place in my heart that will never go away.

Among the golfers was Henri DeFiliquier—Riton—and his wife, André. Wonderful people, full of fun, and truly French in their appreciation of life and good living. Riton was an excellent golfer, with a scratch handicap. For a time, in the late 1930s, he had played in the United States as an amateur, on tour with the pros. We became very close friends.

These people were another part of my French education, teaching me their generosity, humor, appreciation of good things, yet with a serious side about politics and world affairs and people. I came to appreciate the French brilliance in so many fields: art, literature, science, mathematics, and the culture France has handed down. I was a lucky man in Paris.

Layovers are a unique part of a pilot's life. They're times of release from discipline. Once you're on the ground there are no demands beyond getting proper rest before the next flight; aside from that the time is your own, to wander the streets, visit museums, see friends, play golf. I'd walk the streets feeling free, turning this way or that as my fancy directed. That was especially true in the early days of longer layovers—the jet ruined much of that.

Airline pilots aren't any different from an earthbound group of people: most are straight-arrow, some like the opposite sex and constantly pursue its wandering path, a few are religion-centered (one flight engineer I often flew with had his Bible right there with him on the flight deck), some like boats, some love their home workshop, and most are devoted family people; one was a poet who took a year off to teach at a small California college, only to come back to flying saying the politics of a college were too much for him.

Of course anyone so inclined lived in a bright world of sexual opportunity. And now I want to make certain it's understood that the hostesses in Paris were not a collection of easy ladies, but some were available under the right circumstances and understanding—that understanding being a sincere friendship, and the right time and place. American girls at the time were no different, and perhaps the time had something to do with it, because the 1950s and 1960s were the golden age of sex; the pill had been invented, AIDS had not come along, antibiotics still cured VD, and the "freedom" of the hippie age was in the air.

Don't get the impression life was one big sex party, it wasn't, and the occasional encounter involved a certain respect and a warm attachment between two people. It ended there. Well, most did, but there were exceptions.

The exceptions happened when love stepped in. Unfortunately there were some divorces, and sometimes unhappy marriages resulted. But I have seen, through the years, that many of these marriages worked well; I have friends, now in their seventies, living happily with the French or German or whatever partner they met and fell in love with so many years ago.

A few pilots were dumb about worldly things. You could see it happening when a naive, never-been-out-of-the-U.S.A. kind of guy got carried away and bedded down with an attractive European, his first experience off the straight and narrow. Sometime such types would go starry-eyed, ditch home and wife, and screw things up with their new attachment to a wife who pulled toward Europe, while they longed for home in the States. Perhaps later he'd discover it was only a flush that faded and there he was, with an ex-wife getting alimony, his life mixed up. The poor pilot, despite making a good salary, was poor indeed.

The more sophisticated knew what it was about and perhaps settled into an amiable arrangement.

One of these arrangements had a sad ending to which I was a witness. This certain captain was much involved with a German hostess; they were deeply attached to each other and lived together whenever he was in Paris. They traveled some in Europe, and she would occasionally fly to meet him at another layover point. I knew and liked them both.

She was in Frankfurt when I had a layover there, and her paramour was in the United States on a flying task that went sour, an accident resulted, and he was killed. I was in the hotel and went to her when she got the terrible news; she really came apart and no consolation I could offer was of much help. She stopped caring about life; she eventually left the airline, went home, became an alcoholic and let her beauty and form collapse. I lost track of her, but I wonder where and how she is—if she's still alive.

If certain airline people read this I'm sure they will curse me to the skies. But remember, what I'm telling here applies to a small percentage of those who flew. The level of sexual activity probably wasn't any different than with any collection of humans, the same as it is in most offices and businesses in America. These incidents weren't vulgar or tawdry; no, most of them were endearing. And I don't mean to leave an impression that European girls are any more available than those from America, in many cases, au contraire!

The trite expression that we were a big family wasn't trite but true. We helped one another, and if someone had a problem we all went to work on it.

One hostess, an American, had a disastrous experience with a sleazy character who used her and promised marriage; she was really in love with him, and when he dumped her she slid downhill, not caring, vacuous in appearance and spirit. She leaned on alcohol in a serious fashion.

She was on my flight from Paris to New York once, and she drank enough of the ship's liquor to become dead drunk, unable to function. A hostess came up front and in hushed tones, somewhat baffled, told me the situation; what should we do? This hostess said if we could get her inebriated friend off the airplane she'd get her home. So we called ahead to say there was a handicapped passenger who would need a wheelchair. The entire cabin team, working cleverly, got her in the wheelchair, off the airplane, through Customs, and finally home and to bed; the company and the authorities never knew a thing. There's a happy ending to the story: she got straightened out after taking a leave, got off booze and worked until retirement, a great gal we all loved.

We saw all sides of life. On flights arriving late in the evening, after the hotel dining room had closed, we generally wandered to the Jour et Nuit, an all-night restaurant on the Rue Washington—maybe the Rue de Berri, I've forgotten which, but they run parallel off the Champs-Elysées.

The Jour et Nuit was down a level from the street. It was clean and good. I'd have an entrecôte with pommes frites and a glass of red wine. It was always the same, and always good.

Fairly high-level ladies of the night would drift in for a coffee and to get out of the cold. One night, as I sat alone, an attractive brunette came by my table, hesitated, and gave the nod that suggested I might want to go with her.

"No, cherie, too tired." I said it gently because I always like to be polite and kind to ladies no matter their profession—and in some ways I feel that prostitutes are more honest than many righteous women: there's no deception, no games, everything right out front, just, "I'm available for a price."

This lady pulled out a chair next to mine at the table and sat down.

"Honey," I said, "you're wasting valuable time, I'm not interested."

"I understand, but may I just sit and talk with you?"

So we talked. She had problems: the local police demanded certain payoffs from her, she claimed, and said if she didn't pay they'd tell local gangsters she was revealing information about them and then they'd kill her. It was a bizarre story, but it was told seriously and, it appeared, honestly. She didn't want anything from me, except to hear her tale.

"Where are you from?" I asked her.

"Brittany," she replied.

"Why don't you go home to Brittany and escape all this?"

"What—and leave Paris?" She almost sounded like that old joke about leaving show business.

This conversation isn't exact because we talked half in French, half in English, both of us about equal in each other's language. She was attractive, but a sad sort of person. I saw her a few times again in the Jour et Nuit, we had talks, never business, and then I never saw her again. I wonder what happened to her. Was her story true? Did she wind up in the Seine?

Well, that's another side of Paris. One of its attractions is that no matter your desires, you can find satisfaction for any of them.

Now, when I go back there for visits, my first pleasure is simply to walk: along the main boulevards with traffic, but suddenly I turn a corner and I'm two centuries back, on a quiet street with beautiful old mansions and courtyards where I can imagine a horse-drawn carriage discharging guests in all their finery; *hôtels particuliers,* they are called, but *particulier* means a private and not a public hotel, in times past a private home. I walk along the busy Boulevard St. Germain, stop at the Lipp, have a beer outside, sit and watch the people go by, walk some more, a few turns and suddenly there is Place Furstenburg, not two streets from the busy boulevard, a small, subdued, and quiet square. I look up at the second-floor window of an old building on one corner, an apartment, I guess, and I've always fantasized about living there: a quiet room, sitting in a comfortable chair looking down at the strollers—it's my window, my apartment. I have a Renoux poster of it at home and often I gaze at my window, drifting in misty reverie over the 3,000 miles from Vermont to Paris.

The many little parks and small squares of Paris provide sudden tranquillity; trees and flowers, gravel walks, children playing, or just old folks sitting on the green benches, the harsh world far away.

Farther along, winding through Left Bank streets, I come to the Bucci market; busy, stall after stall of all the wonderful foods France can provide: fruits and vegetables, great stores with shelves of cheese from every corner of the country, meats, poultry, pâtés, hundreds of things to excite the eye and stomach. And the mix of people I rub shoulders with: busy, well off, well dressed, also the less fortunate, dressed in clothes acquired, it would seem, from castoffs.

One reason Paris maintains its great feeling is that the city planners have never allowed big glass buildings and business-style development downtown. From the gardens in Vincennes to Neuilly, about eight miles away, the roofline and buildings are the same as in the eighteenth century, many reaching back to the sixteenth. Parks are still there as in those early times; the Place des Vosges, built under Henry IV, dedicated in 1607, stands much as it did then.

My first flight to Paris, my first time there, was July 15, 1947, not long after the end of the war. Paris looked it: the movement of the people reflected postwar scarcities, tourists hadn't yet arrived in numbers, and transportation was by bicycle, motor scooter, and the small Deux Chevaux Renault and diminutive turtlelike Citroën. Young ladies pumped bicycles, dresses flying, often revealing shapely legs, but most all without stockings, which weren't available. Things like soap and Kleenex were hard to find, so we carried our own. We heard that special foodstuffs were not obtainable, but I never experienced such deprivations in the restaurants we visited.

The fancy automobile, the nouveau riche, and American-style snobby sophistication were nowhere to be found. Looking back, I realize it was a time when Paris belonged to the Parisians. It was a good time, a time that reflected the past; I know now how lucky I was to have experienced it.

But Paris even with its modern glitz is still Paris: down the quiet side streets, an elderly man with a ribbon of the Legion d'Honneur discreetly showing on his suit lapel walks alongside a tastefully dressed lady, both purposefully going about their business, reflecting the class of France. For me, such sights overshadow the glitz and I can sit outside a quiet sidewalk café, sip a beer, daydream, and feel the Paris I love.

We had layovers in other places as well: Rome, Athens, Madrid, Lisbon, London, Frankfurt, Geneva, Zurich, Bombay, Hong Kong. As service expanded and new airplanes came in, we found ourselves in some unfamiliar cities, but most places we flew to enough to get a feel for them, and some to know, among them Rome, Lisbon, London, Frankfurt, and Madrid.

The occasional layover in Geneva had special interest for me because of my grandmother's tales of her youth there: climbing Mt. Salève for Sunday picnics that were mostly good bread and chocolate, or playing on Isle Rousseau, the small island at the end of Lake Geneva where the lake narrows to become the Rhône River rushing toward France. When she was born in 1857, Geneva was a small city, about 30,000 population. She went to church at Le Temple de St. Gervais.

So whenever I got to Geneva I did a lot of walking and looking; Mt. Salève sticks up south of the city, flat-topped, in close-by France, a mountain I had to be conscious of in my flying, not to get too close—what a long connection, and how different, since in her days of climbing the airplane hadn't been invented.

I walked on Isle Rousseau, still accessible to Genevoise. Despite its being in the middle of the city, there's a quiet about it, and as I walked I tried to imagine my grandmother as a girl playing there, and of course one cannot bring the misty past into the sharp focus of today, so visits like that leave an element of confusion. I did find the church and the old family home, which was now a shoe store on the bottom floor with living quarters above, located on the corner of two busy city streets.

I went to the old town to find a street called Rue François d'Ivernois, named for an ancestor of mine. That particular walk grew out of a conversation with a hostess one night on a flight from Paris to Rome that would go on to Geneva. This young lady, Dorothy Baschong, came into the cockpit and introduced herself.

"You are French?" I asked.

Very firmly, she said, "No, I am Swiss!"

I asked from where, and she said Geneva. Of course I launched into the story of my Swiss ancestry and went on, "Our family name in Switzerland was d'Ivernois. We have understood there's a street there named after an ancestor who had done diplomatic work for Switzerland. Do you know of such street?"

"Yes," she said, "I live on it."

An amazing coincidence, since the street, as I learned when I finally saw it, is a very short one, only a bit over 300 feet long in a quiet part of the old city.

The system of assignments made it possible to keep life interesting by heading to new places. Each month we "bid" the trips we wanted to fly, so if flying to Frankfurt had gotten repetitious, you could bid for Madrid and fly there for a while, or London, always Paris, or Rome; there were turn-around trips to Paris and back, or long ones to Ceylon. Patterns for a month's flying were posted each month: four round-trips to Frankfurt and one trip to Hong Kong, for example—all sorts of combinations. The pattern showed where one would go and how much flying time there was for pay each month, and, very important, what days off. We called these "lines of time." After careful study, you bid for the line you wanted, and seniority dictated who got the line. If someone was, for example, number fifty on the seniority list, he'd bid on fifty different lines, putting the most desirable first. During my last years on the line I was number one, so I only had to bid one line and always got it; as the expression goes, "I could bid on heaven." Bidding still goes on, and my son, a captain on a major airline, often talks about getting his bids in by tomorrow or some such day. Today it's done via computer and the Internet; in my day we marked our bids on paper and turned them in by a certain date. Somehow most pilots got some line close to what they wanted, and there was always a feeling of expectation, adventure, and excitement to the flying unless you were a very dull person who stuck to the same route and sat in the hotel lobby exchanging airline gossip and talk with a partner of similar "interests." There were a few of these.

One of the first things we learned about each new place was where to eat, where the good restaurants were. In doing that we learned about food, about the specialties of a country. Mama Cesarena's in Rome, start with pasta mista, a plate of various pastas, not a lot, not a big gloppy mess, but delicate little ravioli, tortellini, a sampling; after that a bolito misto, boiled meats of every sort along with a sauce, served from a cart that came to your table. Oh, Rome is a good place to eat.

Lisbon was fish, and Madrid meant paella. In London I remember best the breakfasts—eggs, lean bacon, bread, and delicious jam—while Frankfurt had everything. We stayed in a small town, Bad Hamburg, where in the early 1900s European royalty gathered for the summer. It had a beautiful park with a short nine-hole golf course, said by some to be the first in Germany, one that the czar, the king of England, and other royalty played. There was a casino in the park, pleasant walks, trees, grass, and flowers.

But the hotel was the center, the Ritter's Park, with a dining room that faced the park through large windows. Everything was immaculate, friendly, and the food was great: goulash soup, all matter of meats and dishes not restricted to German, but those of other places in Europe. The waiters knew us after a time, remembered our wants and favorites. Mr. Beal was our favorite waiter, always there, smiling as you entered, greeting you by name, setting you up at your favorite table. The manager was a chunky, smiling man who would rush up behind you saying, "Just a moment, Captain, a better chair." And by ritual he snapped his fingers as he helped you rise, and a bellboy removed the chair you had occupied, quickly replacing it with a bigger chair with arms. "There, das is besser." It happened every time one sat in a straight-back armless chair. And when that manager snapped his fingers, things happened and people jumped. One day, in the lobby, I saw him giving hell to a terrified bellboy, finishing his tirade with a sharp slap on each cheek. Gad, I thought, if he tried that in New York the entire hotel would walk out.

But our interest in cities wasn't just the food. We hunted out the things to see, walked miles because we learned that's the way to grasp a city, by walking it. The places we sought were indications of that crew member's likes and dislikes, background, religion.

There was always shopping for the specialties of that country or city; in Rome, someone found the suit maker Brioni. They weren't big-time then. I had suits made for under $100, five or six fittings, the suits are still good. Not long ago I drifted into their store in New York City; the lowest-priced suit was fifteen hundred dollars! We'd had a real heyday.

We made friends in all places, worked with locals because TWA believed our personnel in a country should be from that country. I met other wonderful people like the Krugers in Bad Hamburg when someone introduced me to them. Helmet Kruger was an architect, and his wife, Ortrude, a sculptress good enough to have her work in the Berlin Museum. I was a guest in their home, and we discussed everything from art to World War II. Ortrude visited us in Vermont.

There was Louie in Tel Aviv; we talked politics, the situation in Israel, Louie's complaints about secular Jews versus the Orthodox—Louie had been born in Israel.

In each country relationships developed and were strengthened by understanding. What were the differences among people? Nothing, really. Of course there were local issues, customs, and economic conditions, but people are people, with the same sorrows, gladness, and worries. One day as I was contemplating this I suddenly realized that my interest was in the people; that I no longer prefaced my judgment of them by their color, or country, religion, or dress, they were all people and I felt comfortable in every land we flew to. Current problems can sometimes upset the norm and require a certain caution, just as we have at home from time to time, but the judgments—or prejudgments and prejudices—no longer existed. I felt I had become a world person.

✶

ANYONE WHO WAS A PART of aviation in the 1950s was very lucky. It was a wonderful era that went from unpressurized, piston-engine-powered airplanes to jet power and eventually the Boeing 747. Actually it was more than a decade; I'm borrowing a few years on each end, from the 1940s and the 1960s. These fourteen years or so were when aviation went from adolescence to maturity.

It wasn't all sweet sailing and we had tears along with the laughter, but basically it was a happy time of adventure, discovery, and advancement. It wasn't just the airplanes that advanced, but also how we used them, how we discovered that by flying boldly we could go anywhere over the planet, which created surprises and the need for adaptation. Little did we realize that we were the harbingers of One World.

There were some exceptions to that bright aura of the times, often the result of changes following the war. Flying into Israel was one of them.

My first landing in Tel Aviv was on March 7, 1948, two months before it became a nation. There was activity and anticipation everywhere, a powerful feeling of cooperation among the people, everyone eager to help, with the only reward being a further step toward the ultimate goal of creating a nation. The feeling was infectious and exciting. We slept on cots under the control tower, brought our own food from Rome and gave much of it away. There was little transportation; people walked along the roadside and you always picked up hitchhikers. Housing was mostly tin shacks or structures made from packing cases. Approaching Lod Airport, as it was then called, we crossed over a radio beacon on the coast seven miles from the airport. The stretch of land from beacon to airport was sandy desert; in the years that followed I watched it become a flourishing orange grove.

Our first flights landed in Tel Aviv and then continued to Cairo, but as soon as Israel became a nation, the Arab countries would have nothing to do with it; an airplane that had been in Israel was contaminated, in their view, and unacceptable.

During that period our airplanes carried a formal logbook just as ships did. When international flying began the various nations didn't quite know how the airplane fit into the international bureaucracy of customs, immigration, and such, so at first they treated us just like ships—hence the logbook, a big, formal thing about a foot long in which were noted any unusual happenings on the journey and what our departure point had been. The purser brought the book up front before each landing and the captain signed it; authorities on the ground inspected and approved it. Arab lands, Egypt included, could easily see if an airplane had been to Israel. To take care of this we based a DC-4 in Rome that only flew to Tel Aviv and back. We called it the Yom Kippur Clipper. I don't remember how long this went on before the old ship's log was dropped for airplanes and the silly business ended—perhaps a year.

Of course Israel started right out in a state of war, and during my time I experienced four of them: May 1948, Israel's invasion of Egypt in 1956, the Six-Day War of 1967, and the Yom Kippur War of 1973. We were not involved in the wars except that a few times, landing at night, I'd see tracer bullets fly through the darkness east of the field. Circling to land west we'd get pretty close to the action, and the tracers seemed almost under us; on one occasion I heard about, they zipped close to the cockpit, actually between the Number 3 engine and the fuselage. For a few days after that we called off service into Tel Aviv, but except for that brief period we continued to fly to Israel all through the wars.

As time went on, Israel grew and developed; our lodging moved from the control tower to a new motel out of town, not fancy, but adequate. You saw the army everywhere, and especially women in uniform. The spirit of the people was as upbeat as ever, and everyone was anxious to show visitors how Israel was advancing.

One of our French pursers had an Israeli girlfriend who was in the army. She offered to show us the country, and off we went in a big old rented car, with driver. We first went to Jerusalem, where we had lunch at a sidewalk place she picked, then across the countryside, with a look from a distance at the Sea of Galilee, 682 feet below sea level. Evidence of past wars decorated the side roads: tanks, burned-out automobiles, and all those other grim sights. Some villages we passed through were abandoned, windows without glass, staring empty, bullet-pocked walls, only the surrounding sand and a spooky feeling. Our guide explained that such towns sometimes contained snipers who took shots at any Israelis who drove through, but not to worry, these particular villages were safe.

We wandered the desolate country feeling secure with our guide, but she and the driver became engaged in serious conversation that became louder and more heated. "Damn," my copilot said, "I think we're lost." And shortly after that we came to a roadblock with Israeli soldiers and pointed barricades across the road. Somehow we had come upon this from the wrong side—the enemy side! There was a lengthy interrogation and finally they waved us through, with instructions on how to get back to Tel Aviv.

As Israel grew we moved from the motel to a new, small, but adequate hotel in Tel Aviv; one excited man told me they had produced the first refrigerator in a new factory, a landmark advance. The feeling of equality and cooperation was strong—people in the hotel were almost insulted when tips were offered, and they were always refused. Now the strip between the coast and airport that had changed from sand to orange groves was becoming part of the expanding Tel Aviv and filling up with housing and business development; at least that's what the buildings seemed to be from the air.

But attitudes were changing, and the change seemed to coincide with the construction of the Hilton Hotel; people I knew complained about the conflict between Orthodox and secular Jews and what it was doing to the country. I began to see a brusque manner in some people, an arrogance that showed here and there; tips were no longer refused, but were sought and expected. Of course, there's still a basic admirable spirit in Israel, but also a somewhat unfriendly feeling one finds in large metropolitan areas. The maturity and advances had taken a toll on the exciting atmosphere of the beginning.

We moved to the Hilton Hotel, enjoying its luxuries, but daydreaming could take me back to the nights of sleeping under the control tower on cots, feeling good about the spirit and aura around me; it was a magnificent time.

The most memorable event of the period was the birth of our son, Robert Orion Buck, on June 5, 1949. I was over the North Atlantic when it happened; when we landed in Gander the TWA dispatcher said, almost matter-of-factly, "Your wife had a baby boy." Jean's brother, Randolph, a lifelong bachelor, got the job of taking her to the hospital and anxiously awaiting the birth. Good experience for a bachelor.

Some aspects of flying were changing as technology brought new equipment. We still carried navigators all through Europe and east, but as nations installed more radio beacons and we learned the land and sea configurations, it was decided to remove the navigators. So now we continued beyond Paris, Madrid, and Frankfurt without them and it worked well; nobody got seriously lost, but the cockpit was a busier place.

Radio operators remained for a longer time because voice communication didn't work well with foreign languages. But eventually, everyone agreed to make English the international language of aviation; no matter where the airport tower is, you communicate with it in English. As soon as this was established, radio operators were removed except for the ocean crossings where navigators were also still used. The problem was that the English used in some places was pretty poor, and at times was almost impossible to understand. One early problem was England itself, where operators often had strong Scottish or Welsh accents and were as difficult to understand as some places whose basic language was not English.

Although we were certified to fly into Switzerland, the Swiss didn't allow us to do so for almost a year after other nations. Why? It was said the Swiss were not satisfied with the quality of their control tower operators' English and wouldn't accept aircraft until they felt it was good enough. When we finally flew into Switzerland, the operators' English was excellent.

Other places weren't as good; the problem was that many operators' English was stylized to the exact aeronautical needs for approach and landing; if some unusual situation came up and you had to deviate from normal procedure, things tended to come apart. A request for a runway different from the one being used, perhaps because of a crosswind, had to be carefully thought out and worded. On one flight out of Rome, the tower operator told me to take off south, but the wind was north and I told him I wanted a north takeoff. He didn't understand and he insisted I take off south. We battled back and forth until finally, in defiance, he stopped talking to me. This was at the old Ciampino airport at a time when things weren't busy. I tried to get a response, but he simply refused to talk. "Well, nuts to him," I told the copilot. "Let's go." I taxied to the south end for a north takeoff, ran up the engines and called for takeoff clearance—still no response, the tower operator wouldn't talk. We looked carefully for traffic, saw none, and took off. He never said a word, and we changed to the en route frequency. It could never happen now.

Gradually, navigation aids and command of English improved, and we got along fine without radio operators and navigators. The farther east one flew, however, the more crude things became, especially in air traffic control. Flying from Tel Aviv to Bombay, across the lonely lands of the Middle East, there was no real control; the long-range radio was sketchy with skips and hard-to-understand operators. We got to know the schedules of other airlines, such as British Overseas, and by talking back and forth between airplanes we provided our own separation as we kept tabs on one another's progress.

During one of the wars we were not allowed to fly direct from Tel Aviv eastward over Syria. We made a big loop going from Tel Aviv west to Cyprus, then north to Turkey, and across Turkey to a radio beacon near

Lake Van almost on the Soviet border, then south over Basra, and finally direct Bombay. These are lonely, empty lands, spooky in the dark night, hardly a light for hundreds of miles until you approach Basra and the oil fields where gas fires from wells dotted the dark below, not lighting up anything, just individual spots of light like candles stuck in the middle of nothing. Past that area, all is empty again as our course crossed the Arabian Sea to Bombay.

You had to be careful with the radio beacon near Lake Van because of the nearby Soviet border. The Russians were trying to suck any American airplane into Russia for political reasons. They placed a radio beacon across the border on the same frequency as Lake Van, but much more powerful, hoping we'd follow it instead of the weaker Lake Van beacon. We were well aware of the setup, but it made receiving the beacon we needed difficult. By careful attention, timing, and great suspicion we avoided their efforts and never got sucked into Soviet territory.

With the war over, the military was releasing things that previously had restricted or secret status. One of these was a Doppler navigation system. Doppler is a radio signal sent to the earth below that bounces back to the airplane with a different frequency. It's called Doppler effect, and we've all heard it when a train blows its whistle approaching a station and we hear the change in tone as the train approaches—that's Doppler effect, named for the Austrian scientist, Christian Johann Doppler, who discovered it.

Electronics can measure the time the signal takes to get down and back and how it changes, then by computer calculation can tell an airplane its speed and drift. With that information you have a new method of navigation.

When Doppler was released by the military I was working as an assistant to TWA's then president, Carter Burgess, and I suggested we get some equipment and try it. We installed it in a 1649 Connie and while there were faults, it looked promising. Little did we realize that the door had been opened to the future of computerized airplanes—humble though this beginning was.

CHAPTER 23

A Summons from
Howard Hughes

✲

NOTHER CALL CAME FROM the West Coast: Hughes had a
flying task he wanted Buck to do. I flew out, a long overnight in
a DC-3, to see what it was. There were messages all over the
place on landing at Los Angeles: a hotel room was reserved at the Miramar
in Santa Monica, and automobile for me, a Chevy—Hughes always used
Chevys. I was to be at a certain gate of the RKO studios at 9:00 P.M.

Nine P.M. I pull up to the studio gate. Everything dark, an iron fence, a
guardhouse, nothing else. A man appears out of the shadows and comes up
to the car; he's dressed in a business suit, late twenties, maybe thirty, neat
and proper looking.

"Captain Buck?"

"Yes."

"Captain, Mr. Hughes is terribly sorry, but he's tied up and wonders if
you'd come back in an hour."

"Okay, see you in an hour."

I drive off and find an all-night lunch wagon, have a coffee and a piece
of pie. Lunch wagon pie isn't the kind your mother makes, but for some
reason it's appealing—my wife disagrees.

In an hour I pull up to the gate: same quiet, empty darkness; same man appears out of the shadows.

"Captain Buck, Mr. Hughes sends his apologies and is very sorry, but he's still tied up—would you return in an hour?" Half an order, half a plea.

"Well, okay, but if this doesn't work out I'm off to the hotel—I'm tired." This comment might sound bold, but I knew that Hughes couldn't fire me, I was protected by seniority and the Railway Labor Act.

Same lunch wagon, just coffee this time. Back to the gate, same atmosphere, same man of the shadows.

"Please park the car there"—pointing—"and follow me."

I get out and we wander through the dark, empty studio streets, a little spooky, past big, lifeless buildings where movies are shot in daytime, around a corner to a row of dressing rooms like small cottages, and we go up to one. The man knocks on the door: "Captain Buck is here."

I hear the sort of twangy voice say, "Come in."

The door opens into a room of little character: a few chairs, a carpet, low light, and, toward the far wall, a desk. Hughes gathers himself and stands up. "Hello, Bob, I'm sorry to have held you up, thanks for coming."

His voice has that polite Texas quality. He's in what I call his uniform: gray slacks, white shirt open at the neck—he hasn't shaved. I can't see his feet, but they're probably in sneakers.

Before we get down to business he wants to know if my accommodations are satisfactory, did they give me a car, do I have petty cash. He's a polite man. Some visualized him as a tough entrepreneur, but I always found him courteous and thoughtful. He was a suspicious person; everything, whether it was necessary or not, was done in secrecy, and it was always emphasized that you weren't to speak about any meetings or actions. Sometimes it seemed silly, but it was his ball game, so I played it.

His quiet, polite attitude made him attractive to women. I once waited in the lobby of his office in the "plant," as the factory was referred to. Also waiting was a most attractive redheaded gal, a starlet type, and we fell into conversation that, for some forgotten reason, became pretty basic when she told me that you didn't go to bed with Hughes because he was Hughes, but because he was a terrific lover.

But back to our night meeting. We settled down to business. Joe Schenck, president of 20th Century Fox, wanted to make a tour of South

America; down the west coast, over to Buenos Aires, then back up the east coast.

Originally the trip was planned using the 20th Century Fox airplane, a twin-engine Beechcraft D-18, with the Fox pilot flying. But one day, as the airplane sat parked on the Santa Monica airport, someone taxied another airplane into it, damaging the wing—nothing serious, not a big repair job, but the drama, emotion, and superstition of actors and movie people read evil thoughts into it and descended on Schenck, warning him that the airplane was jinxed, he shouldn't fly in it ever again. He gave in to this badgering, although as I got to know Joe Schenck he seemed a logical, unemotional man who was just yielding to all the pressure so as not to worry those surrounding him.

So what should he do? In Hollywood, if it involved aviation, you called Hughes; he was the expert and could provide the straight dope.

Hughes said he'd take care of everything. He told me there was a plushed-up DC-3 at Glendale standing by to be leased for the trip—including a mechanic.

"But how about the Fox pilot?" I asked.

"He'll go along as copilot."

I didn't like that, me coming along and knocking a pilot out of his job. "No deal, Howard [we'd spoken on the phone before, and had been on a first name basis for some time]. I'm not about to move in on someone's job."

"No, I'm sure it will be fine—he'll be here in a few minutes so you can meet him."

Almost on cue there was a knock on the door and the man of dark shadows escorted a tall, pleasant-looking person into the room. It was Bill Smith, the Fox pilot. He was a clean-cut honest-looking person, open smile, sincerity covering him like a robe.

Howard suggested we go somewhere and talk it over, then come back in an hour and tell him what we'd decided. He'd realized the implications and had, in his Machiavellian way, set it all up.

So Smith and I went off to my lunch wagon.

"There's no way I'm going to do this, move in on your job."

But Smith came right back with, "No, no, I want to do it, I'll learn how you airline people do things. I consider it an opportunity."

"You sure?"

"Yup."

Bill was an aviation enthusiast, first-class: a naval aviator, experienced in military aircraft, hung around airports, flew anything he could. Unmarried, because I don't think he'd figured out how to marry an airplane. Blond hair, blue eyes, big, with an easy movement to his gait, a soft Western way of talking, never swore and didn't bother with girls—or boys—at all, his love was airplanes.

So we went back to Howard and told him it would be okay.

We leased the DC-3. It was well appointed with big stuffed seats, a daybed/couch kind of thing, thick carpet on the floor. It wouldn't be crowded, just Schenck and Dr. Martin—Docky Martin, as he was known, was a 20th Century Fox fixture, the official studio doctor as well as a buddy to Schenck and other executives, plainspoken joke teller, and husband of the Hollywood columnist Louella Parsons. He'd keep an eye on Schenck's health, but he was there more as a good traveling companion. Bill, the mechanic, and I would make up the rest of the party—small and easy to handle.

I was taken to the studio to meet Mr. Schenck in his palatial office. Harry Brand, head of Fox public relations, took me for the introduction.

Schenck and his brother Nicholas had come to the United States as poor immigrants, but by 1901 they had purchased a pharmacy, and they made big money a decade later managing an amusement park; they joined Marcus Loew and built Palisades Park, and went from there, via vaudeville and nickelodeons, to feature movies and eventually Hollywood. Joe Schenck was part of the wave of people who created the film industry after fleeing Russia, Hungary, and Eastern Europe's poverty and meager opportunity: Zukor, Goldwyn, Selznick, Laemmle, and others all started poor, and through deals—some questionable—buying, selling, and building, combined with a cultural sensitivity that demanded a certain class in their movies, created the industry and made huge fortunes. Considering their interest in films of classics and historic subjects, I imagine these men would be horrified and disappointed to see today's films filled with violence, sex, and crudity.

Schenck rose to greet me, hand outstretched. He had a pleasant, open mien and carried enough extra weight to fill in his wrinkles. We chatted about the trip, and Brand brought up the point that there would be lots of girls along the way.

On this remark, almost sadly, Schenck said, "Yes, it always comes to that."

He continued, "We will go in about a week. Will you be ready, Bobby?" That was the name he used for me—one I don't particularly like, but from him it seemed okay.

"Yes, we'll be ready whenever you are."

"Fine, if you want anything just say so, we're glad to have you with us, make yourself at home."

They gave me an office in the location department, run by a wonderful man named Clarence Hudson. He took care of me: money, studio passes, secretarial help, and always a smile. He was a devout Catholic, a Knight of Malta and active in church affairs. The poor man had leukemia and needed a weekly blood transfusion, but he kept right on working, being cheerful, and you'd never know he had a problem.

After leasing the airplane and getting it to Hughes Airport, we had to obtain flight permits for each country we'd fly through. This was complicated and bureaucratic, but finally it was all put together: permits, visas, assurances of fuel in all countries, and a bunch of annoying details. With all that done I had nothing to do but wait.

This was a time when an antitrust ruling had just demanded that movie studios separate from owning theaters, and Schenck was busy with that, never quite knowing when he'd get free for our trip.

So I cooled my heels, but with a great advantage: being Schenck's pilot gave me status. Everyone was cheerful and cooperative; after all, I was and would be close to the head man. Mornings, as I pulled up to the studio gate it was, "Good morning, Captain Buck," and I was waved through. People in various departments mysteriously knew who I was. I realized I had the run of the place and, with nothing to do except a round of golf now and then at Riviera with Dave Kuhn, a TWA pilot friend, I decided to poke around and learn something about the movie business.

The studios were then at their peak—great films, stars, the glamour, the action, and no place caught the action and feeling like a studio commissary, where everyone came for lunch. You saw stars, directors, technical people, visitors with the studio heads; the place buzzed, the actors were in costume and makeup, and everyone was talking as show people always seem to talk, animated, gesturing, laughing. I seldom missed taking lunch. Ty was there, making a picture about South Africa, and we'd often eat together. My old friend, the director Henry King, was just finishing *Twelve O'Clock High* and we discussed various technical points as well as drifting into airplane talk and trips he'd taken in his Bonanza.

There was a large circular table for those who didn't have a lunch companion; you just sat there and visited with whoever else was alone. One day I sat across from a very attractive blonde. We chitchatted some small talk and she was pleasant and friendly. Later, in Jim Denton's office, I asked him if he knew who that blonde was.

"Oh," he said, "a new gal, named Monroe—Marilyn Monroe."

I wandered over to the Paramount lot and visited Bob Hope and Bing Crosby. They had a sort of court jester named Barney Dean, an ex-burlesque comedian who was always on Bob's or Bing's set, quietly talking with them about the takes, visiting, telling jokes, and being one of the gang. Barney and I hit it off well and we hung out some together. One evening he invited me to the Friars Club, a place where Hollywood people met, mostly comedians, writers, composers. We had a drink at the bar before dinner; George Jessel was there, Milton Berle and others. They chided Barney, in good spirit, about bringing a gentile to the club.

Hope and Barney got off on a joke-telling session one day when I was with them. It was certainly different, and fascinating. Being old pros in this department, they didn't need details, so they skipped the boring long-winded story part of the joke that amateurs seem to delight in dragging out; these two simply told each other punch lines, the rest they filled in from experience and imagination.

I lunched with Barney at the Paramount commissary. The entrance to it was almost a stage; people entered and stood at the top of steps that led down into the dining room. Actors entered, paused, and looked down for their lunch companions, or just stood there to be noticed. One who entered and paused was Elizabeth Taylor—this was the time of her prime, and she was absolutely the most gorgeous woman I had ever seen; she stood there for a moment and the entire commissary became quiet as everyone gazed at her.

The trip was put off from week to week as Schenck wrestled with the antitrust problems. We flew a little; one weekend we went to Palm Springs with Docky Martin along and, a surprise to both of us, Irving Berlin. He remembered me from our Atlantic flying.

"What are you doing here?" I explained and he seemed pleased to see me. We did two of those weekend trips to Palm Springs, always with the same trio.

His comment, which always seemed to open our conversation, was, "I hope you're saving and investing your money."

Another trip was a junket to Death Valley to bring back Henry King from location. Henry rode up front in the cockpit and we made airplane talk.

The only other flying I did was to go to Palm Springs to get John Garfield, who was needed for pickup shots for his most recent movie.

Garfield was nervous, scared to death of flying, asking questions about the airplane, the weather, and anything that came to mind. Bill and I tried to assure him all was well. He was the only passenger and spent most of the time up front with us, casting questions at each bump or change in noise level. Then, as we approached Santa Monica where we were to drop him off, Bill went through the checklist, and when he said, "Mixtures," I responded, "Rich," and as I moved the control levers back, both engines quit! I recognized the problem and reversed the control movement and both engines resumed power, but Garfield went berserk, rushing about like a caged squirrel until we got him calmed down. I had moved the mixtures the wrong way out of habit; all the TWA DC-3 mixture controls moved the opposite way. I didn't make that mistake again.

Even the fairly uneventful landing was a bit hairy for him; it was dark, and the typical fog had rolled in over Santa Monica, but it was thin and we could see the ground down through it. We made a careful approach, lining up with the runway, and then sank through perhaps thirty feet of fog to the ground. As we taxied in, the visibility was almost zero, and despite the fact that we were on the ground, this got Garfield upset. We came to a stop and he climbed out, with profuse thanks, probably brought on by the relief of being safe and sound, got into a waiting limousine, and departed. His cause of death, some years later, was a heart attack; it's a wonder he didn't have one that night.

I took my carte blanche opportunity and roamed the studio. One place to spend hours just poking around was the fantastic back lot, an area that would make collectors and museum curators salivate: old and new automobiles, arms, tanks, potted plants and trees, sets of New York streets, and a multitude of interesting things. I was told, but never able to confirm, that when World War II started and hysteria said that Japan was ready to invade California, the studios provided rifles to the National Guard, which was woefully lacking in arms, suffering from government defense cuts.

I often spent my evenings watching the dubbing of music to a film. It was done at night so there would be less noise than in daytime, when the general hubbub might penetrate the set and spoil the dubbing. A big screen hung from above, and below and next to it was a symphony orchestra led by Lionel Newman. It didn't look like a concert, because the players were dressed in casual clothes, Hawaiian shirts and jeans predominating. They played lovely music to fit the picture being shown on the big screen; of course there were blank spots and interruptions to fit the script, but some wonderful music came through as I sat in a chair, all alone, with my own symphony orchestra.

I learned about the demanding tasks of the camerapeople; they may shoot an outdoor scene and have it interrupted by bad weather and return to the studio for interiors while the weather is bad, then a week later get back to the outdoor scene and pick up where they had stopped. The camera person must repeat exactly the exposure and lighting from the previous week or two. They showed me much of this, letting me look through the viewfinder at a scene about to be shot and then explaining aspects of the lighting and setup. A fascinating experience.

The location department's job, at times, was enormous: moving, feeding, housing hundreds of extras in some unpleasant and unfriendly place on the earth that might be desert or jungle, and responding to the fussy needs of actors, directors, and other people working the shoot. All arrangements, every little detail was anticipated and cared for; it was amazing.

I even had a haircut from Russ, who did the male stars, and the still photo department made a "Hollywood" portrait of me—it didn't improve my looks, but it did sort of gloss me up.

What did I learn from all this? I gained a great respect for the technical and logistic part of the movie industry; there was a lot more to it than stars and stories. Behind them was a large group who made it all work, lighting the screen with their technical excellence—great people, great skills.

The actors and directors I encountered were just folks, once you got past the careful opening greetings as they sized up who you were and what your importance might be to the industry and their careers. After that they settled down to discussing events, problems, and amusements, and I mostly got the impression they were trying hard to be like everyone else.

The days dragged on and a month went by. Finally Mr. Schenck said we were ready, and we'd go on a Tuesday, as I remember. But Monday morning the studio was glum; Joe Schenck had had a stroke. I found out it was minor, hardly enough to keep him confined, but the doctors said no flying—the trip was off.

I returned the airplane, filed the papers, and said goodbye to all the fine people. Schenck was back to work on a limited basis, and I went to say goodbye and to thank him for the kindness and the wonderful way I'd been treated.

"But where are you going?"

"Back to my airline job, flying across the sea."

"Don't you like us here, why do you leave?"

"I like you all, no one ever treated me better, but my life is flying as an airline pilot, that's where I belong."

"We like you, Bobby, stay here—we'll find something for you to do."

I demurred and got my point across—there was a warm handshake and goodbye, my movie days were over.

Bill Smith, who was to have been my copilot, went to work for Douglas Aircraft, teaching airline customers worldwide how to fly the Douglas airplanes they'd purchased. He went from Douglas to Lockheed where he did the same, teaching how best to fly and use the Lockheed 1011. Finally Lockheed put him in flight test and development, where he had a great deal to do with improving the 1011 and making it one of the world's best airline aircraft. Bill retired, and now he lives with his sister in Santa Monica, still going to airports, interested in antique aircraft and flying when he can. A credit to the industry.

Not long after I returned to the airline, Clarence Hudson succumbed to the leukemia he'd been fighting. On my next trip to Rome, knowing how strong his faith was, I went to the Vatican and inquired about having a mass said for him. I wound up in a priest's office, richly decorated with rare tapestries and paintings; he sat behind a large priceless desk. Yes, they could arrange a mass; they came in three different prices. The most expensive wasn't all that much, about $25 as I recall, so I set one up for a specific date, and his family had mass celebrated in California at the same time. I felt a little pleased that I'd repaid, in a small way, that smiling man's kindness to me.

Having said my goodbyes at the studio, I went to bed early, anticipating my flight home. At 2:00 A.M. the phone rang. "Captain Buck?"

"Yes."

"Mr. Hughes wants to talk to you."

The twangy voice came on: "Bob, I have a little job I'd appreciate your doing."

He wanted me to sell his Sikorsky. The Sikorsky was a twin-engine amphibian he'd purchased to practice water landings and gain proficiency before he flew the big boat—the *Spruce Goose.*

He made many practice landings; the popular count was 1,500 before something went wrong on Boulder Lake and the Sikorsky sank. Hughes popped to the surface, safe, but an FAA inspector who was with him never did, and was never found.

The boat was raised and repaired, put back in perfect condition with a very fancy interior of wood-paneled walls, stateroom, and other niceties.

He outlined his idea, which was for me to take it to Miami and try to sell it to some rich South American who was visiting there for the season, as many did: "Rent a good car, get a suite in some fancy hotel, mix with that crowd and you'll find someone."

This sounded like a pretty bizarre operation, though a great opportunity for a freeloader who liked the high life. It took considerable talk to convince him I wasn't the man; in the end I bluntly had to say, "I just won't do it." He finally accepted this, and the phone session ended after more than an hour of back and forth.

There were other calls from Howard during my month stay; one was at the relatively polite hour of 7:00 A.M., on a Sunday.

"Bob, I'd appreciate your doing a little flying for me today." I wondered what it was, as I looked out my window at low clouds and heavy rain. "Fly some people in the Lodestar." This was a twin-engine Lockheed, smaller than a DC-3, but about the same power.

"I've never flown a Lodestar, Howard."

"You won't have any problem, it's just another airplane and the instruments and radios are set up just like TWA's."

A quick thought and decision: I could probably handle it, and I'd always wanted to fly a Lodestar.

"Where am I going?"

"I can't tell you now, and I don't want anybody to know, not even air traffic control."

"I can't get out of here VFR, look at the weather, I'll have to file a flight plan." (VFR—visual flight rules, avoiding other planes by sight and navigating by terrain—allowed you to fly without a flight plan, but it required at least three miles visibility and a 1,000-foot ceiling.)

"Well, it's in Arizona, but I don't want air traffic control to know where."

"They're not going to accept a flight plan with destination Arizona— let me check the weather and get back to you."

"Okay." And he did a rare thing: he gave me his personal phone number—after making me swear in blood, so to speak, that I'd never tell a soul.

The bad weather was mostly in the L.A. basin, but east, over the desert, it was flyable VFR. I called him: "Here's what I suggest, I'll file a flight plan to Palm Springs and cancel it when I'm VFR, then just disappear."

That was his kind of thing. "Okay, go on out to the plant, get the ship and have it at the south gate, engines running, ready to go at 11:30."

The south gate was a gate in the Anchor fence that surrounded the airport, way down away from everything; Hughes often used it for clandestine entry and exit.

At the plant I met up with the manager, Joe, and a mechanic. They had gotten the Lodestar out, run the engines, and fueled it. I climbed aboard and carefully went over all the gadgets, levers, radios, and so on. I checked all the limiting red lines on the instruments, wiggled the controls, looked out the windshield to see where the ground was, and decided I was ready.

Joe came in the cockpit. "Hughes wants you to call him."

I shut down the engines, climbed out, went in an office, and called.

"How much gas have you got in it?" he asked.

"Six hundred gallons."

"Have you got the maps out to Arizona and the Phoenix area?"

"Yup, and the airway and approach charts, too."

This was typical Hughes, he wanted to run everything and all details himself.

"Okay."

There was some time remaining before the south gate meeting, so I returned to the airplane to sit and become more familiar with the gadgetry of the cockpit. Joe climbed up to the cockpit again. "Hughes wants you to call him."

I climbed out, went to the office and called.

"Bob, check with Joe and take four parachutes with you."

"Okay." I wondered what in hell we'd want chutes for.

The time approached. I'd filed with air traffic control, arranging for takeoff at 11:45. Hughes Airport is only about three miles from the LAX tower, so I could talk to it using VHF radio. The L.A. tower approved my clearance with a takeoff time of 11:45; they'd hold L.A. airline takeoffs at that time until I became airborne.

I started the engines and taxied to the south gate, through a wet, sloshy airport in pouring rain. I swung into a position so it would only be a short dash from the gate to the airplane, and I waited, engines running. Eleven-thirty came, forty, forty-five; nothing but the rain and the dismal land-scape.

At 11:45 the L.A. tower called and asked if I was ready to go.

"Just a minute," I replied. No car, no nothing.

L.A. tower called again, said they could only hold my slot a few more minutes. "I'm almost ready," I lied. "One engine's a little rough, I'm clearing it out."

The rain falling, an empty landscape.

L.A. tower again: "I can't hold your time any longer. Call me when you're ready and I'll try to work out something."

"Thanks."

Then from the plant, sloshing across the field, came a Jeep. It stopped next to me, Joe climbed out, got in the airplane, and said, "Hughes wants you to call him. Just leave the airplane and ride with me."

"Nuts to that, I'll taxi back."

I called Hughes. "Bob, I'm sorry, it's all off. I hope I haven't ruined your Sunday. I'm very sorry to have caused you all this trouble. You're free to do what you want." Always polite and thoughtful in our contacts, however strange those contacts might be.

The next day I found out what it was all about: Cary Grant and Betsy Drake were going to be married on a ranch in Arizona, and Hughes said he'd have them flown there. But the weather scared them and they balked at the idea; Hughes said he had a senior TWA pilot to fly them, they'd even put parachutes on board. But the final answer was still no. Grant and Hughes were close friends and Grant often flew with Hughes. My guess is that aside from Grant's charm, Hughes liked to be with him because he could hear him; Hughes was hard of hearing and, of course, Grant had a marvelous voice.

I had another 2:00 A.M. Hughes call when he wanted to talk about the terrain warning device. This was originally a tail warning gadget for bombers that, radarlike, would bounce off unfriendly fighters sneaking up on you.

A smart radio man in the Hughes factory, Dave Evans, took this and mounted it vertically so it would bounce off the ground and warn a pilot that the ground was close. There were three settings, so it rang a bell and lighted a light as you descended through 1,500 feet, then 1,000, and finally 500 feet. It was a good idea, and Hughes got a lot of publicity for "his" invention. Since he owned TWA they installed it on our aircraft.

I had been trying to change the 500-foot setting to 400 feet, and I think we did, because most of our instrument approaches then were to 400 feet, and my feeling was that the bell ringing and red light coming on at 500 feet was a warning that you were approaching the minimum, but not yet there, and while concentrating on a difficult approach a pilot might forget about the 500-foot warning. I wanted it at 400, with the idea that when the bell rang and the light came on, the pilot would know he was at the lowest point allowed and would immediately pull out for a missed approach, or land if the field was in sight.

Howard didn't see it my way and he argued, no kidding, from 2:00 A.M. until 4:00 A.M. He had to have it his way, so in sleepy desperation I said okay, hung up, and went back to bed. As I remember, we never did change it from 400.

I was not party to his later life and don't know what went wrong, but my experience had shown a polite, pleasant man, able to pick good people for his various operations, but tortured by suspicion. Once you were hired by Hughes you were his, and even if he didn't need you, he kept you on the payroll; you became his property. He worked incessantly and wanted to be in on every detail. That was one of his failings, in that he owned an airline, instrument factory, movie studio, tool factory for oil well drills, and a brewery; he wanted to be privy to and have the say on all details, so that while he was working with the movie studio, the airline or other companies sat immobile, often needing important decisions. When TWA purchased the first jets, Boeing 707s, we had no support equipment: ladders for mechanics, steps for passengers, spare parts, any idea where we'd overhaul the airplanes, and some of these decisions were badly needed before the 707s were delivered. Yet when Carter Burgess, a fine man who was then president of TWA, tried to get hold of Hughes for approval, he couldn't. Like everyone else, he'd call the Hughes command post on Romaine in Hollywood, and one of the Mormon lawyers on duty would take the message, but Hughes, busy with other things, wouldn't call back. I remember one three-week period when Burgess sat with his hands tied waiting for Hughes to call. So the entire Hughes domain was like something from *Alice in Wonderland.*

But now I was free of it, or at least released from the West Coast branch. I flew back to New York, ready to resume my normal life.

CHAPTER 24

Farewell to Propellers and All That Drove Them

AIRPLANES CONSTANTLY CHANGE as technology advances. It seems that you've hardly had time to pay for one type of airplane before a bigger, better, more economically attractive one comes on the scene. Frequently, the airline would have been happy to settle down and use the current aircraft that was making comfortable money, but if their competitors got bigger and faster airplanes, they had to get them, too.

When they were still in the development stage, I asked TWA's then president, Charles Tillinghast, if we were going to purchase Boeing 747s. His answer, "Only if [Pan Am President Juan] Trippe does." Trippe did, and so did we even though we would have been far better off financially if we hadn't been forced into the 747 age.

In the early international days we flew the unpressurized Douglas DC-4s, which were phased out in 1951, and no tears were shed. Lots of DC-4 trips were "tough ones," battling head winds in ice and turbulence down at the lower altitudes where we had to fly. I look back on those flights and I'm glad I was young then; later comforts softened us up, and I doubt we'd have had enough stamina to do some of those old tough ones in later years.

So we said goodbye to DC-4s and welcomed Constellations—Connies—with their pressurization that allowed flight close to 20,000 feet, which was above much of the weather, especially those decks of stratocumulus, ice-infested clouds on the western side of the Atlantic.

The 749A model Constellation had a gross weight of 107,000 pounds, engines of 2,500 horsepower each, wingspan 123 feet, and was ninety-seven feet long; the checklist had 104 items. Its cruising speed was about 310 miles an hour, depending on the altitude. They were pressurized and fairly quiet. We carried about forty-four passengers, although eighty-eight could be jammed in if the seats were set closer together. An airplane's passenger capacity depends on how close the airline wants to place the seats; today that's close enough so any passenger is jammed in and uncomfortable. In the early days there was lots more room, even in the most high-density airplane, and air travel was a lot more comfortable.

The Connies were wonderful airplanes, and their higher speed cut down those appalling twenty-plus-hour flights in the DC-4 to about fifteen hours, plus or minus an hour or two. I flew Connies with their big Wright engines for almost three years without a serious problem.

One memorable flight in an early Connie was from Rome to Paris. We knew there'd be weather along the way, some thunderstorms, nothing too tough. But after we departed Rome the pressurization system failed; without pressurization we couldn't go over the Alps because the minimum safe altitude of 19,000 feet would be too high for passengers. After much deliberation we decided to take the old DC-4 route, over the Mediterranean, then toward Marseilles and up the Rhône Valley to Paris. We could fly low on that route, although the trip would be a bit longer. I called the hostess up front to tell her. The hostess was Helen Alexandra, a very attractive and shapely Egyptian with a strong mixture of Greek, hardworking, pleasant. I told her we'd be a little longer and why.

"Oh, that's fine, I have to serve dinner and it will give me more time."

So off we went, but after turning the corner near Marseilles and heading up the Rhône Valley, the weather took on a nasty look: heavy clouds, rain, and an occasional flick of lightning. Eventually we were up to a wall of clouds and it was decision time—where should we go in? We didn't have radar yet, so it was DC-3 best-guess style. I called Helen up: "It may get rough, be sure the passengers are fastened down well, and then go sit and strap yourself in until I tell you it's okay to move about. But stay seated, belt on."

We read the clouds as best we could and went in: rain, choppiness, nothing exceptional. Quite a bit of time passed and nothing changed, but suddenly I felt gusts that said we weren't out of it yet—and then all hell broke loose, really severe turbulence, as bad as the worst I'd flown in the B-17 or P-61. It was the only time my bouncing in the seat and the instrument panel jarring up and down out of phase gave me problems in reading the instruments—it was not impossible, but difficult enough to be frightening. What would happen if I couldn't read the instruments?

And then, as with all thunderstorms, we suddenly flew out of it, into a tunnel of clear air that opened into cloudless sky. I called for Helen, the cockpit door opened, and in came a beat-up, bedraggled young lady, hair a mess, her makeup smeared.

"What in hell happened to you?"

"I was trying to serve dinner, but it was so rough."

"Good God, girl, I told you to stay strapped in."

"Well, it was dinnertime and I thought I could serve it."

I'll always remember that storm as frightening, and Helen's crazy attempt to serve. It happened over Montélimar, France, the nougat capital of the world, which I drove through a few years later to see store windows full of nougat creations, animal forms and shapes invented by the makers. But to me it would always be the home of one of the toughest thunderstorms I've ever flown, and bring to mind a foolish but great young lady.

Our operation had always flown in and out of La Guardia, using the old Marine Terminal; the terminal is still there, all fixed up and used by Delta Air Lines for its Washington shuttle. Original murals still decorate the walls.

But we left La Guardia, and my logbook shows, "4-29-51, moved to KIDL." KIDL was Idlewild, now KJFK, the official aviation code for JFK. (A K in front, as in KJFK, signifies the United States; knowing these code letters tells you what country a weather report is from, and many countries preface the license number painted on the fuselage of an airplane with the same national letter so you can tell what country an airplane is from as it sits on the ramp or taxies by. All U.S. airplane license numbers are prefaced with the letter N, which goes back to the early days of aviation; F is for

France, G the United Kingdom, E for Ireland, I for Spain, and a bunch of others. Why our N has never been changed to K on airplane license markings I don't know; I guess there would be a lot of squawking if everyone had to repaint their Ns to Ks, and it's not earth-shattering stuff anyway.)

On one arrival at Paris we found Orly below limits, so we landed at Le Bourget. Somehow that seemed the closing of a circle: Le Bourget was where Lindbergh landed, and then, finally, so had I.

Ty Power made about four crossings with me during this time, along with his wife, Linda Christian. For a six-month period he deserted Hollywood and did *Mr. Roberts* on the stage in London, at the big Coliseum Theatre. Theater was Ty's first love, and his dream was to someday have a repertory company.

During this time I frequently flew the London flight, arriving Saturday morning, laying over Sunday, and returning Monday. Ty insisted I stay with him and Linda in their flat near Curzon Street. William the chauffeur would pick me up at the London airport on arrival and drive me into town. William was a fine British man, with a full, round, shiny face, and I think he enjoyed picking me up—it was a departure from the usual routine. We chatted, and he always referred to my long sleepless night and ventured, "Bet you're ready for a bit of gin." Which I wasn't.

After a late breakfast with Ty and Linda, I'd retire to bed, then wake and dress at about the time Ty's afternoon performance was coming to an end. On Saturdays in London, the matinees end in the late afternoon and there's not much more than an hour before the evening performance. William drove me to the theater, along with a picnic basket and Ty's supper. We'd chat as he ate, and then I either sat in the wings or out front during the performance. I saw *Mr. Roberts* enough that I almost knew the lines. On a few occasions Ty supplied tickets for my entire crew, which was a bonus much talked about and appreciated, especially after a dressing room visit and introduction.

Following the performance Linda would show up and we'd go off to dinner at some restaurant like the Ivy or White Castle, often with other theater folk, and I mixed in the heady company of Charles Laughton, Rex Harrison, Kay Kendall, and others. *Mixed* is a poor word, actually I sat back, quiet and observing, taking in the enthusiastic talk that overflowed with great stories. Theater people are very enjoyable, especially away from the limelight. This was a great period for me.

After a performance, exiting by the stage door, we were always met by a big crowd, and not a particularly polite one, pushing, shoving—a mounted police officer was there to keep things under control, and was not very successful. But the next day, Ty and I might take a walk and no one would bother him aside from a polite, "Good morning Mr. Power," as we'd pass people. Ty's explanation was that the night before he was theirs, his being on stage made him a commodity for that evening, but the next day his privacy was respected and the polite Brits let him alone. Not like Italy, where he'd be torn apart any hour of the day or night.

I was there the night *Mr. Roberts* closed. I escorted Linda and we sat in the audience—in that time I carried a dinner (in French, a smoking) jacket on my trips to London. It was a gala affair with a packed audience in all their finery. At final curtain the applause kept on until Ty appeared and made a short speech. This is standard British theater practice, and they won't stop applauding until the principal actor comes out and speaks.

Ty graciously thanked them and remarked that he would be back someday. At this the entire audience stood and burst into applause.

We went back to his dressing room while he took off his makeup and changed clothes. When it was time to leave and we'd all started for the door, I looked back and Ty was last, but before leaving he turned and looked back at the room, paused and studied it for a long moment, a moment stopped in time, and I wondered what he was thinking. Then he turned, smiled, and said, "Let's go." It was typical Tyrone, radiating enthusiasm for what was next.

Our routine, pleasant, and tranquil era of the 749A Connie was broken when the G model Connie came on the scene in 1955. This was a bigger airplane, "stretched" as the trade calls it. What happens is that a certain model aircraft is, to put it crudely but accurately, cut in half and a "plug" put between the two halves. Sometimes they cut an airplane in two places, ahead of the wing and behind it. The plug makes a bigger cabin, and more seats mean more revenue. The G Connie was eighteen feet longer, which raised the gross weight by 37,000 pounds. It had the same wing to support it, but bigger engines shoved that wing through the air fast enough so the old 749A-size wing would carry the load.

The bigger engines raised the power from 2,700 to 3,250 horsepower. Fuel tanks, like in a fighter, were installed on the wingtips and held 609 gallons of gasoline, in other words a weight of 3,600 pounds, rather like having an automobile hanging on each wingtip.

This increased the range of the airplane, and we could go nonstop back and forth to Europe. The speed increase wasn't worth talking about, only 10 miles an hour or so; the wing's the thing, and its drag characteristic will only allow so much speed regardless of the amount of power pulling it through the air.

The G was quieter and had other improvements such as better pressurization and interior climate control, but it had one terrible problem: the engines. They were called turbo compound, and we called them turbo complex because they had a weird arrangement of turbines, shafts, and gears that defied reliability. There were three turbines, each driven by the collected exhaust of six cylinders—the engine had a total of eighteen. The turbines spun a long shaft that went down to the engine's crankshaft and helped turn it, adding power. On top of that there was a two-stage engine-driven supercharger; the first stage was used until about 13,000 feet, and then "gears were shifted" and the second stage engaged—with a thump heard and felt through the airplane.

It's easy to see that this engine was a complicated piece of machinery and, as one might expect, there were problems and failures—more than we'd had with any other engine. I had my share of failures: one 350 miles off the coast of Lisbon, another between Bombay and Colombo, Ceylon, and an engine fire on takeoff at Frankfurt. Flying with these engines gave one a slightly uncomfortable feeling that gnawed back there in your mind. One transatlantic flight had a double failure 400 miles off the Irish coast, which was a real sweat for the crew; with two engines out, more power was required from the two working engines, and asking more from these temperamental power plants made the crew very nervous. They were a happy lot when they landed in Shannon.

At the time, I was working in our New York office as an assistant to the president, Carter Burgess. That morning a Connie's landing gear collapsed at the hangar while it was being worked on at La Guardia, killing a mechanic under it. Burgess was at the field where we maintained facilities for domestic flights when it happened, and he took on the sensitive task of going to the mechanic's home and telling his wife. That ordeal over, he came into the city to learn of Captain Fletcher Grabill and crew out over the ocean on two engines hoping to make Shannon. They probably suffered for over two hours the nervousness of feeling they had a good chance of landing in the ocean. When it was all over, Carter sat in my office, put his feet up, and tried to unwind from the ordeal.

"Bob," he said, "these damn airplanes can be dangerous."

"Join the club," I replied. Carter hadn't been president very long and was fairly new to aviation's inner workings. Experience was dished out in a big chunk that day.

We suffered these big engines, but we did learn some tricks. One was that if you never shifted to the second stage of the mechanical supercharger, engine problems dropped dramatically. So many of us flew without using it, but this had its own problems, since the airplane didn't perform very well above 13,000 feet. So we flew lower, and now we were down where more weather lurked, ice and turbulence, back to the DC-4 days in a way.

Then two years later came the next Connie, the 1649, but this one had a new wing, a long, graceful, beautiful wing of 150 feet—twenty-seven feet longer than the G. The fuselage was the same, but the gross weight jumped from 137,500 pounds to 160,000. The total fuel capacity increased from the G's 7,750 gallons to 9,278, and the long wing could carry it all inside without tip tanks. This truly was a long-range airplane, the longest propeller airliner ever, and we flew them, on schedule, nonstop from Los Angeles to London. It was a great airplane with one exception: the engines were the same as the G's, so we flew it lower, too, not using the high-stage supercharger.

The big wingspan allowed designers to put the engines farther out from the fuselage, so the noise level inside was much lower than any previous airplane. To make the long flights comfortable, the 1649 Constellation had sleeper seats that could be stretched out so one was almost in a single bed.

My first Los Angeles to London flight was seventeen hours and one minute. Preparing for the flight, checking weather, the flight plan, and the crew briefing, I felt a little pumped up: this was the longest nonstop I had ever made, and mentally I was back in the days of records and early aviation deeds. After all, Los Angeles–London was a long way. The flight went without problems, and we landed in London early on a foggy, cold morning. The airplane parked, baggage and cargo unloaded, I gathered up my gear and walked down the long stairs to the ground, where personnel hurried about, busy with their chores. One chap in quick passage said, "Mornin', Captain," and went on his way. No one was impressed that we'd just come 4,750 miles nonstop across the United States, Hudson Bay, Baffin Island, the lonely Davis Strait, Greenland's uninhabited icecap, and the cold North Atlantic; it was merely another inbound flight, but to me it was more. I suppose this was what we'd worked for, to make a Los Angeles–London flight a blasé event.

One memorable flight came when President Eisenhower flew to France on a state visit. He flew in his Connie, which wasn't big enough to take the press corps the way the present *Air Force One,* a Boeing 747, can. So a special flight, using a 1649, was set up for the press, and I flew it. First to Washington to load the press; then off for Paris nonstop with extra cabin attendants, lots of fuel and lots of booze, which the press corps used until gone. There were some falling-down drunks, and one woman columnist I had often read and admired passed out in the ladies' toilet. Some were quiet and sedate, but others made up for it, and on arrival in Paris there were some mighty shaggy-looking folks deplaning.

Lurking in the hazy distance was jet power. The air force was using it with dramatic high-altitude, high-speed airplanes. We all knew we'd eventually see a jet transport and we wondered what it would be like; actually, the British had built and flown the first one, the Comet, but development difficulties kept it out of regular service, although a few publicity flights were made. Boeing was developing a transport, and the Brits razzed us about their being ahead of us.

About this time, Colonel Jack Taylor, with whom I'd worked on the thunderstorm project, when we had the P-61, asked me if I'd be interested in attending an officers' jet indoctrination school. I almost jumped through the telephone with my yes.

This was a course set up for senior officers and a few airline chief pilots. I wasn't chief pilot anymore, but I was an advisor to TWA's President Burgess, which gave me enough heft to have me invited, in addition to my friendship with Colonel Taylor.

I should probably explain how I came by the various tasks and positions I had during my career. I feel the appointments were mostly luck; after a few assignments, when someone is searching for a person to do a job, they're apt to remember your name. I'm certain, in every case, there was some other pilot as well qualified, or even better qualified, than I, but as the saying goes, I was in the right place at the right time, and very lucky.

So now I'm at Valdosta, Georgia, on an air force field, with a bed in the officers quarters and instructions to report for ground school in the morning.

The class had a general, a few colonels, and one other civilian pilot. A captain took us through a briefing on what a jet engine was, which is simply a gas turbine: air is compressed by fanlike blades up front, then rushed back into a burner can not too unlike a blow torch; fuel is injected—not much different from the fuel oil a furnace burns—to burn and create a hot stream (around 1,500 degrees) that tears through a turbine wheel in the back. The function of a jet engine is to exhaust the air out the back end faster than it comes in the front, and that's what pushes the airplane; the full theory would require printing pages of formulas. The beauty is that a jet engine just goes around; there's no banging back and forth like pistons in an automobile's engine, no valves, timing chains, or spark plugs (except for starting the jet engine); it's simply the blades and turbine spinning around. It is born for reliability and smoothness.

We also discussed instrument approaches, speeds to use, and how a jet would differ on these from a piston-driven propeller airplane. Then it was time to get to the airplane: a T-bird, Lockheed T-33 jet trainer, grandchild of the P-80. My instructor was a Korean War veteran, a bit cocky—understandably so—and perhaps even bored with the assignment. "Call me Goober," he said.

Outfitted with parachute, air force flight suit, and hard hat, I approach the airplane. I climb up a set of metal steps, curved to the contour of the fuselage, and notice its solid look, strong metal, flush rivets. Then I work my way into the cockpit: nothing plush, all basic, hard green metal rails, seat, serious instrument panel. Goober stands on the metal stairs outside, leaning down toward me, and points out various items we had covered in ground school. He gets in the rear seat, the metal ladder is pulled away and we're ready.

The engine runs smoothly as we taxi, and the whining noise is behind us. We line up and Goober says, "Go ahead." He's given me an airspeed to build to for climb. I open the throttle and we start to move, slowly, and then speed picks up dramatically as we run what seems a long way until I have the speed and gently put back pressure on the stick and we're airborne. I put the gear up and we grab big chunks of the sky and go up fast. I rock a bit side to side, the ailerons are very touchy and it's easy to over-control. That was a surprise, but I settle down to using small pressures left and right, and quickly the aileron control becomes normal, but requiring a gentle touch. At altitude Goober has me do some steep turns, then says to roll it, which I do clumsily because I haven't done rolls in a long time and never in an airplane like this that goes around so quickly.

And so the instruction goes on, landings, takeoffs, instrument approaches, and always aerobatics. Goober, the fighter pilot, doesn't seem happy unless the airplane is cutting up the sky in various maneuvers. I get accustomed to this quickly, my youthful days flinging a biplane about the sky return, a rebirth, a return to childhood.

But one thing bothers me: landings. Landings are always done in a breakaway, fighter fashion with high speed downwind and then a steep turn into final approach. The steep turn is high G and I'm shoved down in the seat. I don't like, and have never liked, high G forces.

"Goober, damn it, when I fly jets it'll be airline style, long, straight-in approaches with no Gs or fancy wingdings—can't we land like that?"

"Hell, that's no way to land a fighter!"

End of effort. I had to catch on to the breakaway landing approach and do it that way, even though I didn't like it.

Other instructors were longtime buddies of Goober's from Korea, and one day Goober decided to rendezvous with one of them who was instructing a colonel to show us some combat flying—dogfighting. We tore around the sky, which seemed below us as much as above, and the Gs had me shoved into the seat a good portion of the time. While I appreciated seeing some of this wartime flying and admired it, I was a happy man when we finally landed.

The air force lingo and stories were fun at the officers club bar each evening, a sharp contrast to airline flying, and an enjoyable interlude. I flew a total of ten hours with Goober—they never allowed any of us to solo, as it would be against air force regulations. It was jet indoctrination, but it was more fighter indoctrination, although we did seven hours under the hood, and an hour and a half of actual instrument flying according to my logbook. All the flying was pretty routine stuff, though at higher speeds than we'd use with a Connie. This wasn't a great revelation, but that jet engine was—the smooth, smooth power. It did have its downside and that was its rate of acceleration going from idle to full power when the airplane might need impetus on approach; the rate was much slower than a prop airplane, and this was an important early jet lesson. I bade farewell and thanks to Goober and the air force. Now I had dreams to dream of a jet-powered airliner—and no G forces.

Boeing was busy working toward a transport. They created a prototype airplane, just one, commonly referred to as the Dash 80. It looked like the 707 eventually did, but was smaller. While working for Burgess I was invited out to Boeing for a look at the 80. Boeing's test pilot, Tex Johnson, took me up along with some others.

I sat in the copilot seat. The cockpit wasn't that strange: familiar instruments, a windshield to look though that had pretty good visibility, an open, horned control wheel that had authority designed into it, but not much different from a Connie's.

Then the takeoff started, only four throttles, no propeller controls, no mixture controls—we were achieving simplicity. No oil cooler controls, no cowl flap controls, just those four throttles that Tex's hand slowly but positively moved forward, and so did the airplane. There was no shove-back-in-the-seat acceleration, and for a period I wondered when this thing would get going—and at about that point, it got going. Tex pulled back, the nose pointed up, and the rumbling of tires on pavement ceased and smooth flight took over. A klunk as the landing gear retracted and tucked away. We climbed in exhilarating fashion, eating away big chunks of sky. And I suddenly realized there was no vibration, no underhanded trembling of the structure, no harsh constant deep quivering, no, it was all smooth.

And there we were, it seemed so quickly, at 38,000 feet. "We're doin' about 600 miles an hour," Tex matter-of-factly said. (That's about 280 mph faster than a Connie.) "Go ahead and fly it."

I reach for the wheel, carefully apply pressure for a gentle turn, then back the other way; a push ahead to see us start down, a pull back to see us go up. It was all natural, except that a small push or pull made for a rapid altitude change. A Connie, at 300 mph, with a small nose-down direction, descends 1,380 feet a minute; but this jet, with the same nose-down degree, descends at the rate of 2,760 feet per minute because we're doing 600 mph. But it's no concern, merely an interesting observation and something to consider in all jet flying, or more precisely our transition to jets.

Back at Seattle, Tex lands, taxis back for takeoff, lines up, and says, "You take her off." I open the throttles carefully and we smoothly start down the runway, gathering speed. The big impression is lack of noise and vibration; the engine roar is subdued because most of the noise is belching out the back of the engine, out the tailpipes, which are far behind the cockpit.

The speed builds, and Tex says rotate her to about 15 degrees, and I pull back the wheel, which has some pressure that's easily relieved by an electric trim button. And there I am climbing, that smooth, swift slide into the sky, seemingly without effort, the earth receding, becoming unimportant, only a distant backdrop to our element, the sky.

"Level her off at 3,000, go on around, and make a landing." He coaches me as to what airspeed to use, which takes some pitch and throttle juggling, but it seems natural, not difficult, as we swing around base leg to final, lining up with the runway. I get on the speed he calls for—one I can't remember, but probably around 130 knots. It all seems effortless as we cross the near end of the runway and Tex says not to flare much. We squeak on and brake to slow speed. My first jet airliner landing is over, and my eyes are wide open to a whole new world that's about to unfold.

THE JETS WERE COMING, but there was a lot of interesting flying remaining before then; each trip seemed to have some adventure, something out of the ordinary. One sunny afternoon we took off from Rome for Paris, but shortly after takeoff the Rome tower asked if I would contact an Army C-119—a twin-engine cargo airplane—that had a problem. We got him and learned he was struggling along on one engine sixty miles southwest of Ponza and wasn't sure if he could make it. We headed out that way and found the airplane, took a position near him, showed him the quickest way back to Rome, and, of course, by being there, we'd know where he was in case he landed in the sea. It all went off smoothly. We landed, renewed our fuel supply, and were off to Paris again; the next day the Rome papers made a big fuss, which was a lot of bushwa, as we hadn't done anything heroic or even difficult; heroes are created too easily.

I remember a takeoff from Geneva, going to Rome, on a day of rain and low clouds that we climbed into and immediately were on solid instruments. Normally, climbing through bad weather, you hit layers of clouds with an area of visibility before you enter another cloud deck up above; the cloud mass is never solid bottom to top, but on this day there weren't any layers, no change in density or color, and the rain, changing to snow up higher, never varied, so we were encased in a white mass. It was a bit strange, leaving a detached feeling as though the world you knew had gone away and here you were surrounded forever in a motionless white mass. Were we certain of our altitude and position? A careful check of the instruments and the condition of the airplane: all normal. The strange feeling lasted until 20,000 feet, and then, whamo, we broke out into clear blue sky, and ahead, stretching out before us to the south, was sunny Italy. Strange how, through all the years, that one climb stays with me so vividly.

There were many breaks in the routine, intervals that interrupted my normal patterns of flying. Maybe that's one reason the job was never boring—it never had time to become so.

In 1952 I sat on NACA's Subcommittee on Meteorological Problems, and then in 1958 on its Subcommittee on Flight Safety. NACA, the National Advisory Committee for Aeronautics, was founded in 1915 as a rider on the navy appropriations bill; its first budget allotment was $5,000 a year, and its stated task was "to supervise and direct the scientific study of the problems of flight, with a view of their practical solution." Its first report was by Jerome C. Hunsaker and E. B. Wilson of MIT, both revered and almost sanctified figures in aviation's technical history; that first report was titled *Report on Behavior of Aeroplanes in Gusts*. In August 1917, funds were provided to the Weather Bureau "to promote safety in aerial navigation." So here we are over eighty years later still worrying about weather and trying to find ways to avoid turbulence, gusts, and shear. Weather never ceases to be flying's torment.

In 1958 NACA embraced the space effort and became NASA, the National Aeronautics and Space Administration, and it's been downhill ever since for aviation, as funds and studies were directed toward space shuttles and things way out there. Aviation has suffered and been neglected.

NACA subcommittees were made up of industry experts to suggest areas needing research, and being a member of two of them made me feel humble and a bit in over my head. My task, among all the lofty theorists, was to inject the practical, what it was like out there in the action, and what pilots needed. We discussed the jet stream and turbulence, which was something I'd been face-to-face with and so could explain what the action was like and what would help. They listened attentively, and I began to feel I might be useful.

The Subcommittee on Flight Safety related directly to my world, and I felt at home even surrounded by experts with impressive degrees and dossiers. One of the subjects we examined and urged was the development of a terrain-warning instrument that would tell the pilot that the ground was too close. Shades of Howard Hughes's effort in 1947 that never went over—mostly, I feel, because other airlines weren't interested because they hadn't invented it. This NIH factor—not invented here—is probably one of the greatest retarding elements in aviation. Eventually the GPWS, ground proximity warning system, was developed and put into limited service, the first being certificated by the FAA on May 7, 1973; it is now required on all transport aircraft.

My time on these committees was worth the effort. We accomplished many things, including better use of the weather that pilots reported over the oceans, and confirming the value of dew point, which some people tried to remove from the weather reports and for whose retention I had to fight. Probably the biggest gain, however, was my own, as I stepped up my reading and study thanks to the inspiration of the learned men I met on the committees, and I think they learned from me, too, about the practical effects of their efforts for pilots flying out there in the stormy skies.

But always in the back of my mind as I returned to the line was my experience with Goober and my short time at the controls of Boeing's Dash 80 with Tex; they made flying Connies feel like driving a used car when you had a new one on order.

The British Comet was prowling the skies, having inaugurated the first commercial jet schedule back in 1952, which was a long time before we'd have jet transports. One day at Ciampino, Rome, when I was getting ready for a flight to Athens, a Comet took off, the first I'd ever seen. It ran the entire length of the runway, belching black smoke and making an earth-shaking noise that to a pilot was thrilling, not objectionable—at least not to this one. It lifted off, it seemed, right at the end of the runway and thundered into the sky. I knew right then the Connie days were numbered.

Having to use all the runway was part of a problem the early Comets had in getting off the ground; they fixed that with a modification to the front of the wing, but then a Comet crashed into the sea near the island of Elba. This was serious stuff; commercial operation ceased, and a thorough research project was done that discovered a structural design weakness. This set the airplane back a long time—about five years. The Comet didn't begin North Atlantic passenger service until 1958, only a few weeks before Pan Am flew the first 707 across.

Between the first Comet and the first American jet service, Sud Aviation of France flew the first Caravelle, in 1955. This was an innovative aircraft with its two jet engines mounted on the rear of the fuselage; Boeing copied the idea for the 727, and the British did the same with their Trident. The Caravelle was the first short-haul jet transport; the early models carried sixty-four passengers. The French were thorough and careful about testing the airplane, and for a lengthy period they flew it on schedule between Algiers and Paris with cargo only.

The Caravelle would arrive in Paris early in the morning, about the time I'd come in from New York in my old-fashioned Connie—at least that's what it was becoming. With considerable envy I'd see the Caravelle land, taxi to the terminal at Orly, and unload; the load always seemed to be crates of oranges from North Africa. The caution was repaid, as the Caravelle was a successful airplane with an excellent safety record through the years. About 400 were eventually built.

Finally, with the blessing of Howard Hughes, TWA ordered Boeing 707s.

Not all pilots welcomed the coming of the jet; some feared their ability to master it and to pass the needed checks. One pilot became so nervous during school he called his wife to come to Kansas City and support him in his frightened state. Harold Neuman, a famous racing pilot who was now a TWA captain, had doubts; in the cafeteria one day he talked seriously of quitting: "The farm's all paid for, and I've saved some money, I can get along." We chided him and pointed out that his skills were among the best; the idea of quitting was ridiculous. He stuck with it, passing with ease, and flying out his years to retirement perfectly in 707s.

A few old-timers passed up the jet, preferring to stay on Connies until retirement—which was silly, since flying the jet was easy, and they missed the benefits of those wonderful engines.

I was still working with President Burgess when I got shipped off to jet school with our chief pilots from various regions and a couple of TWA's operational vice presidents. The school was at the Boeing factory in Seattle and mostly concerned the nuts and bolts of the airplane, its system of electrical and hydraulic controls and such, and sessions on performance. It was easy to see that this was a different world, a high world and the higher the better. Early jet engines, like the Pratt & Whitney J-57, were not fan engines and they were fuel hogs. The way to get the most miles to the gallon was to get up high where the air is less dense and you go fast on less fuel—jet fuel, which isn't a lot different from the stuff the heating company pours into your oil tank in the basement. High meant 35,000 to 39,000 feet.

They taught us about Mach tuck, which is a phenomenon associated with approaching the speed of sound, a spooky area of shock waves where controls act strangely even when you aren't going faster than the speed of sound. Near Mach 1—that's the speed of sound, about 760 miles per hour at sea level, named for Dr. Ernst Mach, who discovered it—the airplane wants to pitch down and dive. It's not difficult to stop or control, you just reduce speed to normal cruising, which was about Mach .82, or 82 percent of the speed of sound. So it was something to know about, but nothing to fret over, especially since we didn't go that fast normally, and a device on the stabilizer trim would automatically take care of the problem if we did.

Swept-wing aircraft also have a flying peculiarity called Dutch roll—the fancy name is yaw-roll coupling. What happens is that the nose swings a few degrees, which makes a wing go down a few also, then it reverses and does it the other way, so the airplane sort of wallows along through the sky. A gadget hooked to the rudder, called a yaw damper, senses this and corrects for it. This wasn't a 100 percent cure, and in the early jets, if you went back to the rear toilet, you could feel this slight swinging back and forth. It did this on a 707 in about a seven-second cycle; it was worse below certain speeds and at high altitude, but it was still no big deal in any case.

So that was the extent of the school. One of the instructors was a kid named Pete Morton; about thirty years later I was back at Boeing and Pete, by then vice president of training, let me fly the latest 747-400 simulator. Nice guy.

In December 1959 I flew my last Connie flight: Frankfurt-London-Idlewild, sixteen hours and fifty-three minutes. A few days later I started 707 training in Kansas City, in our simulator.

Simulators then weren't as sophisticated as they are now; they didn't move, and the visuals were crude and seldom worked. The visual came from a camera mounted on a moving track over a painted landscape in a long room; it only showed the last part of the landing approach, and my recollection is that it worked about 20 percent of the time, and not very well then. Still, we did turns, stalls, instrument approaches, and simulated Mach tuck and Dutch roll.

The other wild bit of instruction was what to do about an explosive decompression, meaning a failure of the pressurization system. If you're in high flight, 25,000 to 41,000 feet, and the pressurization suddenly fails, the cabin atmosphere zooms to the airplane's level, which is very bad for people. The object is to get down fast so the passengers won't all pass out, possibly die, or lose oxygen long enough to damage the brain. Of course oxygen masks fall out of the overhead, and if passengers get them on and breathe the oxygen, they'll be okay. But we were new to high flight and were more dramatic about it, figuring some little old lady or slack-brained man might not get their mask on, so we learned to do a decompression maneuver to get down to livable altitude as quickly as possible.

The routine was to get out in an airplane and actually climb to 35,000 feet—a half hour or more grind—and then the instructor would call out, "Loss of pressure!" Whereupon you banked the airplane and shoved the nose down as you grabbed your oxygen mask, put it on, turned the oxygen to emergency—this meant 100 percent, full-flowing oxygen—and concentrated on not exceeding maximum speed, but went down as fast as possible. Today, thank the Lord, all this is done in a simulator, so the wasteful climb and descent of a real airplane is avoided.

Then it was time for my FAA rating ride to earn my license to fly a 707; an inspector climbed on and had me go through all the hoops for two hours and twenty-five minutes: flying and landing with one engine failed, landing without flaps, doing the decompression drill, demonstrating my ability to handle Mach tuck and Dutch roll and make a few instrument approaches; maybe more, I don't remember, but with all that done he gave me my 707 rating, which said I was proficient to be in command. Big sigh of relief.

Next came a familiarization flight across the ocean with a check pilot, Jack Frier, to Paris and back. It was routine, and I asked for and climbed to 39,000 feet to show Jack I knew how to save fuel. It was a pleasant flight.

Then, on February 1, 1960, I made my first trip as a jet captain, no check pilots or FAA, just me and the crew: Idlewild-London-Frankfurt.

What was different? Simplicity. The cockpit was less cluttered with gadgets: no propeller controls, no concern about engine pressure, the tailpipe temperature was the only serious one to check, the others reflected power settings. The jet engine is simplicity itself, and that's the key to reliability. The instruments themselves weren't much different from a Connie's; we hadn't yet moved into the computer age. The autopilot was a bit more sophisticated, but it wasn't able to land the airplane or do the tricks of today's autopilots. And the visibility was better.

It was easy to feel at home; there was no nervousness of the new, only relief that the engine worries were over. So was much of the concern about weather, because at 35,000 feet you're on top of the nasty stuff. Low-level fog, ice, and thunderstorms would only be a problem when you're descending and landing; at those times, all your experiences of the past, from DC-2s to Connies, come back into play, reminding you that despite the advances, in certain parts of flight the old ways still apply.

Now our vision is up; we are newly interested in those meteorological charts that show what's going on in the high sky, in the 30,000-feet-plus range. The charts point the way to the best course to fly to gain or reduce the loss from the high winds. And the charts show us where turbulence will most likely be—clear air turbulence, a new weather annoyance that comes with high-altitude flying, something added to be wary of. So there were new weather skills to learn, but interesting ones that have a broader sweep and reflect the vastness of the high sky; you have to try to understand and, at times, outguess the invisible movement of air. The closest thing to it in my experience is glider flying, where I fly searching for the lifting air that I know is out there somewhere.

The total flying time New York–London–Frankfurt was eight hours and twenty-six minutes; the last Connie trip for the same route was fourteen hours and six minutes. It was still an all-night affair and I was sleepy, but less dragged out, maybe because I was pretty pumped up.

As the years passed, I realized that the jet speed wasn't a particular advantage to my lifestyle; actually, that lifestyle deteriorated, because with less flying time per trip, we had to fly more trips each month to get those eighty-five hours we normally flew in a month. The result was more commuting to the airport, more time away from home, more nights' sleep missed; the net gain was actually a loss. But flying with those wonderful engines, and the end of so much worry, was like dying and going to heaven.

CHAPTER 25

707 Days

I ATTENDED A REUNION PARTY in Paris, many years after retirement; sitting next to me at dinner was Nicole Sargent Kappler, one of our original French hostesses, still lovely with big expressive brown eyes, a very intelligent lady.

"Tell me, Bob," she asked, "what was the best time of our flying?"

Without a moment's deliberation I said, "The 707 days."

"Yes," she agreed, and went on. "Then we had pride; in our service, the food, and pleasant atmosphere of each flight."

She was right; those were the days, and for many reasons. We flew the same routes we'd been flying, but the atmosphere changed: delays because of engine problems ended, air traffic hadn't grown to plug the sky, the airplanes were quiet and comfortable, even in economy class.

That was when airline flying had class, when passengers looked forward to flights. It was an era between the primitive early days and the modern cattle-car style that makes the journey something to be endured rather than enjoyed unless one has unlimited funds, an expense account, or enough frequent-flier miles to be in first class. But first class or economy, everyone suffers the delays from air traffic and the unpleasant crowded terminals. The 707 time shines above all others, and alas is lost forever.

We strove to make airline flying successful and available to all, but now, those of us who were there from the early days are not proud of the inhuman system it's become. Still, we can take pride in the technical and operational advances we were part of that made it safe and, once the airplane becomes airborne, reliable. But how delightful it is to dream back to those special times when the 707 climbed with character and style into the sky, and our naïveté made us think it would always be like that.

We learned, as we flew the aircraft, the differences between piston and jet in two major areas; one was in landing approach, where the slower acceleration of a jet engine when you need additional power called for new techniques and anticipation. The other was the jet's unquenchable thirst for fuel, especially down low, and especially those first engines, which were not the fan type but rather what we called the straight pipe engines. The key was to fly high, at 35,000 to 39,000 feet, and stay there until we could make a descent to land without loitering; holding for air traffic down low was our nemesis. Fortunately, air traffic was far less then, but a thunderstorm over the airport or very low ceilings that had flights missing approaches could tie things up, and we sometimes found ourselves milling around the holding pattern at 7,000 feet, our eyes constantly scanning the fuel remaining, pestering the flight engineer for his latest figures, while doing math in your mind to figure how much fuel you'd need to get to an alternate, how much longer you could hold, and how the alternate's weather was holding up.

There were unexpected events, like the night I came nonstop from London for New York into strong Atlantic head winds that slowed our flight, requiring more fuel. Close inspection of the winds aloft showed a low pressure area over the ocean a bit north of normal, producing the strong head winds on course. The way to battle this was to fly a course northward and get on top of the low for its east winds; everyone agreed it was the thing to do, but nagging in the back of my mind was the simple question, What if the low was farther north than expected? We made a flight plan northward, and the estimate showed we had enough fuel as long as we could get up high.

So off we went, aiming over Northern Ireland and then Greenland and Labrador, where we should be beyond the low's meanness and able to cut south to New York. The North Track, as we called such detours, sometimes brings jets over my home in Vermont, and on those days I see straight white contrails cutting across the blue sky, forming behind tiny airplanes way up high, boring swift and true through the sky. I look up, and I instantly know what the North Atlantic wind pattern is—I could draw the upper-air chart that has all those inbound airplanes from Europe flying over my mountainside home; there's a lot of nostalgia around when I look up and see the North Track working.

But my flight from London: it started well, and we obtained approval for 35,000 feet. Our times were on flight plan until east of Greenland, when it became obvious the low was farther north than forecast and our hoped for good winds were going to be bad winds. In our favor, however, we did have clearance to 39,000 feet. Lots of computing; little pieces of paper cluttered the shelf to my left with all sorts of contingency figures; while we were slow, we had the fuel, the New York weather was good, and being at 39,000 feet kept the fuel usage modest. But between Goose Bay, Labrador, and the St. Lawrence River, air traffic called me and said descend to 29,000 feet. Disaster! We'd use far too much fuel. Why did they want me down? There was an airspace block for the military where they were refueling aircraft. No amount of argument would change the demand.

More figuring: Go to Montreal? How about Albany? But Albany was not an official alternate. Could we make New York? More figuring, more pieces of paper. It would be tight—tight enough to go to an alternate? Check New York weather, very clear and holding. I contacted the dispatcher, asked him to find out if there were any air traffic control delays anticipated. The answer, none. We kept going toward New York. If things started going to pieces I could always land at Albany; it wasn't legal, but the airport was sufficient, I'd just have to answer to the FAA as to why I went there. Add it all up and I decided to go for New York.

Everything worked as it should: the weather stayed good, no ATC delays, but I flew sitting toward the edge of my seat. No, I wasn't risking running out of fuel, I can always find a place to land before that, but the implications of legality were bothersome.

The night was clear and brilliant as we passed Albany, and I could almost see New York. Normally the entry course is to fly to a point on Long Island, Deer Park, as entry to Kennedy. But Deer Park is east of Kennedy, and going over it would mean an extra thirty miles—not a big amount, but I wasn't interested in dawdling about.

"Any chance," I asked air traffic control, "for direct Kennedy—I'm a little tight on fuel."

"Cleared direct, descend at your discretion." A happy, cooperative reply. It was late at night and there was little traffic.

I cut the throttles and started down, and never touched them until we were turning for final approach to the runway at Kennedy. We landed with a reasonable amount of fuel, although not as much as one would like, a bit less than an hour's worth. It was not a dangerous operation, and the passengers had their nonstop London–New York as promised, but for me it was a tiring flight with many problems and decisions.

The high flying of the first 707 also awakened us to the troposphere. I've mentioned it before as the part of the atmosphere we live in; above the troposphere is the stratosphere, and where the two meet is called the tropopause—or trop, as we call it. What happens above the trop, in the stratosphere? The temperature rises, or at the least it doesn't continue getting colder as one climbs.

Airplanes are temperature-sensitive; the warmer the air the less dense it is and performance deteriorates. So we take off and climb with our heavy load to 35,000 feet. We'd rather go to 39,000 feet, but we can't climb that high right from takeoff, full of fuel and heavy. After two hours or so of flying, we've burned off enough fuel to reduce the airplane weight so it will climb and cruise at 39,000 feet, provided the temperature isn't too high; we want to stay in the troposphere, where we're certain the temperature will stay cold. The question is, "Where's the trop?" At what altitude will we go from cold troposphere to warmer stratosphere? The trop level varies with location and current weather, and it can be as low as 25,000 feet or as high as 50,000.

So we don't want to climb to 39,000 with still marginal performance and fly through the trop into the stratosphere and see the temperature go up and the performance go down. To make it interesting, the trop level is a forecast matter, and we all know how weather forecasting works.

Suppose we're out there and decide it's time to climb to 39,000 feet. The weather charts I've been given before takeoff show that in our present location the trop is forecast to be at 41,000—fine. We call air traffic control and they approve climb to 39,000 feet. Up go the throttles and we climb, everything still fine. But at 38,000 I see a thin line of particulates cutting through the clear sky, probably tiny dust particles even out over the middle of the ocean. As we fly into this level there's slight turbulence, not enough that you'd notice it in the cabin, but it's a signal to me, a bad signal. My eyes dart to the outside air temperature and yes, damn it, it has gone up a few degrees! We're in the stratosphere. We struggle to 39,000 feet and level off. It takes climb power to stay there and maintain speed. I call air traffic control, and ask to go back to 35,000. Sorry, he says, but I gave that to another flight when you left it. So there we are, as the expression goes, "with the nose in the stratosphere and the tail dragging in the water." Meaning we have a nose-high struggling attitude. We're stuck here now at climb power, burning extra fuel until the weight goes down enough to stay in the warm at 39,000 feet using only cruise power.

The trop does other things, related to turbulence. If there's a strong jet stream wind just under the trop you can bet there will be turbulence, and it can be severe. So the question "Where's the trop?" became important and much asked.

We worked through the first year, not a lot different in many respects from past years except for the relief from bad engines. Scanning my logbook's terse notes tells the tale:

"Sophia Loren along."

"In Brussels account Paris strike."

"Two short fire warnings out of Paris."

"First into Fumincino." (Rome's new airport, now called the Leonardo da Vinci. The old one was Ciampino. This was on March 10, 1961.)

"First Doppler."

"Record NY-London—5 hrs 28 mins off to on."

"New record NY-Lisbon—5 hrs 9 mins." (Records fell all over as the jets came into use with their 500 mph versus the old piston's 300 mph. Records never lasted long, as someone would get a big tailwind and do it faster.)

"Returned to London, electric discharge." (That was a lightning strike between two innocent-looking cumulus clouds shortly after takeoff.) "Dumped 90,000 pounds fuel." (A three-foot-long piece of the black nose cone tore off, and the copilot's pressure instruments were out. No big deal, no danger. I was angered by a church group on board that told London reporters how terrifying it had been and that they had prayed and saved us.)

"Natalie Wood into Geneva." (She was very nice, and I let her sit in the jump seat for landing—which she said was thrilling. In that time, before terrorists and heavy security, we often invited people to the cockpit; it wasn't strictly legal, but a lot of it went on and the FAA didn't seem to bother anyone much over the practice.)

"Hugh Downs along."

"Landed KIDL [Idlewild] stab trim out—used spoiler for trim—OK."

"Lahinch—94." (On a Shannon layover I played the wonderful golf course on the coast at Lahinch.)

"Shut down #1 over Mt. Blanc—fuel control unit—1st jet failure." (The engine continued to run, but only at maximum continuous power, so I shut it off and went on to Paris.)

"Minister of War, France, & X. Cugat along."

"La Scala." (Layover in Milan, and I went to the opera.)

"Letter on London noise—113PNDB in letter—92DB by radio after takeoff." (London was very difficult about noise, and measured the amount you made on every takeoff. The ground would then tell you what the reading had been. Evidently there was a screwup between what they told me and what the letter said. It was all straightened out. One Russian airplane exceeded the noise restriction and when admonished by London is reported to have said, "That's good! That is power!")

"Maurice Bellonte aboard—KIDL-LFPO [Paris]." (This was a big event for me, as Bellonte was copilot, mechanic, and navigator on the first nonstop Paris to New York flight, September 1930—the pilot was Dieudonné Costes. Bellonte was a quiet, charming man, and I invited him into the cockpit where he stayed for the entire flight. We discussed his flight and ours. As the Paris lights came in view he became very emotional and shed a few tears. The next day he stopped by my hotel and left a book, autographed, all about their flight with pictures and maps. The most interesting part was a two-page layout map of their course and the weather. It was obvious they knew the weather and went around a mid-Atlantic low to get tailwinds. Way ahead of their time.)

"Returned GVA [Geneva]—gear wouldn't retract."

"New terminal London." (March 3, 1962.)

"Jess Fiser's appendix." (On layover in Frankfurt my copilot had severe pain on his right side and other symptoms. I took him to a doctor, who said it was appendicitis. "What do we do?" I asked. "Ve operate, immediately." Which they did. This was an emotional time, because a hostess on the trip was Jess's fiancée and she went to the hospital with us and was very upset about it all. They eventually married—Jess became a captain and is now retired—and the marriage has been a great success. Jess tended to be chunky and thought maybe he'd lose some weight through all this, but he actually gained weight in the hospital—the reason being that this German hospital served beer with meals.

"Beat Pan Am with Doppler." (We had a constant rivalry with Pan Am, who had flights from Paris and London at the same time we did, so it was often a race.)

The Doppler, that navigation system we tested on a 1649 Connie, was the focus of a long and tough battle between the company and the navigators' union. The airline was trying to phase out the navigators, who used every trick to try to hang on to their jobs and I didn't blame them. Their argument was that Doppler hadn't been proven, and the navigators convinced some people in Congress that horrible things would happen without the navigator.

There followed a proving period in which a pilot would use the Doppler to navigate, while a navigator tracked the flight his way; anytime the airplane wandered more than thirty miles off course, the navigator was to bring it to the attention of an FAA inspector on board the flight. I was assigned to do these proving flights; the equipment was on only one airplane, and every time that airplane flew and I was rested and legal to fly, I was on it.

It was a frustrating task, because I enjoyed the navigation work, but I hated the conflict with the navigators, most of whom were friends. Through all the flights—and there were about fifteen, including the final FAA approval flight—the furthest we went off course was twenty-eight miles, with most deviations falling within fifteen miles, which for an ocean crossing is acceptable, since radio aids will lead you back on the exact course as you approach land.

It was eighteen months before all the negotiations were settled with a severance package for the navigators, as well as passes for life on the airline. I made my first trip without a navigator on October 1, 1962; it was the end of an era, but one that was bound to end as the inertial navigation system was developed, and then finally the ultimate, the GPS, global positioning system, which responds to satellite data, so the only skill needed to navigate is an ability to push computer keys and know what latitude and longitude are.

I look back at my efforts to learn celestial navigation and its use in the B-17 and the early transoceanic passenger service. Now it's all gone; future fliers will never experience the romance and skill of being guided by the stars. It might seem my learning effort was wasted, but it wasn't; it was necessary for its time, and it gave me a treasure, something I realize whenever I stand outside on a crystal-clear, cold winter night and look up to my old friends Sirius, Vega, and Polaris. I made certain my son learned the night sky, its stars, planets, and movements; he has already passed this knowledge on to his son.

Many other logbook entries refer to delays because of weather and air traffic control. It was becoming evident that there were too many flights for the airports available. This was in the early 1960s, and any thinking person could see this was going to get worse simply because airplanes can be built and put in service faster than airports can. As mentioned earlier, the problem can be summed up in one word: runways. A runway can only accept a certain number of airplanes an hour, a figure that runs from forty to sixty. If more flights than that are scheduled, things back up into holding patterns and diversions. At some airports, where there's only one runway, takeoffs must be accommodated, so they back up, too. None of this happened overnight; anyone could see that as more schedules were added the situation got worse—yet no one had the gumption to call a halt.

The problem is old: in 1955, a commission called the Aviation Facilities Study Group was set up to study the air travel problem, and one of the first statements in its report was that "air traffic management had already reached critical proportions." Concern about this goes clear back to the Hoover administration; Truman had it studied, too. But government seems incapable of stopping the push for further profits that has strained the system, and today, the chances for improvement are slim.

The United States needs a transportation plan that would include railroads, buses, trucks, and automobiles. Europe has done a great job with trains; since the TGV—France's fast train—began operating between Lyons and Paris, air travel between the two cities has dropped 65 percent.

New York and Boston are almost exactly the same distance apart; fast trains between Washington, New York, and Boston would reduce the air traffic problem tremendously. How many other short links are there in the United States that trains could accommodate? The air traffic problem may prove to be the most glaring example of government's inability to act.

A note in one of my logbooks from April 1965: "#43 for takeoff JFK, 1 hour and 05 minute delay." I can only conclude that someone thought this was progress.

October 2, 1963, had a short entry: "Mrs. J. F. Kennedy passenger." I was asked to fly this routine New York–Rome–Athens flight with the first lady aboard. There was much fuss and feathers with the food, and a curtain around two first-class seats for her privacy and comfort.

We sat all ready to go, a regular flight except for our first lady passenger. The Kennedy private airplane, a twin-engine Convair, landed from Washington and taxied right up to our gate. Mrs. Kennedy got off, walked to our airplane, climbed the steps, and took her place in first class. The door was shut, the engines started, and we were off to Rome.

It was a beautiful night with a very strong tailwind, so strong we were going to beat schedule by an hour. Everyone knew this well in advance, both in New York and Rome.

The flight went beautifully, and we reached Italy in the early morning ahead of schedule as announced. But Rome traffic control told me to hold at Civitavecchia, a radio beacon thirty miles northwest of Rome's airport. "Why?" I asked. It was clear with unlimited visibility, and I hadn't heard any other flights on the radio. The unexplained answer, "Hold Civitavecchia."

"What's my approach time?" A common question asked of air traffic control when one is told to hold.

Answer, "Indefinite."

I called the company radio, our dispatcher in Rome. "What the hell is going on?"

His explanation: the official government welcoming party hadn't been told we'd be an hour early, so it wasn't at the airport and we were to hold until they arrived.

So we were stuck with it. I called air traffic control and asked if I could cruise around at my own discretion and they said yes, so I flew to Naples, showed the passengers Capri, the bay, and Vesuvius before we were allowed to land. I taxied to the gate and there were the officials, bedecked in fancy uniforms, ribbons across their chests, and backed by a band.

An hour's stop and we were off to Athens. From my seat there was a view available to no one but me: I looked down on the officials wishing the first lady goodbye, and then she turned and climbed the stairs to the airplane; I could look down the steps and see her face while others only saw her back. She grasped the handrail going up with determination, shaking slightly, nervous to be certain she didn't trip or show anything but dignity, which she accomplished. It was a moment when I felt great respect for the first lady.

After takeoff I went back in the cabin to tell her what the landing delay at Rome had been about. She was much amused and said, "Jack will love that." We chatted and she was most gracious, giving me an autographed picture and a *PT 109* tie clasp.

Arrival at Athens was a madhouse. In that time there was a very simple terminal building and most people stood outside. This day there was a mass of people, and they all rushed out toward the airplane. I shut the engines down quickly so as not to suck anyone into one, which is quite possible and has been done.

A few months after this I had another famous passenger, Muhammad Ali. This was an interesting experience. We were going Paris to New York, and Ali had been on a tour to Egypt—I'd seen him briefly in our hotel in Cairo, along with his brother. We were delayed, with French air traffic control giving us trouble; it wasn't a strike, but a slowdown. We sat at the gate waiting for clearance, but they were only giving them out periodically, sometimes it was over an hour between clearances, and then we didn't know who would get the clearance. We couldn't let the passengers off while we waited, because they'd be in the terminal, Lord knows where, and we'd never get them rounded up and on board fast enough once we got clearance for takeoff. So there we sat. I finally got permission for the passengers to get off the airplane for fresh air and to stretch their legs, but to stay nearby, under the wings, so we could instantly climb on board and be off. I explained the slowdown to Ali, telling him I had no idea when we'd go.

"That's okay," he said. "Maybe those fellows need the money."

While the passengers collected under the wing and around the airplane door, Ali entertained them in conversation I wish I could have heard; I was standing by in the cockpit, out of hearing, waiting for a clearance. It was over four hours before our clearance came, and we quickly loaded everyone, fired up, and departed. The passengers seemed happy as they got back on; Ali had done a good job keeping their spirits up. I became a great fan of his, and I still am.

There was a special logbook note on a Paris to Rome flight late at night, a beautiful night. The course was over Dijon, France, Geneva, and Pisa to Rome, but the beauty of the flight was over Dijon, high in the clear sky, the radio silent because there was no traffic. I turned the cockpit lights down low and searched way ahead through the darkness, and yes, there it was, a tiny light in the empty blackness, I knew it, I'd been there, the night light on the Aiguille du Midi, a station in the Alps, 12,400 feet high, perhaps the tallest cable car ride anywhere, and 135 miles from where I could spot it as we flew over Dijon. The jet noise isn't noticeable in the cockpit, and we slipped silently through the night sky. With the crew members quiet, the radio still, and the cockpit lights dim, I almost felt like I was out in the sky. We flew over Geneva and its lights fell behind us, we were in the darkness again, but through the shadowy night below I could see Mont Blanc, the highest of the Alps, 15,771 feet. The mountain seemed close, although 20,000 feet separated us. It was silent, a huge, pure white mass with craggy stone sticking up, nothing moving on the surface. There it was and there we were, with a bond between us that is unfathomable and mysterious. It fell behind us in the night and we looked ahead toward Pisa and Rome.

With the 707 we stretched our wings toward the east, and I flew to Bombay, Ceylon, and Hong Kong. On that particular route we'd fly first to Frankfurt, stay overnight, then to Tel Aviv for another overnight, then across the desert and sea to Bombay for two nights, and then to Hong Kong with stops at Colombo and Bangkok. Every stop had its differences in scenery, culture, sounds, and smells, some kind of mixture between Kipling, Halliburton, and the things Miss Fink talked about in my sixth-grade geography class.

Part of the fun of Hong Kong was landing at Kai Tak Airport. The start of the runway that we'd approach for landing was shoved right up against the city, behind which were 1,500-foot hills, too high to come over and land straight in. So the approach was at a 90-degree angle, over water, away from the hills, toward an island called Stone Cutter. Beyond Stone Cutter, a hill rose that had big red and white checkerboard squares painted on it. So the procedure was to fly over Stone Cutter, descending, then aim at Checkerboard, continuing descent, then just before it make a hard right turn, almost an aerobatic maneuver; by now you were down to 300 feet or less, the tight turn taking you over stacked apartment-style living quarters with wash lines and drying clothes blowing in the wind off the balconies, close enough that you felt your wingtip might tear them off the lines. The runway swung into view, tilted sideways, but coming up level with your wings as you completed the turn; there it was, stretched out ahead and ready to accept your aircraft. After a long boring flight from Bangkok this stirred the blood and got you up on the edge of the seat—careful, but barnstorming with a Boeing 707, having old-style fun.

That's all gone now, with a new airport built away from these problems, just another dull airport with proper, boring approaches. But there's a brotherhood of pilots who flew in and out of Kai Tak, and when any of us come together there's lots of talk, tales, and laughter.

The saddest event for me in this time was the death of Ty Power; he suffered a heart attack in Madrid while making a picture. He was forty-four years old, about the same age as his father when he died of a heart attack in Ty's arms. Ty's passing left a big empty place in my life that never goes away. His movies, many of which I have, bring back that deep, strong voice, his dark eyes and his warm smile, but when the movie ends I realize he isn't here anymore. I've never been able to decide if watching them is a sad event or a happy one—I guess it's a happy one, but there's sadness also.

In August 1962 I got a call from Jeeb Halaby, FAA administrator. Would I be willing to sit on a supersonic transport advisory committee? Indeed . . . indeed.

CHAPTER 26

SST or Not SST

＊

THE FIRST MEETING of the Super Sonic Transport Committee
was impressive; it was held in the FAA conference room, big polished table, chairs all around, notepads and pencils at the ready.
It was led by Halaby, the chairman; around the table were two engineers
from the airlines, the Los Angeles Airport director, a man high in finance
on Wall Street, an airline pilot (me), an engineer from NACA, and a repre-
sentative of the Air Force. Seated behind each were their backup experts
with lots of briefcases and papers—in the case of the Air Force, the experts
were uniformed and ribbon-decorated. I was the only exception; I had no
advisor.

Al White, test pilot of the XB-70 supersonic bomber, was a member,
too, but he dropped out eventually because of a conflict of interest since Al
was chief test pilot for North American Aviation, one of the manufacturers
who would be bidding on the transport.

The first meeting was to introduce us all and for a briefing of purpose
that was simple in statement but difficult to accomplish: we were to decide
if the United States should build a supersonic transport, and if so to what
performance, and how would it get built—cutting down to the nitty-gritty,
that meant who would pay for it.

Early on it was agreed the United States should have a supersonic transport, it should have transatlantic range, carry about 225 people, and cruise at Mach 3. This was the early decision, based on the idea that if France and England were going to have a supersonic transport, the Concorde, we would, too, only a better one. These were easy decisions around a board-room table, but reality was different, and it was our job to face it.

We invited all sorts of experts for their wisdom and knowledge. We traveled far and wide, to aircraft manufacturers both in the States and abroad. We visited the Concorde people, who were cooperative and open about the Concorde project, which was just getting started. In England they let me fly the Concorde simulator, which at that stage was pretty basic; the visual part was a TV monitor stuck in the pilot's windshield, but it still gave an idea of certain flying qualities.

We made many visits to Edwards Air Force Base's test facility and field, where supersonic flight was common stuff. Never having been supersonic, I insisted I get at least a whiff of supersonic flying.

My first was in a T-38 with Major H. Evans, Mach 1.2. I did assorted air work, including, at Evans's urging, a roll at supersonic speed. I also made some simulated ILS instrument approaches.

Going supersonic was rather a disappointment, because nothing much happens; as you pass the speed of sound—once called the sound barrier, at sea level it's about 760 miles per hour and in the stratosphere about 660 mph—all that happens is that the pressure instruments (airspeed, altimeter, vertical speed) give a small wiggle and then settle down. But there's no big impression, a roll is a roll, and because the airplane is small and sleek it goes around quickly and easily, not much different from a subsonic one, just quicker.

I was sent to Fort Worth to fly a B-58 supersonic bomber. This started with a lengthy session in a simulator to gain some familiarity with the air-plane before I flew it. But the flight never happened; the B-58 had a shaky safety record, and while I was learning in the simulator a B-58 crashed under mysterious circumstances—meaning they didn't know why. Wash-ington grounded all B-58s, which cut me out of actual flight. I can't say it was a big disappointment, as I was a bit cool about charging off in this air-plane with its suspect reputation.

So it was back to Edwards, this time to fly an F-104, the sexy Lock-heed fighter with tiny wings and big speed. This time it was at Mach 1.5

for fourteen minutes. I was strongly told, "Landing, don't cut the throttles until touchdown." The reason was that bleed air from the engine was directed over the wing flaps to reduce landing speed. Closing the throttle reduced the bleed air enough to increase the landing speed, which wouldn't be too much trouble on the long runway on Edwards—but if, when the throttle was pulled back, the bleed air didn't reduce evenly, meaning there was more on one wing than the other, the airplane would do a rolling maneuver that was probably uncontrollable and very bad for one's health—it would probably kill you.

It was a great ride. The check pilot told me, "Hold it down till 450 indicated," meaning airspeed, "and then rotate to 30 degrees." The performance was really impressive to a big transport pilot like me; in a little over three minutes we were at 41,000 feet!

The airplane didn't feel as smooth and gentle as the T-38, and the big engine seemed to creak and groan behind me. Everything reacted fast with a serious feeling that said do it right or it'll kill you. I've only flown two airplanes in my life that made me say, "Be careful, this baby could kill you"; the F-104 was one of them. (The other was a two-place low-wing open-cockpit job powered by a Ford V-8 engine. This was a long time ago, back in the 1940s; it spooked me and I did one circuit of the airport and landed, glad to be out of it.)

There were various simulators to fly at NASA's Ames in California; one was especially interesting because it gave a preview of what might happen with an engine failure at supersonic speed. It consisted of a tiny cockpit for one person very well strapped in, with a metal plate on each side of your head in case the simulator went ape. The cockpit, called the cab, was mounted on gimbals so it could roll or turn over in any direction. The entire contraption was on the end of a centrifuge arm that could swing in a circle.

Climb in, fasten seat belt and shoulder harness tight. Check the communications with the outside world, close the hatch cover, and there I was, head between the steel plates, locked down very tight, the instrument panel not fancy but simply equipped with the controls necessary for keeping the airplane upright and flying, or getting it back that way if it wasn't.

The object of this particular session was to see if a pilot could control a multiengine large airplane going at Mach 3 in event of a sudden failure of two engines on one side. It was set up without any control augmentation at first.

So there I was staring at the instruments, 70,000 feet, Mach 3, and suddenly whamo, two engines cut, the airplane yawed and rolled, and nothing I could do would stop it. The cab rolled over quickly, and the centrifuge arm swung around firmly. It wasn't pleasant.

"Okay, Captain Buck?"

"Yup, okay."

Then we tried it with a bit of control augmentation, meaning computer inputs that could move faster and recognize the trouble better than a pilot.

So up we go, 70,000 feet again, Mach 3—engine cut. I almost caught it, but it rolled and yawed and went upside down. They brought it back to level.

"Okay, Captain Buck?"

"Yup, okay." But I was fibbing a bit, because the tumbling and swinging around had me woozy.

So we did it with more augmentation, and with that I could catch it and prevent the upset.

So now we went the other way: they put in augmentation so I could fly it, then removed bits of augmentation until I couldn't handle it. With this opposite approach they were bracketing my capability.

A few more of these resulted in a very strong woozy feeling akin to wild amusement park rides. I was getting close to saying I'd had enough, but I didn't want to say uncle because I just knew outside they were thinking, "Let's see how much an airline pilot can take." And they included a NASA test pilot who I was certain felt that way in spades.

But I was saved: the operator called, "I'm sorry, Captain, but it's lunchtime and we're going to have to shut down."

Oh, I thought, happy words, but I didn't show it; rather I replied, in a disappointed tone, "Oh, all right." And that was that.

There were two technical problems that were tough to handle: one was the sonic boom that everyone in creation objected to. Somewhere in our studies we wanted to learn how much boom the populace would stand. So the entire committee went to Edwards Air Force Base to be boomed. The boom measurement is called overpressure, meaning pressure over normal atmospheric pressure.

The idea at Edwards was to have us boomed with different overpressures by various military supersonic aircraft. We got there late at night and retired to the barracks facilities, with the test to start the next day. At about 4:00 A.M. the world blew up. We all tumbled out of bed, awakened by an explosion—but it wasn't that, it was the diabolical humor of the commander who'd had a fighter dive and turn toward our barracks in the maximum boom fashion that produced an overpressure of about 30, which breaks windows and is very loud.

The next day we were boomed at various levels and we all pretty well decided that an overpressure of 1.6 was fairly acceptable. Of course, that was us and not the public.

To follow on, a program was set up near Oklahoma City where we would boom a community at 1.6 overpressure and see what the reaction would be. The people were told they would be boomed and to send comments, and to apply for compensation if any damage was done. The results were mixed, but it was obvious that airline aircraft couldn't go over the country even at the modest 1.6. An interesting sidelight came one day when we announced there would be a sonic boom flyover, but then we didn't do it. Nevertheless calls came in complaining about the boom, and there were a few claims for broken windows and dishes. Imagination or dishonesty?

I was told that in England there was concern that the Concorde boom might break the valuable stained glass windows in old cathedrals. A test was made, and the results showed that the church bells created a bigger overpressure than the sonic boom. Still and all, the Concorde only goes supersonic with the boom when it's over the ocean.

The other technical problem was our call for Mach 3. Heat was the name of the game; up to about Mach 2.2, a normal airplane structure with minimum modification can stand the heat, but at Mach 3 the heat generated while tearing through the atmosphere is too much for normal structure. The temperature difference between them—and this is subject to a lot of nitpicky stuff having to do with time at high Mach number and other factors—is roughly 400°F, Mach 3 being that much hotter. This meant using titanium, and titanium is tough stuff to work with and has certain quirks. (It does seem to be great for golf clubs, but that's a recent development.)

What's the difference? Why fool with Mach 3? The difference is about 600 miles an hour (this varies with altitude and temperature, but not by a large amount), and 600 miles an hour means the Mach 3 airplane gets to Paris from New York about forty-five minutes sooner than the Mach 2 one. Actually, the Concorde cruises up to Mach 2.2, which cuts the difference down a little bit.

That difference hardly seems worth the agony of going to Mach 3, but people like to ride the fastest, and in the growing Pacific market for business travel Mach 3 really begins to make a big difference over the large distances. Also, when airline schedules are taken into account, the Mach 3 airplane gets more usage, more trips per day, than the Mach 2. This gets into some pretty esoteric stuff dealing with airplane turnaround, crew work hours, and other things we don't have to get into here.

So we decided on Mach 3, and the word went out to manufacturers to prepare proposals. Boeing created a movable wing concept, rather like the B-1 bomber, but changed later to a delta wing with tail and flaps. Lockheed went for the delta wing along Concorde lines, and North American did likewise. Douglas said they weren't interested, because they felt a Mach 3 transport was an interim airplane and that we were close to the technical possibility of hypersonic aircraft cruising at Mach 6 or more.

We made a sobering visit to the B-70 bomber. The huge airplane sat in the hangar with stands, tubes, wires strung across the floor and into it, workmen in various places on the airplane reaching up to the structure, fiddling, looking, working at many tasks. One impressive setup was a battery of hair dryers, plain hairdressers' hair dryers, the best solution to get heat onto some strange liquid in the fuel tank that would solidify under heat and seal the leaking tank. Of course there were many tanks, and through them went tubes and lines of liquids to be cooled by the fuel in the tanks. Another indication of the heat battle was the use of silver-colored tires that would reflect heat, even though retracted and inside, and not absorb it like regular black tires. I could imagine all this effort transferred to an airliner, and I realized it was going to be a very difficult and expensive airplane to create and then maintain and operate. The B-70 made many successful flights, reaching Mach 3 during some of them, but after each flight there was a long period of maintenance and correction of the new problems discovered.

The B-70 came to its end with a crash caused by a collision in the air during a photo mission. Al White bailed out successfully with some injuries, but the copilot was killed.

The research and development for a new transport would cost in the billion-dollar range—and not just one billion. No manufacturer could take that on, so government had to help, and that meant congressional approval. It was legislation designed for conflict; and it was ultimately killed through the efforts of Senator William Proxmire, who was famous for his close watch on government spending. He felt the SST wasn't worth the cost, and he was supported by environmental groups imagining all sorts of catastrophes, ranging from polluting the air, changing the climate, and using up all the oil.

We were disappointed by the failure, but in retrospect it was a good thing: the R&D costs would have grown to gigantic size, airlines wouldn't have been able to afford it, and its fuel use would have been gluttonous. The Concorde, which carries about 100 passengers, burns on a Paris–New York flight about the same amount as a Boeing 747 with 400 passengers. So the most efficient use of fuel isn't at SST speeds.

The Concorde's costs have never been totally revealed, but its R&D cost went well over the mark, and no one ever mentions the cost of tooling to build it, which is often as much as the R&D cost itself. Just how much a Concorde would cost with all factors included has never been revealed. An Air France operations officer I asked about Concorde's cost to operate, hence to make a profit, answered with a Gallic shrug and said, "We have a very good arrangement with the government." It's all lumped in with promoting tourism.

Both the French and the British often claim that the Concorde makes a profit, but industry people smile at this, knowing the actual cost of the airplane has never been established. Perhaps profit is possible if only the crew costs, fuel, and maintenance are counted, but that's far from realistic. I can hear yowls when certain people read this, but that's the way it is. But regardless of costs, the Concorde is a well-built and well-designed airplane the French and British can be proud of. The accident that temporarily shut them down was just one of those things and not a basic flaw.

NASA has a modest group that keeps some work going on an SST, but it's largely technical in the sense of staying apprised of what's new that would apply if we ever built one. The French talk about an enlarged new Concorde, but there doesn't seem to be any real action. It will be a very long time before the United States has an SST—perhaps never, because what Douglas (now part of Boeing) had to say, calling it an interim aircraft, may have been right; years from now we probably will be zooming over the earth in vehicles powered by rockets or their derivatives, and making it to Paris in minutes.

The latest Boeing claim is that their next airplane, the Sonic Cruiser, will cruise at Mach .95, just shy of supersonic. Some have said, why not go supersonic in a modest way—to Mach 1.1, for example, where heating will not be a problem and the sonic boom will be much less. No one knows exactly where this more modest path will lead, in an aviation world that's very different from the one in which we studied the question.

CHAPTER 27

Home, and Above

J EAN, A GENTLE LADY, a lover of beauty, home, children, and
nature as expressed in her work and her loving care of the garden,
saw fit to be my wife and the mother of our children, Ferris and Rob.
Her focus is home, and she never ventured to become part of the aviation world except to climb on an airplane and go to Paris, or to fly with me in a small airplane.

Our daughter, Ferris, went through all the girl things, including ballet and theater, finally becoming, in later years, a leader in stress management and mindfulness, which fits her kind and sympathetic character; she is a fierce protector of the rights of all people. Her brilliant mind has always been a stimulus and joy when we're together. Her interest in aviation is as an airline passenger, with a certain worldly interest in the science behind it.

Our son, Robert Orion, Rob, was born nine years after Ferris. From the time he first walked, there was always a model airplane in his hand. As he grew, the models became more serious, and he built them first with rubber bands and then with engines. I tried to aim him in other directions, fearing that he was interested in airplanes only because I was a pilot, but there was no changing his course, and his engagement with things like Little League was halfhearted.

At age twenty-three months I took him for his first airplane ride in a

Piper Pacer. From then on, my logbook often notes, "Rob along," and then, in time, "Rob flew." That meant he'd held the airplane straight or made simple turns, since his legs were not yet long enough to reach the rudder pedals. A year or so later, "Rob landed." As time passed, there were more comments until he was flying, from takeoff to landing.

He did learn to swim; I insisted that both Ferris and Rob learn two things, how to swim and how to touch-type, for which they have both thanked me.

I don't mean to imply Rob wasn't a regular boy, that he didn't spend time with his friends, playing games, running, yelping, making a raft for the pond, and fishing. But when his aviation interest turned to gliders, around age twelve or so, that awakened memories for me of *Diving Dottie,* our home-built glider, and I thought I'd like to try modern gliding. So off we went to Elmira, New York, and the Schweizer Aircraft Company school.

The gliders I'm talking about aren't hang gliders, but sleek aircraft, with a cockpit you slide into and sit in a reclined position, almost lying down, the sides of the aircraft right there at your shoulders; the wings stretch out right behind your back so it almost seems like they're a part of you. The cockpit is comfortable and compact with an instrument panel well filled with interesting things; a plexiglass canopy closes over you and the visibility is big, you can see all over. Inside there's a stick and rudder, and a lever to move spoilers that come out of the wing on the pilot's command to kill lift, because these machines are so efficient, so refined, they would float three feet off the ground across an entire airport without landing unless there were spoilers to create drag and spoil some lift. They are part of the glider's energy management; while the glider will fly at 40 miles an hour, we make descents and approach to landing at 60 mph, plus or minus, depending on wind and conditions. So there's 20 mph of energy to play with; pull out the spoilers and the glider descends—sinks might be a better description; if the sink is too much, close the spoilers, and smooth, long flight comes right back. So the spoilers are almost like the throttle on an airplane, with the exception that you will eventually run out of altitude and have to land. But the performance and control mean that you can easily maneuver to land on the airport or field you've chosen; our present glider descends at a rate of 150 feet per minute, so if we're at 3,000 feet it will take twenty minutes to reach the ground, and that's plenty of time to work and maneuver.

In glider language we talk of L/D, Lift over Drag, which is a measure of how far you can go from a given altitude. For example, if the L/D is 30, and you're a mile high, you can glide thirty miles before reaching the ground. An L/D of 30 is modest; our present glider has 42, and some go as high as 60. So a glider is not just an airplane with a failed engine, it's a different and unique aircraft, probably the most efficient in the sky. (A Boeing 747 has an L/D of about 18; the Concorde is closer to 9.)

Another point is that it doesn't need wind to stay up. Laypeople often ask glider pilots, "But what happens if the wind stops?" Well, not much. Wind can be helpful if there are mountains; it blows up the side of them, creating a rising current you can fly in, brushing along the mountainside, maybe only 200 feet above it. That's called ridge soaring. Some days, with wind across a mountain, a wave forms in the sky downwind of the mountain; get in it with a glider and you can reach great heights depending on the mountain and the wind. In Vermont we frequently get to 15,000 feet and on rare occasions to 20,000 from the 4,000-foot Green Mountains; the glider altitude world record is 49,009 feet made in the lee of the California Sierras.

But the main way gliders climb is in thermals, rising currents of air, areas that have been heated and break away from the earth and go up like bubbles. Thermals are best when the wind is light, or even no wind. We circle and rise with them. Climb to 7,000 feet in a thermal, then glide off in the direction you want to go until you're down to, say, 4,000 feet—then find another thermal and climb back to proceed on course again; you've gone about twelve miles in that 3,000-foot glide. Along the course, gliding between thermals, you don't just glide along fixed at one angle, but as you pass through these areas of lifting air you pull back on the stick and zoom in the lift, gaining altitude; if there's down air, we push forward, increasing the speed to get through the bad air quickly. So we go through the air like a dolphin does the sea. Sometimes it's possible to go a long way before you have to stop and circle in a thermal, because you've gained altitude by dolphining through the sky.

If the wind stops when you're flying a ridge or a wave, you glide over to the nearby valley and either find some thermals, or you land. A good glider pilot always keeps in mind a landing spot that's within range.

Gliders have radios, and oxygen if you're going to play with the wave. Many now have computers with GPS, too.

They're a wonderful way to start flying, because you learn to appreciate weather from its broad picture down to minute detail; your touch with the controls improves, becoming delicate with great feel and awareness of the terrain, fields, and your location in relation to the entire picture of lift available and performance. These factors and a host of others make glider pilots very good pilots. (In Europe many airlines give preference to pilot job applicants if they have a glider background.) The art creates a desire to know more, and glider pilots constantly study weather, performance, terrain, and anything else that might be useful in soaring. On the ground, glider pilots gather in bull sessions that are a mixture of experience, theory, and tall tales, but they're absorbing, and you might catch a bit of technique that's new. It's a throwback to the old days of hangar flying.

So that's where Rob started his flying career, with Bernie Carris as his instructor, and also Ernie Jones. Rob soloed at age fifteen. His dad, in the meantime, got checked out, beginning a new epoch of flight.

Aside from all the technical aspects, soaring creates an aesthetic experience that's almost impossible to duplicate. Once the yellow knob is pulled that drops the tow rope and sends the noisy tow plane back to earth, the environment becomes soft and quiet; there's a slight swish of air flowing over the sleek body, nothing more. You are alone, with all the world of nature spread out below, and blue sky and white clouds up above. There is no aid or command from the outside, all decisions will be yours alone, only the weather dictates and, if you're wise, it becomes an ally until it warns you that it's time to land and quit for the day. Soaring is one of the few things remaining where thought and action are completely yours, and as you recognize this, it shuts out the mundane world and lifts you to an ethereal state.

Sometimes I go aloft just to cruise the sky, find thermals, circle in them, leaving one to find another and to try better ways of entering it, working to improve my climb and circling techniques. I play in the sky, carefully, as smoothly and expertly as possible, yet without pressure or concern. I can see the Green Mountains below me in a way not otherwise available to us humans. I may circle with a hawk, and I once shared a thermal with a golden eagle. I land and am surprised to check the time and realize I was up there for perhaps three hours—it felt like three minutes. The wonderful aspect of glider flying is that you can make it a careful, scientific task, or you can go up simply to smell the flowers; you can cruise around, carefully studying the ground, or—as I have done in the fall—you can slide in near a flock of southbound geese to see how fast they were flying (almost 50 miles per hour). There are two worlds at your call, the aesthetic and the scientific, sometimes a mixture—take your pick.

So gliders became a part of our life. We purchased a Schweizer 1-23, metal, L/D 31 or so, and took it to Marfa, Texas, where Rob flew in the national competition at age seventeen—he had already learned to fly an airplane a year earlier. From then on we have owned four other gliders. The second was a German Libelle, an early fiberglass model with L/D up to 38, a wonderful machine. Each one was a little better until our current ASW-20 with its L/D of 42. In a way, airplanes became transportation, but gliders are still flying. Between airline flights, Rob is often aloft in the glider, still captivated by its charm and challenge, as am I.

All the years I flew airliners, I still felt my aviation heart was back in smaller airplanes that fit into what's called general aviation, which is all flying except military and airline. G/A, as it's called, goes from 40 horsepower Cubs and less, to big corporate jets, but the core to me was what we once called a private airplane, and that's the group from two-place airplanes to small twin-engine models that carry about six people. But it's that two-to-four-place category—place meaning the number of seats including the pilot—that I've always felt a part of; though my logbook goes from DC-2s to 747s, there are monthly flights noted in things like a Piper Pacer, Cessna 180, Culver Cadet, Cessna 170 or 172, Skylane, and others. Whenever I get in one of these I have a feeling of coming home, I suppose because that's where I started. Private flying has a freedom that airline flying doesn't; one can fly without even talking to the ground, without a bunch of procedures and rules. Aside from the FARs—Federal Air Regulations—private pilots operate mostly by inbred, unwritten rules, dos and don'ts engraved in your brain, obtained by experience, learning, and fright time, those times when you got in a frightening situation and got away with it and were put in your mental "I'll never do that again" file.

When you don't have all the written rules and procedures that airline flying burdens you with, there's a great sense of freedom as soon as you get airborne. It's possible to avoid the airways and their restrictions, especially if you live in a remote part of the country such as here in Vermont; you don't have to talk to an air traffic controller and be confined to what they say to do.

Private flying is free flight, and of course that's also true of flying the glider and soaring. These are different kinds of flying under very different disciplines, but inside all flying are some basic principles, and sometimes, when things go awry in an airliner, one of those basics can surface from deep inside and save you.

So while Jean tended her garden and ran our home, and Ferris pursued her intellectual, sympathetic ways, the family always understood that airplanes and gliders were there, too, not overbearing, but wafting softly in the background.

CHAPTER 28

Around the World—
Upside Down

✳

TWO TWA CAPTAINS, Fred Austin and Harrison Finch, attended a dinner at the Explorers Club in New York in 1963. The speaker was Lowell Thomas, who said there were no more great flying adventures to be accomplished in the earth's lower atmosphere. Not so, said Austin and Finch—how about around the world vertically, over both poles, in one continuous flight? They took up the challenge and spread out to organize such a flight.

The job took two years: finding sponsors, deciding on a route, getting permits and an airplane, and involving various scientists who might find useful data on such a flight. Austin and Finch wanted it to be more than just a stunt.

Almost as a side issue was a chance to break the round-the-world speed record, which meant only short stops for fuel. Two pilots couldn't do all that, so they enlisted two others: Jim Gannett, a Boeing test pilot, and me. The airplane, a Boeing 707-349C, belonged to Bob Prescott, president of Flying Tiger Line—so Jack Martin, Tiger's chief pilot, was added to the entourage.

There would be some long hops, so extra fuel tanks were installed in the forward cabin, big ugly black bladders that carried 4,000 gallons. It was a cargo airplane, so the bladders were tied to the floor via the cargo tie-down rings. Behind this section was a passenger cabin fitted with seats—I never did know how many, and I didn't spend any time back there; my spot was either in a pilot's seat, at the navigator's table, or down under the cockpit floor in a warm, quiet place next to the radio equipment where I had a sleeping bag. When there was an opportunity I crawled down through a kind of trapdoor, snuggled into my sleeping bag, and escaped the crowd above.

The flight carried a total of forty people. There were five pilots, three flight engineers, three navigators, and two radio operators. John Larsen was TWA's chief navigator and someone I had flown many flights with, I knew his skills and how he worked, so Johnny was my focus in the navigation department—although the others, including Flying Tiger's chief navigator, Ernie Heckman, were well qualified, too. Austin and Finch got the best people available in all categories. I'm not sure that includes this pilot, but Austin and I were old friends, going back to the day he came to work for TWA as a copilot and I was teaching copilot school, so maybe he called on me from our long association—and I also knew Finch well. They were both excellent captains.

There were various scientific projects being undertaken, and so there were ten scientists on board to run them. I think the basis for the research was that we'd make a continuous flight across both polar regions, and the equatorial ones, in a short space of time. The science projects involved measurement and collection of samples, correlating radiation with solar activity—examining how it could affect crew members and passengers. Meteorology was a big item, too, and the man in charge of that was an old friend, Newt Lieurance of the Environmental Science Service Administration. I first knew Newt when he was a TWA meteorologist, and an excellent one. In World War II he was a navy captain, making films to teach pilots about weather, and he ran much of the navy's meteorological service in the Pacific.

There were thirteen airmen, six people from radio and newspapers—one of them, ironically, Lowell Thomas Jr.—ten scientists, and eleven observers. Quite a few seemed, to my cynical eye, to be just along for the ride.

I got to Los Angeles ahead of time and was handed the job of double-checking the courses and fuel required; when I'd finished that I kind of had a feeling of, "Well, no sweat, the 707 can do it—why don't we just accept that and stay home?" That didn't fit the excitement they were generating for the real thing.

First we were going to fly to Honolulu from Palm Springs—some aviation event was being held in Palm Springs, and our departure would add to the festivities. But the actual round-the-world would be Honolulu to London over the North Pole, then London to Buenos Aires, from there to Christchurch, New Zealand, over the South Pole, then back to Honolulu. The effort was called the Rockwell Polar Flight because Colonel Willard F. Rockwell, CEO of Rockwell-Standard Corp., had put up the necessary money; he also came along on the flight—a delightful, spunky, elderly man.

I'll dwell little on the scientific aspects because I never had a detailed briefing about each experiment or data gathering. The data collected on one flight is a pretty small sample and the results shouldn't be taken as earth-shattering information. In Newt Lieurance's experiments he found more carbon dioxide in the Southern Hemisphere than in the Northern, and that was a surprise because most of the industrial junk poured into the atmosphere comes from the Northern Hemisphere. But Newt, being a realist, added that this one sampling wasn't enough and more investigation was needed before drawing any conclusions.

The crowd gathered, came on board, and we were off. I made the takeoff, with Jim Gannett acting as copilot. It was a typical easy flight to Honolulu, except for the unusual situation of a storm parked over the islands, so we landed through an 800-foot ceiling in heavy rain.

After a few hours to eat and get fuel we were off and headed for the North Pole. As luck would have it, I was flying as we crossed Alaska, which I knew well from my B-17 experience. A dark night, no weather, and stars bright above as we went past the Alaskan north coast and headed across the Arctic Ocean. I could see my old friend, the North Star, high in the sky. I viewed it through the eyebrow window all 707s have, a small rectangle almost directly above the pilot's head.

It was peaceful, the world not really part of my consciousness; I was suspended in space, everything black below, no lights, no sign to assure me

I was over anything at all. Above was the northern sky, billions of stars stretched across its canopy, and my friend Polaris climbing higher and higher in my eyebrow window as we flew north.

There were people gathered and much excitement around the navigator's station as we approached the Pole. Sights were being taken, timing done carefully to announce our passage. I twisted a bit to keep the North Star in sight as it climbed higher and higher in my window. For nearly all of my flying life it was over my shoulder, but now it was almost above me, and then, as I craned my neck to see up, there it was directly over my head. I didn't need anyone to tell me we were over the Pole; the star above did that.

From there we followed the Prime Meridian, zero longitude, the Greenwich Meridian—take your pick for a name—to London where we landed in the dark thirteen hours and fifty-four minutes from Honolulu. I made the approach and landing because I was familiar with London.

A sleepy terminal, few people, but there was a problem: the long runway was closed for repairs, which meant using a shorter one, and that restricted our fuel load and put Buenos Aires out of nonstop reach—what should we do? I knew Lisbon had a big long runway, I'd used it many times, so I suggested we go there and then go to Buenos Aires. London to Lisbon was a short flight, only two hours and nineteen minutes.

We almost didn't get out of Lisbon. To get to the weather office, it was necessary to use an elevator. Too many of us crowded into it and it sank to the bottom of the shaft, where we faced a door secured with a big padlock for which no one seemed to have a key. We were locked there for the better part of an hour before a man with a hacksaw appeared and got us out. The hour was interesting because we were crammed in tight, and I could observe the various reactions of people that ran from a calm, "Let's relax, they'll get us out," to one sweaty-faced individual in a near panic; there were two others who were not much better, and I mentally put them on my list of who not to count on if we had any emergencies. Fortunately, none of the panicky types were crew members.

Freed at last, we were off to Buenos Aires, still dark, weather good. I opened the trapdoor, climbed down to my private sleeping quarters, and slept about eight hours. Back in the cockpit, bright sunshine greeted me with the coast of South America off to the right.

Eleven hours and fifty-seven minutes from Lisbon we landed in Buenos

Aires at one o'clock on a hot afternoon. The stop was about three hours, while our flight engineers looked over the airplane and we took on fuel— jet fuel for the airplane, Argentine beef for the rest of us.

There was a question about the weather, because Buenos Aires didn't have the latest information for New Zealand, which is understandable— who flies Buenos Aires to Christchurch? So we stared at an old weather map and tried to look wise. Newt stood there, too, and I said, "What's your guess, Newt?"

"I think a front's going through Christchurch and we'll get there behind it—probably be good weather." So armed with that we were off.

The afternoon was hot. The runway was a bit over 10,800 feet long, which may sound big, but with our heavy load and the high temperature it was tight. I was elected to make the takeoff with Jim Gannett in the right seat.

Let me tell you a bit about Gannett; he's an ex–air force pilot, a graduate of the air force test pilot school, test pilot for Boeing, and the primary pilot who took the 707 through its original test flights to certification. He's a dark-haired, medium-sized man, very quiet and unemotional, with the sweetest touch on an airplane's controls of anyone I've flown with. So with that kind of a pilot as the other half of the team we were in excellent shape.

I taxied to the end of the runway and turned around to takeoff position, the runway stretched out ahead of us.

"Let me show you something," Jim said and turned the airplane around again, taxiing toward our starting end. He taxied until I thought we were off the runway, certainly the cockpit was hanging out over the ground before the runway. The nose wheel, however, being back of the cockpit, was still on pavement. "Now swing her around," Jim said, and I turned again to aim down the runway. "Now we're using all of it." The maneuver had given us perhaps another 100 feet of runway, but that 100 feet could, under some circumstances, make the difference.

We were cleared to go and I advanced the throttles, careful to do it at the rate that would give us maximum acceleration, but not jamming things on too fast. I was really flying by the book not only because I wanted to do the best possible, but I wanted to be as precise as I could be for Gannett's eyes. Jim was not making any suggestions or telling me how to fly, he sat there acting as copilot, never saying a word except, "Vee one," then "Vee R," as we reached rotation speed. I pulled back and tried my best to rotate at the prescribed rate of 3 degrees per second, to our climb-out pitch angle. As I pulled back and the nose came up, and we broke ground, the end of the runway flashed by under us and we were over dirt ground; we'd used every foot of it.

"Up gear!" and Jim flipped the gear lever. As altitude was gained we retracted the flaps and settled into our normal climb speed. It all felt good, and I was satisfied I'd done it with Jim's approval. As we took up a southerly heading, the thought of where we were going sank in: it wasn't the destination, Christchurch, but that we were headed for the South Pole, across a piece of the globe few had flown, and that we'd go abreast of the rugged southern end of South America where Saint-Exupéry had flown the mail—actually, that was way off to one side, but there was a connection and I liked how it felt.

A brilliant day, few clouds, bright sun, ocean below. It was a sleepy time, most people had sacked out somewhere and the cockpit was almost empty with me in the captain's left seat and Jimmy Jones, flight engineer, at his station; the copilot seat was empty.

As I looked down on the sea I felt someone come into the cockpit. I turned to see who it was, and it was the person who had the most right to be there: the great Arctic and Antarctic pilot and explorer Bernt Balchen, who had come along as an observer.

Born in Norway, Balchen worked with Roald Amundsen, the great Arctic explorer and the first to reach the South Pole. In 1925 Balchen rescued Amundsen and Ellsworth when they were forced down on Spitsbergen. He went with Byrd on the first North Pole flight, teaching Byrd and Bennett about Arctic flying and designing special skis for Byrd's airplane. When Byrd attempted a New York–Paris flight right after Lindbergh, Balchen was one of the pilots. The flight flew through terrible weather for almost forty hours. To their dismay, Balchen was the only pilot on board who could fly instruments, so he flew almost the entire flight, which finally landed just off the coast of Normandy near Ver sur Mer. All were able to get to shore, and the airplane was retrieved when the tide went out.

Then when Byrd made the first-ever South Pole flight, he picked Balchen to be the pilot.

Balchen became a U.S. citizen and flew for the Air Corps, leading an operation from Norway against the Germans. Balchen rose to the rank of colonel and did much to make our northern operations successful. And here he was, this impressive man who looked like the Arctic, eyes set back as though they had spent a life squinting, bold head that seemed to dare any adversity. "Please, sit down," I said, motioning him to the copilot seat, which he settled into.

So here I was with the only qualified Antarctic tour guide in the world! I had met him before, once during the war as I stood over a weather map in Iceland, studying a very messy setup for a flight to Goose Bay, Labrador. A low was in the Davis Strait spreading snow, clouds, and Lord knew what over most of the course, especially Greenland, which I had to pass to go on to Goose. He stood beside me, looking at the map, saying nothing. I knew there was snow and ice and that we'd be on instruments most of the time; I didn't mind that, or snow, but the idea of ice was making me a bit nervous. I turned to him and said, "Going to be a long night—lots of snow."

"Yes," he said. "Lots of snow." And that was his total comment. He wasn't going with us, he was just there on some other mission, but he knew what I was going to have to deal with, and there wasn't any use making a lot of conversation about it.

We started to see ice below, and as we flew over the Weddell Sea, way off to our right was the Antarctic Peninsula. He pointed into the distance and said he could see the mountains. I studied the area, and across the ice-covered sea below I could make out white humps that stuck up over 13,000 feet. Our course took us over the Ronne Ice Shelf, and then to the continent, which is ringed by mountains, some 12,000 feet high. I remember reading of the struggle he'd had getting Byrd's Ford Tri-Motor over those mountains. He looked out and down at all the white landscape, and I wondered what he was thinking.

"I'll bet it's pretty tough down there."

"Yes," he said. "Especially if you are alone."

I thought, if we're forced down for some reason, I know who I want to see as leader of this troop.

It was a rare privilege, one I often think of, sitting there over the Antarctic with this giant of history. I wondered if he was thinking of the contrast as we flew so far above the snow, ice, and mountains, the sun pouring in, warm, in shirtsleeves, cruising at 500 miles per hour; did he think of the bitter cold and wind, the times of Amundsen, Scott, Shackleton, and others? His thoughts were certainly different from mine; I didn't feel any connection with the vast whiteness below, I'd never been there, suffered, and fought; I was simply looking down from a lofty perch, insulated from reality. I might as well have been looking at a postcard.

Once beyond the surrounding mountains, we were over a plateau of ice about 9,000 feet thick. The actual South Pole land is about sea level, but there's 9,000 feet of ice over it.

As we approached the Pole, people again gathered in the cockpit and around the navigator's station. Balchen, almost unnoticed, slipped out of the seat and went back, and Gannett took his place.

The excitement grew, and heads stuck up toward the windshield to get a glimpse below. We had been told there was an omni station at the Pole and we had a frequency, but all it would produce was a distance-measuring response—it was a DME station. I was following the navigator's heading and Johnny was taking sun lines with the sextant, and he was also able to get a shot on Venus. I was waiting for him to announce the Pole, but others wanted to get in the act. "Turn and see if the DME increases or decreases," someone said—this is the schoolbook procedure to get over a DME. I told whoever it was to shut up and let things work out. Other unwanted and annoying suggestions came from the bundle of people crowded around.

The early inertial system that we had in the back on test was tracking us, too, and suggestions came up from that quarter as to what to do. I nixed them, saying, "Let's let the navigator do his job."

Then I called the South Pole on a radio frequency we had been given. Immediately a voice came back, loud and clear, "Go ahead."

I chitchatted for a moment, and then told the operator we were coming up on the Pole at 39,000 feet; could he see us?

"Wait a minute."

In a bit, a breathless voice came back—he was underground and had to go upstairs to get a look outside.

"I see you—if you turn 10 degrees west you'll go right over."

"Where in hell is west down there?" Of course, everything is north.

"Oh, turn left about 10."

I did, and then asked, "How's that look?"

Another wait, then a breathless, "You're goin' right over."

I stretched over the glare shield to see down better, and there it was—not much to see, a few antennas, lumps of dark color I guess were the roofs of buildings. So there we were, over the South Pole, found by visual with a bow to the old methods. I was amused afterward when serious navigation papers were printed showing how the South Pole navigation had been done in very scientific fashion. Well, the instruments did a fine job, but hell, I know how we found it, pretty much the way you might find a local airport, by looking out the window for directions.

We circled the Pole and then Johnny furnished a heading and we pointed north. I got out of the seat and Jack Martin took my place.

Polar navigation is different from navigating anywhere else. A compass doesn't do much good because variation, the difference between the geographic pole and the magnetic pole, is changing so fast that compass navigation is about impossible. The lines of longitude are all converging toward the pole, so every few minutes of flight is likely to cross one of them, making the task of getting a course reference almost impossible. So we use a different type of navigation called G navigation—G for grid. Parallel lines representing longitude and latitude are drawn on the map, all referenced to the zero meridian. Courses are measured against these parallel lines, which don't all bunch together at the pole. Next, you don't use the magnetic compass; instead you follow the heading of a gyro, which doesn't have magnetic-seeking properties but just spins along giving a constant heading. Nothing is perfect and that includes the gyro, which precesses—that is, it wanders off a little bit over time. So the navigator takes sights with an astrocompass and periodically resets the gyro for its precession. These rates are pretty constant, so if one knows the gyro's rate, a graph can be drawn for periodic corrections.

So to sum it all up, we fly by reference to phony lines of latitude and longitude, using a nonmagnetic gyro.

Circling makes the gyro precession lose its constant rate, so when we finished circling the Pole our gyro was not precisely accurate, but it was good enough for a start. So Johnny handed up a heading that was something to get started on while he took astro sights to correctly set the gyros and give a precise heading. He knew it wasn't a precise heading, and so did I because we'd been through a lot of this at other times, and I knew within a few minutes he'd tighten it all up.

But the people in the back running the test inertial system determined that our heading was about 17 degrees off course for Christchurch, about 3,200 miles away. They sent this information forward and Martin got excited, and Gannett questioned it, too. I stood there and tried to explain that this was no big deal, just hang on a minute and we'd have a corrected heading. This didn't convince Martin; to do something, he reached up and flipped the switch to change the display of our heading information from the gyro to the magnetic compass. Fortunately we had two systems, and before he could flip the other I grabbed his arm and said, "Damn it, don't turn that other one off!" He didn't, but they both looked at the magnetic compass, and it was changing heading rapidly as we crossed the isogonic lines—the lines that show compass variation on a map. In polar regions these lines are bunched together, while they're miles and miles apart in places like Indiana. We were flying straight on the gyro heading, but the magnetic compass was constantly changing because of the quick variation change.

"We're circling the Pole!" he said in loud voice.

"Bullshit, Jack, hold on a minute, give the navigator a chance."

Our course was planned a bit east of McMurdo Sound, where there is a large air base that supplies the Pole station and does other scientific work. There was a radio beacon there, so once we got settled down, I went back to Johnny and said to change the course so we'd go near McMurdo and they could observe us passing the beacon. Gannett is still unhappy about our course, and to this day, when I see him, he's apt to say, "We were in real trouble over the Pole."

But things settled down, especially when the beacon started to come in and the automatic direction finder needle waved toward it. I had been flying since the Buenos Aires takeoff and was tired, so I went below and slept almost to Christchurch, where we landed in the dark. The night was clear; Newt had called the weather perfectly.

We'd been in darkness over the North Pole, dark from southern Alaska to London, and now it was the opposite in the south where it was daylight from Buenos Aires, over the pole, and partway to New Zealand—November 14–17, 1965; spring in the Southern Hemisphere, fall in the Northern.

We were only there two hours and ten minutes, then off at 2:00 in the morning local time for Honolulu. Jim made this takeoff with me as his copilot. It was an easy departure, 39,000 pounds lighter than out of Buenos Aires, but flying with Jim is always a pleasure; every move he makes is smooth as silk, his anticipation of what's called for next is almost mystic, his commands loud enough to hear but soft so there's no sense of domineering or impatience. It's a demonstration I wish everyone who flies could experience.

Finch and Austin soon came up and relieved us. I crawled down through the trapdoor again and slept a few hours. We landed in Honolulu and it was still raining, although the storm moved off and the sun came out as we had lunch.

Martin flew us back to Los Angeles and that was it. The flight had broken or established eight speed records including the big one, sixty-two hours and twenty-seven minutes around the planet, and new records between each pair of cities we'd flown.

It was an impressive flight, well prepared and well managed, but it didn't attract much attention; after all, by then they were in space, twirling around the planet in less than three hours. But it demonstrated something else that airline passengers should realize and be comforted by: that a regular airline aircraft had accomplished such a feat with no problems or need for dramatic action. In the business, we'd call it a routine flight.

CHAPTER 29

Grande Dame

I N THE LATE 1960s, the 747 loomed as the next aircraft—not just another airplane, but the biggest ever built for airline use. Boeing had introduced the 727 in the early 1960s, and it became one of the most popular aircraft ever built. The 727 was meant for domestic short and medium hauls; in its original configuration it carried ninety passengers, though it was eventually stretched—longer fuselage, more powerful engines—to carry around 150 or so, a little more if you really wanted to stuff them in. Its range was limited, with nonstop New York–Miami about its practical maximum, but once it was stretched its range increased, and it could go nonstop coast to coast if the head wind wasn't too strong. It had three engines, two mounted on the sides of the fuselage in back, and a third inside the fuselage, again in the back. Boeing ultimately built 1,832 of them.

The 747 was going to be a quantum leap forward, and it was exciting to think about. Rumors flew everywhere: something that big would be a new flying problem; how could anyone judge their height off the ground to flare for landing; something that big would be slow to accelerate and therefore make an aborted takeoff from low altitude impossible; it would be too difficult to taxi on the narrow airport taxiways and turn tight corners. Boeing tried to put the concerns of this last rumor to rest when they made a great big kiddie-car kind of rig with wheels spread just as they'd be in the 747, with a pilot's station at the same height and geometry as the 747 cockpit—and then had Jack Waddell, who would be the 747 test pilot, drive this rig around the airport in Seattle to show it would work. He said there wasn't any problem, but people still shook their heads.

Another rumor was that the number of passengers it would carry— 400, give or take a few—would use up all the travelers available at an airport in a single hop; on an hourly schedule from Chicago to New York, it would eventually empty Chicago and move it to New York! There was some pretty wild stuff going around.

As mentioned earlier, Pan Am's Juan Trippe put in orders, so TWA did, too. There were a few years between the orders and the first airplane delivery. This made me nervous, as I was getting close to retirement, only five years or so to go, and rumors went around that the company wouldn't check anyone out in the 747 who was fifty-five and over. This was not because of proficiency, but economics: it costs a lot to check someone out, and a pilot over fifty-five might not be worth the ante.

This issue came to a head while I was attending the Reading, Pennsylvania, air show, and someone told me the decision had been made by TWA not to check anyone out over fifty-five—I'd be that age when the first one was to be delivered in 1969. In a panic, I found a pay phone and called Roy Simpkins, our VP of flight operation. What about it? It was all wrong, he told me, anyone could get checked out on it even if they were fifty-nine—retirement age being sixty. A great sense of relief. When the airplane came on the scene I was number one on the seniority list, so I was in the first batch of pilots to go through the hoops of checkout and FAA licensing.

In December I went through ground school, learning the nuts and bolts of the airplane. It wasn't difficult because, in many ways, the 747 was just a big, improved 707, and the constant refrain from the instructor as he pointed his stick at some diagram was, "Same as," meaning it was the same as a 707's system. Airplanes, like people, have certain character traits that reflect their ancestors; in airplanes their lineage is the company that made them, with design quirks handed down. A few things on the 747 were obvious enough to remind me of my B-17, such as the footrests in the cockpit.

The class consisted mostly of old senior captains at an age where retirement wasn't something years and years off, but within sight. And I'd like to get it said right now: when the 747 came into service, it was flown by the oldest pilots, and there were no accidents in the first four years of operation, which says something for old pilots. By the time of the first accident, on takeoff from Nairobi, a good portion of the original 747 pilots had retired.

Ground school lasted three weeks, passing grade 80. We all made it. It was like all ground schools, mostly boring, but in this case a few things made us sit up and pay close attention; the big one was the INS, inertial navigation system, like the early test one we'd carried on the pole-to-pole flight, now refined, proven, and designed for easy pilot use.

It was a shock when we realized this would be the only navigation system on the airplane. No navigator and sextant, no loran, nothing except the INS to lead us across the wide ocean. (We still had omni and DME [distance measuring] equipment on board for airway navigation over land.)

What is INS? It's based on the forces of inertia, and in detail it gets pretty involved, but the simple and useful explanation we pilots could absorb was that precise accelerometers, mounted on a gyro-stabilized platform, sensed any movement of the aircraft—its inertia in any direction. That information is passed into computers, and they tell you everything you need to know. (Modern INS uses laser beams chasing around a triangle rather than accelerometers.)

Using Inertia, as we got to calling it, was easy: before takeoff we entered the airplane's position very precisely in latitude and longitude, not merely for the center of an airport, but for the gate where the airplane is parked. (All this information is in the manuals pilots carry in our black bags.) The first movement of the airplane is sensed by the accelerometers, and the INS control unit starts reading speed and direction. This was useful even on the ground because it's hard to judge speed from the high perch of the cockpit, three stories above the ground; the tendency is to feel you're going slower than you are, and it's a shock when you think the speed is around 20 miles per hour to look down at the instrument and see it at, say, 60, especially when a sharp turn is coming up.

In the air INS tells the pilot exact longitude and latitude all the time; it tells ground speed and drift, gives a time estimate for the next checkpoint, and some additional ancillary information. It operates independently of anything outside the airplane—no ground radio stations or anything else that could go wrong or be blown up by an unfriendly nation or terrorist. It's a good feeling; the earth below could be in the midst of a disaster, but the old INS would keep right on functioning. But what if it breaks? To take care of that we had three separate systems, and the chance of all three going bad was infinitesimal.

This all sounded great, but there was some nervousness about it at first. How did it turn out? In almost four years of operation I only had one failure, and that was on just one of the systems. Accuracy? We tallied the miles off course after each crossing and wrote them up in the ship's maintenance log; New York to Paris was generally within about three miles, which is remarkable for a flight of over 3,000 miles. (This didn't mean we came flying into Paris three miles wide of the airport, because as we came to shore we picked up the airway radio aids, omni, and beacons, and made a slight correction to center ourselves.) The largest error I ever had was thirty-seven miles, and that was on one of the three systems; the other two were normal.

INS is used in many places; submarines, missiles, and on most long-range airplanes. The earliest INS was developed by Charles S. Draper of MIT toward the end of World War II. The first major demonstration was a B-29 coast-to-coast flight to show the military how good it was; it worked perfectly, which was a happy surprise even to Draper. That first INS weighed over 3,000 pounds and had to be cooled by a special air-conditioning system; today it's about as big as a shoebox.

INS is being replaced in many uses, including airplanes, by GPS, which pinpoints position by satellite. GPS is wonderful, but I still like the independent feeling INS gives, not depending on satellites or anything else. After all, an unfriendly nation doesn't have to blast us with a nuclear missile, just blast the satellites and we're mute. INS would keep right on showing the way. It isn't as accurate as GPS, but it's close enough. Most modern airplanes still use INS and its gyro to feed information to blind-flying instruments and other chores.

After ground school came the simulator, and that's where the size of the airplane ceased to intimidate us—because a cockpit is a cockpit is a cockpit. It wasn't noticeably larger, the instruments, knobs, and gadgets were mostly familiar, and the new ones were interesting advancements that were easy to understand.

Settled in the seat, we programmed the INS, learned how to start the engines, which was a bit tricky, taxied out, and flew to do the usual maneuvers such as steep turns and stalls, tried different flap settings, coped with shut-down engines and various other emergencies as our knowledge progressed. I spent about ten hours in the simulator, which included sessions with an FAA inspector along and finally an oral exam by him on the airplane. It was extensive and included normal and emergency operations.

This oral exam always precedes an actual flight for your final rating approval by FAA, and no one ever looks forward to it. The word passed along was, "Just answer the question as simply as possible—don't enlarge on anything," since a few pilots had gotten into trouble trying to explain details that were beyond their knowledge. Some played this to excess, and an FAA inspector told one of our pilots, "You'll have to answer with more than just yup or nope."

Then into the airplane for actual instruction. Starting the engines was emphasized, because if it wasn't done properly the fuel would light up in the burners and quickly go over temperature limits, which could cause expensive damage. The procedure was to turn on the start switch, then watch the engine turn; when it reached 20 percent revolutions per minute you moved up a start lever and fuel entered the combustion chamber and was lit. Now came the tricky part: when the fuel ignites, a temperature gauge shows a light-off; at that point you have to watch the temperature rise, and if it climbed quickly and zoomed past 400 degrees, you'd slam down the start lever to stop the fuel flow to the engine and put out the fire before it did any damage. The engine was sensitive to this, and each engine start, all four of them, was a serious business with all eyes on the gauges ready to act.

There wasn't any feeling of the airplane's size, except for how high I was off the ground and how small the taxiway looked—and where were those eighteen wheels under and behind me, on the pavement or off?

Lined up and ready for takeoff, checklist read and cleared to go, it was just another airplane. Rush down the runway—it isn't as noisy as the 707—and lift it off, pulling back on the control wheel; no feeling of its size, the control movements didn't feel much different from a 707, and the results were the same as a Piper Cub; pull back to raise the nose, push ahead to lower it, turn the wheel or push a stick one side to bank—like all airplanes, push the way you want to go.

I flew seven hours with three different instructors, all line pilots I knew well: A. H. Smith, Mel Rogers, and Jim Hendrix. It was just like any checkout, the maneuvers, instrument approaches, engines cut, nothing startling or different; it stalled like any airplane, started to shake as the speed got too low, control response sluggish; push ahead, power on, and fly out of it. That's what you do as you approach a stall, you learn to correct it before it gets too deep into the problem. But I wanted to see a real stall, and I goaded my instructor, I think it was Jim Hendrix, to let it go further. He was reluctant, but we did another approach to stall and instead of the fly-out procedure, I kept hauling the wheel back until the nose wanted to fall and the airplane squirmed a bit to one side. It shook like a wet dog and I wondered about that big rudder and the horizontal surfaces hanging on, but I was certain Boeing test pilots had taken it far deeper into stall than I did. Before she really paid off I pushed the wheel ahead and then brought in power. There were various expletives and laughs as we flew back normally, but it reinforced my conviction that all airplanes, big or small, did the same things.

The INS was useful on a nonprecision approach. A nonprecision approach is a leftover from past days, but used for odd runways that aren't normally into the wind, or minor airline stops that haven't been updated. You cross a radio beacon and then head for the airport, descending; there isn't any beam to follow, so the last reference is a beacon or omni in back of you. Tracking away, using information from a needle pointing behind you, is a bit tricky, and it requires quick math and visualization to find drift. But the INS gave you exact drift and ground speed; apply the drift and you'd produce an exact course. The ground speed took care of time, so my nonprecision approaches were right-on. It doesn't take long for pilots to find new ways to use gadgets that the original designer and developer never considered.

My only problem was some uncertainty about taxiing. I finally got that under control in simple fashion. We were doing our training at the Salina, Kansas, airport where there wasn't any airline traffic and we pretty much had free rein, so the atmosphere was relaxed. I borrowed a company station wagon and then followed one of the 747s going out to the runway; I couldn't follow too close because the jet exhaust felt as though it would blow me away. But I was close enough to see where the wheels were in relation to the taxiway, especially turning. There was lots of room, and the turn it made seemed as tight as a 707's.

There are a lot of wheels on a 747. The nose wheel has two tires, and we steer it with a small control wheel on the left side of the cockpit. There are four main-wheel trucks with four wheels each: a truck on each side under the wing, and a truck on each side of the fuselage—I don't know why, but the manual always refers to this as the "body" when all the world calls an airplane's body the fuselage. The body gear trucks are the reason a 747 turns easily and tight; they swivel, just like the rear wheels on a hook-and-ladder fire engine. There's no one to steer these, but they react to the position of the nose wheel; if it's turned over 26 degrees, then signals go to the body trucks and tell them to start turning—more nose wheel turn, more body gear turn. Once I'd watched this from the station wagon, my fears about taxiing disappeared, and in service, taxiing around JFK Airport with its maze of complicated taxiways, other airplanes and trucks darting around, I found I could weave through there as well as any other airplane.

Theoretically I was now a checked-out 747 captain, but not fully until the FAA rode with me and had me go through a rating ride, which repeated much of what we'd done during training. The inspector was pleasant, with little to say after our two-hour-and-fifteen-minute session. His only complaint was that I exceeded 200 knots airspeed in the airport landing pattern; this was during a no-flap approach, and I reminded him that the no-flap minimum allowed airspeed was 205 knots. He sort of nodded his head and that was that. So now my license said I could be an airline captain flying a Douglas DC-4, Boeing 707/720/747, Lockheed Constellation, and Cessna 500 (Citation).

But it's not over yet: now I have to have a line check, and that was done with Marv Horstman, TWA's international chief pilot—that wasn't his exact title, but that's what it meant. He was an old friend, one seniority number under mine, a superb pilot. My line check was TWA's inaugural 747 flight from JFK to London: Marv flew it over and I flew it back. That was on March 20, 1970, and now I was a fully qualified pilot on the new machine.

Six days later I flew my own first New York–London round-trip in the 747. It was a bad weather night with things backed up at JFK, and my logbook has a note, "4+07 waiting ATC @ JFK—engines running." Yes, that's four hours and seven minutes. The skies were getting crowded.

Things were different back in the passenger cabin; first of all, we now had twelve cabin attendants, most of them female and young. The older hostesses looked at the 747 and said, "Not for me." They imagined mobs of passengers and problems, so they didn't bid to fly on it. The most junior women on the airline wound up with the assignment; many were wide-eyed at the idea of going to Europe, and nervous about the service. Some were off to Paris on their first trip—not only first trip to Paris, but first trip as a hostess!

Before each flight we held a briefing with the entire crew. During that I'd tell them what the flight was going to be like—weather and time. Then we'd review various emergency procedures. During the briefings I'd try to relax the new hostesses, tell them we were there to cooperate and to answer questions—that they always had friends and a place for answers in the cockpit. They were so new and young that we felt fatherly about them.

What happened? Nothing. They caught on quickly, did a great service job, and after a few flights they were as good as anyone. It didn't take long for the older hostesses to learn the 747 wasn't a bad thing after all, and they began to show up on the roster, too. Many of the new ones, even with their low seniority, managed to stay on.

For a period of about a year we had an additional crew member, a sky marshal, who was put on to counter any potential hijackers. Hijacking was just coming into play and there were great fears, so an armed, experienced marshal was added to every flight. Pilots viewed this with considerable skepticism and concern, because we didn't relish the idea of having gunplay in midair, with holes shot in the fuselage affecting pressurization as air escaped through them. It must have been a boring job, just riding back and forth. On one trip I had, the marshal enjoyed the first-class dinner—with wine—and was well in his cups by the time we got to New York. We got along with them okay, however, and I never heard of any shots fired in any of our airplanes.

Security now is a serious business, and its solution is difficult. To properly screen all passengers would take hours, with much more involved than simply walking through the magnetometer, since small knives such as my Swiss army knife often don't ring the bell. It will take detailed examination and questioning as they do in Israel. (My wife's hair dryer was ruined when a guard in Tel Aviv plugged it in to make sure it was a hair dryer—unfortunately, their electric current is 220 volts and Jean had the dryer set on 110—end of dryer.) There are great gaps in security in the ramp area where passengers don't go, and a terrorist could get through easily and toss a bomb. If I had a solution I'd be a hero—I don't have one, and it will be a frustrating problem for a long time.

Everyone seems agreed now that the cockpit should have a door that's impregnable, and perhaps a camera so the flight crew can see what's going on in the passenger cabin. Security is like everything else; people become sloppy at times, and it takes a big event to get all on their toes. One night at JFK, years ago, I stood talking to a passenger agent before getting on my flight to Paris; as we stood talking near the metal detector I did a double take as I saw a guard—with a gun on his hip and a belt of bullets—walk through it and it never made a squeak! I hit the ceiling, stopped everything, and called a vice president away from his dinner to get out to the airport and start changing things and raising hell. When questioned, the passenger agent said, "When we have a big load and want to get out on time we turn that thing down." I'm not certain, but I think the present devices cannot be adjusted by local personnel.

But that shows what can happen, and it points out that the system must be such that it functions almost automatically. The ground search is all to the good, but it's not perfect, so we need more foolproof measures on the airplane: make the cockpit impossible to invade, cameras for the pilots to see what's going on in the passenger cabin, have sky marshals, arm the pilots. All these ideas have pluses and minuses and need sorting out to create a foolproof system.

I was always careful in this area, but I was never scared because of it; after all, the odds are pretty good—or at least were.

Walking down the jetway to a 747 through the crowd of passengers waiting to board, I had a feeling of pride. On board, the big empty fuselage seemed long and large. I'd always walk the length of it, stopping at each galley station where the attendants for that area were checking their gear or standing and gossiping. I felt a jovial hello would relax them, and perhaps create a good mood that would be reflected in how they treated passengers—and it was a good opportunity to see if any special beauties were part of the crew.

One thought differently about the 747 than other airplanes; it didn't fly any better, or need new tricks, but it commanded respect. It was, and still is, the grande dame of airliners. Watch one taxi, headed for a takeoff runway: she stands tall, the raised deck and nose carried high, appearing to look down on everything around her, moving slowly, gracefully, regally. It thrills me still.

This grandeur is part of flying a 747. One flies precisely, by the book; there's no reversion to old barnstorming ways—although she'd respond to them if circumstance required. But flying the 747 is to fly with dignity.

Since ours were the early ones, they had certain troubles. We now had an automatic landing system; just put it on ILS, sit back, and fold your arms while it descended on the beam and landed—well, not quite. The system hadn't been perfected, so you turned it on and then kept your hands lightly on the throttles and controls, watching the indicators to make certain it was doing things properly. But sometimes it didn't, and during an approach, with all going well, only a few miles from the runway, a red light might glare on and a warning horn sound, loud, startling. You took over then and flew the rest of the approach by hand, and wrote up what had happened so the engineers could dig further into the system and improve it.

There was another engine problem that showed up when you'd land the airplane, then go into reverse, which slides big pieces of engine cowling and changes the jet flow. The method, even today, is to get into reverse at high speed just after touchdown, pour on power, benefit from its action early, and then later use the wheel brakes. Our problem was that the airflow wasn't sufficient at lower speeds—anything under 100 knots—and using power would cause a compressor stall with a loud banging noise and, if it continued, a hot engine, causing damage that cost $250,000 to fix; four engines, $1 million. So we had to be careful, use reverse on touchdown, then stop it before slowing to 100 knots. With a short runway or wet and slippery conditions, you wondered if the wheel brakes could get it stopped before you slid off the end, or if you should continue in reverse and possibly ruin the engines. It didn't happen often, but a few engines were damaged. Just another one of those pilot judgment things you get paid for.

But it was good, interesting flying, with less worry; the navigation was simple and foolproof, the engines reliable, the cockpit comfortable. It wasn't as much fun as the 707, which still had links with the past, but it gave off a solid feel that not much could go wrong. Perhaps that's why its safety record is excellent. All those worries and rumors that had been circulating before it was built disappeared into never-never land.

I flew our inaugural flight of the 747 to Paris on April 13, 1970. I landed at Orly Field and taxied to the terminal; there, neatly lined up on the tarmac, was a line of lady ground agents, all people I knew, specially dressed for the occasion with flowers in their hair. There were wide smiles on their faces and mine, and the weather smiled, too, as spring and Paris greeted the latest new age.

CHAPTER 30

Fin

F AA RULES SAY THAT after sixty a pilot may not fly in scheduled
air carrier service. There's no good reason they picked sixty, but they
did, and its arrival was only months away. I would spend it all flying.

To do one's monthly stint took four and a half Paris trips. My logbook
is full of JFK-ORY (ORY for Orly Field,) and ORY-JFK. There were other
places, too, that I went to see again before I hung it up: Madrid, Rome,
Frankfurt, London, Tel Aviv, and the so-called polar flight, JFK to London
overnight, then London to Los Angeles overnight, back to London
overnight, and then to JFK. These polar flights aren't polar: Take a string,
stretch it on a globe between London and Los Angeles, and you've got the
Great Circle course. It doesn't even cross the Arctic Circle—66°33'
north—but goes across the southern tip of Greenland, northern Quebec
(almost to Baffin Island), the lower end of Hudson Bay, and then over
Manitoba to the United States via North Dakota.

But that wasn't always the track we took. We played the winds and
took tracks to fit the current pattern; time, not distance, is what counts.
Each flight was a careful study of the meteorological setup with computer
analysis, but the final okay was the captain's, and he might want it different for some reason. One reason might be turbulence; when I saw that the
computer track was going to put us through a jet stream close up against

the trop, I'd request a change to avoid it. (Those were the days when the captain had a lot to do with the final flight plan and flight strategy. That's beginning to change; there are many more flights now, and the dispatcher may be miles away in a flight center busy with all of an airline's flights. Unless the captain is assertive, gets on the phone and argues for his idea, the dispatch's choice is the one you'll use. This will become more and more the case as the number of flights increases and operations become frantically busy. Envisioning such a future made retirement easier; this wasn't the way I'd done things for the past thirty-six years. Modern dispatch's increasing control, plus air traffic control's inflexible demands, prevent pilots from exercising judgment. I discussed this with a current working pilot, who agreed: "Pilot judgment is used less and less," he said. "We're just there to take the blame.")

On the London-L.A. flights, we'd sometimes go as far north as 70 degrees, which is way up there, crossing the northern part of Hudson Bay. Our final track, when we turned south toward Los Angeles, would be farther west, close to Calgary, and entering the United States over Idaho. Those far north tracks were fascinating, and I'd sit up front for almost the entire flight. Westbound it was all daylight because we were keeping up with the sun; it didn't change position much, and we'd land in L.A. in the afternoon, having departed London only a few "daylight" hours earlier.

I loved to stare at the wide Arctic land, snow-covered and seemingly empty of people or settlement, no trees because we were north of the treeline. This far north it doesn't snow like it does farther south because it's too cold for there to be much moisture in the air to form snow; in a big part of the Antarctic, for example, it never snows. So the weather on far north flights was generally clear.

I'd look down on the tundra, and the land of Baffin Island, Southampton Island, and lonely Coral Harbour, the frozen shore of Hudson Bay. It is a cold, lonesome land, with a certain mystery. I wondered how we'd ever get along if we were forced down. My concern was eased during a dinner when I sat next to the Canadian Air Force general in charge of land and sea rescue, Major General H. McLachlan.

"Tell me," I asked. "What would happen to us if forced down up there?"

"Don't worry," he answered with assurance. "We'll get to you, no matter where you are, within two and a half hours." He was that strong Canadian type, and I believed him.

Flying south from the vast, white, seemingly empty Arctic, the land changed to subarctic, trees reappeared, and then we'd come to Manitoba and the open lands of Saskatchewan with its thousands of lakes, and Alberta with the Rocky Mountains looming in the distance. It was a fascinating flight, never boring. I flew many of them.

The westbound took about eleven hours and the eastbound a bit under ten. Eastbound, within a few hours after takeoff from L.A., it became dark, and we landed in London not long after daybreak.

Long flights give much time for reflection, something I'm not generally prone to do, but the thought of approaching retirement allowed for some musings—not simply about what had gone on before, but what it would mean to the future. The last thing on earth I want to be is a prophet, but certain directions seem inevitable based on what we did and what comes next.

Part of the flavor of early aviation was its heroes, performing deeds that seemed impossible in their time; the history book is full of names, some deserving and some not, as lucky one-shot stunts put a few people on the front pages. Some of the great names I look up to for their skill and courage. But my heroes are the unknown, unheralded airline pilots who fly without incident or accident, making decisions, stopping potential disasters before they happened, flying all night to see dawn through scratchy, tired eyes; fighting bad weather in all seasons from ice to thunderstorms; away from home and family at least half of every month. You see him, and now her, walking through the airline terminals wheeling their black brain bags and overnight cases, unnoticed except for the uniform. They will retire and disappear into the world of senior citizens. They have taken thousands of people safely from one place to another, across continents and oceans, but few know them or bestow on them the laurels they deserve—these are my heroes. I do not include myself in this category, because our days were so different; while they were scary at times, they were never dull. We had fun, and the flying never felt like drudgery. Pilots of recent times have a tougher job, harassed and intimidated by a multitude of regulations, the overpopulation of the skies, and the lack of freedom. We were explorers, but those who maintain their concentration and command in today's conditions are heroic in ways that are all too easy to ignore.

Thinking back, way back, to my Monocoupe days with a map and compass for navigation, then to radio ranges, celestial, Doppler, loran, and INS along with GPS, made me realize I had seen aviation grow from adventure to practicality. I had flown in the days when we worried because of navigation's inexactness and the early airplane's lack of long-range fuel supply—a nasty combination. Celestial sights were often cut off by overcast, loran by static, Doppler by smooth-sea outages and inaccurate variation. You constantly asked yourself, Are we really where we think we are? How high is the terrain within our range of possible positions—which would tell me how high I should be flying. What was the weather at destination: was it holding, or were there indications it might go downhill? There were all kinds of questions and doubts that made a skeptical nature an essential part of your makeup, a characteristic that protected you and everyone on board with you.

Now, of course, position is certain as you navigate with radio aids, INS, GPS, and monitors in the cockpit that show what the terrain is ahead and below, removing the old doubts. A pilot's skill can be limited to the ability to punch keys on a board.

We lived in a world where engines failed and your skills included knowing how to handle the situation, especially if it became more complicated than a simulator can create in its make-believe environment; engines failed in bad places, during high winds and turbulence, at night, in bad weather—they didn't give you a choice. The jet engine of today almost never fails; it will be a common thing in the future for a pilot to go through an entire career and never have an engine failure. When I talk to retired pilot friends I often ask how many jet engine failures they had. The answer, generally, is none.

So I picture the pilot of today, trained in recent times, having computer skills, but lacking some of the skills that early flying demanded and taught you, often in dramatic fashion. Does this modern pilot have the skeptical nature we had that kept us from trouble? Can you develop that nature without experiencing the fright time we all went through at some time or other? We hope pilots will have some skepticism about their computers and watch them for errors. But as the computerized flying world becomes more and more reliable, will this skeptical nature diminish? I suppose it will, but I hope not.

Will the modern pilot need all the skills we learned through the rough-and-tumble early days? Probably not. As automation, reliability, weather information, radar, and instruments as yet unknown are developed to fight weather and failure, most old skills will drift into the haze of the past. Of course, rare though the occasion might be, some old skill still might save the day; if it isn't there we may lose an airplane, but it will be rare and will affect the safety statistics only slightly, and get relegated to the "That's the way it is" column. As technology improves and grows, though, this will happen less and less. And while I speak in glowing terms of the good old days, I know that those days were far more dangerous than these. We have progressed remarkably.

So the outlook is bright for safety, except that the increase in flying will give more chances for problems; the record will be good, but now and then human error will occur, or some mechanical part fail.

Air traffic will get worse, and delays will get longer. The industry will have to cooperate: reschedule, fly at different times, and realize that scheduling 100 flights into or out of an airport at the same time just doesn't work. This awakening and correction will probably only come after two airliners collide—something that seems increasingly possible as safety margins involving the distance between airplanes are reduced to accommodate the increased traffic created by thoughtless growth.

The growth of traffic will gradually take away the freedom of flight as restrictions become tighter; I can feel it coming even when I'm flying my glider over the Green Mountains of Vermont, and I look up and see an airliner not so far above me descending and heading for Burlington, the airway going right over our gliding area. It seems inevitable that flying in this close proximity will cause conflict and constraint.

And most likely we will never reach all-weather operation. Mother Nature will always hold the trump card, and often that card will be a thunderstorm.

How fortunate I was to have been part of aviation's growth through adolescence to maturity, a time no one will ever experience again. Now my days of flying live only in reverie, when I dream of the quiet, dimly lit cockpit of a 747, high over the North Atlantic, swiftly cutting across the sky, creating a precise contrail in the moonlight, headed east to Paris, with my old friend, the North Star, over my shoulder.

*

AND THE FLIGHT this narrative started with, how did it end? The Paris early winter visibility slowly improved enough to land, which we did through a cold fog, the runway showing up only 600 feet ahead— the kind of approach that lets you use your experience and skills and leaves you with the good feeling of a job done well.

As the wheels rumbled across the runway pavement, all the concerns about fuel and alternates, winds and turbulence, ceased; now my thoughts turned to hot chocolate, croissants, and a warm bed. And tonight, at JFK, another pilot will prepare for his own flight to Paris, taking on the worries I had just tossed off. That's the way it is all across this flying world.

Index

433

ABOUT THE AUTHOR

BOB BUCK is the author of four previous books, including *Weather Flying* and *The Pilot's Burden*. He lives in Fayston, Vermont.